CHILDREN'S LANGUAGE

Volume 6

edited by
Keith E. Nelson
and
Anne van Kleeck

IASCL

This book is dedicated to the International Association for the Study of Child Language, IASCL. Shorter foundation papers for each of the chapters in the book were presented originally at Austin, Texas, as part of the third international congress for IASCL (1984). Earlier congresses were held in Tokyo, Japan (1978) and Vancouver, British Columbia (1981). IASCL invites international applications from all professionals who share an interest in enhancing understanding of children's acquisition and use of languages.

Lund, Sweden, is hosting the Fourth International Congress for the Study of Child Language just as this book reaches the presses, in July, 1987. The theme of this Lund meeting is "The Active and Creative Child." In the long light days of this summer meeting, we wish for continued progress, openness, sharing, and light among co-workers in the field of children's language.

CHILDREN'S LANGUAGE

Volume 6

edited by

Keith E. Nelson
The Pennsylvania State University

and

Anne van Kleeck
The University of Texas at Austin

LEA LAWRENCE ERLBAUM ASSOCIATES, PUBLISHERS
1987   Hillsdale, New Jersey   Hove and London

Lawrence Erlbaum Associates, Inc., Publishers
365 Broadway
Hillsdale, New Jersey 07642

ISSN 0163-2809

ISBN 0-89859-760-9

Printed in the United States of America
10   9   8   7   6   5   4   3   2   1

Contents

Contributors

NAN BERNSTEIN-RATNER
University of Maryland, College Park, Maryland

GINA CONTI-RAMSDEN
University of Manchester, Manchester, England

CATHY H. DENT
Miami University, Oxford, Ohio

SANDY FRIEL-PATTI
University of Texas, Dallas, Texas

ALISON GOPNIK
University of Toronto, Toronto, Ontario, Canada

DAVID INGRAM
University of British Columbia, Vancouver, British Columbia, Canada

HELEN LIST
University of British Columbia, Vancouver, British Columbia, Canada

SARA MANNLE
Emory University, Atlanta, Georgia

YO MATSUMOTO
Stanford University, Stanford, California

ANDREW N. MELTZOFF
University of Washington, Seattle, Washington

DEBRA NATHAN
Harvard University, Cambridge, Massachusetts

KEITH E. NELSON
The Pennsylvania State University, University Park, Pennsylvania

RIVKA PERLMANN
Harvard University, Cambridge, Massachusetts

CLIFTON PYE
University of Kansas, Lawrence, Kansas

PRISCILLA L. ROTH
Harvard University, Cambridge, Massachusetts

MARILYN SHATZ
University of Michigan, Ann Arbor, Michigan

CATHERINE E. SNOW
Harvard University, Cambridge, Massachusetts

GISELA E. SPEIDEL
Center for Development of Early Education, Honolulu, Hawaii

MICHAEL TOMASELLO
Emory University, Atlanta, Georgia

LYDIA WHITE
McGill University, Montreal, Quebec, Canada

Preface

This series, *Children's Language,* reflects the conviction that extensive work on entirely new fronts along with a great deal of reinterpretation of old-front data will be necessary before any persuasive and truly orderly account of language development can be assembled. For all volumes in the series there is a common scheme of operation with two tactics. First, to give authors sufficient planning time and freedom to arrive at a chapter-length account of their area of thinking which vividly shows both the progress and the problems in that area, with the author of each chapter free to find a workable proportion of new experimental contributions, review, and theory. This flexible approach means that formats vary. It also insures that none of the chapters are simply reviews, and that none of the volumes are "handbooks" or "reviews" or introductory texts. Rather the volumes try to capture the excitement and complexity of thinking and research at the growing, advancing edges of this broad field of children's language. The second tactic concerns the selection of topics for each volume. Again eschewing the general handbook or review approach there is no stress placed on representing all of the facets of children's language in one volume. The chapters placed within one volume are chosen because there are some common themes that tie subsets of them together and because each chapter is "due" in the following sense—the author's theoretical and experimental program has come to a point where a systematic account will be stimulating and perhaps catalytic to the work of other investigators.

In line with these goals for the *Children's Language* series the present volume includes coverage of a fairly wide range of topics and subtopics. The authors for each chapter will weave their own story and we leave to them the introduction of their main plots and the major and minor characters in their scientific stories.

Here we will just briefly emphasize a few important themes and connections across the varied chapters.

We find four overlapping areas in which the authors of the present chapters have particularly interesting insights and data. The first area encompasses children's language structures at successive developmental points. Perhaps this is the area where progress over time would most be expected, because the study descriptively of children's language structures is the oldest and most differentiated part of the field. The present investigators contribute by providing new and more differentiated accounts of structures in syntax, semantics, phonology, discourse, and discourse timing. A second area of study in the present volume is individual differences in the ways in which children learn complex language systems. Part of this contribution focuses on what the child manages to do across time in constructing language, but increasingly the literature generally, and the present chapters in particular, show how individual differences in interactional patterns with others influence children's language acquisition and language use. A third line of interconnection between chapters is the increasing differentiation of the processes and mechanisms involved in language acquisition. The authors move well beyond any simple nativist account and any simple interactional account to provide intriguing details about postulated learning mechanisms and how they are applied to the actual data and evidence available to individual children.

The final theme we would like to emphasis across chapters is a concern with how children stretch their current language and cognitive resources to help themselves make further progress without yet knowing exactly where they are headed in the next rounds of advance. This kind of process involves going beyond the information given and also going beyond the operations and hypotheses so far constructed. In many cases, as the child takes new steps forward, interactions with others will provide facilitators and stepping stones and bridges that help to explain the fascinating ways in which a child with only a few kinds of phrases or a few kinds of sentences increasingly incorporates more and more complexity in language at each new level. But in certain ways the child in any culture will find at certain points that he or she must in effect provide pieces of their own scaffolding. Children sometimes must actively forge new bridges and new hypotheses relying on the language chunks and rules already in place and the resources of their own active mind. As we will see in the current volume, there are many metaphors for this child centered learning activity. But in one way or another they all point to a kind of boosting up or a kind of winding up for the next stages of analysis that the child provides to herself or himself.

In Chapter 1, Shatz prefers the metaphor of bootstrapping. In her account she considers several different operations by which the child may bootstrap. One kind of operation involves procedures for eliciting from others the kinds of information and the kinds of support that can be helpful in working out new levels of language structure. A second kind of related activity by the child concerns entering into conversation and entering into representational systems many pieces of language or frames of language that are not fully understood. Here the child succeeds in maintaining active communication and active representation of both known structures and puzzling structures for an interim time so that more complete analyses can be worked out. A third area of bootstrapping discussed by Shatz concerns various expansions and manipulations of language structures as part of an active process of analysis. Children do not simply use language rules and language structures, they actively organize and reorganize the language resources they have and in discourse often lay out sequences of manipulated structures in ways that invite new comparisons and analyses. As Shatz notes, "Children use what they know to learn more, thereby achieving their own success. In idiomatic language, they pull themselves up by their bootstraps" (p. 1). These processes are held to apply for each child, but to assume different patterns for different children and their interactional partners.

Mannle and Tomasello in Chapter 2 use a bridge metaphor to capture the kinds of stretching of linguistic resources that a child may engage in when confronting nonprimary caretakers in conversation. Consider a child who spends most of her stime talking with her mother, but spends some time talking with a sibling or a father for a short stretch of conversation towards the end of the day. The child then may confront challenges that simply did not arise in the more everyday, familiar, smoother exchanges with the mother. The data presented by Mannle and Tomasello indicate that fathers and siblings are in fact less "tuned in" than mothers to the child's language level. In the course of stretching and bootstrapping to meet the needs of conversational partners who are different from the child's most frequent caretaker, the child may also learn to construct appropriate discourse structures of a code switching sort that allow towards the end of language mastery a smooth accommodation and a quick accommodation to new communication constraints. In addition, the material in Chapter 2 fits with the theme of individual differences. Both in terms of differences between children and in differences between varied fathers and varied siblings in their conversational behavior, it is evident that any adequate theory of language development will need to accommodate individual differences both on the child's side and on the input side.

Instead of looking at variations between conversational partners, Chapters 3, 4, and 5 look in considerable detail at the structure of communicational exchanges in particular kinds of situations. There is much valuable data and discussion in the chapter by Conti-Ramsden and Friel-Patti and in the one by Snow, Perlmann, and Nathan concerning direct comparisons between situations that vary in these terms: (a) the degree of familiarity of the situation, (b) the toys and books and other available materials, and (c) the predictability or "scriptedness" of the situation. In these analyses the child in each case converses with his or her mother but the situation varies across analyses. In Chapter 5 by Speidel, the focus of analysis is on a reading setting for children who are acquiring standard English dialect after having first acquired Hawaiian English. Here the co-conversationalists for each child are teachers and other children in the class. Despite the school setting, there is strong evidence that the teachers have achieved a naturalistic, conversational quality of communicative exchange. The authors of these three chapters do a good job of discussing the complexities of understanding how the tasks, the situations, the co-conversationalists, and scripts may all influence what occurs in a particular session of conversation and what the child learns over stretches of many months. In addition, individual differences arise that illustrate quite powerfully that not every script or task or situation will bring out the same communication quality in either children or adults. Nevertheless, there are some common suggestions that arise from the laboratory situations examined in Chapter 3, the home situations examined by Snow et al. in Chapter 4, and the classroom situation examined in Chapter 5. In contrast to the consideration of certain advantages arising from unfamiliarity provided by Mannle and Tomasello, these three chapters point up certain potential advantages of familiarity of situation, sequence and conversational partners. Given familiarity and predictability, the child may do a fair amount of risk taking and bootstrapping to push the use of his or her available linguistic resources as far as possible. Less attention and less processing capacity needs to be given to analyzing the situation and making and monitoring new plans for behavior in the situation. For the adult, the circumstances that are high in familiarity and predictability may motivate the adult to provide more flexibility and space for the child in discourse to initiate and to try out their linguistic resources. The adult also may have a greater readiness when the child does offer a conversational gambit to come back with a reply that is contingent on what the child says, but which goes beyond that and provides some kind of challenge linguistically. Putting the observations of these three chapters together with the chapters by Shatz and by Mannle and Tomasello provides a good antidote to a highly simplified view of language learning that posits standard input to a child who behaves in a stereotyped and consistent way. Instead new data and theory takes us in the direction of seeing how children with considerable individual differences in language skills and language styles encounter adults whose own skills and styles are deployed in different ways in different tasks and situations. Older reports in the literature primarily concentrated on what children were learning in language acquisition. The present accounts move us closer to differentiated pictures of who learned what from whom when.

Roth's work in Chapter 6 brings us to a consideration of children who are very early in language learning level, around 12 months-of-age. Here again we see considerable individual differences. Babies vary in their rate of vocalization and mothers vary in how much they share the child's attentional focus, how quickly they respond to the child's vocalizations, and in how often they provide semantically relevant encoding of the child's actions and other foci of attention. At these early points in language learning prompt and semantically relevant responses from mothers may provide very important stimulation for the child's analysis of language units and of relations between language and context.

In Chapter 7 Bernstein-Ratner also looks in fine detail at the kind of maternal input provided to children in the early stages of language learning. She argues that there are rich acoustic clues provided in adult speech to children, but that on the methodological level considerable care and sophistication is required to detect these clues. Her discussion converges with those in earlier chapters in stressing that adult speech will not always be rich in the same ways regardless of the goals and tasks and situations in which adult-child conversation occurs. So it is essential to look for those circumstances in which useful rich acoustic information is provided to children even though not every adult or every situation will contain rich clues to language structure. Another important caution urged by Bernstein-Ratner is close attention to the child's language level. This injunction applies to researchers who need to look for possible sensitive adjustments by adults to the child's language level and also to reduction of cues to children after they achieve certain levels of mastery. In addition, the injunction takes the form of advice to parents. In her view, parents may be better facilitators of language learning if they do adjust their cuing to the child's language level, if they provide clarification phonologically of new information and messages, and if they provide frames for analysis of word and phrase boundaries by using different instances and different realizations of the same words and phrases. You might say that even if children are going to have to do a lot of bootstrapping in the early stages of language learning, the responsive adult can do a lot through timing and emphasis and discourse structure to make the bootstraps a bit closer and more noticeable for the child.

Cross cultural comparisons have proved a valuable tool in revealing variations in the nature of language and in the nature of conversational interaction. Any adequate theory of language acquisition will have to take into account important cross cultural observations. In Chapter 8, Pye, Ingram, and List apply the cross cultural research strategy to consonant acquisition by babies learning a Mayan language (Quiché) in Guatemala and babies learning American English. In this case, good attention to the structural detail of the child's phonological systems helps to guide inferences towards more detailed conceptions of the processes by which children abstract language structure from the input they hear. The authors find systematic differences between the babies in the two cultures which challenge all prior theories of phonological acquisition. They emphasize children do not just learn sound systems but learn sound systems in connection with meaningful differences in language. Theories that rely heavily on factors such as ease of articulation will have difficulty dealing with their findings. Part of the bootstrapping process, even in very early stages of language learning, is that children will bootstrap by learning how to learn, by letting the results of early hypothesis testing against the particular local language influence the kinds of new hypotheses that they construct. The further the child goes in learning a language, the more the child is able to rely upon prior categories and rules and structures that have already been abstracted to selectively form new hypotheses that have high probability of success in their local language (for example, Quiché) but which would be less likely to succeed for a child working out the structure at a similar level of mastery for a different language (e.g., English). As the authors say, "Children must monitor the speech of others for forms with detectable meanings. Once these are found the forms can be stored by reference to their meanings. . . The adult phonological system inserts its influence during the child's search across different lexical types since the more frequent phonological contrasts should be the easiest to find (p. 181).

As we have just seen, sound analysis and semantic analysis do not proceed independently. Similarly, the analysis of new semantic lexical entries does not proceed independently of the analysis of nonlinguistic events and objects. Gopnik and Meltzoff show us that new word acquisitions of particular types tend to co-occur with new levels of understanding for related nonlinguistic events. For example, advances in understanding disappearances of objects are correlated in time with the acquisition of words for describing disappearance, such as "all gone." In line with many of the other chapters in this volume, the emphasis here is on the fine structure of acquisition. It is argued that if very broad measures of semantic development and of nonlinguistic development are used or if very global time periods are employed then interconnections would be missed. With new data of the sort reported in this volume, models of acquisition gradually will be able to specify links between language and cognition, ties between input variations and the acquisition of phonology, syntax, semantics and discourse, and links between development in each of these areas.

Relations between verbal representations and nonverbal representations are also the focus of the next chapter, Chapter 10 by Dent. Four-year-old children may be quite competent at verbally telling you about their concepts of giraffes and buildings and horses and dancers. The same children may also understand quite a bit about metaphor without being able to explicitly verbalize some of this knowledge. Dent provides insights into the children's nonverbal understanding by having them create novel hybrid constructions to show metaphor meaning. A child confronted with the metaphor, "The building is a giraffe," or the metaphor, "The horse is a dancer," could form a hybrid construction piece by piece to specify topic-vehicle relations. The task is new and the metaphor is new to the children. But by using what they know as a firm foundation, children are able to twist, turn, stretch and bootstrap their way to reasonable new constructions.

Across metaphors and across languages there are many ways of dividing up and representing the world and mapping these representations to distinctions in language. Matsumoto, in Chapter 11, reviews the ways in which Japanese carries information about multiple objects such as pencils and boats and mountains. These classes of objects, and many other classes as well, require differentiation of classifiers. For example, the classifier *"-hon"* in *"ni-hon-no enpitsu,"* "two pencils," would not be used for referring to cars or boats or horses. By attending to the interesting fine structure of classifier use in adults, Matsumoto is able to generate many experimental tasks to reveal information about the order of acquisition of these classifiers by Japanese children. One important result is some striking individual differences. A second general result is that a full account of the details of acquisition order requires moving beyond semantic complexity theories and input frequency theories to a more complex and differentiated theoretical account.

As in chapters by Dent, Matsumoto, and Nelson, White in her chapter (12) relies on focused experiments as a prime tool for revealing details of children's language and language growth. Her analyses concern children's systems for dealing with various verbs and their direct and indirect objects. Children in her experiments were asked to act out sentences such as "The monkey is drawing a picture for the doll," or "The doll is opening the monkey the door." Children often overgeneralize constructions that are appropriate for one verb to verbs that will not accept the same construction. The result is acceptance of sentences that are ungrammatical from an adult point of view, such as the second sentence above. It is essential to see that these errors do not occur at the early points of syntax development. Instead they develop when children are about 4½ to 5½ years-of-age, after they have built up a firm foundation both for appropriate generalizations and for active generalizations that prove to require correction in the longer run. Her theoretical argument again leads us to close consideration of the particular input that children receive and how differences in examplars presented to children may lead to different rules and different generalizations for certain periods in development. Nearly all children work out in English the correct object verb relations, but different children get to mastery through different sequences of steps.

Nelson in Chapter 13 considers together and helps to integrate many of the observations and theoretical discussions of the preceding chapters. The theoretical framework employed is one labeled "a rare event cognitive comparison theory of language acquisition." As in previous chapters stress is laid on describing and accounting for individual differences rather than aiming for one overall simplified model of how a child ("the child") acquires language. Each child is held to approach language acquisition with RELM, a powerful general learning mechanism that opens the way to considerable individual variability. Precisely because RELM is so powerful, children are sensitive to input but they are not overly dependent upon closely tailored, finely adjusted, explicit input that points out to children each new step they need to take in order to become more fluent in language. By relying on powerful long-term memory storage and retrieval systems and powerful analytic mechanisms, the child is able to put together for analysis related examples that are spread out over many days, weeks, and months of conversational interaction. From the dance of conversations on many separate stages and situations, the child is able to extract important but rarely occurring patterns. This kind of model attends to the fine structure of the child's current hypotheses, the fine structure of the child's storage and retrieval and analysis processes, and the fine structure of the interactional conversational patterns that individual children encounter. Together with the insights of the preceding chapters this kind of work indeed takes us closer to a differentiated and persuasive account of how children work out the mysteries of language. In line with the imagery of the following poem by Elizabeth Bishop, we have come to some clear angles of understanding and some clear patterns of explanation, with many startling revelations in what we have thus far come to understand.

Across the floor flits the mechanical toy,
fit for a king of several centuries back.
A little circus horse with real white hair.
His eyes are glossy black.
He bears a little dancer on his back.

She stands upon her toes and turns and turns.
A slanting spray of artificial roses
is stitched across her skirt and tinsel bodice.
Above her head she poses
another spray of artificial roses.

His mane and tail are straight from Chirico.
He has a formal, melancholy soul.
He feels her pink toes dangle toward his back
along the little pole
that pierces both her body and her soul

and goes through his, and reappears below,
under his belly, as a big tin key.
He canters three steps, then he makes a bow,
canters again, bows on one knee,
canters, then clicks and stops, and looks at me.

The dancer, by this time, has turned her back.
He is the more intelligent by far.
Facing each other rather desperately—
his eye is like a star—
we stare and say, "Well, we have come this far."*

---

*This poem, *Cirque d'hiver*, appears in *Elizabeth Bishop, The Complete Poems* published by Farrar, Straus and Giroux in New York in 1977.

1 Bootstrapping Operations in Child Language

Marilyn Shatz
University of Michigan

When children start to talk, they often produce naively inappropriate and even contradictory, if cooperatively intended responses, as exemplified in (1)–(3).

(1) E: What do you wear on your head? (to an 18-month-old)
     C: (looks at E, smiles, pats the top of her head)
(2) E: What color is this? (holding out a yellow ball to a 24-month-old)
     C: Green.
     E: What color?
     C: Red.
(3) M: Do you want a cookie? (to a 14-month-old)
     C: (reaching for the cookie) No.

Instances such as these are often passed over as merely charming indications of the young child's ignorance or contrariness. However, child language researchers should take them more seriously, for they are evidence of the kind of partial knowledge children have and regularly make use of as they simultaneously try to solve the dual problems of interacting and learning to communicate conventionally. Children must engage in the unfamiliar world of conventional communication from a very early age, and they have a variety of behaviors that help them get by on the little they know while at the same time assisting in the construction of a more adequate knowledge base. That is, children use what they know to learn more, thereby achieving their own success. In idiomatic language, they pull themselves up by their bootstraps.

The idea of bootstrapping is not new to child language theory. However, the scope of the notion and the diversity of its functions proposed here are new. Previous notions of bootstrapping were proposed primarily as part of endeavors

1

to explain the acquisition of syntax. In these earlier uses of the term, syntactic knowledge was said to build on some more basic understanding, either semantic or pragmatic, and one of two assumptions underlay the relations between the more basic level and the derived syntactic level. One assumption was that the structural relations in the two levels were isomorphic; hence, understanding in one level made the other necessarily apparent. One well-known example of isomorphic bootstrapping is Bruner's (1975) suggestion that the structure of agent-action-object-recipient relations in the world is revealed through parent-child interactions with objects and then reflected in basic word-order patterns. However, as Slobin (1982) has noted, languages that do not adopt this pattern as their basic order are no more difficult for children to learn than languages that do.

The other assumption is somewhat weaker, postulating one-to-one relations, rather than isomorphic ones. Pinker's (1984) system exemplifies this approach. For example, in his theory, the child's early understanding that some words designate objects and others actions forms the basis for distinguishing the grammatical categories of nouns and verbs. Although the formal basis of grammatical categories is given innately, the child discovers the particular expression of grammatical categorization in her language by mapping the simple semantic categories to the syntactic ones. Since the one-to-one assumption does not require that the structural description of the derived knowledge be strictly related to that of the more basic kind, it is weaker and less reductionist than the assumptions of isomorphic description. Nevertheless, it does assume that semantic distinctions are more transparent or available to the child than syntactic ones. (See Pinker, 1984 for further discussion of the Semantic Bootstrapping Hypothesis.)

The notion of bootstrapping proposed here is even weaker and more fluid than Pinker's. It is weaker in that it is less restrictive because some instances of bootstrapping do not have to obey even the one-to-one constraint. That is, the ways in which bootstrapping operations promote learning are assumed to be more varied than just by the creation of one-to-one correspondences. It is more fluid than earlier approaches in that bootstrapping operations are assumed to function as mechanisms of acquisition for all sorts of knowledge about communication and not just for syntax. Thus, the child is expected to use whatever aspects of language are available to her to illuminate the unknown, even, for example, using primitive syntactic understandings to shed light on pragmatic or semantic conventions.

WHY BOOTSTRAPPING?

There are several reasons for extending the bootstrapping construct in these ways. The first is that, although syntax has been the focus of the question of how language gets learned, it is not the only complex aspect of language a child must master. The child must also learn her culture's way of cutting up semantic space as well as its pragmatic practices, and these are hardly ever error-free or speedy acquisitions (Carey, 1985; Shatz, 1981). It seems unreasonable then to assume that semantic understandings for all facets of language are more transparent than some relevant syntactic knowledge, or that the social rules underlying language use are always in place before the rules of grammar. Rather, if the child has to acquire a complex array of communicative knowledge on various levels, it seems likely that she uses bits and snatches of whatever she knows to learn more. Thus, in this approach, the direction of facilitation is not limited to that from semantics or pragmatics to syntax, but can vary.

The second reason for extending the bootstrapping construct concerns the role of the child in the acquisition process. Over the last decade, there have been repeated claims that the child is an active participant in the creation of her language (Newport, Gleitman, & Gleitman, 1977; Shatz, 1981, 1982). Much of the evidence in favor of this position has been of a negative sort. Direct interpretable correlations between maternal linguistic input and subsequent child behaviors have been relatively few (Newport et al., 1977; Gleitman, Newport, & Gleitman, 1984; also see Hoff-Ginsberg & Shatz, 1982, for a review). Similarly, attempts to identify maternal pragmatic or nonlinguistic behaviors that can function as explanatory bases for the course of communicative development have not been especially successful (Shatz, 1982, 1984). In addition, there is some positive evidence for an active child, in both the child's selective uptake from input (Kuczaj, 1982) and the child's creative speech, from overregularized past tenses (Cazden, 1968; Ervin, 1964) to overgeneralized causatives (Bowerman, 1982) and specifically marked form-function distinctions (Karmiloff-Smith, 1979). Among the most compelling of such examples is Karmiloff-Smith's discovery that children sometimes formally mark a functional distinction that the adult language user does not. She found that French children progress through a stage of using two different forms to mark explicitly the determiner and numerical functions expressed by single form *un(e)* in the conventional language. These examples, and others like them, indicate that the child's route to mature language use is not determined wholly by all and only the input received. A comprehensive effort is needed to integrate data like these with a model for how the child controls the building of a communicative system over time. The extension of the bootstrapping construct forms the basis for describing the set of mechanisms required to explain the child's progress over time in achieving a conventional communicative system.

Three types of bootstrapping operations proposed here, elicitation, entry, and expansion operations, allow the child maximally to utilize the social environment for the learning of her culture's communicative system. Although the operations have different functions and different behavioral manifestations, taken together they form a larger complimentary set motivated by two characteristics of the child learner. Some of the operations are required because the child controls her own progress and hence must assure adequate input to the learning device. Others are a consequence of the learner's limited processing capacity, and the fact that the child must do other things while language learning progresses.[1] Neither of these two characteristics of the child as learner, limited processing capacity and self-control over the learning process, are presently well understood, but the latter is perhaps more controversial than the former and thus warrants a more explicit defense.

Executive control of language learning could be housed externally in the environment or internally in the learner. If it were located in the environment, that environment would have to be extremely sensitive to the state of the learner to be effective and efficient. This is true especially because the learner is a limited capacity processor and cannot learn anything and everything provided for it at any moment in time. Moreover, even if the environment were sensitive to the limited capacity of the learner and provided information in orderly, suitably sized packets, it would still have to be able to monitor the learner's uptake of such packets and frequently adjust its output to provide just the information needed by the learner to maintain continued development. In this model, even moderate deficits of monitoring sensitivity in the environment might have serious consequences, leaving the learner highly vulnerable to disruptions of the growth process.

By contrast, learners with internally directed developmental programs can select from environments differing in sensitivity but still relatively rich in information the amount and kind of material they need when they need it. The environment needs only to be sufficiently rich that the learner can at any point in time discover what she needs; it need not be especially sensitive to just what it is that the child requires at a given time. Hence, disruptions of the developmental program due to misreadings of or insensitivity to the state of the child are avoided.

This is not to derogate the role of the environment. There is ample evidence that absence of a communicative environment, or a highly impoverished one, is devastating to language learning (e.g., Curtiss, 1977). The point is that an internally controlled acquisition system does not need an especially sensitive environment, although it must still have an available one; whereas an externally controlled one must have both. Evolution theorists suggest that one of the main problems faced by organisms is the maintenance of developmental integrity despite environmental vagaries (Waddington, 1957, 1974). Hence, it seems reasonable that an important acquisition such as communication would be protected from all but the most severe environmental deficiencies by housing the

---

[1]Note that the question of whether the child has less processing capacity than the adult is irrelevant here. Even if the child processes as much as an adult, adult limits must be her asymptote, and hence limited on-line processing is a given (e.g., Anderson, 1983).

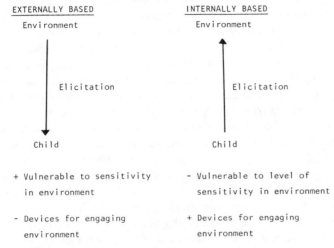

FIGURE 1.1.   Alternative control systems for language learning.

primary engine of development in the learner. (See Shatz, 1985, for further discussion of this point.)

However, there is a price to pay for the robustness an internally controlled system displays in the face of relative insensitivity in the environment. If one were designing an externally controlled system, satisfying the requirement of sensitivity could allow easy satisfaction of the requirement of availability. In an internally controlled system, where sensitive monitoring devices in the environment are no longer required, the learner must have some means for assuring ready availability to relevant data. This tradeoff between the vulnerability of the learner and the learner's need for ways to engage the environment is illustrated in Fig. 1.1.

This brings us to one new function for bootstrapping operations: Children need them to elicit data for their language induction processes to operate on. Devices that allow learners to use what they already have to gain more information from the environment are called elicitation operations.

The other two kinds of bootstrapping, entry and expansion operations, are more directly motivated by the processing capacity limitations of the learner. They compensate for those limitations by allowing preliminary representations of data that can be analyzed and elaborated over time. Thus, entry operations allow new elements to enter the language store, even in the absence of full analysis or understanding of them. Expansion operations allow understanding to grow as capacity becomes available to analyze in more depth and detail what has been stored in preliminary fashion.

Before we turn to some examples of operations and evidence for them, some clarifications are in order. What the three kinds of operations have in common is that they all help the child to use partial knowledge she already has to acquire more. Although there is an obvious logical order for any particular acquisition, from elicitation to entry to expansion, no stage theory of development is implied. Rather, it is assumed that all of these operations go on for extended periods of time, in waves, as it were, with ongoing analysis and reanalysis as more data arrive. Essentially, the operations are strategies for language learning. Although some may be specific to language learning, others may be more general learning strategies. Which are specific and which more general is an empirical question I do not address here. Similarly, whether all children or just some manifest partic-ular operations is an empirical matter. However, because I have claimed that the three types of operations are consequences of characteristics of the language learner, it is essential that every normal child normally acquiring language man-ifest at least some behavioral evidence for each of the three types of operations. Indeed, predictions about language learning deficits can be made on the basis of the tripartite model and the presumed absence of a particular type of operation. I shall return to this point in the last section of the paper. Finally, whereas some behaviors the child produces may clearly function as only one type of operation, others may have multiple functions. Communicative behaviors are not meant to be categorizable exclusively as one kind of bootstrapping operation or another. Again, how they function is an empirical question. This becomes clearer as we examine now in more detail examples of the various kinds of operations.

ELICITATION OPERATIONS

Since most children in normal environments are surrounded by speech, one might ask why children need special devices to elicit input. Why can't the child just make use of what she hears, or overhears? The problem is that the child occasionally has to know what is being talked about. Every current theory of language acquisition assumes that some meaning can be assigned to the strings to be analyzed (e.g., Anderson, 1983; Pinker, 1984). At the very least, the child needs to be able to identify the objects and events being talked about some, if not all, of the time. One way to assure this is for the child to identify what she wants talked about. Even before the child is capable of indicating this in speech, she can do so via an intermediary interaction system. Gestural behaviors are a good candidate for such a system. Unlike other prelinguistic devices for interaction such as smiling and crying, hand gestures can be used to direct the attention of an interlocutor towards objects and events beyond the dyad. If the interlocutor then responds to those gestures with language and appropriate gaze direction, the child can be fairly certain what the referential space of the language is. At the stage in which word learning is particularly important, gestural indicators on the part of the child are likely to elicit referent-matching statements (Hoff-Ginsberg & Shatz, 1982). For example, children pointing to objects in books or during play sessions often have those objects named for them (see Masur, 1982; Murphy, 1978).

If child gestures serve the function of eliciting speech rich in referential information, they should be especially frequent during the period in which the child is acquiring a vocabulary of labels. The data on early gesturing confirm this. Children begin to gesture communicatively sometime between 9 and 12 months, at just about the time they become mobile and start word learning in earnest. These early gestures drop out as the child becomes more proficient in word use, particularly as combinations of words become more frequent (Goldin-Meadow & Morford, 1985). Certainly gestures return to the communicative system at a later point in development; as we know, adults gesture when they talk. However, it is not until about 10-years-of-age that the full array of mature gestures is found in children's communicative behavior (McNeill & Levy, 1982). The hiatus in gestural behavior, and its change in form as well, supports the proposal that the early gestural system has a different functional role from the later system. (See Abrahamsen, Cavallo, & McCluer, 1985, and Shatz, 1985, for similar arguments.)

Further evidence that early gestures are not an integral part of a growing linguistic system but something preliminary to it comes from experimental studies of children's responses to gestured and ungestured language. Children under two were very likely to respond to gestured language by producing some action in response, regardless of whether gestures and language were consonant with one another or in conflict (for example, a speaker pointing to a cow, but asking, "What says woof-woof?"). In response to ungestured speech, children were more likely to vocalize (Allen & Shatz, 1983). Moreover, 2-year-olds also tended to respond with action to gestured language, and when so doing, produced less appropriate verbal responses than when they responded to ungestured language with speech only (see Shatz, 1984, for a report). Nor were the children's action responses a substitute for appropriate speech. For example, in response to "What says woof-woof?" a child might have simply pointed to a toy dog that was close at hand. Nevertheless, only a small fraction of the children's nonverbal behaviors were of this appropriate sort. Rather, the studies on young children's responses to gestured and ungestured language suggest that gestures and language are not yet integrated into a single communicative system.

Another study, examining the influence of maternal gestures on child language, is highly compatible with the view that early gesture serves to focus joint attention beyond the dyad on objects and events that can be talked about. Schnur & Shatz (1984) found that maternal gesturing functioned to direct the child's attention to a common focus, but had little influence on the appropriateness of the child's responses. Thus, taken together, the studies of both maternal and early child gesturing suggest that gesture serves to situate parent-child attention at a time in the child's development when the child's knowledge of language itself is insufficient to do so.

A repertoire of attentional gestures is unlikely to suffice as elicitors of speech for very long, however, Parents get bored with naming games, and children eventually need to know more than names for things. The child has to have other means as well for keeping the linguistic interaction going. Normal children very early on demonstrate a variety of response behaviors that convince parents they are cooperative interlocutors and that keep parents conversationally engaged. For example, having learned common actions on commonly labeled objects, children pull familiar labels from utterances and act accordingly on the objects mentioned, without having to analyze much about either the intention behind the utterances or the grammatical relations expressed in the string. Thus, 2-year-olds and under often respond with action to a variety of utterances which do not explicitly request it (Shatz, 1978).

Children also early on learn that some kinds of utterances require something more than or other than action. Even before 18 months, they recognize that yes/no questions take a special response, and they often use either *yes* or *no* indiscriminately in response to such questions, although their use can be totally inappropriate from the semantic or pragmatic point of view. For example, one 24-month-old observed in England responded to her mother's question, "Do you want your Teddy?" by saying, "No, please." At about the same time, children learn that wh-questions require some sort of verbal response different from *yes* or *no*, but they do not know just what it should be, and they produce some other vocal responses that are often semantic hash. (See Shatz & McCloskey, 1984, for a review of children's early question-answering behavior.)

Other response strategies gleaned from adults' discourse behavior have also been reported. Children pick up words or phrases they observe being used as responses, but they adapt them in often inappropriate ways to their own need to respond in circumstances when their knowledge is insufficient. One child picked up the *hmmm* that her mother regularly used in responding to her child when the child had said something incorrect but the mother did not want to criticize or correct directly. (4) is an example of such an instance of the mother's use of *hmmm*.

(4)   C: (showing the mother an object) A basket.
      M: Hmm. I think it's a bowl.

The child's use was quite different.

(5)   M: Where does it (a toy car) go?
      C: Hmm.
      M: Where does it go?
      C: Hmm.
      M: Does it go in the garage?
      C: Hmm.
      M: Yeah, it goes in the garage.

All of the above response behaviors, action responding, common question-response pairs, and frequent but idiosyncratic response modes, recruit partial knowledge of language use to the task of signaling to the interlocutor that the child is an attentive and cooperative participant in the interaction. Research on parents of autistic and retarded children tells us that, in the absence of such child behaviors, whatever propensity parents have to talk to and interact frequently with their children is diminished (e.g., Cunningham, Rueller, Blackwell, & Deck, 1981). Thus, the children's ability to take turns in conversational interactions, even when they can make only partial touch with the thread of the discourse, importantly functions to keep parents engaged with them.

The use of partial understandings to carry on discourse results in some rather surprising findings about children's semantic knowledge. It is often assumed that children first learn basic level or specific labels for referents before having an idea about the superordinate domain to which a term belongs. Color terms, however, appear to follow a different developmental course. Even children who cannot reliably identify the proper referent for color terms are able to answer the question, "Do you know the name of a color?" with at least one color term (Bartlett, 1977; Rice, 1980). Hence, they know the domain to which specific words belong before they know particular referents for those words. Moreover, they know the set of words appropriate to answer the question "What color is this?" before they are able to answer the question correctly, as (6) illustrates.

(6) M: What color trousers has she got on?
     C: Um-blue.
     M: No.
     C: Red.
     M: No.
     C: Blue.
     M: No.
     C: Red.
     M: No. You said those. Try another one. G—
     C: G—
     M: G—for?
     C: Red.
     M: G—for green.
     C: G—for green.

As with the children who knew something about the discourse domain for yes/no responses before understanding their particular semantics, this 29-month-old understood something about the appropriate discourse contexts for color words before understanding their particular meanings. Her willingness to use her partial knowledge elicits a language lesson on color terms from her mother.

An especially intriguing aspect of these elicitation behaviors is that the child does not appear to be particularly conservative about using the little language she knows to keep the interaction going. Unlike some other aspects of language learning, for which it has been argued that the child is a rather conservative learner, typically avoiding constructions she is unsure of, here the child seems willing to risk using a response she does not have full semantic or intentional control over. One reason why these liberal uses of partial knowledge may occur is that, inadequate though they may be, the child may discover early on that the best way of getting speech input is to try talking. For example, Masur (1982) and Ninio & Bruner (1978) both found that parents label more in response to their children's labeling attempts than to their gestures.

As for the kinds of facilitation that might occur as a consequence of these behaviors, I have already noted that gestural behavior would likely result in labeling under easy referent matching conditions and hence might facilitate word acquisition. Discourse cohesive but semantically inadequate responses might elicit specific language lessons or corrections. Indeed, Brown & Hanlon (1970) report that parents correct their children's semantics, and a study now being done suggests that children about the age of two elicit many language lessons similar to the one illustrated in (6) (Shatz & Ebeling, 1987). However, direct corrections or lessons are not a necessary outcome for facilitation to occur. Parental responses may be more subtle. For example, a reformulation of the situation using the correct form might occur and could be helpful if the child had a means for comparing what she had just said with the parent's reformulation. The work of Nelson and his colleagues (Nelson, Denninger, Bonvillian, Kaplan, & Baker, 1984) and of Hoff-Ginsberg (1985) shows that parents do make such reformulations and that children can take advantage of at least some of them.

However, it is important to note that these are examples of how facilitation could occur. No one-to-one correspondence between a given operation and a particular sort of linguistic information to be gained is being postulated. Rather, what particulars the child might learn from conversation-eliciting behaviors will more often than not be governed by factors other than the particular behavior produced. Primarily the behaviors function to keep the child and parent engaged in linguistic interaction and to provide opportunities for the child to gain data on which to work. For example, one of the most primitive devices available to the child is that of imitation. Children have been reported to use imitation as a response that indexes attention to the conversation and the willingness to take a turn in it. Yet, clearly, it does not direct subsequent parental behavior toward any specific additional information need. Indeed, longitudinal research suggests that continued reliance on imitation may not be an efficacious strategy past the early periods of language learning (Nelson, Baker, Denninger, Bonvillian, & Kaplan, 1985). In contrast, the much more sophisticated direct questioning about language that many 30-month-olds do, as illustrated in (7) (from Shatz & Ebeling, 1987), affords the opportunity to receive quite specific and relevant information.

(7)   Mother and child are looking at a picture book.
       M: I can see something that begins with B.

C: Bicycle.
M: Bocycle (in teasing tone).
C: What are bicycle call means?
M: Bicycle? Bicycle's a bike with two wheels.

Thus, elicitation behaviors can result in the reception of either general or focused information, and their appropriateness and usefulness can vary depending upon the linguistic level and age of the child. Without even the most primitive of them, however, it is unlikely parents would have the fortitude and diligence to stick with the often unrewarding task of talking to an unresponsive listener.

ENTRY OPERATIONS

Thus far, the focus has been on how the child elicits information from the environment. However, that information is only as useful as the child's ability to utilize it. Entry operations get the information into the language learning system in a format that promotes further analysis and learning by the child.

There are several reported phenomena in the literature that qualify as entry bootstrapping operations. Taken together, they suggest two characteristics of the data entered into the child's memory store for language. First, entry operations regularly take as the unit represented something larger than the word, for example, a noun phrase composed of modifier and label, or a discourse sequence, comprised of an overture-response pair. Second, words are often stored along with more familiar words or in typical utterance frames, even though they themselves are poorly understood. Thus, items enter the memory store in a linguistic context that will facilitate their eventual analysis and elaboration.

Examples of larger-than word size, unanalyzed or partially analyzed units abound. They include some of the discourse sequences already mentioned, contracted terms such as *where's, what's,* and *gonna* and *wanna,* and rote phrases such as *what's that?* (Brown, 1983; MacWhinney, 1982). Children often use words in contexts that help explicate them, although they do not know the exact meanings of the words. For example, a 4-year-old said, "I pricked my finger" after she had stuck herself with a needle. She then asked, "What does prick mean?" Keil & Carroll (1980) report that early adjectival terms are often used with a range of familiar exemplars only, with no apparent understanding of their meaning in specific featural terms, and the same is reported for the first uses of comparative forms. (Also see Carey, 1978). Children who are comfortable using the comparative of *big* find it hard to do so for *dirty* and *red* (Gathercole, 1979). These data suggest that representing some new or only partially understood information in the presence of old may help to cue the meaning of the new; it seems to be easier to assign meaning to *tall* with reference to *tree* rather than to *column* (Keil & Carroll, 1980). Moreover, storing new information with some context allows for comparison of contexts across instances and provides further insights into meaning and privileges of occurrence. Recent data on word learning in children suggests that this is just how lexical acquisitions occur (Miller, 1984).

Evidence for the representation of larger than word-size units can also be found at a more abstract level. Slobin & Bever (1982) investigated whether children assigned agent-patient relations on the basis of a first noun agent, second noun patient strategy. Whereas that strategy seemed to apply to N-V-N sentences, the children performed randomly when verbs were in first or final position. That is, the children had a sense of the basic configuration of declarative English sentences, and could not apply their rule of case relation assignment when that sense was violated.

In addition to the advantages already mentioned, the storage of strings of words allows analysis to go on at a more leisurely pace with less serious loss of information. Resources can be devoted to representing more of the string, rather than doing on-line analysis of only a part of it. This helps to mitigate the limited capacity problem, which constrains the ability to analyze on line more than it apparently does analysis and reorganization off line. It is hard to imagine a child doing instantaneous analysis of new elements of grammar as she hears them, at the same time that she also has to generate a response in a conversation.[2] It is more reasonable to assume that she has some capacity to represent strings of only partially analyzed speech for later comparative analysis.

To summarize, we now have a child who has various ways of using what she knows to stay in interactions, and she manages to elicit speech as a consequence. She can relate some of what she hears to her ongoing activity and/or perceptions of the world, and she has stored snatches of that speech and scanned it for basic sentence patterns. Now, there have to be ways that she can operate on these representations to create a more elaborated system.

EXPANSION OPERATIONS

There are various behaviors documented by child language investigators (e.g., Braine, 1971; Clark, 1982; Kuczaj, 1983; Rogers, 1978; Weir, 1962), that seem to involve common opportunities for language analysis. These behaviors include language practice, language play, and spontaneous repairs. They all involve substitutions of words into sentence frames, or the combining and separating of words into larger and smaller strings or segments. For example, a 24-month-old produced the following sequence as part of a conversation about the family wash with her mother.

---

[2]There is evidence that engaging in discourse is a drain on cognitive resources. Children produce less sophisticated utterances as responses than they do as spontaneous initiations (Bloom, Rocissano, & Hood, 1976).

(8)   My tight.
       My tight.
       Penny tight.
       Penny tights.

The same child at 28 months, in an argument with her older sister, modified her utterance until it was clear and grammatical.

(9)   No my read!
       My read!
       Me read!
       Let me read!
       Let me read the book!

Of course, some repeated tries do not result in better-formed utterances, as spontaneous sequence (10) illustrates.

(10)   C: (to her older brother) Do it properly.
              Do properly.
              Do your properly, Scott.

Possibly some of these buildup and breakdown operations, as Kuczaj (following Weir) called them, are a consequence of difficulties in the motor programming of speech; that is, children may think more extended or complex strings than they can say. (See Scollon, 1976, for a similar argument.) Even so, they are also opportunities for the child to examine the components of the strings, as well as to manipulate strings stored previously as incompletely analyzed wholes. Other examples illustrate this kind of experimentation with language very clearly. For example, a 26-month-old had learned a new phrase, and in a period of about 10 minutes, produced the following utterances as she trailed her mother around the kitchen.

(11)   Cheese, isn't it?
        My chair, isn't it?
        Heavy, isn't it?

At still younger ages, one sees children not only experimenting with word order and word substitutions but attending to phonological similarities as well. Sound play examples between children have been reported (Keenan, 1974); even children playing by themselves produce them (Garvey, 1977), as in (12), said by an English 24-month-old playing with the vacuum cleaner.

(12)   Hoover up. Hoover, Hoover here. Hoover here.
        That's your ear. That's your ear. That's your ear.

Spontaneous repairs are also evidence of the child's monitoring of her own productions and working towards some internalized model. The first turn of (13) was produced by a 24-month-old, who monitored her speech at the phonological level, but Scollon (1976) has reported phonological repairs in a one year old. A 30-month-old produced the semantic repair in (14) and the morphological repair in (15) 2 months earlier.

(13)   C: Hom here. Home 'ere. Come here.
        M: Can't you open it?
        C: No. Come here.

(14)   A dolly - baby stuck.

(15)   And a pears.
              And a pear.

Categorization, generalization, and reorganization are other devices for expansion of the knowledge system. The evidence for these operations often appears somewhat later in the language learning process, after 2-years-of-age. This is not surprising if some of the earlier productions are rote or partially analyzed segments. However, even primitive grammatical categories would help children gain knowledge because they could make inferences about common uses for terms of the same class on the basis of limited experience. There is at least some evidence for early classification of nouns. Girls as young as 17 months are able to use the presence or absence of a determiner to decide on the common or proper noun status of a label (Katz, Baker, & Macnamara, 1974; also see Gelman & Taylor, 1984), and even 2-year-olds have the beginnings of a mass and count distinction (Gordon, 1985).

Other evidence for the formation of grammatical categories is found in the third year-of-life. In a study of auxiliary acquisition, children who received enriched input consisting of the auxiliary *could* in initial sentence position grew faster in their use of modal auxiliaries than did children who received sentences with *could* in middle position. Moreover, their learning was not limited just to *could* or to front position, although it was limited only to modal auxiliaries (Shatz, Hoff-Ginsberg, & MacIver, 1986). This finding suggests that the children had some idea of the common privileges of modal words. A more explicit description of their knowledge and how they acquired it awaits further research, but Maratsos and Chalkley's (1980) distributional analysis proposal and Pinker's (1984) suggestion of paradigm representations seem particularly promising avenues to investigate further.

Some productions from 2-year-olds suggest that children often generalize on the basis of surface configurations without fully understanding the syntactic implications of those configurations. British children often hear positive tag questions such as, "Got it now, have you?" The post-posed subject construction was transferred inappropriately to declaratives by 3 of 6 children in my sample, although it never attained high frequency. (16) lists examples of their utterances, with meanings in parentheses.

(16)   Have one me. (I'll have one.)
       Want see it me. (I want to see it.)
       Sort you out. (You sort it out.)
       You show me. (I'll show you.)

Such instances, I believe, are less common in American children, who are more rarely exposed to post-posed subjects, and hence less likely to generalize.

Many other examples in the literature show that overgeneralizations can be explained as the outcome of reorganization processes consisting of analysis and errorful or constrained reassembly. For example, Bowerman described her child who used verbs prefixed with *un-* correctly, but then when she analyzed them into the prefix-verb construction, she made overgeneralization errors such as "I'll never unhate you" or "Wait 'til it unfuzzes" (about a Coke). Not until the further semantic constraint of applying *un-* to verbs with a "covering, closing, or surface-attaching meaning" was learned did the child realize the proper scope of her analysis (Bowerman, 1982). Thus, expansion operations can sometimes result in interim stages of excessive productivity.

Internal organization operations also have been the explanation for distinctions children sometimes make that do not appear in the input language. As noted earlier, Karmiloff-Smith (1979) reported that French children go through a stage of marking the difference between indefiniteness and singularity, even though in French *a* and *one* are both expressed by *un(e)*. The overmarking of such distinctions clearly indicates that the child goes through a process of actively analyzing the input data and organizing and reorganizing the results of that process.

To summarize expansion operations, I suggest that children manipulate sequences of words by substitution, build-up, and breakdown operations that allow them to explore common privileges of occurrence and to notice similarities and differences in patterns at a variety of levels of analysis. These commonalities that are thus noticed and explored probably provide the basis for preliminary categorization and generalization operations, which in turn allow more productivity that invites feedback and increased input. As more information comes into the system and can be absorbed, the child reorganizes her information to approximate more fully the adult model.

SUMMARY AND DISCUSSION

I have argued for a description of the language learner that includes a set of devices allowing the child to be an active participant in the language acquisition process. The child is equipped with procedures for eliciting language input in

TABLE 1.1
Examples of Types of Bootstrapping Operations

Elicitation	Entry	Expansion
early gestures	rote phrases	language practice
action responding	familiar exemplars	language play
discourse pairings	canonical sentence	spontaneous repairs
imitation	patterns	categorization
direct questions	sentence frames	generalization
		reorganization

relevant situations, for maintaining discourse, for entering linguistic information into her representational system even without full understanding, and for subsequently analyzing those representations. Such a system takes account of the inability of the child to do much on-line processing of unfamiliar material, it allows for reorganization and reanalysis in light of new data, and it is sensitive to environmental influences without being completely at the mercy of them—an evolutionarily sound system. Evidence for the description comes from a review of the literature reporting a variety of behaviors children produce over the course of language learning. These are summarized in Table 1.1. The list is meant to be exemplary rather than fully inclusive.

In addition to the studies already mentioned, other work in the field bears some similarity to one aspect or another of the proposed model. Holzman (1984) has suggested a reciprocal model of language acquisition that gives considerable weight to the role of the child. Grimm (1987) suggests that normal language acquisition depends on early gestalt-like processes, and Keil and Ballerman (1984) note that storing unanalyzed wholes may be a basic strategy for naive learners. MacWhinney (1982) has suggested that many early productions are essentially unanalyzed, and Peters (1983) has proposed that early language units may differ in size from those in the adult language.

Some researchers have suggested that approaching language holistically versus analytically may simply be a function of personal style rather than a necessary stage through which all children pass (e.g., Nelson 1973; Nelson et al., 1985). Undoubtedly children differ in degree to which a particular approach to language is utilized. However, it is difficult to imagine even the most analytic of children not occasionally using a word or construction stored in memory before it is fully analyzed. The opportunities for learning via such use are just too great to pass up completely. It is important to remember that style characterizations of children in the literature as "gestalt" or "analytic," (or equivalent labels) are gross dichotomies. They can not be taken as evidence that some children learn language without recourse to the entry operations involving rote or unanalyzed wholes. Indeed, how much children use unanalyzed segments is likely to depend on their level of language competence as well as on the structure of the language they are learning.

Nonetheless, acquisition models utilizing unanalyzed segments, including the model proposed above, must ultimately deal with the knotty problem of how analysis of early internal holistic representations proceeds. What triggers analysis? How much data must be entered into the system for analysis to proceed? What are the constraints on analysis and reanalysis? These are difficult questions on which language acquisition researchers are just beginning to make some progress. (For example, Nelson et al., 1984, show that the level of complexity in maternal recasts of child utterances is a determinant of language learning facilitation.) Questions like these recall concerns for which earlier cognitive development theories positing serious reorganization were criticized. (See, for example, Fodor's (1975) critique of Piaget's and Bruner's theories of changes in modes of representation.) Despite such problems, there seems to be no viable alternative that accounts as well for the *developmental* data of language acquisition. Children simply do not learn language instantaneously; the evidence points to a system that expands over time as piecemeal organizations and reorganizations are accomplished, leaving a trail of often charming and revealing errors behind.

In addition to being a developmental model, the present proposal has the advantage of going beyond the nature-nurture debate that has for so long bedeviled the study of language acquisition. The present model is compatible with whatever degree of innate mechanisms is found to constrain the shape of natural human languages. The problem addressed here has been the question of how the child learns the particular language she is exposed to, not how she learns any language at all. The larger question of language acquisition involves both issues, and must take into consideration the developmental factor as well.

The current model has some implications for three areas of research closely allied with work on first-language acquisition: second-language learning, language disorders, and individual differences in learning. As for second-language learning, the main implication is the prediction of serious differences between patterns of first- and second-language learning, especially as the ages at which the two languages are learned diverge. Whereas both first- and second-language learners are likely to utilize the same general set of active learning operations proposed, the particulars of those operations are likely to differ. For example, elicitation operations may be different because something like early gestures to set up mutual interaction may no longer be available. Rather, other kinds of behaviors for keeping interactions going may be available, but they surely will have different meanings attached to them and carry social implications that are different from those pertaining to the social role of the young child.[3] Second, while entry operations may in principle be similar, they may be harder for second language learners to carry out. Adults may be too analytic to pay as much

---

[3]Certainly adults use gesturing to communicate in a foreign country, but they often are mimetic gestures going far beyond the simple attentional ones young children produce.

attention to prosodic or other cues that facilitate the storage of unanalyzed segments, and they may focus more on individual words and neglect surrounding
context. Their strategies for later analysis and expansion are also likely to be
different from first-language learners, given their different cognitive and linguistic levels of experience, and they will be variably advantaged and disadvantaged by those differences.

As for language disorders, different sorts of disorders should result from
disruption of different kinds of operations. For example, children unable to enter
unanalyzed segments would be expected not to achieve broad productive expression, but only narrow ranges of expression having little in common with the
patterns of the input language. This is just what Grimm (1987) claims to have
seen among dysphasic children studied in Germany. On the other hand, retarded
children might be able to represent the gestalt-like sequences, but not perform the
full program of analysis and reanalysis necessary for the complete learning of
more complex constructions. Although surface forms might look quite adequate,
the subtleties of the language would be beyond them. Preliminary data suggest
this may indeed be the case (Gleitman, 1983).

Finally, as already noted, although it is assumed that all children must have
some of each of the elicitation, entry, and expansion operations, not every
particular operation must be exhibited or utilized to the same degree by every
child. Thus, there is the opportunity to account for individual differences in
language acquisition paths as a consequence of differing utilization patterns of
operations. Given this, one might ask whether the model overpredicts individual
differences in learning. A more fully elaborated version of the model would not.
For one thing, the selection of certain operations is undoubtedly constrained by
cognitive development. Thus, 18-month-olds might look more like one another
than 30-month-olds would because their repertoires are more limited. Second,
some of the operations may indeed be universal, and mandated by innate constraints. Only further research will clarify which operations are universal and
which highly probable due to cognitive developmental factors.

In summary, the problem of becoming a native speaker is a complex one for
the child; it involves juggling many balls at once. Reaching equilibrium in the
adult language system is not a linear process, building syntax on top of semantics
on top of pragmatics. To think that only one kind of information necessarily
forms the foundation for another limits us from appreciating the full range of the
child's achievement. The child has to use what she knows about language,
communication, and interaction to learn more. She is equipped with processes
that allow her to do just that. If a homely and homey metaphor might be allowed,
it is more like getting a fitted sheet on a bed. The best way to do so is by a system
of approximations, adjusting one corner a bit as another is partly fit into place.
Thus, bootstrapping is a pervasive process, facilitating the child's gradual but
determined progress toward communicative competence.

ACKNOWLEDGMENT

This work was facilitated by a visiting scholar fellowship at the Max Planck Institute for Psycholinguistics, Nijmegen, The Netherlands, in 1984 and by a Senior Research Scholar Fulbright Award in 1985. I thank Judy Dunn and the Medical Research Council Unit on the Development and Integration of Behaviour for making available to me the British mother-child data from which many examples are drawn. I also benefited from discussions with Pat Bateson, Melissa Bowerman, Robert Hinde, and Judith Johnston.

REFERENCES

Abrahamsen, A. A., Cavallo, M. M., & McCluer, J. A. (1985). Is the sign advantage a robust phenomenon? From gesture to language in two modalities. *Merrill-Palmer Quarterly, 31,* 177–209.

Allen, R., & Shatz, M. (1983). "What says meow?": The role of context and linguistic experience in very young children's responses to what-questions. *Journal of Child Language, 10,* 321–335.

Anderson, J. R. (1983). *The architecture of cognition.* Cambridge, MA: Harvard University Press.

Bartlett, E. (1977). The acquisition of the meaning of color terms: A study of lexical development. In P. Smith & R. Campbell (Eds.), *Proceedings of the Stirling Conference on the Psychology of Language* (pp. 89–108). New York: Plenum.

Bloom, L., Rocissano, L., & Hood, L. (1976). Adult-child discourse: Developmental interaction between information processing and linguistic knowledge. *Cognitive Psychology, 8,* 521–552.

Bowerman, M. (1982). Reorganizational processes in language development. In E. Wanner & L. R. Gleitman (Eds.), *Language acquisition: The state of the art* (pp. 285–306). Cambridge, England: Cambridge University Press.

Braine, M. (1971). The acquisition of language in infant and child. In C. Reed (Ed.), *The learning of language* (pp. 7–95). New York: Appleton Century-Croft.

Brown, R. (1973). *A first language: The early stages.* Cambridge, MA: Harvard University Press.

Brown, R., & Hanlon, C. (1970). Derivational complexity and order of acquisition in child speech. In J. R. Hayes (Eds.), *Cognition and the development of language* (pp. 11–54). New York: Wiley.

Bruner, J. S. (1975). The ontogenesis of speech acts. *Journal of Child Language, 2,* 1–20.

Carey, S. (1978). The child as word learner. In M. Halle, J. Bresnan, & G. A. Miller (Eds.), *Linguistic theory and psychological reality* (pp. 264–293). Cambridge, MA: MIT Press.

Carey, S. (1985). Constraints on semantic development. In J. Mehler (Ed.), *Neonate cognition: Beyond the blooming buzzing confusion* (pp. 381–398). Hillsdale, NJ: Lawrence Erlbaum Associates.

Cazden, C. (1968). The acquisition of noun and verb inflections. *Child Development, 39,* 433–448.

Clark, E. V. (1982). Language change during language acquisition. In M. E. Lamb & A. L. Brown (Eds.), *Advances in developmental psychology, vol. II* (pp. 171–195). Hillsdale, NJ: Lawrence Erlbaum Associates.

Cunningham, C. E., Rueller, E., Blackwell, J., & Deck, J. (1981). Behavioral and linguistic development in the interactions of normal and retarded children with their mothers. *Child Development, 52,* 62–70.

Curtiss, S. (1977). *Genie: A psycholinguistic study of a modern-day "Wild Child."* New York: Academic Press.

Ervin, S. (1964). Imitation and structural change in children's language. In E. Lenneberg (Ed.), *New directions in the study of language* (pp. 267–302). Cambridge, MA: MIT Press.

Fodor, J. A. (1975). *The language of thought.* New York: T. Y. Crowell.

Garvey, C. (1977). Play with language and speech. In S. Ervin-Tripp & C. Mitchell-Kernan (Eds.), *Child discourse* (pp. 27–48). New York: Academic Press.

Gathercole, V. C. (1979). *Birdies like birdseed the bester than buns: A study of relational comparatives and their acquisition.* Unpublished doctoral dissertation, University of Kansas, Lawrence.

Gelman, S. A., & Taylor, M. (1984). How two-year-old children interpret proper and common names for unfamiliar objects. *Child Development, 55,* 1535–1540.

Gleitman, L. R. (1983). *Biological dispositions to learn language.* Unpublished manuscript, University of Pennsylvania, Philadelphia.

Gleitman, L. R., Newport, E. L., & Gleitman, H. (1984). The current status of the motherese hypothesis. *Journal of Child Language, 11,* 43–79.

Goldin-Meadow, S., & Morford, M. (1985). Gesture in early child language: Studies of deaf and hearing children. *Merrill-Palmer Quarterly, 31,* 145–176.

Gordon, P. (1985). Evaluating the semantic categories hypothesis: The case of the count-mass distinction. *Cognition, 20,* 209–242.

Grimm, H. (1987). Developmental dysphasia: New theoretical perspectives and empirical results. *The German Journal of Psychology, 11,* 8–22.

Hoff-Ginsberg, E. (1985). Some contributions of mother's speech to their children's syntactic growth. *Journal of Child Language, 12,* 367–385.

Hoff-Ginsberg, E., & Shatz, M. (1982). Linguistic input and the child's acquisition of language. *Psychological Bulletin, 92,* 3–26.

Holzman, M. (1984). Evidence for a reciprocal model of language development. *Journal of Psycholinguistic Research, 13,* 119–146.

Karmiloff-Smith, A. (1979). *A functional approach to child language.* Cambridge, England: Cambridge University Press.

Katz, N., Baker, E., & Macnamara, J. (1974). What's in a name: A study of how children learn common and proper names. *Child Development, 45,* 469–473.

Keenan, E. O. (1974). Conversational competence in children. *Journal of Child Language, 1,* 163–183.

Keil, F. C., & Ballerman, N. (1984). A characteristic-to-defining shift in the development of word meaning. *Journal of Verbal Learning and Verbal Behavior, 23,* 221–236.

Keil, F. C., & Carroll, J. J. (1980). The child's conception of "tall": Implications for an alternative view of semantic development. *Papers and Reports on Child Language Development, 19,* 21–28.

Kuczaj, S. A., II (1982). On the nature of syntactic development. In S. A. Kuczaj II (Ed.), *Language development: Syntax and semantics* (pp. 37–72). Hillsdale, NJ: Lawrence Erlbaum Associates.

Kuczaj, S. A., II (1983). *Crib speech and language play.* New York: Springer-Verlag.

MacWhinney, B. (1982). Basic processes in syntactic acquisition. In S. A. Kuczaj II (Ed.), *Language development: Syntax and semantics* (pp. 73–136). Hillsdale, NJ: Lawrence Erlbaum Associates.

Maratsos, M., & Chalkley, A. (1980). The internal language of children's syntax: The ontogenesis and representation of syntactic categories. In K. E. Nelson (Ed.), *Children's language* (Vol. 2). New York: Gardner Press.

Masur, E. F. (1982). Mothers' responses to infants' object-related gestures: Influences on lexical development. *Journal of Child Language, 9,* 23–30.

McNeill, D., & Levy, E. (1982). Conceptual representations in language activity and gesture. In R. J. Jarvella & W. Klein (Eds.), *Speech, place, and action: Studies in deixis and related topics* (pp. 271–295). Chichester, England: Wiley.

Miller, G. (1984). Some comments on the subjective lexicon. In D. Schiffrin (Ed.), *Meaning, form, and use in context: Linguistic applications* (pp. 303–312). Washington, DC: Georgetown University Press.

Murphy, C. M. (1978). Pointing in the context of a shared activity. *Child Development, 49,* 371–380.

Nelson, K. (1973). Structures and strategies in learning to talk. *Monographs of the Society for Research in Child Development, 38*(1–2), 149.

Nelson, K. E., Denninger, M., Bonvillian, J. D., Kaplan, B. J., & Baker, N. D. (1984). Maternal input adjustments and non-adjustments as related to children's linguistic advances and to language acquisition theories. In A. Pellegrini & T. Yawkey (Eds.), *The development of oral and written language in social context* (pp. 31–54). Norwood, NJ: Ablex.

Nelson, K. E., Baker, N. D., Denninger, M., Bonvillian, J. D., & Kaplan, B. J. (1985). *Cookie versus Do-it-again:* Imitative-referential and personal-syntactic-initiating language styles in young children. *Linguistics, 23,* 433–454.

Newport, E. L., Gleitman, H., & Gleitman, L. R. (1977). Mother, I'd rather do it myself: Some effects and non-effects of maternal speech style. In C. E. Snow & C. A. Ferguson (Eds.), *Talking to children* (pp. 109–149). Cambridge, England: Cambridge University Press.

Ninio, A., & Bruner, J. (1978). The achievement and antecedents of labelling. *Journal of Child Language, 5,* 1–15.

Peters, A. (1983). *The units of language.* Cambridge, England: Cambridge University Press.

Pinker, S. (1984). *Language learnability and language development.* Cambridge, MA: Harvard University Press.

Rice, M. (1980). *Cognition to language.* Baltimore, MD: University Park Press.

Rogers, S. (1978). Self-initiated corrections in the speech of infant-school children. *Journal of Child Language, 5,* 365–371.

Schnur, E., & Shatz, M. (1984). The role of maternal gesturing in conversations with one-year-olds. *Journal of Child Language, 11,* 29–41.

Scollon, R. (1976). *Conversations with a one year old: A case study of the developmental foundation of syntax.* Honolulu: The University of Hawaii Press.

Shatz, M. (1978). On the development of communicative understandings: An early strategy for interpreting and responding to messages. *Cognitive Psychology, 10,* 271–301.

Shatz, M. (1981). Learning the rules of the game: Four views of the relation between social interaction and syntax acquisition. In W. Deutsch (Ed.), *The child's construction of language* (pp. 17–38). London: Academic Press.

Shatz, M. (1982). On mechanisms of language acquisition: Can features of the communicative environment account for development? In E. Wanner & L. R. Gleitman (Eds.), *Language acquisition: The state of the art* (pp. 102–121). Cambridge, England: Cambridge University Press.

Shatz, M. (1984). Contributions of mother and mind to the development of communicative competence: A status report. In M. Perlmutter (Ed.), *Parent-child interaction and parent-child relations in child development* (pp. 33–59). Hillsdale, NJ: Lawrence Erlbaum Associates.

Shatz, M. (1985). An evolutionary perspective on plasticity in language development: A commentary. *Merrill-Palmer Quarterly, 31,* 211–222.

Shatz, M., & Ebeling, K. (1987). *Two-year-olds work at language learning.* Paper presented at the biannual meeting of the Society for Research in Child Development, Baltimore, MD.

Shatz, M., Hoff-Ginsberg, E., & MacIver, D. (1986). *The effects of differentially enriched input on the acquisition of English auxiliaries.* Unpublished manuscript, The University of Michigan, Ann Arbor.

Shatz, M., & McCloskey, L. (1984). Answering appropriately: A developmental perspective on conversational knowledge. In S. A. Kuczaj II (Ed.), *Discourse development* (pp. 19–36). New York: Springer-Verlag.

Slobin, D. (1982). Universal and particular in the acquisition of language. In E. Wanner, & L. R.

Gleitman, (Eds.), *Language acquisition: The state of the art* (pp. 128–172). Cambridge, England: Cambridge University Press.

Slobin, D. I., & Bever, T. G. (1982). Children use canonical sentence schemas: A crosslinguistic study of word order and inflections. *Cognition, 12,* 229–265.

Waddington, C. H. (1957). *The strategy of the genes.* London: Allen & Unwin.

Waddington, C. H. (1974). A catastrophe theory of evolution. *Annals of the New York Academy of Sciences, 231,* 32–42.

Weir, R. H. (1962). *Language in the crib.* The Hague: Mouton.

2 Fathers, Siblings, and the Bridge Hypothesis

Sara Mannle
Michael Tomasello
Emory University

> *We do not presently have evidence that there are selection pressures of any kind operating on children to impel them to bring their speech into line with adult models. It is, however, entirely possible that such pressures operate in situations unlike the situations we have sampled, for instance, away from home or with strangers. It is also possible that we should look more closely at the small number of child utterances which turn up in most samples where the adult just does not seem to be able to make out what the child means. Perhaps these are the leading edge where the pressures operate.*
>
> (Brown, 1973, p. 412)

A language is a set of conventions. Regardless of any biological predispositions for language that may exist, children must begin their linguistic careers by establishing with some person or persons a set of social and/or linguistic conventions. In the beginning, these conventions typically are established with only one or a few persons: Infants' early protoconversations normally run smoothly only with the primary caregiver (Bateson, 1979), and many of children's early linguistic productions are comprehensible only to those very familiar with the idiosyncracies of their behavior. As the child's social world expands during the second and third years-of-life, she must also learn to communicate with persons less familiar with her unique set of experiences and predispositions. If, for example, an 18-month-old expects the new babysitter to understand that *doos* means *juice* and that this refers only to orange-juice served in a bottle, the child is likely to be disappointed. It is intuitively appealing to suppose that communication pressures of this sort lead the child to seek in her linguistic environment means of communication that are conventional for a wider and wider community of persons.

23

In 1975, Jean Gleason proposed that fathers play a special role in this developmental process:

> Fathers are not as well tuned in to their children as mothers are in the traditional family situation. . . . There are probably serious and far-reaching good effects that result from (this). . . . Children have to learn to talk to their fathers and other strangers . . . (They) try harder to make themselves both heard and understood. In this way, fathers can be seen as a bridge to the outside world, leading the child to change her or his language in order to be understood. (p. 293)

The underlying assumption of the Bridge Hypothesis—which is not shared by all developmental psycholinguists—is that communication pressure is beneficial to the child's development of communicative competence, including the acquisition of linguistic skills. The status of the hypothesis is uncertain at the present time because, although there is a reasonable amount of research on fathers' speech to their language learning children, most of this research is concerned only with structural/linguistic features. Because its focus is on processes of communication, the Bridge Hypothesis is primarily concerned with the *pragmatic* aspects of linguistic interaction: how language is related to the linguistic (conversational) and the nonlinguistic (referential) contexts. Consequently, assessing the validity of the hypothesis on the basis of existing research is far from straightforward.

If the essence of the Bridge Hypothesis is that fathers are less "tuned in" to the child than primary caregiver mothers but more tuned in to him than total strangers, it would seem reasonable to extend the hypothesis to other persons exhibiting a moderate degree of sensitivity to the child and his communicative conventions. In particular, it might be extended to persons who interact with the child on a regular basis, but who are not as intimately involved as the mother in the child's daily activities. An interesting case in this regard is the other member of the immediate family, the sibling. We might reasonably expect that, like fathers, siblings are less tuned in to the child than mothers and that the young child must make a special effort to communicate with them. Unlike fathers, the siblings' lesser degree of sensitivity may not be due only to a lesser degree of familiarity, but also to the sibling's relatively high degree of egocentrism—as preschool-age children, for example, are notoriously poor at relating language to the particularities of the referential and conversational contexts (e.g., Dickson, 1981). This might result in a different type of bridge with different implications for the infant's developing communicative skills. Once again, however, most of the relevant research on sibling speech to infants is concerned with structural/linguistic features, and it is thus unclear in this case as well whether siblings do in fact place communication pressure on the language learning child and thereby act as a linguistic bridge.

An adequate test of the Bridge Hypothesis would consist of demonstrations that: (1) compared to the primary caregiver mother, the father and sibling are less tuned in to the young child in their communicative interactions with him; and (2) these styles of communicative interaction facilitate in some way the development of the child's communicative skills. In this chapter, we review the existing research on fathers' and siblings' linguistic interactions with young children, including some recent research from our own laboratory. In an effort to assess the Bridge Hypothesis, we first examine the claim that the father is less tuned in to the young child than the mother. This is followed by a similar assessment of siblings. We then examine the claim that these "other" members of the family have beneficial effects on the young child's communicative competence. In a final section, the role of communication pressure in the language acquisition process is explored briefly, and several directions for future research are proposed.

One caveat. Fathers and siblings come in many shapes and sizes. Most of the existing research concerns the prototypical—perhaps stereotypical—working father who serves as secondary caregiver. Research with siblings has almost uniformly focused on preschool age siblings. Consequently, our review and conclusions are restricted to these two exemplars, keeping in mind that an examination of different types of fathers and siblings might lead to different conclusions. Nevertheless, though we may not know the particularities in all cases, our own proposal is that with proper modifications the Bridge Hypothesis may be applied to anyone—male or female, young or old—who plays an important role in the child's life but whose communicative interactions with her are in some way less "tuned in" than those of the primary caregiver.

FATHERS

In the traditional family situation, fathers spend significantly less time than mothers interacting with their children (Clark-Stewart, 1978, Rebelsky & Hanks, 1971), and so presumably are less familiar with the everyday behavioral routines that are so important for early language acquisition (Bruner, 1983; Snow & Goldfield, 1983). It is thus reasonable to assume that they might be less tuned in to their child's early language than primary caregiver mothers. However, early research on this question seemed to contradict the Bridge Hypothesis. Results from a variety of studies suggested that fathers were very similar to mothers in the way they adjusted their speech when talking to young children. Golinkoff and Ames (1979) reported that fathers' language resembled mothers' in both free play and structured situations. In their study of 12 families, similarities included mean length of utterance (MLU), mean length of conversational turn, and mean number of verbs per utterance. In addition, both parents used the same proportion of questions, declaratives, and imperatives. Kavanaugh and Jen (1981) found no significant differences in a number of similar measures, and Kavanaugh and Jirkovsky (1982) found no differences in three major categories: complexity (MLU, repetitions), sentence type (declaratives, interrogatives) and semantic content (modifiers, locatives, absent object references). Lipscomb and Coon (1983) found very few differences in the 20 couples they studied, and concluded that the similarity of mothers' and fathers' speech was striking given the differing amounts of time each parent spent with the infant. Even the very recent research of Hopman (1985) and Kruper and Uzgiris (1985) found for the most part very few differences between mothers' and fathers' speech to young children.

These findings of similarity have led many researchers to conclude that fathers are redundant with mothers as linguistic interactants. However, most of these studies focused exclusively on structural/linguistic measures. Other research has demonstrated that in the pragmatic/communicative domain—which is where familiarity should play a key role—fathers do differ in important ways from mothers. Killarney and McCluskey (1981), in a study of 32 parent-child dyads, found that fathers had shorter mutual dialogues with their children, and Golinkoff and Ames (1979) reported that fathers had fewer conversational turns than mothers. In a study of two 3-year-olds, Hiadek and Edwards (1984) found that fathers initiated fewer conversations with their children and responded less to child utterances. In the only experimental research of mothers' and fathers' linguistic interactions, Weist and Stebbins (1972) found that fathers were not as adept as mothers in understanding child speech.

Rondal (1980) investigated the speech of five French-speaking couples with their male children, ages 18–36 months. Results indicated that, for the most part, fathers employed the same structural simplification processes that were found in maternal speech. The one exception to this was in MLU, which was shorter for fathers (a finding also reported by Malone & Guy, 1982). More importantly, however, pragmatic differences emerged between the parental styles. Relative to mothers, fathers had fewer conversational turns and requested clarification of the child's utterances more often.

Masur and Gleason (1980) also focused on pragmatics. They documented that parents differed in their production and elicitation of lexical information: Fathers produced more label and function requests, which encouraged the children to provide greater lexical information. Consistent with these findings were the findings of Malone and Guy (1982). In their study of 10 parent-child dyads, fathers were more controlling in conversation as evidenced by their more frequent use of imperatives and directives, and their minimal use of questions. These authors argued that their findings supported Gleason's hypothesis because the fathers' more directive conversational style forced the child to exert herself more in an effort to communicate.

Although these findings were not perfectly consistent, the overall pattern would suggest that mothers and fathers are very similar in the linguistic/structural adjustments they make for young children. On the other hand, in the pragmatics of their communicative interactions—the way they relate their language and their child's language to the linguistic and nonlinguistic contexts—they do differ. For this reason, Tomasello, Farrar, and Kaley (1984) focused exclusively on pragmatic factors of mothers' and fathers' communicative interactions with their young children.

Before their first birthday, most children are capable of engaging in communicative interactions with their parents, relying exclusively on nonlinguistic devices to maintain a shared attentional focus—usually on some concrete object or activity (see, e.g., Lock, 1978). At some later point in development, children learn to use linguistic devices to initiate and maintain a shared focus, that is, they learn to engage in conversations. Unlike earlier interactions, these linguistic interactions are no longer limited to concrete objects. If it is true that fathers are less tuned in to their young children than mothers, this should manifest itself on both of these levels. In our study, therefore, we had two sets of hypotheses. First, on the nonlinguistic level, we expected that the father would be less likely to maintain a state of joint attentional focus with the child and, consequently, would relate his language to the child's current focus of attention less frequently—both of which are argued to be of crucial importance to early language acquisition (Bruner, 1983; Tomasello & Farrar, 1986). Second, on the linguistic level, we expected that fathers would be less likely to understand and respond appropriately to the child's utterances. This presumably is important to early language development as well (cf. Howe, 1981; Nelson, Denninger, Bonvillian, Kaplan, & Baker, 1984).

Subjects for the study were 24 white, middle-class children 12–18-months-of-age (mean age = 14.6 months). There were equal numbers of males and females, firstborns and laterborns. Children spent an average of 23 hours per week alone with their mothers and 8 hours per week alone with their fathers, $t(23) = 4.36$, $p<.001$. Subjects were videotaped in their homes in dyadic interaction for 15 minutes each with mother and father, with order of interaction counterbalanced across subjects. Experimenters provided toys—a novel set for each parent, counterbalanced across subjects—and gave no special instructions to the parents, except to "do what you normally do."

Videotapes were coded by two research assistants in three ways. First, states of joint attentional focus were determined by identifying episodes when the adult and child were both visually focused on the same object or action at the same time. It was required that the child be aware of the interaction, as evidenced by some overt behavior toward the adult (e.g., a look to the face) during this period (see Tomasello & Todd, 1983, for details of the coding scheme). Second, within these periods, each adult reference to an object was coded for whether it was made in an attempt to redirect the child's attentional focus to a new object or to follow in to the child's current attentional focus on an object. The success or failure of the attempt—i.e., whether or not the child visually attended to the referent object immediately after the adult made the reference—was also coded. Third, all of the parents' contingent replies to the child's utterances (both inside and outside periods of joint attentional focus) were placed into one of seven mutually exclusive and exhaustive categories. Four of these would seem to indicate a high degree of sensitivity and understanding of the infant's language in that they maintain the child's topic—acknowledgement (e.g., "yes" or "okay"), imitation (exact repetition of some or all of child utterance), recast (partial repetition with additional material), and topic continuation. The remaining three would seem to indicate a lesser degree of sensitivity in that they are off the child's topic—nonacknowledgment (no verbal response), request for clarification (e.g., "what?"), and topic change. Because the children were just beginning to learn language, only one general measure of conversation was obtained—average number of child turns per conversation. Conversations were defined as at least one child and one adjacent adult utterance on the same topic. Reliability for these measures was established by having a second pair of assistants code 20% of the videotapes in these same ways. Percent agreement ranged from 80–85% for Joint Attention; from 83–89% for Object Reference; and from 82–100% for the Conversation and Contingent Reply measures.

Results of the study showed that fathers were different from mothers in the predicted direction on some of each of the three types of measure. Means for all measures are presented in Table 2.1. First, fathers spent less time than mothers in joint attentional states with their children, $t(23) = 2.37, p<.01$. Second, within these states, fathers referred to objects a fewer number of times than mothers, $t(23) = 2.35, p<.01$. Fathers were also different from mothers in the proportional distribution of the types of object references they provided. Both parents directed the child's attention to new objects equally often and equally successfully. However, when the attempt was made to follow in to the child's current focus of attention on an object, fathers were successful less often than mothers, $t(23) = 1.87, p<.05$, and unsuccessful more often, $t(23) = 1.74, p<.05$.

The third group of measures concerned the parents' responses to the child's utterances. Analysis of these responses used only 17 of the 24 children as some children produced very little language with either the mother or the father. As can be seen in Table 2.1, overall, mothers made more replies that were on topic than fathers, while fathers made more off-topic replies, $t(16) = 2.26, p<.05$. In terms of individual response categories, mothers recast their child's utterances more often, $t(16) = 2.43, p<.05$, and there was a tendency for fathers to request clarification more often $t(16) = 1.56, p<.10$. The average number of child turns per conversation did not differ for mothers and fathers.

These results support the hypothesis that fathers are less tuned in to the young child than mothers. It is important to note in this regard that the children in the current study were at different levels of development in their use of linguistic and nonlinguistic communicative devices. Our 15-month-olds were quite familiar with nonlinguistic joint interactions, but they were just beginning to learn the role of language in initiating and maintaining a shared focus. Nevertheless,

TABLE 2.1
Means for Mothers and Fathers for All Measures

	Mothers	Fathers
Joint attention (secs)	608	493[a]
Object references (in joints)	29.51	18.34[a]
% follow-successful	.29	.18[a]
% follow-unsuccessful	.03	.12[a]
% direct-successful	.44	.46
% direct-unsuccessful	.25	.24
Contingent replies (N=17)		
% imitation	.31	.23
% acknowledgment	.06	.04
% recasts	.20	.10[a]
% topic continuation	.23	.31
on topic	.80	.68[a]
% topic change	.03	.04
% nonacknowledgment	.15	.22
% request clarification	.01	.06
off topic	.20	.32[a]
Child turns per conversation	1.5	1.4

[a] $p < .05$

fathers in the current study differed from mothers on both of these levels: They engaged in less nonlinguistic interaction with a joint attentional focus, and their linguistic interactions were not as tuned in to either the child's visual focus or conversational topic. Although mother-child and father-child conversations were of the same average length, on many occasions fathers failed to acknowledge or requested clarification of the child's utterance and so a conversation did not ensue. Undoubtedly, these differences between mothers and fathers diminish as the child becomes more and more linguistically capable. Nevertheless, along with previous research on differences in mother-child and father-child conversations, these results provide strong support for the first part of the Bridge Hypothesis, namely, that, compared to mothers, fathers are less tuned in to the young child in their social and linguistic interactions.

SIBLINGS

As with fathers, the research on siblings' communicative interactions with young children has just begun. This is unfortunate because more than 80% of American children have one or more siblings, which means that a considerable amount of their linguistic interaction is with brothers and sisters (Brody & Stoneman, 1982). Although sibling relations have long been considered important (Abramovitch, Corter, & Lando, 1979; Lamb, 1978), little research to date has focused on the part siblings play in the language acquisition process. Because young children often experience difficulties in tasks in which they must take the point of view of another person (see, e.g., the papers on referential communication in Dickson, 1981), it might be expected that they would have difficulties taking account of the linguistic limitations of infants and adjusting their speech accordingly.

Two early and well-known studies, however, demonstrated that preschool age children do modify their speech when speaking to infants, in much the same way as mothers modify theirs. Shatz and Gelman (1973) reported two studies which sought to determine if 4-year-olds made systematic speech modifications when talking to a 2-year-old. In the first study, the subjects were shown a new toy and then asked to discuss it with an adult and then a 2-year-old. In the second study, subjects' spontaneous speech with an adult and with the younger child were compared. Results from both studies indicated that 4-year-olds shortened their MLUs, used fewer complex constructions, and used more attentional utterances (*hey, look,* etc.) with 2-year-olds than with adults.

Sachs and Devin (1976) added two conditions to the Shatz and Gelman study. In one, 4-year-olds were asked to pretend to talk to a babydoll "who is just learning to talk." This manipulation was included to make it impossible for the children to modify their speech on the basis of cues from the listener. Results showed that the children adjusted their speech, even without listener feedback. The childrens' speech to the babydoll, as compared to their speech to a peer/adult, was characterized by shorter MLUs and preverb length, simpler tenses, a greater number of imperatives, labels, and self-repetitions. The second manipulation was a role-playing situation in which children were to "talk like a baby." When given these instructions, 4-year-olds showed shorter MLUs and preverb lengths and simpler tenses than in their normal speech. One measure that was expected to be the same for preschoolers and adults yielded results contrary to expectations: preschoolers asked fewer questions than adults (see also, Warren-Leubecker & Bohannon, 1983).

These two studies laid the foundation for the subsequent research on sibling language models. Although neither of these studies examined sibling behavior per se, they did establish that preschool age children are not egocentric when it comes to making structural speech modifications. Like the early research on fathers' linguistic interactions, these results encouraged a more thorough examination of sibling language models, especially with regard to pragmatics.

An effort to understand more precisely the nature of sibling linguistic interaction was undertaken by Dunn & Kendrick (1982) who systematically compared mother-infant dyads to sibling-infant dyads. Thirteen mother-sibling-infant triads were audiorecorded in their normal daily interactions in the home. Infants were 14-months-of-age and their siblings were 2- to 3-years-of-age. Many of the modifications in the siblings' language were similar to those previously reported.

Like their mothers, siblings adjusted their MLUs, used simpler tenses, and employed many self-repetitions and attentional utterances. However, in comparing siblings to mothers, Dunn and Kendrick observed important differences as well, especially in the pragmatics of the infant directed speech. For example, sibling use of self-repetitions and attentional devices occurred almost invariably when the sibling was attempting to prohibit or restrain the infant. The mothers' use of these same devices occurred most often in more "positive" interactions, such as those in which she was attempting to show the child something novel. Dunn and Kendrick suggested that, while it is true that preschoolers are capable of making structural adjustments when addressing language learning infants, there nevertheless exist important differences between the modifications of adults and siblings, especially with regard to their integration into the ongoing social-interactional context.

Tomasello and Mannle (1985) investigated more thoroughly the differences between the language models provided for infants by mothers and preschool age siblings, with a special emphasis on pragmatic factors since this is where we might expect to see the most significant differences. As with fathers, we expected that if the siblings were less tuned in to the infant than the mother, this would manifest itself in two ways. The first was nonlinguistic. It was expected that, like fathers (though perhaps for different reasons), siblings would be less likely than mothers to engage in social interactions with a joint attentional focus and to follow in to the infant's attentional focus when referring to objects. The second set of expected differences concerned the linguistic or conversational context. It was expected that, again like fathers, preschool age siblings would make fewer on-topic replies to infant utterances (imitations, recasts, acknowledgments, and topic continuations) and as a consequence engage in shorter conversational sequences with the infants. Conversely, it was expected that they would make more off-topic replies to infant utterances (nonacknowledgments, requests for clarification, and topic changes) than mothers.

Subjects were 10 white, middle class infant-sibling-mother triads. Five infants were male, five were female. Siblings were 3- to 5-years-old (mean = 4.1), and there were seven males and three females. Each was videotaped in their home for 30 minutes on two separate occasions: once when the infants were between 12- and 18-months-of-age (mean = 14.1) and again 6 months later. Mother and infant interacted in a free play situation for the first 15 minutes of each session, followed then by 15 minutes of sibling-infant interaction. In addition to structural measures of the infant directed speech (MLU, Questions, Directives, etc.), videotaped interactions were coded by a team of two researchers for the three types of measure also coded for the fathers in the Tomasello et al. (1984) study (with slight modifications): Joint Attention, Object Reference, and Contingent Replies. Reliabilities were established by having an independent researcher code a random sample of 20% of the videotapes. Percent agreements ranged from 88–

TABLE 2.2
Means for Mothers and Siblings for All Pragmatic Measures

| | 12-18 Months | | 18-24 Months | |
	Mother	Sibling	Mother	Sibling
Joint attention (secs)	583	85	634	62[b]
Object references	38	6	26	15[a]
% follow	.26	.14	.34	.12[a]
% direct	.74	.86	.66	.88[a]
Contingent replies				
% imitation			.06	.02
% acknowledgment			.09	.02
% recasts			.25	.03[a]
% topic continuation			.25	.03[a]
on topic			.65	.09[b]
% topic change			.09	.06[b]
% nonacknowledgment			.21	.83[b]
% request clarification			.05	.01[b]
off topic			.35	.91[b]
Child turns per conversation			1.3	.5[a]

[a] $p < .05$
[b] $p < .01$

100% for Structural and Object Reference measures; 89–100% for Joint Attention; and 83–100% for Conversation and Contingent Replies measures.

Mother-sibling comparisons on infant directed speech measures showed that siblings produced fewer utterances, $F(1,9) = 41.37$, $p<.001$, used a higher proportion of directives $F(1,9) = 29.49$, $p<.001$, and asked a smaller proportion of questions $F(1,9) = 95.23$, $p<.001$ than mothers. MLUs were equivalent for mothers and siblings (both between 2.5 and 3.0). These results correspond to those previously reported on structural differences in sibling and mother speech.

Means for the pragmatic measures are presented in Table 2.2. First, siblings were engaged in joint attention with infants for proportionally less time than mothers, $F(1,9) = 258.39$, $p<.001$. Second, siblings provided the infant with fewer references to objects than mothers, $F(1,9) = 8.21$, $p<.05$. Those references that they did present were mostly presented as directives, rather than as attempts to follow in to the infant's attentional focus, $F(1,9) = 9.70$, $p<.05$. The third group of measures concerned contingent replies. Because infants produced very few utterances in the earliest session, replies to infant utterances were analyzed for the second time point only. Siblings failed to acknowledge infant utterances 83% of the time, as compared to 21% for the mothers, $t(9) = 23.57$, $p<.001$. Siblings replied with topic continuations significantly less often, $t(9) = 8.81$, $p<.05$, and they recast the infant's utterance less often as well $t(9) = 5.53$, $p<.05$. Overall, siblings responded on topic less often than mothers, $t(9) = 5.56$, $p<.05$, and off topic more often $t(9) = 5.76$, $p<.05$. The average number of infant turns per conversation was significantly less when they were interacting with siblings $t(9) = 2.32$, $p<.05$.

Clearly, compared to mothers, siblings are less tuned in to young children in both their linguistic and nonlinguistic interactions. Like fathers, siblings in these interactions engage in fewer and shorter joint attentional episodes, are less likely to refer to objects by following the child's attentional focus, and are more likely to respond to infant utterances with off-topic replies. The explanation for this pattern of results is not entirely clear. Preschool age siblings may be less capable of tuning in to the infant's attentional focus simply because they are cognitively less sophisticated than adults. They may be less capable of providing appropriate linguistic feedback because they are less capable than adults at understanding and reconstructing the infant's background knowledge and point of view. It is also possible that they are unmotivated to do either of these. In any case, the current data make it evident that, like fathers, when compared with mothers, siblings are less tuned in to infants and so it may be said that they too conform to this first claim of the Bridge Hypothesis.

LINGUISTIC BRIDGES

It is clear that both fathers and siblings display characteristics which, according to Gleason's hypothesis, should serve to function as bridges to a wider community of speakers. However, the similarity of fathers and siblings in this regard does not imply that as bridges they serve identical functions. Our hypothesis is that they affect different aspects of the child's communicative competence, and so serve as bridges to different communities of speakers. We must acknowledge at the outset, however, that in assessing the effect of fathers and siblings, there are few directly relevant data. Nevertheless, we may employ several lines of indirect evidence to evaluate our hypothesis.

Two preliminaries. First, we must recognize that being less tuned into the child is not in all cases beneficial. If the interactant's speech (input) is not related to the referential context in a way comprehensible to the child, it is likely that the input simply is not processed by the child and no direct effects result. On the other hand, the interactant's responses to the child's communicative attempts (feedback) no matter what their nature—tuned in or not—provide the language learning child with information about the efficacy of her communicative skills. For this reason, feedback is the only aspect of communicative interaction directly addressed by the Bridge Hypothesis, and we will therefore focus on this aspect alone.

Second, we must also be precise about which aspects of the infant's competence might be affected by linguistic bridges. In particular, it is unclear whether traditional measures of language development such as MLU or vocabulary size are the most appropriate outcome measures since they are at best imperfect indicators of the child's ability to communicate effectively. One might argue that communicative strategies—for example, those involving the integration of language and gesture or those involving the choice of an appropriate response when a listener signals noncomprehension—might be more plausibly related to the child's exposure to different types of communicative interactants. Thus, in addressing the question of effects, we must remain open to the possibility that the effect of fathers and siblings is on aspects of communicative development not typically measured in studies of language acquisition.

In the two sets of data reported here, the striking difference between fathers and siblings was in the nature of the feedback they gave to the infant's utterances. Fathers usually responded (78% of opportunities) to the child's utterances with linguistic responses (many of which were off-topic). Siblings, on the other hand, responded a vast majority of the time (83%) with nonverbal (non-acknowledgment) responses. Our hypothesis is that these different styles of feedback lead the child to make different inferences about the efficacy of referential, as opposed to expressive, means of communication. We believe that this process works in the following way. When the child receives feedback that her initial effort to communicate is unsatisfactory, she first attempts to identify the reason for the failure (though, of course, she may be unable to do so), and she then devises an appropriate means for resolving it (though, again, this attempt may be unsuccessful). The nature of the feedback from an interactant is an important influence on the child's inference as to the cause of the communication failure and so on her choice of a communicative response. For example, if the father responds to the child's utterance "I want soup." with "You want what?", the child is given relatively specific information about the reason for communication failure: She may reasonably assume that the father heard the utterance, that he wanted to respond, but that he misunderstood a part of it (and she may even infer which part). If the sibling, on the other hand, does not even acknowledge the child's utterance, a variety of inferences about why her communication failed are possible: the sibling did not hear, did not understand, did not want to respond, and so forth. If the child is responded to in this way often enough, she may make the inference that referential means of communication—e.g., naming a desired object—are not always effective. She may thus come to prefer more expressive means of communication—e.g., whinning and pointing at the desired object—which may be more effective when interacting with a sibling.

This account is supported by further evidence from our father study (Tomasello et al., 1984). We correlated mothers' and fathers' contingent replies to child utterances at 15 months with the child's subsequent vocabulary size and percent general nominals (as a measure of referential-expressive orientation) at 21 months. Pearson Product Moment correlations, controlling for child age, are presented in Table 2.3.

In interpreting these relationships we must of course be careful when attribut-

TABLE 2.3
Pearson Product-Moment Correlations (Controlling Age) of Contingent Reply
Measures with Child Language at Follow-Up

| | Mothers | | Fathers | |
	Vocab	% Nominals	Vocab	% Nominals
Contingent replies (N=17)				
% imitation	--	$-.75^{b}$	--	$-.42^{a}$
% acknowledgment	--	--	--	$.55^{a}$
% recasts	--	--	$.51^{a}$	--
% topic continuation	--	$.46^{a}$	--	--
on topic	--	--	--	$.41^{a}$
% topic change	--	--	--	--
% nonacknowledgment	--	--	--	$.62^{b}$
% request clarification	$.53^{a}$	--	--	--
off topic	--	--	--	$.41^{a}$

[a] $p < .05$, one-tailed
[b] $p < .01$, one-tailed

ing a direction of causality. However, it is important to note that (a) the child measures were taken 6 months following the parent measures, (b) child age is controlled in the correlations, and, (c) the parent measures are proportions and thus it is unlikely that the amount of child speech affected them.

If we may interpret the correlations causally, it is clear that fathers do make a difference—especially with regard to the child's language acquisition style. Five of nine father measures correlated with the proportion of general nominals in the child's vocabulary. The positive correlations all involved minimal and/or off-topic replies. This would seem to suggest that fathers who provide high proportions of such replies encourage children toward a referential orientation, that is, they encourage children to choose object labels as communicative devices for requesting and drawing attention to objects, in preference to more expressive devices such as pronouns and/or rote formulas. Because words are the most widely conventional way to accomplish these aims, we might thus argue that off-topic replies of the sort used by fathers help the child to identify her unconventional means of expression and to find more conventional ones. It is also important to note that these correlations also imply that some fathers do not act in this way and so may have different effects on their children.

We do not wish to posit on the basis of these relationships that different response types are important for mothers and fathers. There is a complex relationship with overall parent frequency of response that makes such an interpretation of the current data problematic. Children in the current study were not speaking much (7 of the 24 children used very little language with either adult). Also, some parent responses were very infrequent, for example, maternal requests for clarification, which nevertheless correlated with child vocabulary size. Although we should remain open to the possibility that a given response may have different effects on the child depending on who makes it, it is just as likely that it is the response alone, no matter who it is from, that determines its effect on the child. Differential effects of the mother and father nevertheless may result from the fact that they produce different frequencies of these responses. In any case, as these are the only father-language correlations we are aware of, future research should attempt to corroborate our findings and to find more sensitive ways to assess the effects of fathers on early language development.

We are aware of no data correlating sibling interaction to child language development. However, some indirect support for our hypothesis is provided by the finding that laterborn children employ more expressive styles of language acquisition (Nelson, 1973; Nelson, Baker, Denninger, Bonvillian, & Kaplan, 1985). Tomasello and Mannle (1985) hypothesized that because siblings ignore so many of the child's utterances, their presence might initially encourage an expressive style. For example, having her object labels habitually ignored may lead the infant to infer that these labels are not as effective a means of communication as pronouns or rote formulas or even nonverbal means of communication.

It should be noted that, if indeed laterborns are more oriented toward expressive styles of communication, this would make them appear on traditional measures to be slower in their early acquisition of language (McCarthy, 1930) or no different from firstborns (Bretherton, McNew, Snyder, & Bates, 1983; Hardy-Brown, Plomin, & Defries, 1981). This would seem to be discrepant with the hypothesized beneficial effect of siblings. However, it is possible that the beneficial effect of siblings is not apparent until the child is older. Nelson et al. (1985), found that at 4-years-of-age, children who had earlier been classified as "expressive"—many of whom were laterborn—were now superior on some language measures. Another possibility is that siblings affect aspects of communicative development not investigated by studies of birth order. It is clear that none of these studies focused on the child's communicative competence broadly defined (Gleason & Weintraub, 1978). For example, they did not investigate differences in nonverbal communication, nor did they explore the possibility that the effect of siblings is on communicative strategies children use when their initial attempts at communication fail. Perhaps in these situations children with older siblings are more adept than firstborn children at finding some way, linguistic or nonlinguistic, to make themselves understood.

We should thus remain open to the possibility that the effect of siblings on the infant's communicative competence may be at ages or in ways we have not studied. In this regard, there is some research which suggests that laterborn children are qualitatively different in their social interactions with preschool peers (Pepler, Corter, & Abramovitch, 1982). It is not implausible to suppose that general, including perhaps pragmatic or nonverbal, communication skills—which may not be detectable by typically used language measures—may be involved in this difference. This suggests to us the possibility that siblings serve as a bridge to facilitate communication with peers. We of course realize that the evidence for this is indirect. Nevertheless, we believe that it is a plausible hypothesis and that at the very least it is worthy of further research.

Our overall hypothesis then is that, early in the child's language development, fathers and siblings serve as bridges to different communities of speakers. Unfamiliar adults are one group. These potential interactants are cognitively and linguistically more mature than infants and they are usually motivated to make sense of the child's speech, but their lack of familiarity may sometimes make understanding the child difficult. The child's father is also cognitively and linguistically mature and motivated, however he is typically of a moderate degree of familiarity: less familiar than the mother, but more familiar than other adults. His communicative interactions with his child will be similar to, but more tuned in than, the interactions of strangers with the child, and thus they should be good preparation for communicating with unfamiliar adults. Peers are another important group. They are closer to the child's level cognitively and linguistically, but they are often egocentric and/or unmotivated to converse with the infant. Siblings share these characteristics but are more familiar with the child (though less than the mother) and so presumably are better than peers at understanding his language. Again, this would seem to be good preparation—in this case for communicating with peers. Thus, in our conceptualization, it is their moderate degree of familiarity with the child that makes fathers and siblings serve as bridges, and it is their particular cognitive and linguistic characteristics that defines the community of speakers for whom they serve as bridges.

It must be remembered in all of this that many different family constellations are possible: Some children grow up without mothers, or without fathers, or without siblings. Still other children grow up with multiple siblings of varying ages and/or with significant roles being played by nonparent adults such as grandparents or sitters. In addition, however, even when two children have identical family constellations, they may still experience different language learning environments. Parents and siblings display individual differences in how they interact with young children and thus, for example, some fathers and siblings may interact in ways similar to mothers, and thus have different effects on the child's language. Also, family members differ in the amount of time they spend with their children and in the role they play in his or her life. Individual children also have different amounts and types of experiences with unfamiliar adults and peers. All of these considerations are of crucial importance if we are to document in full the language learning environments of young children and the processes by which they acquire the linguistic conventions of those around them.

COMMUNICATION PRESSURE

We have attempted here to begin specifying the nature of the child's communicative interactions with persons other than the primary caregiver mother. We have demonstrated that fathers and siblings communicate with young children in ways that differ systematically from the way mothers do—especially with regard to pragmatics. We have hypothesized that the effect of these types of interaction is to place the child under communication pressure, and that in adapting to this the child's communicative skills broaden in such a way that communication with a wider community of speakers is facilitated. Unfortunately, we know very little about the hypothesized mechanism of communication pressure.

This is beginning to change, however. In going beyond the demonstration that mothers provide their child with very few explicit corrections of their linguistic productions (Brown & Hanlon, 1970), recent research has demonstrated that mothers do provide their children with "implicit corrections" of their unconventional utterances by recasting them into conventional adult form (Demetras, Post, & Snow, 1986; Hirsch-Pasek, Trieman, & Schneiderman, 1984; see Rondal, 1985, for a review). If these recasts may also be considered a form of communication pressure—they make salient for the child a discrepancy between his and his caregiver's language—then it follows that even when adults understand children perfectly well, they still sometimes place them under pressure to conform to adult conventions. If this is the case, then perhaps we may generalize the cognitive comparison mechanism proposed by K. E. Nelson (1981) to include all cases where the child receives some indication that he is not speaking as adults speak. In some cases (recasts) he is receiving simultaneously an appropriate adult model to help reduce the discrepancy, while in others (requests for clarification, nonacknowledgments) he is not and must rely more on his own devices. If communication pressure and cognitive comparison may be generalized in these ways, we have a very powerful language learning mechanism, akin to general cognitive mechanisms such as equilibration (Piaget, 1977). Moreover, the operation of this mechanism depends in a vitally important way on social factors associated with the child's exposure to different communicative interactants.

There is much to be done in investigating the specific interrelations among interactants, feedback, and child strategies. Two lines of research seem especially important. First, we have yet to document in full the types of feedback provided children by different social interactants: mothers, fathers, siblings, strangers, peers, teachers, to name a few. Are there differences in the devices these interactants use when attempting to maintain a conversation? Do they rely on different types of feedback when they do not understand the child? Information on the extent of the child's contacts with these interactants at various developmental periods, in combination with information on the types of feedback they provide, would allow us to construct detailed profiles of the totality of the child's real-world language learning environment. Second, we need to make greater use of experimental approaches. In particular, we should manipulate experimentally different types of conversational responses to the child's utterances and examine the immediate effect in terms of the child's response to the feedback (see, e.g., Anselmi, Tomasello, & Acunzo, 1986, on children's responses to neutral and specific contingent queries). Also, we should investigate the long-term effects of different types of feedback—perhaps using a training paradigm where children are provided with predetermined numbers and types of feedback and their communicative development subsequently assessed (e.g., Nelson, 1977). We should also investigate the interactions among these, that is, we should investigate the possibility that the same feedback is responded to differently by the child depending upon the interactant (see, e.g., Tomasello, Farrar, & Dines, 1983, on children's responses to queries from the mother and a stranger).

The information provided by this type of research will allow us to evaluate the hypothesis that the child's expanding social world provides incentives, in the form of communication pressure, for her to broaden her communicative skills and so become fully socialized into the conventions of her culture. It will also allow us to evaluate more fully the specific claim of the Bridge Hypothesis that fathers, and in our extension siblings, play a special role in this process. Regardless of our specific hypotheses, it is clearly time for us to go beyond the mother—important though she may be—in exploring the child's language learning environment and the effects this has on the development of communicative competence.

ACKNOWLEDGMENT

Portions of this chapter were presented to the International Association for the Study of Child Language, Austin, Texas, 1984. The authors would like to thank Jeff Farrar and Lisa Kaley for assistance with data analysis and coding. Also thanks to Keith Nelson, Anne van Kleeck, and Ann Kruger for helpful comments and discussions. Thanks to Lena Beatenbough for assistance in preparing the manuscript.

REFERENCES

Abramovitch, R., Corter, C., & Lando, B. (1979). Sibling interaction in the home. *Child Development, 50,* 997–1003.

Anselmi, D., Tomasello, M., & Acunzo, M. (1986). Young children's responses to neutral and specific contingent queries. *Journal of Child Language, 13*(1), 135–144.

Bateson, M. C. (1979). The epigenesis of conversational interaction: A personal account of research development. In M. Bullowa (Ed.), *Before Speech* (pp. 63–79). New York: Cambridge University Press.

Bretherton, I., McNew, S., Snyder, L., & Bates, E. (1983). Individual differences at 20 months: Analytic and holistic strategies in language acquisition. *Journal of Child Language, 10*(2), 293–320.

Brody, G., & Stoneman, Z. (1982). Family influences on language and cognitive development. In J. Worrell (Ed.), *Psychological development in the elementary years* (pp. 321–357). New York: Academic Press.

Brown, R. (1973). *A first language: The early stages*. Cambridge, MA: Harvard University Press.

Brown, R., & Hanlon, C. (1970). Derivational complexity and order of acquisition in child speech. In J. R. Hayes (Ed.), *Cognition and the development of language* (pp. 11–54). New York: Wiley.

Bruner, J. (1983). *Child's talk: Learning to use language*. New York: Norton.

Clarke-Stewart, K. A. (1978). And daddy makes three: The father's impact on mother and young child. *Child Development, 49,* 466–478.

Demetras, M. J., Post, K. N., & Snow, C. E. (1986). Feedback to first language learners: The role of repetitions and clarification questions. *Journal of Child Language, 13,* 275–292.

Dickson, W. P. (Ed.). (1981). *Children's oral communication skills*. Orlando, FL: Academic Press.

Dunn, J., & Kendrick, C. (1982). The speech of two and three year olds to infant siblings: Baby talk and the context of communication. *Journal of Child Language, 9,* 579–595.

Gleason, J. B. (1975). Fathers and other strangers: Men's speech to young children. *Georgetown University Rountable on Language and Linguistics* (pp. 289–297). Washington, D.C.: Georgetown University Press.

Gleason, J. B., & Weintraub, S. (1978). Input language and the acquisition of communicative competence. In K. E. Nelson (Ed.), *Children's Language, Volume 1* (pp. 171–222). New York: Gardner Press.

Golinkoff, R. M., & Ames, G. T. (1979). A comparison of fathers' and mothers' speech with their young children. *Child Development, 50,* 28–32.

Hardy-Brown, K., Plomin, R., & DeFries, J. (1981). Genetic and environmental influences on the rate of communicative development in the first year of life. *Developmental Psychology, 17,* 704–717.

Hiadek, E., & Edwards, H. (1984). A comparative analysis of mother-father speech in the naturalistic home environment. *Journal of Psycholinguistic Research, 13*(5), 321–332.

Hirsh-Pasek, K., Trieman, R., & Schneiderman, M. (1984). Brown and Hanlon revisited: Mothers' sensitivity to ungrammatical forms. *Journal of Child Language, 11,* 81–83.

Hopman, M. (1985, April). *Mothers and fathers as playmates and teachers*. Paper presented at the Biennial meeting of the Society for Research in Child Development, Toronto.

Howe, C. (1981). *Acquiring language in a conversational context*. New York: Academic Press.

Kavanaugh, R. D., & Jen, M. (1981). Some relationships between parental speech and children's object language development. *First Language, 2,* 103–115.

Kavanaugh, R. D., & Jirkovsky, A. M. (1982). Parental speech to young children: A longitudinal analysis. *Merrill-Palmer Quarterly, 28,* 297–311.

Killarney, J., & McCluskey, K. (1981, April). *Parent-infant conversations at age one: Their length, reciprocity and contingency*. Paper presented at Biennial meeting of the Society for Research in Child Development, Boston.

Kruper, J., & Uzgiris, I. (1985, April). *Fathers' and mothers' speech to infants*. Paper presented at the Biennial meeting of the Society for Research in Child Development, Toronto.

Lamb, M. (1978). Interactions between eighteen-month-olds and their preschool-aged siblings. *Child Development, 49,* 51–59.

Lipscomb, T., & Coon, R. (1983). Parental speech modifications to young children. *Journal of Genetic Psychology, 143,* 181–187.

Lock, A. (Ed.). (1978). *Action, gesture and symbol*. Orlando, FL: Academic Press.

Malone, M., & Guy, R. (1982). A comparison of mothers' and fathers' speech to their three year old sons. *Journal of Psycholinguistic Research, 11*(6), 599–608.

Masur, E., & Gleason, J. B. (1980). Parent-child interaction and the acquisition of lexical information during play. *Developmental Psychology, 16*(5), 404–409.

McCarthy, D. (1930). The language development of the preschool child. *Institute of Child Welfare Monograph,* Minneapolis: University of Minnesota Press.

Nelson, K. (1973). Structure and strategy in learning to talk. *Monographs of the Society for Research in Child Development, 38,* (serial no. 149).

Nelson, K. (1981). Individual differences in language development: Implications for development and language. *Developmental Psychology, 17,* 170–187.

Nelson, K. E. (1977). Facilitating children's syntax acquisition. *Developmental Psychology, 13,* 101–107.

Nelson, K. E. (1981). Toward a rare event cognitive comparison theory of syntax acquisition. In P. S. Dale and D. Ingram (Eds.), *Child language: An international perspective* (pp. 229–240). Baltimore, MD: University Park Press.

Nelson, K. E., Baker, N., Denninger, M., Bonvillian, J., & Kaplan, B. (1985). Cookie versus do-it-again: Imitative-referential and personal-social-syntactic-initiating language styles in young children. *Linguistics, 23,* 1–29.

Nelson, K. E., Denninger, M. M., Bonvillian, J. D., Kaplan, B. J., & Baker, N. D. (1984). Maternal input adjustments and non-adjustments as related to children's linguistic advances and to language acquisition theories. In A. Pellegrini & T. Yawkey (Eds.), *The Development of Oral and Written Language in Social Contexts* (31–56). Norwood, NJ: Ablex.

Pepler, D., Corter, C., & Abramovitch, R. (1982). Social relations among children: Comparison of sibling and peer interaction. In K. H. Rubin & H. S. Ross (Eds.), *Peer relations and social skills in childhood* (pp. 209–227). New York: Springer-Verlag.

Piaget, J. (1977). *The development of thought: Equilibration of cognitive structures.* New York: Viking Press.

Rebelsky, F., & Hanks, C. (1971). Fathers' verbal interaction with infants in the first three months of life. *Child Development, 42,* 63–68.

Rondal, J. (1980). Fathers' and mothers' speech in early language development. *Journal of Child Language, 7,* 353–369.

Rondal, J. (1985). *Adult-child interaction and the process of language acquisition.* New York: Praeger.

Sachs, J., & Devin, J. (1976). Young children's use of age-appropriate speech styles in social interaction and role playing. *Journal of Child Language, 5,* 391–402.

Shatz, M., & Gelman, R. (1973). The development of communication skills: Modifications in the speech of young children as a function of the listener. *Monographs of the Society for Research in Child Development, 38* (5, Serial no. 152).

Snow, C., & Goldfield, B. (1983). Turn the page please: Situation-specific language acquisition. *Journal of Child Language, 10,* 551–570.

Tomasello, M., & Farrar, M. J. (1986). Joint attention and early language. *Child Development, 57,* 1454–1463.

Tomasello, M., Farrar, M. J., & Dines, J. (1984). Children's speech revisions for a familiar and unfamiliar adult. *Journal of Speech and Hearing Research, 27,* 359–363.

Tomasello, M., Farrar, M. J., & Kaley, L. (1984, July). *Lexical and conversational differences in mothers' and fathers' speech to one-year-olds.* Paper presented at the International Association for the Study of Child Language, Austin, Texas.

Tomasello, M., & Mannle, S. (1985). Pragmatics of sibling speech to one-year-olds. *Child Development, 56,* 911–917.

Tomasello, M., & Todd, J. (1983). Joint attention and lexical acquisition style. *First Language, 4,* 197–212.

Warren-Leubecker, A., & Bohannon, J. W. (1983). The effects of verbal feedback and listener type on the speech of preschool children. *Journal of Experimental Child Psychology, 35,* 540–548.

Weist, R., & Stebbins, P. (1972). Adult perceptions of childrens' speech. *Psychonomic Science, 27,* 359–360.

3 Situational Variability in Mother-Child Conversations

Gina Conti-Ramsden
University of Manchester

Sandy Friel-Patti
University of Texas at Dallas

Variability in language use is an area that has received much attention in the last 2 decades. We now know that there are differences between the speech of different speakers. Middle-class speakers speak differently than working-class speakers (Labov,1966; Trudgill, 1974); adults speak differently than teenagers, who in turn speak differently than children (Macaulay, 1978; Romaine, 1984); and male speakers speak differently than female speakers (Cheshire, 1982; Lakoff, 1973; Smith, 1979). But linguistic variation also occurs within the speech of a single speaker. Stubbs (1983) has emphasized that all speakers are multidialectal or multistylistic, in the sense that they adapt and change the way they speak in accordance with the situational context they find themselves in. Thus, who we speak to, where we speak, what we talk about and what we are doing affects our language use in many ways such as our politeness strategies (Brown & Levinson, 1978), our address systems (Ervin-Tripp, 1973) and our turn-taking patterns (Sacks, Schegloff, & Jefferson, 1974).

TWO RESEARCH TRADITIONS

In child language research, the questions of linguistic variation in children's use of language has been addressed from two rather different, though related, angles. First, some researchers interested in child language have focused on the influences of contextual variables on the language produced by children. The key area of concern has been the effect of situational variability on the task of determining children's language abilities. Are we in danger of misrepresenting children's linguistic abilities if we only look at the child in a particular situation? What sorts

43

of situations are more conducive for children to display their current linguistic abilities? Cazden (1970) has suggested that the topic, task, conversational partner and the nature of the interaction can significantly affect how a child uses language and, thus, can affect our perceptions of their abilities. In terms of topic, she has reviewed the work of Strandberg (1969) who found that 4- and 5-year-old children talked more about either a toy or a 20 second silent film about that toy than they did about a color photograph of it. As far as task, Cazden has found that lower-class black American children use longer utterances in informal tasks than in highly structured ones. The work of Smith (1935) has suggested that the characteristics of the conversational partner can significantly affect language use. In this study preschool children were found to use longer utterances at home when speaking with adults than at play when speaking with other children. Lastly, Cazden had suggested that the nature of the interaction can play an important role in language use. For example, in adult-child interaction conversations that are initiated by the child are usually longer than conversations initiated by the adult.

More recent research corroborates Cazden's early suggestions. Atkins and Cartwright (1982) have found that 3- to 5-year-old Head Start children talked more and used longer utterances and a greater number of inflections in picture interpretation tasks than in tasks involving responding to imperatives or story retelling. Much like Longhurst and Grubb (1974) and Longhurst and File (1977), these authors have found that less structured conversational settings resulted in language of greater quantity and complexity than the more structured conversational settings.

In the same vein, Stalnaker and Creaghead (1982) have suggested there may be different situational effects on different aspects of language. They have found that although retelling a story produced the longest utterances, natural play with toys and playing with toys while asking the children questions produced more utterances in 4- to 5-year-old Head Start children. Similarly, the work of Dore and his colleagues (Cole, Dore, Hall, & Dowley, 1978; Dore, 1978) has pointed out that preschool children's conversational performance varied in terms of the amount, type and range of speech acts they used in a classroom versus a supermarket situation. In these studies, it is the topic of conversation as well as the nature of the interaction which affects children's language use. The effect of the conversational partner, also suggested by Cazden (1970), is discussed at length by Mannle and Tomasello (this volume).

The second perspective on linguistic variation has come from research on mother-child interaction. In this tradition, investigations have attempted to identify specific contexts which may be conducive for language learning and language use. Bruner and his colleagues (Bruner, 1978; Ninio & Bruner, 1978; Ratner & Bruner, 1978) have argued that routines involving games such as peek-a-boo provide the child with an excellent opportunity to master a variety of language forms and functions. It is within these routine contexts, with their predictable, simple format, that children often attempt to use what they are learning. Thus, routine contexts not only provide the framework within which language develops but they also provide an opportunity for children to exhibit their most sophisticated linguistic behaviors.

Snow and her colleagues (Snow & Goldfield, 1983; Snow, Perlmann, & Nathan, this volume) have also suggested that conventionalized routines involving mother-child interaction form the basis from which language develops. Snow and Goldfield (1983) have investigated in great detail the book-reading routine of a child and his mother. They have found that the child used utterances in the book-reading context which could be directly traced to what his mother had said in previous occurrences of that context. The authors thus view not only the routinization of the situation but the predictability of the utterances used by mothers in these situations as important factors in language learning. In this volume, Snow, Perlmann, and Nathan have further argued that in familiar, routinized situations children's speech is more complex and more sophisticated. Children use longer utterances (as measured by mean length of utterance) and they use a greater number and variety of grammatical morphemes in routinized versus nonroutinized contexts. Furthermore, these researchers have suggested that routinization also affects maternal speech. They have hypothesized that maternal speech is more complex and less semantically contingent during routine than during less routine situations. Once again, taking the results of both sets of studies jointly, it is argued not only that routinized situations are the basis from which language develops but also that they are the type of context in which children exhibit more sophisticated linguistic behaviors.

Katherine Nelson and her colleagues (Luciarello, Kyratzis, & Nelson, 1983; Luciarello & Nelson, 1982; Nelson & Gruendel, 1979, 1981) have attempted to explain the facilitative role of routines for language learning and use with the notion of the script. They have suggested that young children may form event representations for the routinized events they participate in. These event representations or scripts when shared by mother and child may enable the mother-child dyad to indulge in more sophisticated linguistic behaviors and thus serve as scaffolding for further language growth. Nelson and her colleagues have argued that sharing scripts is sharing knowledge about sequences of events and thus, such sharing can provide a structure within which interaction and understanding can take place. Also they have argued that knowledge of scripts frees the child from having to spend a great deal of time in trying to understand the situation itself and instead the child has the time and the opportunity to try new skills, including language.

RATIONALE FOR THE STUDY

The present study is an attempt to marry the two research traditions on cross-situational variation in children's language using the script as a unifying theme. In the first tradition, we found researchers concerned with determining children's linguistic abilities across a variety of situations. Such research has usually focused on one member of the dyad, the child, and on traditional structural-linguistic measures such as mean length of utterance or vocabulary size. Conversely, research of the second tradition has usually involved the mother-child dyad and although structural-linguistic measures have been commonly used, they have been applied to both conversational partners.

In the present study, the question of situational variability of children's linguistic abilities are expanded to involve the entire mother-child dyad. Mother-child dyads are observed in three different contexts. A play context, a no-toys context, and a new-toy context. This study is also designed to expand the range of measures previously used. Traditional structural-linguistic measures of maternal and child language are used in order to replicate existing research but in addition, dyadic conversational measures are investigated in an attempt to explore the effect of situational variability at the pragmatic level. Much like Mannle and Tomasello (this volume), we think that conversational behaviors such as the ability of the child to share in conversation, to choose what the dyad will talk about, and the extent to which the child can hold the floor as speaker, may more plausibly be related to the child's participation in different types of situations than traditional structural language behaviors might be.

From the research tradition on mother-child interaction we have learned that routinized contexts are scripted and thus provide an opportunity for the child to use more sophisticated language (Luciarello et al., 1983; Nelson & Gruendel, 1979, 1981). Nonetheless, it can be argued that scripts, although originating from particular contexts of routinization, can be used by mothers and their children outside these routinized, scripted contexts (Lucariello et al., 1983). Indeed, the mother-child dyad can apply scripts to highly similar new contexts. Consequently, it is possible that young children bring scripts from the different situations they engage in. Indeed, it could be argued that an important source of children's and indeed mothers' language variation may be the degree of scriptedness of the contexts they participate in. The present study was designed to examine this possibility.

Intuitively, the three situations to be observed in this study—play, no-toys, and new-toy—vary in the degree of scriptedness they can afford. First, free play appears to be the most scripted of the three. In the free play situation with toys children know that balls are for throwing or rolling, seriated cups are for stacking and nesting, toy vehicles are for pushing along the floor, toy telephones are for talking to absent people, and so forth. Thus children have some routine sequences of events available to them for use. Second, the no-toys context appears to follow in degree of scriptedness. The no-toys, waiting context might be reasonably familiar to children from similar activities such as waiting at the doctor's or dentist's. The children may have acquired a certain knowledge of the routine behaviors engaged in this type of situation, for example, sitting on mum's lap, pointing to and labeling things which can be seen, or talking about what they will do next. And finally, the new-toy situation would, in our opinion, be the least scripted situation of all three. In our study, the children would have to play not only with a new toy they had not seen before, but a toy that was challenging for them in terms of learning how to use it and be successful at it. In this situation, children would have less access to routine behaviors they could rely on.

In terms of maternal speech, more scripted situations can provide an opportunity for mothers to use more complex and less semantically contingent language (Snow et al., this volume). In more scripted situations, mothers can afford to be less finely tuned to their children because they both share knowledge of the sequences of events they are engaging in. The predictability of more routinized, scripted contexts can serve as the basis for mother-child communication. In more scripted situations, children do not have to process maternal speech in the same way they have to in unfamiliar situations. Children can respond to scripted language without having to fully analyze it because they know the routines.

Specifically, the research was designed to address the following questions:

1. Are mothers' and children's language more complex in more scripted situations?
2. Is maternal language less semantically contingent in more scripted situations?
3. Are dyadic discourse behaviors more sophisticated in more scripted situations?
4. Are children's discourse behaviors more sophisticated in more scripted situations?
5. Can we reliably measure degrees of scriptedness in different situations?

METHOD

Procedures

The present investigation examined some characteristics of mother-child conversations across three situations in the laboratory. The first situation, free *play*, is typical of those used in child language acquisition research. In this context, mother-child pairs played with a set of toys (a stuffed ball, a shopping cart, a stuffed doll, a toy telephone, a large box full of leggos, cars and trucks). The second situation was the *no-toys* context. Mother-child pairs were brought into a room barren of toys and were asked to wait for a few minutes. Lastly, the third situation was called the *new-toy* context as it consisted of presenting the mother-child pairs with a toy selected to be somewhat challenging for children in their third year-of-life (an etch-a-sketch skodoodle toy). Mothers were instructed to try to show their children how to play with the toy.

Ten mother-child dyads, six girls and four boys aged between 2;3 to 2;9 years, were audio and video-recorded through an observation window while interacting in a laboratory playroom. All children were from white, apparently middle-class families living in a large southern city in the United States. All children scored at or above their age level in the *Sequenced Inventory of Communication Development* (Hedrick, Preather, & Tobin, 1975). Thus, all the children were normal language learners learning English in monolingual homes. The mothers were nonworking or worked part-time so that they were at home with the children most of the time.

The interactive session lasted for 15 minutes for each mother-child dyad: 5 minutes of the no-toys context, 5 minutes of play and 5 minutes of the new-toy context. The order of presentation of the conditions was counterbalanced only for the play and new-toy conditions. All sessions began with the no-toys condition as this facilitated having the children wait with their mothers (in the hope that there would be an opportunity to play later).

The three 5-minute interactions were transcribed from the videotape recordings. Transcriptions included verbal and behavioral events and the context in which these events occurred. Thirty percent of the data were transcribed by an additional transcriber working independently. Interater reliability based on percentage agreement between the two transcribers was 94%.

The Measures

In order to address the questions outlined in the introduction the following measures were taken:

1. *Children's language measures.* Each child's mean length of utterance (MLU) was calculated using the guidelines suggested by Brown (1973) for all child utterances in each of the situations. The mean length of five longest utterances (MLU5) was also calculated to facilitate comparisons with Snow, Perlman, and Nathan (this volume).

2. *Maternal language measures.* Mothers' mean length of utterance (in words) was calculated for all maternal utterances in each of the situations. In addition, the percentage of maternal utterances which were semantically contingent on preceding child utterance was calculated. Like Snow et al. (this volume), we defined semantically contingent utterances as those utterances which followed the same topic.

3. *Dyadic discourse measures.* The number of conversations and the number of turns per conversation were calculated. The definition of a conversation was taken from the work of Luciarello et al. (1983) in order to facilitate comparisons with this study. A conversation was defined as two or more turns linked together

by a focus on a particular topic. Thus, every time either conversational partner changed the topic, the start of a new conversation was noted. Conversations thus could vary in length depending upon how long the dyad purposely continued to maintain the established topic. The length of conversations was calculated by counting the number of turns between topic shifts. Luciarello et al. (1983) found that in more routine, scripted contexts mother-child dyads engaged in more lengthy conversations.

4. *Children's discourse measures.* Three discourse measures of children's ability to initiate and maintain conversations were calculated. The first measure involved child-chosen topics. The percentage of time conversations were initiated by the child was calculated in an attempt to capture the degree of the child's involvement in the management of conversations. It was thought that a low percentage would reflect the child's reliance on mother to introduce new topics, while a measure of around 50% would reflect the child's ability to equally share with mother the responsibility of initiating new conversations and thus, keep the dialogue going. In the same vein, the number of child-initiations within conversations were calculated as the second measure. Once the topic of conversation has been established, this topic needs to be maintained. The child then has the choice of being more passive, that is mainly responding, or of being more active, that is actively pushing the conversation forward with initiations on the *same topic*. The ability of the child to initiate within a topic (within conversations) reflect the ability of the child to take the speaker role within the contraints of a particular topic. In early mother-child dialogues it is the mother who usually initiates and the child who responds (Bruner, 1978). But gradually the child develops towards a more active participation through initiations such as comments, questions, and commands. Following this line of argument, it was thought that a greater percentage of child-initiations within conversations would suggest greater sophistication on the part of the child to engage in dialogue within the same topic. Finally, children's mean number of utterances per turn were calculated. Cazden (1970) has discussed the variability in children's length of response in different situations. In some cases, children tend to be very brief and hardly control the conversation for any length of time. In other cases, children tend to indulge in their turn more. They use more utterances and often these utterances are more complex. It was thought that the measure of number of utterances per turn could reflect children's ability to hold the floor of the conversation for a period of time. The greater number of utterances children use per turn, the greater the chance they have to influence the conversational partner, by exchanging information, requesting action, or emphasizing their point of view.

A reliability index was obtained for the five discourse measures used in this study. Cohen's (1960) kappa based on one-third of the transcripts was .92, suggesting good interrater reliability for the discourse analysis.

TABLE 3.1
Child and Maternal Language Measures by Context

Measures	Play (X)	No-Toys (Y)	New-Toy (Z)	P
child MLU	3.54^a	3.22^b	2.95^c	X-Y < .007 Y-Z < .05 X-Z < .005
child MLU 5	7.04^a	6.34^b	5.30^c	X-Y < .06 Y-Z < .03 X-Z < .005
maternal MLU (in words)	5.08	5.25	5.22	no signif. difference
percentage of maternal seman- tically contingent utterances	44.2^a	43.9^a	24.2^b	X-Z < .005 Y-Z < .005

[a,b,c]Numbers sharing superscripts within a row do not differ significantly. Conversely, those with different superscripts do. Each set of comparisons is specified and the P level reported according to the Wilcoxen Matched-Pairs Signed-Ranks Test.

RESULTS

The results for the children's and mothers' language measures are presented in Table 3.1. In this table the situations are ordered in terms of their degree of scriptedness from play (most scripted) to new-toy (least scripted). It was found that children's speech was more complex the more scripted the situation. Specifically, the children's MLU was significantly greater in the play situation than in the no-toy situation and new-toy situation. In turn, children's MLU in the no-toys situation was significantly greater than in the new-toy situation. The identical set of results were obtained when the analysis was done using MLU for the five longest utterances per child (MLU5).

As far as maternal speech, no significant differences were found in mothers' language complexity across contexts as measured by MLU. In contrast, mothers' percentage of semantically contingent utterances was significantly smaller in the new-toy, least-scripted context than in the play and no-toys contexts.

The results for the discourse measures examined in this study are presented in Table 3.2. With respect to the dyadic discourse measures, it was found that mothers and their children engaged in significantly more conversations in the no-toys context than in the play and new-toy contexts. Not surprisingly, the number of conversations though was inversely related to the length of the conversations. In the new-toy context the mother-child dyads had fewer but much longer conversations than in the play and no-toys conditions.

The second section of Table 3.2 looks at the children's discourse behaviors in more detail. In general, it was found that the more scripted the context, the more sophisticated the children's discourse behaviors. First, children initiated conver-

TABLE 3.2
Discourse Characteristics of Mother-Child Conversations by Context

Dyadic Discourse Measures	Play (X)	No-Toys (Y)	New-Toy (Z)	P
mean number of conversations	8.5^a	11.7^b	6.9^a	X-Y < .02 Y-Z < .05
mean number of turns per conversation	9.1^a	5.7^b	21.6^{ab}	X-Y < .02 X-Z < .02 Y-Z < .01

Children's Discourse Measures				
mean percentage of conversations initiated by child (child chosen topics)	67.1^a	54.3^a	37.8^b	X-Z < .10 Y-Z < .05
mean percentage of child's initiations within conversations	56.2^a	54.7^a	32.1^b	X-Z < .005 Y-Z < .02
child's mean number of utterances per turn	1.44^a	1.13^b	0.75^b	X-Y < .05 X-Z < .005

[a,b]Numbers sharing superscripts within a row do not differ significantly. Conversely, those with different superscripts do. Each set of comparisons is specified and the P level reported according to the Wilcoxen Matched-Pairs Signed-Ranks Test.

sations and turns within conversations significantly more often in the play and the no-toys context than in the new-toy context. That is, the mother and child shared the conversational floor more equally in the play and no-toys contexts, while in the new-toy context the child was in the listener-responder role two-thirds of the time. Second, children had significantly more utterances per turn in the play situation than in the other two situations. In the play context, children were saying more when they took a turn and thus were contributing more to the conversation.

DISCUSSION

Maternal and Child Language Measures

Our results corroborate earlier research which suggests that children's speech is more complex in more familiar, routinized, scripted situations than in less scripted situations (Ratner & Bruner, 1978). Like Snow et al. (this volume) we found that children's MLU and MLU5 were significantly greater the more scripted the context. It appears that the more familiar the situation, the more likely children are to use what they know linguistically. Unlike Snow et al. (this volume), though, we found no effect of situation on maternal MLU. Maternal speech was equally complex in the three situations. In other words, there was no relationship between maternal MLU and child MLU. We did not find that the relative complexity of maternal MLU was highest for the more scripted situations. This finding puts in doubt the claim made by Snow et al., that in more routinized situations, a powerful process is that of delayed imitation. If the child were imitating what mother has said and she was using more complex language, then it would follow that the child's language would also be more complex. Instead, what we found was that the children in this study used more complex language in more scripted situations although they were exposed to language of equal complexity from their mothers throughout the three situations. Nevertheless, it could be that initially, when routines are being established, delayed imitation plays a very important role but as mothers and children become more and more familiar with the routine, children are freed from having to imitate and can choose how to say what they want to say. The children in this study were in their third year of life (2;3–2;9 years) while the children in Snow, Perlman, and Nathan were mostly in their second year of life (1;5–2;3 years), and this may well have been a factor affecting our results. But, this possible variable cannot explain why Snow, Perlmann, and Nathan found maternal MLU to increase with routinization while we did not. One possible explanation for the discrepant findings is the nature of the routines. Snow et al. argue, based on the work of developmental psycholinguistics and ethnographers interested in cross-cultural research, that routines usually involve more complex language, that they are usually arbitrary and not semantically contingent. We would like to cast some doubt on the first claim, that is, that routines involve more complex language on the part of mothers by suggesting that, although this sometimes may be the case, it is not always necessarily so. Routines may vary in their degree of complexity and thus in the degree of complexity of the language used by mothers when participating in those routines with their children. Granted, Snow et al., when reviewing cross-cultural research, identify routines such as the *elema* teaching device used by the Kaluli mothers of Papua New Guinea (Schieffelin, 1979) which involve highly complex language, but this is more than likely the end of a continuum rather than the norm. A catalogue of routines from a variety of cultures would probably reveal a great deal of variability as to the degree of complexity involved in them. Another possible explanation comes from the work of D'Odorico and Franco (1985). These researchers have argued that syntactic aspects of maternal speech may be the consequence of the particular context in which data are collected. The contexts used in our study were different from those used by Snow et al. and this itself could have affected our results for maternal MLU.

Our finding on maternal semantic contingency casts some doubt on the second claim made by Snow et al. (this volume) that routines are arbitrary and not semantically contingent. Indeed, we found the opposite trend. Our results suggest that the less scripted the context, the less semantically contingent the maternal speech, and not vice versa. Once again, some routines like the *elema* routine of Kaluli communities may indeed be arbitrary and not semantically contingent but on the other hand, other routines such as feeding, bathing and dressing in western societies are not arbitrary and are semantically contingent. In our view, routinization and contingency are not necessarily in conflict with each other. It is a matter of degree and it is highly dependent upon the nature of the routine. Thus, although we found that the least scripted context yielded the least semantically contingent speech, we do not believe that this is a trend that will be necessarily replicated unless the type of situations used are highly similar to the ones we used. As we have said before, the nature of the routines shared in the different contexts could affect the degree of semantic contingency of maternal speech.

In addition, factors other than the degree of scriptedness could influence semantic contingency. One such factor could be the nature of the task we put forward to the mother-child dyads in the new-toy (least-scripted) situation. Mothers were instructed to try to show their children how to play with the new toy. Mothers succeeded very well in this task. They maintained children's interest and they encouraged children's attempts to draw the different shapes available as part of the toy but they did not do so by following the children's leads but instead, imposed their focus in the interaction. The mothers directed and encouraged, and the children complied. Thus, although our results in the dyadic measures show that in the new-toy context mother-child dyads engaged in their longest conversations, this may not have been because the mothers were semantically contingent on the child's preceding utterance and/or nonverbal actions, but it may have been because mothers dictated the focus and sequence of the interaction and the children tended to comply.

Discourse Measures

The dyadic discourse measures of number of conversations and number of turns per conversation did not appear to be directly related to the degree of scriptedness of the contexts in any clear way. We did not find the clear trend found by Luciarello et al. (1983) that in more routine, scripted context mother-child dyads engage in more lengthy conversations. Indeed, we found that the less-scripted, new-toy context yielded the longest conversations. In the previous section we pointed out that the length of the conversations may not have been an index of the child's ability to engage in sustained dialogue, but a major effort on the part of the mother to keep the conversation around a particular topic—the new toy. Thus, although we do not think the degree of scriptedness was the only major variable affecting our results, it is a variable which cannot be easily discarded.

What other factors besides scriptedness could have influenced our results? We found that mothers and their children engaged in significantly more conversations in the no-toys context than in the play and new-toy contexts. The absence of toys and thus the lack of perceptual support for mother-child dialogue may be at least partly responsible for the increased number of conversations in the no-toys context. These conversations were significantly shorter when compared to those in the other two contexts. Simplistically, in the no-toys condition, mother and child went from topic to topic quickly in order to pass the time. Conversely, in the new-toy condition, the mother-child dyad had fewer but much longer conversations owing at least in part, to the availability of only one, rather challenging toy and the mothers' continual efforts to keep the child playing with that toy. Finally, the results of the play context fall truly in between those of the other two contexts. In the play context, mother-child dyads engaged in an average of 8.5 conversations with a mean length of 9.1 turns each. Thus, it appears that the physical set up of the situation and the functional everyday considerations such as passing the time so that the child will not get bored or fussy or maintaining the child's interest in a particular toy, may influence the number and length of conversations mother and child share together.

Scriptedness did seem to play an important role in children's discourse behaviors. We found that, relative to their discourse in the new-toy context, the children's discourse was more sophisticated in the two more scripted, familiar situations. In the more scripted situation, the children initiated conversations more often. They also maintained the floor as speakers for a longer period of time. They initiated more often within topics and they took longer turns. These results are very much in line with what Nelson and her colleagues have hypothesized is the role of scripts in dialogue (Luciarello et al., 1983; Luciarello & Nelson, 1982; Nelson & Gruendel, 1979). Scripts allow children to share knowledge of the immediate situation and thus, they can engage and manage dialogues in a more sophisticated manner. It is not thought, though, that all discourse aspects will be equally affected by degree of scriptedness. There is still much to be done in investigating the range of behaviors that are affected by scriptedness and identifying those that are not.

Implications for Current Research

The present study put forth the suggestion that the degree of scriptedness of situations may be an important source of children's and mothers' language variation. We furthermore suggested that scripts are not confined to routine situations such as taking a bath or getting ready for bed, but that indeed young children can bring scripts to the different situations they engage in such as playing, waiting, and talking to strangers. The results of the present investigation indeed supported this view. It appears that children share scripts in nonroutinized situations and the degree of scriptedness of the situation affects how the dyad interacts at both the linguistic-structured level and the pragmatic-discourse level. This position has implications for current research in child language. The work of Snow et al. (this volume) is based on the assumption that routine situations are quite different from nonroutine situations. In contrast, we are saying that it is not a black and white situation but a matter of degree. It is thought that children bring scripts to nonroutinized situations and thus, we cannot make a prior separation between which situations are scripted and which are not. We need to find out what the degree of scriptedness of a situation is; we can not assume it. In the Snow, Perlmann, and Nathan study this question is very relevant. For example, the results of their first case involving five children aged 1;5 to 1;10 years interacting in three situations, a routine situation, a routine-format situation and free play, did not confirm their original hypotheses. They found that in general maternal and child speech were more complex during free play than during the routine situation. They point out that they had experienced unresolvable methodological problems in the scheduling of the filming of the three contexts which could affect the findings. We point out that another possible confounding variable is the degree of scriptedness of the nonroutinized situations. It is not possible to assume that free play is script-free. The effects of routinization and scriptedness can be present in free play and other situations, thus marring the boundaries between routinized and nonroutinized contexts. Snow et al. allude to this in study 2 when they discuss the possibility that some children may have had better established routines than others, with possible confounding of their results. It appears that degree of scriptedness is a variable we need to take into account and in doing so we are adding an important new dimension to this tradition of child language research.

But, degree of scriptedness can also serve as an explanatory tool. Mannle and Tomasello (this volume) argue that in the pragmatic/communicative domain fathers differ in important ways from mothers. Fathers engage in shorter conversations with their children (Golinkoff & Ames, 1979), they initiate and respond less (Hiadek & Edwards, 1984) and they are less successful in following the child's focus of attention (Mannle & Tomasello, this volume). In the study of Mannle and Tomasello, comparisons between mothers and fathers were possible by keeping the situation constant. Both parents interacted with their 12–18 month-old children in a free play situation involving a novel set of toys. Nonetheless, these authors point out that fathers spend significantly less time interacting with their children and so may be less familiar with the routines the children are interested in. We take this further and suggest that mother-child play is probably more scripted than father-child play given that mothers in the Mannle and Tomasello study spent an average of 23 hours per week alone with their children while fathers spent only 8 hours. Thus, the degree of scriptedness is not only a relevant variable but one which can serve as an explanation for the differences observed in children's interactions with a variety of partners.

Measuring Degrees of Scriptedness in Different Situations

The preceding discussions on the possible role of degree of scriptedness on children's language acquisition and use assume that degree of scriptedness is something we can measure. Indeed, the area of child language research we have been discussing is based on this assumption. We ranked the three situations in our study from most- to least-scripted by intuitively assessing the opportunities each of the situations provided for mother and child to share scripts. Other researchers have made their decisions a priori by defining a scripted, routinized situation as a situation which mother and child engage in a specified number of times per week (Luciarello et al., 1983; Luciarello & Nelson, 1982; Nelson & Gruendel, 1979, 1981; Snow et al., this volume). Usually, everything else which falls outside the particular definition is thought to be nonroutinized. Both approaches, the intuitive approach and the a priori approach, share a common problem. Once the situations are categorized in terms of their degree of scriptedness, can we go back and identify talk which is script-based and talk which is not? That is, can we reliably measure degree of scriptedness?

We thought that the task of determining the extent to which our mother-child dialogues were script-based was a possible one until we began to try to operationally define a script and obtain some sort of acceptable reliability on our judgment.

Scripts: What Are They?

The term script as used in child language acquisition research has been defined as a temporally organized representation that describes an appropriate sequence of events in a particular context. Thus, scripts may represent "any number of routine, sequential events" (Nelson & Gruendel, 1979, p. 78) such as going to bed, attending a birthday party, eating at a restaurant, taking a bath, having a telephone conversation, and so on. Each script includes information on actors and their roles, thus specifying who does what and when. The script is constructed from the point of view of one of the actors, thus, in the case of a young child, scripts will be constructed from the child's perspective.

Although this information provides a flavor of what a script is, it does not give us an indication of what does *not* constitute a script. First, in a loose sense, most events can be thought to be sequential and thus there is no clear way of confining those sets of events which constitute scripts from those which do not. Second, it is not clear when a set of sequential events are a routine and when they are not a routine. One, of course, could say that when a set of sequential events become routinized that is when a script emerges, but this is circular and does not help us understand what scripts are in the first place. Snow et al. (this volume) touch on this issue in their second study. They point out that three of the five children studied had routines that appeared to be better established, more predictable and, thus, more scripted. They then continue to focus on these children. But, they do not provide us with an explanation as to what factors made them decide that some routines were more scripted than others. Indeed, we think this is essential information if we are to develop a set of indices for identifying more scripted versus less scripted routines. One of the key problems is the fact that scripts are constructed by children from their perspective and thus will probably differ in important ways from those of adults. So, what constitutes a sequence of events may be different for the child and the adult. The task of the researcher-observer is thus complicated by this factor.

Consequently, when confronted with an excerpt of mother-child dialogue with 2-year-olds, one of the main problems is deciding what is not script-based rather than what is. During the analysis we found ourselves drawing longer and longer lists of possible scripts as we went along. Is talk about dressing and undressing dolls, riding a tractor and clearing toys away script based? How do we know where to stop?

The work of Lucairello et al. (1983) and Lucariello & Nelson (1982) highlights some of the problems but also indirectly points to some possible ways of dealing with them. These investigators studied ten mother-child dyads aged between 2;0 to 2;5 years in three contexts. A routine situation (such as bathing, getting dressed or having lunch), a free play situation and a novel situation where mother-child pairs were asked to play with a model castle they had not seen before. These authors found that the routine situation yielded the most sophisticated language behaviors on the part of the child. But, in addition, they noted that mother-child dyads appeared to share scripts, not just in the routine situation but in the other situations as well. Unfortunately, they only state that and do not attempt to evaluate, in any systematic way, the degree of scriptedness of the situations. Nonetheless, their methodology suggests some possible productive ways of doing this. Instead of looking through all the dialogues and trying to decide when talk is script-based and when it is not, these authors first analyze the dialogues in terms of categories such as future talk and spatial displacement. Once they identify the categories they are interested in, then they ask the question. What percentage of talk is script-based? Once again, they state the percentage but do not tell us how they arrived at such a decision, especially how they decided when future talk was *not* scripted. Furthermore, they do not provide us with any reliability measures for their decisions. However, the idea of concentrating on a particular category of talk, such as future talk, and analyzing it in detail in terms of script-sharing, is one worth pursuing. We would like to emphasize that when doing this, it would be very important not only to give examples of, let's say, future talk which is script-based, but also examples of nonscript-based talk with reasons why and how those decisions were made.

Another problem concerns the generality of scripts. Nelson and Gruendel (1979) talked about "general social scripts" such as conversational scripts which describe the structure of conversation itself. But, they also talk about specific scripts such as Joshua's "coming home from shopping" script (p. 78). This script describes the sequence of opening the door, putting the stroller with Joshua inside, and then picking up the groceries. Furthermore, Barrett (1983, 1986) describes scripts that are much more limited in scope than those hypothesized by Nelson and her colleagues. He describes the early usage of the word *duck* by his first son Adam Bruno. Adam uses the word *duck* when hitting one of any three yellow toy ducks while standing next to the bath. Thus, Barrett postulates that Adam has acquired a mental representation of this event and he only produces the word *duck* whenever he recognizes the occurrence of that particular script.

It is obvious that there are differences in the level of abstraction of scripts as well as their generality and it is not clear what comes in between these levels of abstractness and generality. Indeed, the scope at present is so great that it was not very difficult for us to think up scripts (although it was not easy to agree on what those scripts would consist of) that would account for most of the mother-child dialogues we collected. Granted, intuitively we were able to identify a "middle" ground involving talk about routine activities such as phoning a friend, making something to drink, but the literature in principle did not constrain us enough for us to reliably discard a number of mother-child dialogues as being nonscripted nor to draw reliable boundaries for scripts.

Finally, when trying to define what scripts are, we found it difficult to know where scripts start and where they finish. Nelson and Gruendel (1979), for example, think of the lunch script as consisting of three basic events: playing, eating, and napping, with less important or optional events such as washing hands, getting food, etc., etc. It is not clear to us why the lunch script should consist of playing, eating, and napping and why should not napping be considered a separate script, or similarly, why should not playing be considered separately. We are aware that some scripts are easier to define than others and we are also aware that there is a great deal of variation and individual differences in children's routines but it is also true that in general, it is difficult to know on what basis should one group events to form scripts. Especially in cross-sectional studies like ours, the researchers are not familiar with the everyday routines the particular set of dyads they are investigating are engaging in, thus complicating the decision-making process in analysis. In this respect, longitudinal research like that of Snow and Goldfield (1983) and Snow et al. (this volume) may be more enlightening.

In summary, we found the concept of a script intuitively appealing but at present too vague and difficult to work with in dialogue analysis. Given the aforementioned problems it was not possible for us to determine reliably the extent to which our mother-child dialogues were script-based. Granted, in those instances where mother and child enacted and talked about a specific daily routine, for example, taking the bus to school, the decisions were not particularly difficult. But, those cases where our criteria coincided were not great in number.

Of further consideration was the presence of conversational routines. Are conversational routines more than verbal scripts?

Scripts and Conversational Routines

Although it is thought that what is ritualized in conversational routines are the conversational management techniques such as turn-taking, one could argue that some conversational routines are also ritualized in terms of substance, that is in terms of the actual content of the talk that is shared in dialogue. The most obvious example of such routines are nursery rhymes where the exact words are used each time mother and child engage in reciting them. Snow et al. (this volume) also suggest that in other cultures verses are used extensively to accompany routine activities such as dressing, bathing, and feeding. These verses are repeated every time the activity takes place. Thus, in these cases, it is not only the activity which is ritualized, but the structure and content of the talk.

Given that scripts are representations of routine, sequential events and conversational routines can be ritualized sequences of dialogue, it is not difficult to imagine some confusion arising. They both share the predictability and repetitiveness characteristic of routines. Can one simply argue that scripts are mental representations of events while conversational routines are the verbal enactment of those scripts? Let's take an excerpt of dialogue from our data.

CR and her mother in the no-toys context
CR: Where's Jessica (a friend of CR)
Mother: Jessica is probably at school
CR: No, Jessica's here
Mother: I don't think so

In this example we have the child initiating a conversation about the location of a unique referent, in this case, an absent friend. This example is typical of many of the conversational routines we encountered in our data in the no-toys context and to a lesser extent in the play and new-toy contexts. Children asked about the location of the absent parent, absent friends, and particular toys. Every child in our study initiated a conversation about nonpresent objects in the no-toys condition. Much like Sachs' (1983) data on her daughter Naomi, in our study talk about absent objects seemed to be similar across dyads. Such talk involved a small set of topics which followed a particular format, usually of the type "Where_____?"

The question then arises, are mother and child verbally enacting a script when they engage in a conversational routine about the location of an object? Scripts are said to "represent events that occur over time and thus the links between its component acts are temporal links, one act following another; in the most tightly woven structures, they are causal as well" (Nelson & Gruendel, 1981, p. 138).

In the conversational routine about absent objects there are no temporal links between events. The mother and child are not talking about a sequence of events. What is routinized and predictable is first the structure of the conversation itself, and in this general sense, it could be argued that mother and child are sharing a script. We suggest that the topic of conversation, such as asking about absent objects and people is also routinized and predictable, and this aspect of conversation does not necessarily refer to a routine sequence of events. It could be that conversational routines may originate within scripted contexts but with time they can evolve their own internal coherence and thus, can proceed independently from the original scripts. Once again, cross-sectional research does not provide a large enough framework in which such a question can be answered. Detailed longitudinal research is necessary to study the evolution of conversational routines.

A piece of research which serves as an example of how research in this area could be carried out is that of Snow and Goldfield (1983). These authors have studied in detail the book-reading routine of a child and his mother. The book-reading routine is of particular interest because in such a situation, not only are the sequence of events scripted but the topic of conversation and the actual talk used also appears to be routinized. In this activity events such as sitting down, opening the book, turning the pages, etc., is routinized and the structure of the conversation between mother and child as well as much of the content of what they say to each other is also routinized. One could argue that such situations provide a very strong context for language learning. Indeed, Snow and Goldfield (1983) found not only that the child became very familiar with the sequence of events involved in book reading (the child knew when to turn the pages, close the book, etc.), but that the child began to produce utterances which his mother had produced on earlier occurrences of the situation. The child had not only identified the situation and had developed a script for the sequence of events involved in the situation, but he also had established memories of the utterances produced during the situation. In this sense, one could argue that scripts which provide a representation of the sequence of events in the child's memory can function to support language. In turn, language itself can function to help establish and enrich scripts (Sachs, 1980).

It would be of interest to investigate further the child's use of the utterances he learned in the book-reading context in different contexts. In this way we could begin to trace the evolution of conversational routines and their relationship to scripts.

Closing Remarks

The purpose of this chapter was to study variations in mother-child conversations across different contexts and to explore reasons why such variations occur. It was suggested that a factor in language variation is the degree of scriptedness of the contexts mother and child participate in. It was argued that the notion of degree of scriptedness adds an important dimension to current child language research and that it also provides a basis for explaining different aspects of child language development and use.

Methodologically, it was pointed out that we have a lot of work ahead in developing a workable, reliable set of indices for measuring degree of scriptedness. The concept of a script is a notion which may be too often in the eye of the beholder alone. An adequate operational definition of a script has not been provided and the evidence that scripts have any psychological reality for the child has not been forthcoming, especially in the area of dialogue analysis. It is important that the notion be better defined and examined if we are going to make full use of its potential. Otherwise, the claim that scripted contexts facilitate language in dialogue appears suspiciously circular.

Furthermore, there is a need to clarify the relationship between scripts and conversational routines. We have suggested that for language development what is said in dialogue may be as important as knowing what to do, when, and to whom in a particular situation. Camaioni and Laicardi (1985), in their longitudinal study of three children, found that the most linguistically advanced child in their sample was not only the child whose participation in conventionalized routine games was more frequent, but also was the child whose mother most frequently *linguistically* marked her child's participation. Much research lies ahead before we can fully understand the contribution of the different types of routines to the children's language development and use.

ACKNOWLEDGMENTS

We appreciate the many useful comments from our colleagues, particularly Martyn Barrett and the members of the Developmental Group at the Psychology Department, University of Manchester.

Portions of this chapter were presented at the International Association for the Study of Child Language, Austin, Texas, 1984 and at the Child Language Seminar, Durham, U.K., 1986.

REFERENCES

Atkins, C. P., & Cartwright, L. R. (1982). An investigation of the effectiveness of three language elicitation procedures on Head Start children. *Language, Speech and Hearing Services in Schools, 13,* 33–36.

Barrett, M. D. (1983, September). *Scripts, prototypes and the early acquisition of word meaning.* Paper presented at the British Psychological Society Developmental Section Annual Conference, Oxford.

Barrett, M. D. (1986). Early semantic representation and early word-usage. In S. A. Kuczaj & M. D. Barrett (Eds.), *The development of word meaning* (pp. 39–67). New York: Springer-Verlag.

Brown, P., & Levinson, S. (1978). Universals in language usage: Politeness phenomena. In E. Goody (Ed.), *Questions and politeness* (pp. 56–289). Cambridge, England: Cambridge University Press.

Brown, R. (1973). *A first language.* Cambridge, England: Cambridge University Press.

Bruner, J. S. (1978). The role of dialogue in language acquisition. In A. Sinclair, R. J. Jarvella, & W. J. M. Levelt (Eds.), *The child's conception of language* (pp. 241–256). New York: Springer-Verlag.

Camaioni, L., & Laicardi, C. (1985). Early social games and the acquisition of language. *British Journal of Developmental Psychology, 3,* 31–39.

Cazden, C. B. (1970). The neglected situation in child language research and education. In F. Williams (Ed.), *Language and poverty* (pp. 81–101). Chicago: Markham Publishing Company.

Cheshire, J. (1982). *Variation in an English dialect.* Cambridge, England: Cambridge University Press.

Cohen, J. (1960). A coefficient of agreement for nominal scales. *Educational and Psychological Measurement, 22,* 37–46.

Cole, M., Dore, J., Hall, W. S., & Dowley, G. (1978). Situation and task in young children's talk. *Discourse Processes, 1,* 119–176.

D'Odorico, L., & Franco, F. (1985). The determinants of baby talk: Relationship to context. *Journal of Child Language, 12,* 567–586.

Dore, J. (1978). Variation in preschool children's conversational performance. In K. E. Nelson (Ed.), *Children's language, Volume 1* (pp. 397–444). New York: Gardner Press.

Ervin-Tripp, S. M. (1973). *Language acquisition and communicative choice.* California: Stanford University Press.

Golinkoff, R. M., & Ames, G. T. (1979). A comparison of fathers' and mothers' speech with their young children. *Child Development, 50,* 28–32.

Hedrick, D., Prather, E., & Tobin, M. (1975). *Sequenced Inventory of Communication Development.* Seattle: University of Washington Press.

Haidek, E., & Edwards, H. (1984). A comparative analysis of mother-father speech in the naturalistic home environment. *Journal of Psycholinguistic Research, 13,* 321–332.

Labov, W. (1966). *The social stratification of English in New York City.* Washington, D.C.: Center for Applied Linguistics.

Lakoff, R. (1973). *Language and women's place.* New York: Harper & Row.

Longhurst, T., & File, J. (1977). A comparison of Developmental Sentence Scores from Head Start children collected in four conditions. *Language, Speech and Hearing Services in Schools, 8,* 54–64.

Longhurst, T., & Grubb, S. (1974). A comparison of language samples collected in four situations. *Language, Speech and Hearing Services in Schools, 5,* 71–78.

Lucariello, J., Kyratzis, A., & Nelson, K. (1983, September). *The interrelationship between event representations and language use.* Paper presented at the British Psychological Society Developmental Section Annual Conference, Oxford.

Lucariello, J., & Nelson, K. (1982, March.) *Situational variation in mother-child interaction.* Paper presented at the Third International Conference on Infant Studies, Austin, Texas.

Macaulay, R. (1978). Variation and consistency in Glaswegian English. In P. Trudgill (Ed.), *Sociolinguistic patterns in British English* (pp. 132–144). London: Edward Arnold.

Nelson, K., & Gruendel, J. M. (1979). At morning it's lunchtime: A scriptal view of children's dialogues. *Discourse Processes, 2,* 73–94.

Nelson, K., & Gruendel, J. M. (1981). Generalized event representations: Basic building blocks of cognitive development. In A. Brown & M. Lamb (Eds.), *Advances in Developmental Psychology, Volume 1* (pp. 131–158). Hillsdale, NJ: Lawrence Erlbaum Associates.

Ninio, A., & Bruner, J. S. (1978). The achievement and antecedents of labelling. *Journal of Child Language, 5*, 1–15.

Ratner, N., & Bruner, J. S. (1978). Games, social exchange, and the acquisition of language. *Journal of Child Language, 5*, 391–402.

Romaine, S. (1984). *The language of children and adolescents.* Oxford: Basil Blackwell.

Sachs, J. (1980). The role of adult-child play in language development. In K. H. Rubin (Ed.), *Children's play* (pp. 33–48). San Francisco: Jossey Bass.

Sachs, J. (1983). Talking about the there and then: The emergence of displaced reference in parent-child discourse. In K. E. Nelson (Ed.), *Children's language, Vol. IV* (pp. 1–28). Hillsdale, NJ: Lawrence Erlbaum Associates.

Sacks, H., Schegloff, E. E., & Jefferson, G. (1974). A simplest systematics for the organization of turn-taking for conversation. *Language, 50*, 696–735.

Schieffelin, B. B. (1979). Getting it together: An ethnographic approach to the study of the development of communicative competence. In E. Ochs & B. B. Schieffelin (Eds.), *Developmental pragmatics* (pp. 73–108). Orlando, FL: Academic Press.

Smith, M. E. (1935). A study of some factors influencing the development of the sentence in preschool children. *Journal of Genetic Psychology, 46*, 182–212.

Smith, P. (1979). Sex markers in speech. In H. Giles & K. Sherer (Eds.), *Social markers in speech* (pp. 109–137). Cambridge, England: Cambridge University Press.

Snow, C. E., & Goldfield, B. A. (1983). Turn the page please: Situation-specific language acquisition. *Journal of Child Language, 10*, 551–569.

Stalnaker, L. D., & Creaghead, N. A. (1982). An examination of language samples obtained under three experimental conditions. *Language, Speech and Hearing Services in Schools, 13*, 121–128.

Strandberg, T. E. (1969). *An evaluation of three stimulus media for evoking verbalizations from preschool children.* Master's thesis, Eastern Illinois University.

Stubbs, M. (1983). *Discourse analysis.* Oxford: Basil Blackwell.

Trudgill, P. (1974). *The social differentiation of English in Norwich.* Cambridge, England: Cambridge University Press.

4

Why Routines Are Different: Toward a Multiple-Factors Model of the Relation between Input and Language Acquisition

Catherine E. Snow
Rivka Perlmann
Debra Nathan
Harvard University

What features of the social interaction the child engages in are facilitative of or prerequisite to language acquisition? This recurrent question has become, as more and more research is directed to it, not easier but more difficult to answer. Results of different studies are often contradictory. Even more serious, the best candidates for highly facilitative, even prerequisite features generated by one research tradition ("straight" developmental psycholinguistics, as practiced by Anglo-American psychologists and educational researchers) are revealed by another research tradition (cross-cultural or ethnographic studies by anthropologists) to be irrelevant to language development. Clearly, under these conditions, a simple answer to the question posed is impossible and a complex one cannot be formulated unless we succeed in relating the various contradictory research traditions to one another. It is the goal of this paper to compile and interpret findings from both these research traditions, in an attempt to design a study that would integrate the seemingly disparate findings. Results from a small-scale version of such a study are presented, and interpreted in light of the previously separate research undertakings.

The developmental psycholinguistics research tradition has generated two major hypotheses concerning features in the speech addressed to children that facilitate language development: (a) fine-tuning of the syntactic and semantic complexity of input speech to the child's level, and (b) semantic contingency of adult utterances to the child's previous utterances or focus of attention. Evidence relevant to each of these hypotheses is reviewed below. First, we review studies that lead to the conclusion that, though fine tuning does often occur, and may facilitate language development, it certainly isn't necessary to language development. Second, studies about the occurrence and facilitative effect of contingency to infant and toddler behaviors are reviewed as well as studies on cultures within which semantic contingency is rare and clearly not a major facilitator of language development. The contradictory findings about the roles of fine tuning and semantic contingency lead to a model within which their contributions to language development are contrasted to the role played by routinized interactions, which have the same effect of placing the child's own behaviors and utterances in context. Finally, two small studies are reported, which were undertaken to assess semantic contingency and fine-tuning in maternal speech and the complexity of child speech as a function of the degree of routinization of the interactive setting.

FINE-TUNING

Evidence That Fine-tuning Occurs

After the publication of the first studies which demonstrated that caretakers simplify and in other ways modify their speech when addressing young first language learners (see Snow, 1977b for a review), it was widely proposed that speech to children could be thought of as "fine-tuned" to the child's own language level (e.g., Berko Gleason, 1977). Fine-tuning implies that, as the child's own language ability develops, the caretakers decrease the amount of simplification or modification in their child-directed speech, thus providing a continually adjusted optimal discrepancy between the language system of the child and the language system the child is exposed to.

The notion of fine-tuning fit in well with many of the early results about caretakers' speech to children (see Table 4.1 for a summary of many of the relevant studies). Snow (1972) found large and significant differences in the speech addressed to 2-year-olds versus 10-year-olds; Phillips (1973) found differences between speech to 18 versus 28 month-olds; Longhurst and Stepanich (1975) found differences in speech addressed to 1-, 2-, and 3-year-olds. All these cross-sectional studies confirmed that the syntactic complexity of the adult's speech correlated with the language ability of the child addressed. In all these studies, however, the age differences between the groups of children being compared were relatively large and the children's language levels were inferred from their age, rather than being tested directly.

A more conservative test of the fine-tuning hypothesis requires looking for correlations between caretakers' and children's speech during much shorter spans of development. The cross-sectional studies, which tested groups of children differing in age by at least a year, could be said to give evidence for "gross-tuning," not for fine-tuning. A longitudinal study in which the speech of mothers and their children was recorded at 6-month intervals (Newport, Gleitman, & Gleitman, 1977) reported only nonsignificant positive correlations between the child's MLU and maternal MLU or other measures of maternal syntactic com-

TABLE 4.1
Summary of Results on Fine-Tuning

Study	Effect on Maternal MLU	Effect on Maternal Content
Bellinger, 1979	increase with age, 1 to 5 years	
Bellinger, 1980	MLU weighed heavily in discriminant function which correlated significantly with child MLU, and which discriminated child age effectively	
Bruck, 1978	not related to language ability (LD or normal) of kindergarteners (teachers' talk)	more concrete teaching and explanation to language delayed children
Chapman, 1981 (summary of several studies)		vocabulary diversity, as measured by TTR, increases with age
Clarke-Stewart et al., 1979	positively correlated with children's comprehension	
Cross, 1977	positive correlation with child MLU; higher positive correlation with child comprehension	
Engle, 1979	mothers of 2 vs. 3-year-olds differed significantly; fathers showed no difference	
Fraser & Roberts, 1975	significant increase between 1;6 and 2;6	
Furrow et al., 1979	positive correlation with child MLU at 2;3; significant difference between 1;9 & 2;3	
Kaye, 1980	no change with age, 3 to 26 weeks	
Kaye & Charney, 1980	no change, 2;2 to 2;6	
Longhurst & Stepanich, 1975	positive correlation with age, comparing groups of 1, 2 and 3-year-olds	
Nelson et al., 1984	correlates with no child measure at 22 mos., positively with child's longest utterance at 27 months, but not with other child language measures	
Newport et al.,1977	no correlation to child MLU	
Phillips, 1973	increase from 18 to 28 months, decrease from 8 to 18 months	
Retherford et al., 1981		no change in maternal semantic relations with child age; child changed to match mother

Study	Effect on Maternal MLU	Effect on Maternal Content
Rondal, 1978		very minor changes from 1;11 to 2;6
Rondal, 1980	mothers' and fathers' MLU and syntactic complexity increased with child age/MLU (range 1;6 to 3;0/1.3 to 4.1)	mothers' and fathers' TTR increased with age/MLU of child
Sachs, 1979, 1983		some adjustment to child not perfect limitation to child's level
Schaffer & Crook, 1979	correlated to child age for directives, not for attention-directing utterances	
Snow, 1972	significant difference between 2 and 10-year-olds	
Snow, 1977a	no change, 3 to 18 months	increasing reference to objects, more complex content with age, 3 to 18 months
Snow, 1977b		no change over child stages I to IV in semantic relations expressed
Stern et al., 1983	no change, 2 to 12 months; some increase between 12 and 24 months	
Van Kleeck & Carpenter, 1980	lower to developmentally delayed children, but not lower to children with deficits in comprehension	both generally & specifically comprehension-delayed children hear fewer non-present references & receive more nonverbal cuing.

plexity (e.g., maternal S-nodes per utterance). It is not clear from the report if these correlations are based on data from the first or second recording of mothers and children, or both. An alternative way of testing for fine-tuning would be to determine if the maternal speech was significantly more complex at the second recording than the first, 6 months previously; Newport et al. do not report any such analysis, but concluded: "There is no compelling evidence in our data that mothers tune their syntactic complexity to the growing language competence of their children through this crucial age of syntax acquisition, the period from one to two and a half years" (pp. 123–124).

Similarly, total absence of support for fine-tuning of maternal MLU to child MLU has been reported by Nelson, Bonvillian, Denninger, Kaplan, and Baker (1984) for 25 children aged 22 to 27 months. However, maternal auxiliary use to 27-month-olds was correlated with concurrent child auxiliary use, and maternal auxiliary use to 22-month-olds predicted child MLU at 27 months. These and a few other correlations (both maternal MLU and maternal verb complexity with length of child's longest utterance, and with child auxiliary use, all at 27 months) suggest that some aspects of adult speech may be more finely tuned than others. However, Nelson et al. emphasize that many possible correlations did not emerge, and that those that were significant were nonetheless only moderate (.42–.53). Cross (1977) carried out a study which had considerable potential to test for fine-tuning, since all the children she observed were very close to one another in language level. If significant correlations are found between maternal speech variables and measures of child language level in this kind of sample, where the variance on one factor is sharply truncated, then the support for the conclusion that maternal speech is fine-tuned is strong. Cross found evidence for fine-tuning, some of which directly contradicts the findings of Newport et al. For example, Cross found significant positive correlations between child MLU and maternal MLU, as well as significant negative correlations between child MLU and several measures of maternal repetitiveness, and between child MLU and maternal use of various sorts of expansions. Furthermore, in almost all cases, an even stronger relationship was found between the maternal speech variables and measures of the child's receptive language ability, suggesting that mothers are adjusting speech complexity to their children's ability to understand, even more than to their expressive ability.

In contrast, seeming total absence of syntactic fine-tuning by mothers to changes in children's development has been reported by Snow (1977a) and by Kaye (1980), both of whom collected longitudinal data for the period spanning early infancy through early language use. They both found that the mothers' speech was as short and simple to the infants as to the children who could talk, and concluded that fine-tuning to children's language level was not a major source of many of the "baby-talk" modifications. However, Snow did report changes in the *content* of maternal speech and kinds of maternal repetition, both associated with changes in the babies' behavior. One version of the fine-tuning hypothesis, in which the fine-tuning mechanism is presumed to be adjusting the complexity of maternal speech in response to the child's syntactic complexity, would predict no simplification in speech to very young prelinguistic children, who give no cues, either of speech production or of comprehension, to which the maternal speech could be adjusted. The preponderance of short, simple, and repetitive utterances in speech to infants clearly suggests, then, that this version of the fine-tuning hypothesis is incorrect, as does the finding that some adjustment occurs during this period (Sherrod, Friedman, Crowley, Drake, & Devieux, 1977). Maternal speech may be finely tuned to children's comprehension or production ability, but other aspects of the child also have an effect on the nature of the maternal speech. In fact, some characteristics of speech to young children are also typical of speech to pets and plants (Brown, 1977; Hirsch-Pasek, & Treiman, 1982), and, as already noted, of speech to preverbal infants, clearly confirming the conclusion that fine-tuning to children's language is not the *only* source of the modifications in mothers' speech. The occurrence of such modification in these other speech situations does not, however, in any way cast light on the question of whether fine-tuning to children's language abilities also occurs.

The Cross (1977) finding that maternal speech was better correlated with receptive than productive measures of the children's language raises an interesting question. Given that some adjustment to language knowledge of listener occurs (as obviously it does: No one disputes the fact of listener-adjustments in western societies, only the degree to which they are finely tuned), to what characteristics of the listener are adjustments made? Newport et al. assumed adjustments to productive language ability. Cross demonstrated that receptive language ability worked more powerfully, at least for mothers with their own children, women who could be assumed to be very knowledgeable about their addressees' comprehension. Bohannon with his colleagues has done a series of studies (Bohannon & Marquis, 1977; Bohannon, Stine, & Ritzenberg, 1982; Stine & Bohannon, 1983; Warren-Leubecker & Bohannon, 1983) which suggests that fine-tuning occurs, and that it is driven by very specific cues of noncomprehension, such as 'What?', 'Huh?', or by imitation of the previous utterance. Van Kleeck and Carpenter (1980) on the other hand, found rather few differences between the speech addressed to normally comprehending vs. comprehension-delayed 4-year-olds, though generally developmentally delayed 4-year-olds received speech adjusted syntactically, semantically, and pragmatically. Whereas Newport et al. and Cross treated fine-tuning as a predictive process, in which the mother chooses a level of complexity based on her knowledge of the child's ability, Bohannon sees it as a much more interactive process, organized and manipulated at the level of conversation, and reactive to specific cues rather than to more global characteristics of the child.

Another question that arises is what aspect of her own speech the mother chooses to manipulate or tune. Cross found considerably stronger relationships with discourse measures in the maternal speech (e.g., use of expansions, use of imitations, use of repetitions) than with measures of mothers' syntactic complexity. As noted earlier, Snow (1977a) found that mothers adjusted the content of their speech to changes in their babies' cognitive level and looking behavior; Similarly, Cross (1977) found that maternal reference to nonimmediate events correlated with children's MLU and with their receptive language scores. Van Kleeck and Carpenter (1980) also found that reference to nonpresent entities, but not formal measures of complexity, differentiated speech to comprehension delayed and to normal comprehending language-delayed children, and Mannle and Tomasello (this volume) found that mothers are better than fathers or siblings in talking about the child's focus of attention, though not much different in syntactic complexity. However, Sachs (1979, 1983) presents evidence showing that the fine-tuning of parental content to child level is not perfect; the parents in her study infrequently but regularly addressed questions to their child which were too complex for her to understand. The frequency of the complex question types (questions demanding answers about nonpresent events) increased after the child started to answer them correctly, suggesting some sensitivity to child level, but their presence before that time suggests less than perfect tuning, since they resulted in conversational breakdown. Neither Retherford, Schwartz, and Chapman (1981) nor Snow (1977b) found any evidence for fine-tuning in analyses of semantic relations expressed in mothers' speech to 18- to 36-month-old children.

Yet another suggestion concerning what aspect of their own speech the parents are adjusting comes from Kaye and Fogel (1980). They explain the various adjustments in maternal speech patterns, and the changes in those adjustments with the child's growth, as manipulation of timing. They argue that the crucial behavior of the child, especially in infancy, which the adult has to take into account during interaction, is the episodic structure of activity and attention cycles. Parents use short and repetitive utterances to babies because these fit in well with the timing of the babies' behaviors. Monologic structures, or even long and complex utterances, would be inappropriate for addressing infants simply because their timing does not match the infant's rhythms well.

Another possibility is that mothers are indeed adjusting the syntactic complexity of their speech to some aspect of their children's language ability, but that the adjustments are situation-specific, occurring exclusively for some types of speech or speech acts, or perhaps representing different kinds of adjustment in different kinds of speech. Hints that this kind of complexity may be at the root of the rather confusing pattern of results for fine-tuning exist: Snow et al. (1976) found that mothers' speech was significantly more complex in a book-reading than a free-play task, suggesting that levels of fine-tuning may be different in the two tasks, and thus that an analysis that merges maternal speech across situations might miss the fine-tuning that occurs. Schaffer and Crook (1979) found that the MLU of mothers' directives correlated with child age but not the MLU of mothers' attention-directing utterances. Snow and Goldfield (1982) found evidence for semantic fine-tuning which emerged only if the mother-child pair were observed engaged in the same activity—reading one book over several months. The study presented here addresses this issue directly, by comparing fine-tuning in routinized vs. nonroutinized interaction situations.

What can be concluded from this review of studies of maternal speech adjustments? Almost any conclusion could be justified by referring to one or more of the studies reviewed. There is evidence that maternal MLU increases with increased child age, child MLU and child receptive ability (Bellinger, 1979, 1980; Bruck, 1978; Clarke-Stewart, Vanderstoep, & Killian, 1979; Cross, 1978; Engle, 1979; Longhurst & Stepanich, 1975; Phillips, 1973; Rondal, 1978, 1980; Stern, Spieker, Barnett, & MacKain, 1983). However other evidence indicates that maternal MLU to babies is as short as to 18-month-olds (Kaye, 1980; Snow, 1977a), to older 2-year-olds as short as to younger 2-year-olds (Kaye & Charney, 1980; Nelson et al., 1984), and to poor comprehenders as long as to good comprehenders (Van Kleeck & Carpenter, 1980). But further contrast comes from reports that MLU decreases after signals of noncomprehension (Bohannon & Marquis, 1977; Stine & Bohannon, 1983). The strongest and most consistent patterns of results suggest very different adjustment patterns for MLU and for semantic content. Results from a number of studies converge on the conclusion that maximum change in maternal MLU occurs between 18 and 28 months (Bellinger, 1979, 1980; Phillips, 1973), presumably in response to the changes occurring then in children's syntactic production and/or comprehension. The semantic content of maternal speech, on the other hand, shows rather great shifts between 3 and 12 months as reflected both in what is talked about and in the degree of repetitiveness, but no change at all between 18 and 28 months, as reflected by use of semantic relations (Snow, 1977a, 1977b; Kaye, 1980; Retherford et al., 1981).

Evidence That Fine-tuning Helps

Despite the considerable evidence that fine-tuning does occur, at least in some cases and for some domains of input language, there is rather little evidence that it helps. This does not mean, however, that many researchers have found no relationship between fine-tuning and subsequent gains in language skill. Rather, it is very hard even to ask the question whether fine-tuning helps, for a number of methodological reasons:

1. Mothers may show equal tendency to shift input complexity as their children advance, but may start at different levels, i.e., with different "gaps" between the complexity of their own and the child's utterances. One mother may match her child's MLU closely, while another maintains a gap of 4–5 morphemes (see Nelson et al., 1984, for evidence that this happens). Only longitudinal analysis would show that each of these mothers was fine-tuning her utter-

ances to her child's growing linguistic sophistication. Throwing their data from one time-point into a correlational analysis would suggest an absence of fine-tuning.

2. Mothers may adapt the complexity of their speech to the child's language level with different "gaps" for different activities. For example, teaching a new skill might elicit a very small gap between the complexity of maternal and child speech, whereas reading a familiar book elicits a much larger gap. Both situations might show fine-tuning, in that the adult speech gets more complex as the children get older, but failure to track the complexity separately for the different activities, or to distinguish the activities carefully in assessing the adult and the child speech, would make it difficult to recognize the fine-tuning. Furthermore, some activities may elicit fine-tuning while others do not, again obscuring its occurrence and its effects.

3. Similarly, fine-tuning may occur but with different gaps at different stages of child development. The model that has been used to test for fine-tuning is a linear one with the expectation of parallel adjustment. What if adaptation to child's language level is not linear but divergent or curvilinear?

4. The measures which have been assessed in search of fine-tuning are typically quite global—maternal MLU, for example—whereas fine-tuning may occur for parts of the language system and be reflected only in more specific measures. For example, the Nelson et al. (1984) results suggest that maternal auxiliary use is adjusted though maternal MLU is not. The facilitative effect of fine-tuning in some part of the language input may, furthermore, depend on the child's stage of acquisition of the relevant structure.

The one study which has presented evidence in support of the facilitative effect of fine-tuning (Furrow, Nelson, & Benedict, 1979) selected children all of the same linguistic level, at the late one-word stage. Furrow et al. found that children whose mothers spoke more simply—i.e., with less of a "gap" compared to the children's one-word speech—learned more over the successive 9-month-period than children whose mothers' speech had been more complex. While it cannot be ruled out that the children were at Time 1 already different in unmeasured ways and thus that the correlation between maternal MLU and child growth is an artifact of child effects at time 1, nonetheless these results suggest that fine-tuning may be particularly facilitative during early stages of language acquisition.

Evidence That Fine-tuning Is Not Necessary

Almost all the evidence presented above, showing that modification of the syntactic complexity of speech to children occurs and that this modification may even be quite finely tuned to the child's level, comes from studies of English-speaking children in Britain, Australia, or North America. The picture given us by Ochs and Schieffelin (1984) of speech to children in Samoa and among the Kaluli of Papua-New Guinea is very different. They observe that speech to children is typically not adapted to the children's level—in fact, children have the responsibility of adapting to the adult's level in those cultures. In both societies, children are often given messages to pass on or models of utterances they are meant to repeat: It is striking to see in the dialogues Ochs and Schieffelin reproduce how syntactically and semantically complex such utterances can be. Kaluli mothers, for example, direct their 2-year-olds to imitate rhetorical questions, a form considered very sophisticated and late to appear in English-speaking children. These Kaluli mothers are quite clearly not fine-tuning the complexity of their input to the child's comprehension or spontaneous production level.

SEMANTIC CONTINGENCY

Contingency during Infancy

Observations of mother-child interaction from infancy through the first several stages of language acquisition have revealed consistently that mothers respond contingently to their children's utterances and, during the prelinguistic period, to behaviors that signal something about the infant's internal state. It seems very likely that such contingency provides opportunities for learning.

Caretakers respond predictably and reliably (under certain circumstances, at least) to infant behaviors such as vocalizing, burping, coughing, and looking intently (Snow, 1977a). Experiencing such contingencies is the perfect way for the infant to learn how to use these behaviors to control the world. Furthermore, since the adult responses tend to be rather stereotyped, they function to help classify and identify events for the infant (Watson, 1972).

Joint attention in early interaction is achieved in the first instance by virtue of the mother's contingent responses to the child's shift of attentional focus. By following the infant's gaze, and by talking about the thus jointly established topic, caretakers achieve joint attention and model a basic structure of communicative events—topic/comment relationships. Such joint attention is, furthermore, prerequisite to referencing, a major task in linguistic communication.

The paradox emerging from studies of contingency in early social interaction is this: though it is an abundantly rich source of information about communication and language and though there is considerable evidence that access to this rich social experience facilitates language acquisition (see Snow, 1979, 1981, for reviews), there is also evidence, primarily from cross-cultural work, that children without such experience grow up quite normally, and become competent native speakers of their language (in which, of course, their rules for interaction are governed by local, not universal, norms). Many observations have now been recorded of parent-infant interaction in nonwestern cultures which make clear that the interactive, reactive, conversational style typical of American, British, Australian, and Western European mothers is absent, or even proscribed (see, for example, Schieffelin, 1979, 1984, and the papers in Liederman, Tulkin, & Rosenfeld, 1977). Many groups of African, Polynesian, and Austronesian infants evidently receive little experience with face-to-face social interaction, and little contingency to their own communicative behaviors.

The evidence that experience with contingent responses to one's own actions and vocalizations facilitates language development comes primarily from three sources: (1) Case studies, which demonstrate that specific language behaviors first emerge as protocommunicative behaviors in the child's early social experiences (e.g., Bruner, 1977, 1983; Bruner & Sherwood, 1976). For example, Bruner (1983) describes how his subjects Jonathan and Richard adopted versions of their mothers' marking vocalizations (e.g., *pick* and *peeboo* respectively) during hide and find games. The games were observed dozens of times, during which maternal language use was highly predictable and contingent to the child's attention, before the children's vocalizations started to approximate the adult form. (2) Studies with various at-risk populations, which demonstrate that risks which increase the likelihood of later language disabilities also cause disturbances in patterns of early parent-child interaction (see Snow, 1981, for review). Interpreting these studies as support for the role of contingency in language development involves an inferential leap, but does nonetheless provide some support for the position given the large sample sizes and robust effects found. For example, Cohen and Beckwith (1976) found that premature children (who are at risk for language disorders) experience less contingency in maternal responses during infancy. Similarly, language delayed children typically receive rather low levels of semantic contingency, and intervention programs incorporating semantically contingent responses often result in considerable language growth. (3) Studies which have found correlations between certain patterns of early mother-infant interaction and later indices of cognitive or language development (e.g., Clarke-Stewart, 1973). This set is perhaps the strongest evidence for some effect of early social interaction, though of course correlational relationships cannot by themselves allow a causal interpretation. These three sets of data taken together seem to be a strong basis for concluding that access to rich social interaction during infancy contributes to language acquisition. However, descriptions of infant caretaking practices in other cultures make quite clear that the pattern of contingent reciprocal interaction we consider desirable is not only minimally available, but thought of as inappropriate, in many parts of the world.

Thus, while it is likely that, just by virtue of the caretaking that goes on, infants everywhere in the world have access to some semantically contingent responses, nonetheless the levels of semantic contingency normally available to many African, Polynesian, and Austronesian infants are lower than the level available to American infants who subsequently experience language delay. (See

Cross, 1983, for a review of speech to children at risk of delay.) If these low levels of semantic contingency have such negative effects on language development for American babies, why do they not retard language development in babies elsewhere in the world? Put more positively, how do the babies who do not typically experience high levels of semantic contingency learn what American babies learn from semantically contingent interactions?

Semantic Contingency during the Period of Language Development

Perhaps the most robust finding in the large literature on the role of input in language acquisition in the western, American-European mainstream culture is the facilitative effect of semantically contingent responses to child utterances on language acquisition. Since first reported by Cross (1978), many other researchers have confirmed and extended this finding in various ways. For example, Snow (1982) found that semantically contingent responses to very early stage 1 children's focus of attention were powerful predictors of their vocabulary. Barnes, Gutfreund, Satterly, and Wells (1983) found that semantic contingency predicted language gains in a group of English children of mixed social classes. Goldfield (1985) found that maternal naming responses to infants' showing of objects predicted the child's learning of nouns.

Semantically contingent responses have been shown in experimental studies to facilitate the learning of grammatical structures. Presumably one way this happens is by triggering a procedure of comparison between the child-version and the adult-versions of utterances—a comparison which is enlightening to the child if the adult version is either an "expansion" (a correct version that adds no new semantic information) of an incorrect child utterance, or a "recast" (a reply that structurally changes one or more major components of the child's utterance, but repeats the rest) of a correct child utterance. Nelson and his colleagues have demonstrated significant effects of expansions and of recasts, which might be seen as the semantically contingent responses par excellence (Baker & Nelson, 1984; Nelson, 1977, 1981; Nelson, Carskaddon, & Bonvillian, 1973; Nelson et al., 1984), and others have confirmed this finding (e.g., Hovell, Schumaker, & Sherman, 1978; Schumaker, 1976; Wells, 1980; Whitehurst & Novak, 1973). But as early as 1965, Cazden, in a study designed to demonstrate an effect of expansions, showed that "conversational responses" (most of which would probably be classified as semantic extensions or complex recasts) did relate to improvement of children's language skills. The availability to American children of semantically contingent responses varies as a function of interactant (see Mannle & Tomasello, this volume for a review). Fathers and especially siblings are less likely than mothers to talk about the child's focus of attention, to provide recasts and to make responses that continue (rather than disrupt) the conversation. However, the less semantically contingent style of fathers is probably related to their role as secondary caretakers; primary caretaking fathers are no doubt more like mothers. The reduction in access to semantically contingent speech associated with being second born has been related to delays in later-borns' language acquisition (see Snow, 1979, for a review).

Despite the strong and widespread evidence for the positive effect of semantic contingency on language development, we again find that the cross-cultural literature identifies societies where semantic contingency is not the model for parent-child interaction, notably Samoan, (Ochs & Schieffelin, 1984), Kaluli, (Schieffelin, 1984) African (LeVine, 1977), and rural blacks in North America (Heath, 1983; Ward, 1971) (others have not been looked at in this regard). Needless to say, children do nonetheless learn to talk in all these cultures. As is the case for fine-tuning, one of the reasons why semantic contingency fails to occur is the sense that it would be inappropriate, perhaps even demeaning, for adults to adapt themselves so extensively to the level of children. Among the Kaluli, furthermore, it is considered impossible to "guess" at another's intentions—the responsibility to make the message clear lies with the speaker, not the listener. Accordingly, clarification questions and expansions, frequent subcategories of semantically contingent speech, are not typical or frequent responses.

SEMANTIC CONTINGENCY AND FINE-TUNING: WHERE DO WE GO FROM HERE?

In the last two sections, we have reviewed some evidence concerning the nature of social interaction with prelinguistic children and the language spoken to children who are themselves just starting to talk. While there are demonstrations that carrying on conversation-like interactions with infants can facilitate later language acquisition, it is nonetheless clear that some children learn to talk without such early experiences. While there is considerable support for some notion of fine-tuning in maternal speech, clearly many other factors than adjustment to the child's language level play a role in determining syntactic complexity in maternal speech. Furthermore, given the unreliability of the fine-tuning mechanism, it seems very unlikely that fine-tuning could be in any sense crucial to normal language acquisition, though it looks very much like it is facilitatory.

These findings leave us with a dilemma. How does language acquisition occur for children who receive little semantic contingency and no fine-tuning? What is their source of information about the possibilities of communication and the structure of language? Why does it seem to be the case that low levels of access to early social interaction or to finely-tuned adult speech have negative consequences for children in western cultures, yet are without bad effects for children in other cultures?

In the following sections, we present an attempt to reanalyze the nature of social interaction between caretakers and children so as to resolve the paradoxes and dilemmas discussed above.

DISCOURSE

In this section we briefly sketch a few assumptions about language acquisition which will be prerequisite to understanding the proposal in the next section concerning how the conflicts in the research results might be isolated.

1. Children's utterances need to be interpreted in context, originally in the context of the child's activities but increasingly, as the child develops, in the context of the ongoing discourse, if they are to be interpreted or analyzed correctly by the adult interlocutor or the observing psycholinguist.

2. A central measure of children's developing linguistic knowledge during the first few years of language acquisition is their growing ability to encode meaning within utterance boundaries, i.e., syntactically, rather than across utterance boundaries, i.e., conversationally (see Ochs, Schieffelin, & Platt, 1979).

3. Children acquire language, i.e., vocabulary and grammar, during the early stages of acquisition, by virtue of hearing their own utterances placed in context, primarily, though not exclusively, in discourse contexts.

The point we emphasize is that this set of assumptions represents a departure from the general treatment of the language addressed to the child. For example, the comparison/analysis process that Nelson (1981) proposes is triggered by expansions and recasts, is assumed to function because the syntactic information in the adult utterance is displayed with greatest clarity and saliency in expansions and recasts. While this is undoubtedly a part of the story (indeed, Baker, Pemberton, & Nelson, 1985, have shown for slightly older children that interactive presentation of recasts is not prerequisite to their facilitative effect), we would argue that—at least for young children—the maternal recasting of the *child* utterance is important. In our opinion, the major function of the speech to the child in the early stages of language acquisition is, not displaying information about syntactic structure, but rather providing a context for the child's utterances—putting language before it and after it so that the utterance is part of a longer, coconstructed text. It has previously been generally assumed that the major interface between parents' speech and the child's language system was in the child's head, where the parental speech was processed, comprehended, and analyzed such that the information about it could stretch or modify the child's own language system. We are suggesting, on the other hand, that the major interface between adult speech and child language is at the level of utterance— that information about the structure of the adult language becomes available to the child from the contrasts and the completions provided by the juxtaposing of child and adult utterances. Thus, we believe the effects of adult speech must be sought at that interface before one can expect to see any impact on the child's internal system. Language learning goes on in the space between child and caretaker, before it can happen in the space between the child's ears. Perhaps the clearest statement of this premise is Roger Brown's, from 1968:

> It may be as difficult to derive a grammar from unconnected sentences as it would be to derive the invariance of quantity and number from the simple look of liquids in containers and objects in space. The changes produced by pouring back and forth, by gathering together and spreading apart are the data that most strongly suggest the conservation of quantity and number. The changes produced in sentences as they move between persons in discourse may be the richest data for the discovery of grammar. (p. 288)

The first and major task, then, of the caretaker interested in his child's successful acquisition of language, is to create discourse around the child's utterances. If children reliably hear their own short utterances embedded in discourse, they will discover ways to create longer linguistic contexts for themselves, instead of relying on their caretakers to do it. It is a commonplace that children start to talk by producing short utterances, and move to longer ones. We are proposing that it is their participation in the two party construction of longer utterances when children are in the one word stage that enables them to move to a stage of producing two word utterances autonomously.

ANOTHER CONTINUUM

Broadly speaking, there are two ways caregivers have available to them to build the discourse frames we believe children need for learning to talk (and for learning to act like members of the culture in other ways). The caregivers can build chunks of discourse by being highly responsive to the child's actions, gestures, or vocalizations, thus embedding those child behaviors into conversation-like structures. Or they can build discourse by imposing predictable "texts" on the child often enough that the child comes to recognize what the structure of the texts is. The first technique utilizes contingency to child behaviors: it is child-driven, though highly mother-managed, and results (when it works) in well-integrated conversational sequences which have highly variable content. Perhaps the most extreme examples of such contingency driven interactions involve infants, whose burps, coughs, and nonlinguistic vocalizations elicit responses from adults, or count, when they occur fortuitously at the right time, as responses to adult questions. The second technique exploits predictability: it is almost exclusively mother-driven, at least until the child is well-schooled in any particular text. This mode results, when exploited effectively, in well-practiced routines and games, in which the successive moves follow one another because that sequence is imposed by the format. This is not to say that the form of the games and routines is always nonsensical (though "this little pig went to market" and "Ride a cock horse to Banbury cross" are not the most clearly sense-ful of rhetorical forms), but rather that understanding the forms is not crucial to performing them, because their predictability (and, in some cases, other memory supports such as rhythm and rhyme) provide adequate basis for correct performance based simply on delayed imitation. Obviously, the first several run-throughs of the routine may not generate effective two-party discourse, but as children learn their roles, and as adults start to demand child participation, responsibility for parts of the sequence are shifted to the child. Furthermore, it is obviously possible, and likely, that children do come to understand some parts of the routines they engage in; the issue is, though, that the understanding is not essential to the performance.

These two modes of building discourse should not, at least not at this early point in exploring their usefulness, be reified into two styles of interaction. Rather, they should be seen as defining two endpoints of a continuum, which can help us to place and to relate the different kinds of episodes of caregiver-child interaction that have been hypothesized to be of importance to language acquisition. Thus, it is obvious that routines can incorporate contingent speech to greater or lesser degrees, that contingent conversations can be embedded within such events as bathtime or bedtime, for which much of the structure is routinized and predictable. Conversely, even events such as toy play, in which talk is typically quite contingent for American mothers and children, may have some highly predictable subroutines (e.g., tutorial questions about toys' names, colors, characteristic noises, etc.). Thus, in the real world we rarely encounter pure examples of routines or of semantically contingent conversations. As d'Odorico and Franco have argued (1985), micro-situations may need to be distinguished, rather than macro situations such as "free-play," in order to see the effect of context on maternal speech. It is, furthermore, difficult to establish clear criteria for identifying routines, especially for dyads one does not know well. Thus, we wish to emphasize that in the discussion of routines vs. contingency that follows, we are considering the rare ideal: The routine in which the internal structure of utterances and behaviors is unknown to the child, who nonetheless performs them properly because of their predictability and the amount of practice he has had, vs. the contingent interaction within which the child's utterance or behavior sets the topic for the succeeding adult utterance, and the sequence is quite novel.

A large number of factors might be expected to influence the utilization of a mode of interaction closer to one end or the other of the proposed continuum. These factors probably include, but are not limited to, culture, situation, task or goal of the interaction, individual differences among caretakers, and individual differences among children. Each of these will be considered in turn, though in most cases too little is known to be able actually to assess the relationship between any given factor and the utilization of contingency versus predictability in the interactions.

Culture

The culture of the caregiver is a major factor in the availability of games and routines for utilization in caregiver-child or caregiver-infant interaction. Familiar games which are exploited by parents in England for use with their 3- to 6-month-old infants include tickling games ("Round and round the garden," "Eentsy weentsy spider") and body-part games ("This little pig went to market," "Shoe the horse, shoe the mare"—see Snow, de Blauw, & van Roosmalen, 1979; Snow, Dubber, & de Blauw, 1982). In addition, lullabies ("Rock-a-bye-baby"), counting songs ("One, two, buckle my shoe"), and other nursery rhymes are accessible for use in interaction with infants and children, because they constitute part of the cultural knowledge available to adults in general.

There is some evidence that cultures differ from one another in the availability of such games, songs, and verses for children, and it seems likely, furthermore, that there are important cultural differences in the degree to which they are considered appropriate, desirable, or helpful in child care and education. Schieffelin (1983) has described the negative attitudes of Kaluli mothers toward their children's sound-play, toward the use of baby talk, and toward talk which is considered to be "to no purpose"; it seems unlikely that such mothers would have very positive attitudes toward verses such as "hey diddle diddle, the cat and the fiddle, the cow jumped over the moon" or "hee haw, Margery Daw," even if they were available within the Kaluli repertoire of songs and verses.

On the other hand, the utilization of children's songs, verses, and games is, though wide-spread, nonetheless relatively infrequent, as far as one can tell, among English, Dutch and North American mothers (see Snow, de Blauw, & van Roosmalen, 1979). Reports of interaction between mothers and their children in other cultures suggest that verses are used extensively during dressing, bathing, feeding, and other caretaking activities; for example, Landers (1983) reports that in Southern India specific lines of songs and verses are meant to accompany the various actions involved in bathing and dressing activities, and such songs are repeated at each repetition of the caretaking activity.

Task

Certain tasks which must be accomplished in the course of child rearing lend themselves very obviously to routinized styles of interaction and accompanying talk which is highly predictable. Tasks which have an inherently routine nature, and which recur frequently, such as feeding, bathing, and dressing, are easier to make predictable than unstructured activities such as free play, or than infrequent activities such as visits to the doctor.

Goal

Relatively routinized versus contingent styles of interaction may be employed by one person in pursuit of different goals. For example, in North American pre-school and kindergarten classroom settings, the contingency mode is considered appropriate for presenting new information, on the assumption that children learn new material best when they are motivated by their own spontaneous interests.

On the other hand, teachers in these classrooms rely extensively on routines (morning meeting, clean-up, snack), and devote considerable attention to getting children socialized into correct participation in these routines. The purpose of using such routines may be explicitly identified by the teacher as "calming the children down," "maintaining discipline," or "establishing order," though the use of such routines has also been analyzed as a way of imposing and strengthening group membership among the children, identifying them as members of the class group by their knowledge of the routine (Dickinson, 1985). Precisely because the routine is arbitrary, knowledge of it serves as a badge of membership. Wallat and Green (1982) give a good example of the way in which one teacher used a routine to smooth transition from clean-up to meeting, and document how the children learned the routine in the course of the school year.

In addition to events like preschool routines, games and nursery rhymes, which are truly arbitrary, many events in the child's life may be represented as scripted and arbitrary routines, though from the adult point of view the event sequence is nonarbitrary. Studies of children role-playing "scripts" such as grocery store or doctor's office make quite clear that the organizing goal structure in the adult enactments of these events (obtaining food by exchanging money for it, obtaining diagnosis and cure of disease) are often not accessible to the child, who therefore reenacts events from these episodes in inappropriate sequences for obtaining the goal (e.g., giving the cashier money, then selecting food, then wheeling the cart around a bit, then putting food back on shelf) (Gearhart, 1983). Children seem quite prepared to operate with such arbitrary scripts—in fact, they seem very willing to develop a script, based on exposure to only one or two model episodes of an event (Nelson & Gruendel, 1979). Furthermore, they seem fully prepared to do so without understanding the goal structure that, for the adult, organizes the episode—they often develop scripts as it were, without plots. No doubt children's readiness to represent events as scripts (or mental representations that incorporate routine elements) is a prerequisite to the contribution of routines to language development hypothesized here. Furthermore, such willingness to operate with scripts would support the child's use of deferred imitation as a communication strategy if the predictable features of the event include some language.

It should be noted that the reliance on contingency modes for teaching new material is highly culture-specific. The Koranic schools throughout the Moslem world (Wagner, 1983, 1985) as well as traditional Yeshivas, rely on routinization and rote memorization as ways of teaching the sacred texts, and as the major method for teaching reading. The ultimate goal of these educational systems is skill in independent analytic thinking, yet routinized teaching methods are considered appropriate for reaching that goal.

Individual Differences

There are undoubtedly individual differences among caretakers in their preference for one style of interaction over another. In addition, there may well be individual differences among children in their ability to function well with one or the other mode. Highly imitative children may be those who function better in routinized interactions—they need to have appropriate responses available for situations before they can start to analyze the situation and develop the ability to produce novel behaviors in them. Nonimitative children, on the other hand, may be those who are relatively unwilling to produce utterances or actions simply because they are predictable from the context, without understanding the rules that generated them.

The question of individual differences in aspects of children's language learning is now starting to attract serious attention from language researchers (e.g., Katherine Nelson, 1981; see Goldfield & Snow, 1985, for a review). Clearly it is an enormous oversimplification to assume that ''fine-tuning'' will work identically for all children or that the same features in the input language will be helpful to all children. A recognition of the reality of individual differences in children's styles and strategies for language acquisition is prerequisite to drawing sensible conclusions about the existence of fine-tuning or of facilitatory effects of input speech. It would, for example, be very interesting to compare the effectiveness of highly routinized interactions vs. semantically contingent interactions in promoting the acquisition of syntax and lexicon in imitative vs. nonimitative children. The naturally imitative child should learn more easily and quickly from the routinized interactions, and the nonimitator more from the semantically contingent ones.

Implications

What are the implications of the continuum sketched above for our understanding of the results relevant to fine-tuning and early social interaction? By definition, routinized styles of interaction need be neither fine-tuned, nor semantically contingent. There is, of course, no reason to fine-tune the complexity of the routinized speech, since it need not be processed by the child in the same way as contingent speech needs to be. Children can respond to routinized speech without analyzing it, because they know the routines. Thus, the presence of a complex syntactic structure within the routine is no hindrance to its use by the child. Feld and Schieffelin (1981) report no adjustment of the utterances Kaluli mothers model for child imitation using the *elema* teaching device; it is natural that such utterances are not tuned to the child's level, because they are being presented for rote repetition, precisely the mode which will rely least on fine-tuning. If a large sample of adult speech is analysed, globally calculated measures such as MLU may appear not to be fine-tuned, because the finely adjusted, simple utterances are offset by utterances which constitute parts of routines. Before assessing finetuning, it is necessary to determine if the utterances being analyzed by the investigator are those which could be expected to show fine-tuning at all. Which utterances those are could, as discussed above, vary grossly depending on culture, situation, task, caretaker, and child.

However, it is also important to point out that different learning mechanisms are called into action by the different facilitating conditions (Snow & Gilbreath, 1983). One cannot expect that the same items will be learned nor that they will be learned in exactly the same way from finely tuned semantically contingent interactions and from routinized interactions.

The model presented here suggests that highly routinized interactions will differ from nonroutinized interactions in a number of ways. It is predicted that adult speech will be (1) more complex; (2) less semantically contingent; (3) less well finely tuned to the child's level in routinized situations. At the same time, children's speech in the routine event is presumably modeled on adult speech heard at equivalent points in previous run-throughs of the routine: furthermore, the child might be thought of as having more cognitive capacity available for language production in routine events, in which it is easier to comprehend what is going on, than in nonroutine events during which adult actions and objects are unfamiliar. Accordingly, one would expect the child's speech in routine events to be (1) more complex; (2) more correct; (3) less scaffolded. A study was undertaken to test these hypotheses. Preliminary results are presented here.

STUDY 1

Procedures

Five children (four boys and one girl) aged 1:5 to 1:10 at the beginning of the study were the subjects, together with their mothers. These five participated in a larger study in which their interactions with their mothers were recorded at weekly intervals over a period of 12–30 weeks in two highly routinized situations per child. The specific situations were selected by each child's mother as the best examples of recurrent contexts for interaction which were highly predictable and seemed to have 'rules' for the child. Typical contexts were bath, bedtime, playing with a favorite puzzle or posting toy, or reading a favorite book. During the last few weeks of data collection for each child, new observation situations were introduced: (a) a context that was very similar to the child's best routine in terms of format but which involved novel content (e.g., reading a new book for a child whose book-reading routine had been observed regularly); (b) a free-play session between mother and child using a set of novel toys; and (c) a role-play session, in which the child was induced to play the mother's role in the routine activity which had been observed. Because of the disparity across children in the nature of the routines being observed, cross-child comparisons, especially of the role-play sessions, are very difficult to interpret. A partial analysis of the book-reading role-play sessions has been presented in Snow, Nathan, and Perlmann (1985).

The basic hypotheses this research was designed to test were:

1. Child speech is more complex, more correct, and less scaffolded during routine than during unstructured, unfamiliar play situations.

2. Maternal speech is more complex, less semantically contingent, and less finely tuned during routine than during less routine situations.

3. The facilitating features of maternal speech in routine situations are different from those of nonroutine situations: specifically, semantically contingent responses are more frequent and more helpful in nonroutine situations, whereas repetitiveness or predictability might be the facilitators in nonroutine situations.

Speech Measures.   In order to test these hypotheses, the following measures were taken:

1. Child language measures. Each child's mean length of utterance (MLU) was calculated using the standard rules (Brown, 1973) and procedures for at least 100 child utterances during each of the situations. The rules stipulate that the 100 utterances on which the calculation is based not be taken from the very start of the interaction, exclude partially transcribed utterances and exclude fillers and false starts from the count. Exact repetitions, rote-learned utterances, and exact or reduced imitations of preceding maternal utterances were excluded from the count.

2. Maternal language measures. In analyzing maternal language, we were interested in two major questions: is it more complex during the more routinized activities? and does it show the same incidence of features previously found to facilitate language acquistion as nonroutine speech? Accordingly, we calculated the percentage of maternal utterances which were semantically contingent on

preceding child utterances. Semantically contingent utterances were defined to include the following categories:

Exact and reduced repetitions.   Maternal repetitions of child utterances.

Expansions and recasts.   Maternal utterances which, though including new constituents, repeated at least one major constituent and content word from the preceding child utterance.

Clarification questions.   Maternal utterances which, though perhaps not repeating any part of the child utterance, nonetheless were directed to clarifying its meaning (e.g., Huh? What did you say?)

Extensions.   Maternal utterances which, though repeating no words from the child utterances, continued and extended the child's topic, e.g.,

Child: It's a doggy.
Mother: With a huge long tail.

Responses.   Maternal utterances which responded to children's requests for information or for help, e.g.

Child: What's this?
Mother: That's an octagon.

Child: How do you open this?
Mother: (Trying) I think it's stuck.

A first approach to testing these hypotheses involved a comparison of the three observation sessions which can be ranked in terms of routinization: the routine itself, the routine-format with novel content, and the free play.

Results

The results for child MLU, maternal MLU, and maternal use of semantic contingency are presented in Tables 4.2 through 4.4. Casual inspection of the tables reveals that, except for the child we call Ben, our expectations were not con-

TABLE 4.2
Children's MLU's in Three Situations

	Age Range	Routine	Routine-Format	Free Play
Josh	1;7.19-1;11.21	1.2	1.5	1.3
Ben	1;10.3-1;11.25	1.2	1.4	2.8
Amy[a]	1;11.0-2;3.20	1.4	1.8	2.8
Jim	1;11.8-2;0.25	2.1	3.0	2.8
Alex	2;0.24-2;3.16	2.5	2.9	3.9

[a]Order of sessions: Routine, Free Play, Routine-Format.

TABLE 4.3
Mothers' MLU's (in Words) in Three Situations

	Routine	Routine-Format	Free Play
Josh	4.4	3.7	4.2
Ben	6.2	5.6	5.1
Amy	4.4	5.1	5.4
Jim	4.2	3.8	4.5
Alex	5.6	5.6	6.1

firmed. In general, maternal speech was more complex and less semantically contingent in the free play situations, and child speech was similarly more complex during free play and least complex during the routine.

An unfortunate confound may, however, reduce the value of these findings as direct tests of our hypotheses. Although our goal had been to do the three comparison sessions as close together as possible, in fact scheduling problems meant that sometimes a span of several weeks elapsed between the last routine observation and the completion of the comparison observations.

We had chosen to carry out the nonroutine observations after the routine in all cases, so that any development that occurred in the child's language ability would work against the possibility that we would find the result we wanted. In fact, it is possible we succeeded too well; we were observing children during a period of rather rapid language growth, and changes in their language due to development may have overwhelmed the differences due to situation.

One way to test this possibility is to look, not at absolute levels on complexity measures, but at the relation between maternal and child complexity, in fact, at the degree of fine-tuning. Our hypothesis, with a developmental perspective added to it, is that maternal speech could be relatively more complex than the child's level in routine than in nonroutinized situations, and that unstructured situations would elicit a highly fine-tuned maternal style. Table 4.5 presents the difference scores between maternal and child MLU for each of the three situations. Although the routine-format does not behave predictably, the routine vs. free-play comparison yields very consistent results: In all cases the relative complexity of maternal MLU was highest for the routine situation. This finding is especially strong because one would expect the child's developmental level to

TABLE 4.4
Percent Semantically Contingent Responses in Mothers'
Speech in Three Situations

	Routine	Routine-Format	Free Play
Josh	13.2	49.6	24.6
Ben	11.8	22.3	46.3
Amy	33.0	23.5	12.3
Jim	65.3	56.2	21.1
Alex	21.3	17.4	15.5

TABLE 4.5
Difference Scores Between Maternal and Child MLU's
in Three Situations

	Routine	Routine-Format	Free Play
Josh	3.2	2.2	2.9
Ben	5.0	4.2	2.3
Amy	3.0	3.3	2.6
Jim	2.1	0.8	1.7
Alex	3.1	2.7	2.2

affect these difference scores precisely as it would affect MLU scores: older and linguistically more competent children can handle less finely tuned maternal speech. In seems, then, that aspects of the routine may support children's comprehension sufficiently that, even at earlier stages of language development, they can handle relatively more complex input.

While these data are, partly because of the timing of the observations, much less strong than we had hoped, other data in support of our prediction are available. Conti-Ramsden and Friel-Patti (this volume) compared three situations that, like ours, varied in degree of predictability for the child: an old-toys, no-toys, and new-toy situation. Their old-toys situation (most routine) was like our free-play (least routine) in some ways—the availability of many toys, for example—but different in that our free-play session introduced many toys novel to the child, for which no standard play-scripts were available, whereas theirs introduced very familiar toys (balls, blocks, etc.). Their new-toy situation introduced one very complex and very unfamiliar toy, and was thus quite different from our free-play, with its mix of familiar and unfamiliar toys. Conti-Ramsden and Friel-Patti found that child MLU and MLU5 were lowest in their new-toy situation, but that mothers' MLU's showed no differences (i.e., were closest to the children's in the novel situation). They also found, as we did, that semantic contingency was *lowest* in the new-toy situation, a fact related in their data to lower incidence of child initiations and a more didactic style adopted by the mothers when playing with the unfamiliar toy. Thus, the Conti-Ramsden and Friel-Patti data, like ours, suggest that children display their linguistic competence best in routine situations, that mothers may be less well-tuned to child level in routine situations, but that semantic contingency is highest in routine situations.

Clearly, one factor affecting this pattern of results is that "semantic contingency" as coded by us (and, presumably, by Conti-Ramsden and Friel-Patti) encompasses both maternal utterances that are on topic but relatively difficult for the child to process (e.g., semantic extensions) and utterances that are completely limited to the child's topic (e.g., simple recasts and clarification questions). High semantic contingency can be seen as a measure of conversational cohesiveness. In the "ideal" semantically contingent interaction such conversational cohesiveness is the product entirely of maternal work in following the child's topic. In the conversations we actually analyzed, it was the product of a general tendency for mother and child to talk about the same topics, both in the routine and in the less routine situations.

STUDY 2

Procedures

The results of the study just described were rendered somewhat tentative by the time elapsed between the comparison sessions. A more powerful comparison between routines and nonroutines, and between more and less structured interactive situations, is offered by looking more precisely at smaller segments of the data from this same group of children. Three of the five children were different from the others in that their routines were better established and more predictable, and in that their routine-format observation situations were quite similar to the routine in terms of the details of how they were carried out. The very strongest case, in our opinion, is provided by a comparison of child and mother reading the routine-book with their reading of a different book, precisely because the book-reading format constrains the situation so as to reduce the influence of irrelevant factors. This comparison was possible for three different children, on two occasions for two of the children and once for the third. Another contrast is provided by a comparison of the children's talk during routine play with a set of familiar toys, and during reading of a familiar book. This comparison of two routines allows one to see the effect of greater or less structure imposed by the routine activity. This contrast occurred three times, all three in the corpus from one boy.

Speech Measures.   In order to have standard assessments of the length, complexity, and correctness of the children's speech during these various situations, we used the following measures, in addition to MLU calculated as in Study 1:

1. Mean length of five longest utterances (MLU5). It has been suggested that the MLU5 is a better reflection of competence than MLU, since it is less affected by the vagaries of the discourse.

2. Use of grammatical markers. For children aged 16 to 24 months and in the early stages of combining words, there is considerable variability in the percent grammatical morphemes supplied in speech, and in the number of grammatical markers used at all. We used as an index of morphological complexity the number of grammatical markers used in at least 80% of obligatory contexts, basing our analyses on the list of 14 morphemes first identified as undergoing development during this period by Brown (1973).

3. Percent scaffolded utterances. Scaffolded utterances are defined as those that incorporate content words from immediately preceding adult utterances, i.e., immediate reduced, exact and expanded imitations. Since imitation is a frequent child response to an adult utterance that has not been understood (Stine & Bohannon, 1983) and since scaffolded utterances are less demanding to produce than spontaneous utterances, a higher rate of use of scaffolded utterances can be seen as a negative indicator in an assessment of the children's language. Since all comparisons were carried out within subjects, individual differences in tendencies to imitate should not affect results.

The maternal language measures used in Study 2 were the same as those used in Study 1.

Results

Child Language. The results for the comparison of the familiar with the unfamiliar book are presented in Tables 4.6 and 4.7. It can be seen that the results strongly support the hypothesis: In four out of five cases, the measures of grammatical complexity and sophistication (MLU, MLU5, and Number of Grammatical Markers) show that child speech during routine situations was more complex and more sophisticated. The exception was Josh's first session, which happened to occur right at the beginning of multiword speech for him. Again, in four out of five cases, more scaffolded utterances were produced in the novel-book situation, suggesting lower comprehension rates or greater processing loads for the children in this context.

The comparison of a structured, familiar play routine with a less structured, though equally familiar play activity on three occasions for Alex shows much the same picture, though perhaps not quite so strongly (see Table 4.8). His MLU was noticeably higher in the more structured situation only once, but his MLU5 was considerably higher in all three comparisons, and his use of grammatical morphemes also considerably greater two out of three times. His imitation rate throughout was so low as to make comparison unenlightening.

Adult Speech. The mothers' utterances were generally shorter during the reading of the unfamiliar book (Josh I was the only exception), but were more

TABLE 4.6
Child MLU's (MLU5's) While Reading Familiar Vs. Unfamiliar Book

	Age Range	Familiar Book	Unfamiliar Book
Josh I	1;5.7-1;5.11	1.00 (1.0)	1.06 (1.6)
Josh II	1;8.6-1;8.10	1.57 (2.2)	1.25 (1.4)
Jim	1;11.20-1;11.27	2.36 (4.2)	1.57 (3.2)
Alex I	1;10.28-1;11.0	1.28 (2.8)	1.10 (1.6)
Alex II	1;11.17-1;11.17	1.79 (4.0)	1.56 (2.6)

TABLE 4.7
Indicators of Productive Language Use During Reading of Familiar
Vs. Unfamiliar Book

| | # Grammatical Features Used | | % Scaffolded Utterances | |
	Familiar	Unfamiliar	Familiar	Unfamiliar
Josh I	0	1	9	15
Josh II	2	1	0	0
Jim	11	3	2	5
Alex I	2	2	0	2
Alex II	5	2	0	5

semantically contingent in only one of the five cases and were less semantically contingent in three cases (see Tables 4.9 and 4.10). Thus, while the hypothesis concerning complexity was confirmed, the relationship of semantic contingency to routinization is not what we had predicted. For these children, at least, levels of maternal semantic contingency are not related to the degree of routinization associated with the activity being engaged in.

DISCUSSION

We have presented evidence suggesting that children's speech is more complex in familiar, routinized, structured situations, and that maternal speech is more finely tuned in nonroutinized activities with unfamiliar toys. We did not find the expected relationship between degree of semantic contingency in the maternal speech and the nature of the activity being engaged in—if anything, routine events generated more semantically contingent maternal utterances.

There are a number of possible explanations for our failure to find differences in semantic contingency. Perhaps the most routine formats we could isolate were simply not routine enough to qualify as equivalent to the routinized interaction formats with highly predictable accompanying language that children in other cultures engage in. The children we observed produced very few deferred imitations or repetitions of identical utterances from one routine session to the next, partly because the mothers' speech was quite variable in these routines. Even in

TABLE 4.8
Indicators of Complexity and Grammatical Productiveness in Alex's Speech in Relatively
Structured Vs. Unstructured Routine Situations

| | Age | MLU | | MLU5 | | # Grammatical Features | | # Scaffolded | |
		Str	Unstr	Str	Unstr	Str	Unstr	Str	Unstr
I	1;10.30	1.10	1.09	2.8	2.2	2	2	0	0
II	1;11.17	1.79	1.58	4.0	3.4	4	2	1	2
III	2;0.24	2.42	2.51	4.8	4.2	7	4	0	0

TABLE 4.9
Maternal MLU While Reading Familiar Vs. Unfamiliar Book

	Familiar Book	Unfamiliar Book
Josh I	4.96	5.08
Josh II	5.52	5.17
Jim	4.63	4.46
Alex I	5.50	4.81
Alex II	5.03	4.90

the book-reading routines, reading the text was rare, and constituted less than 5% of all maternal utterances. Alternately, perhaps the "semantic contingency model" is so strong in this culture that it is applied by mothers even in situations where it is not a necessary device for keeping the child's utterances within a discourse context. The children might have been capable of processing less contingent maternal speech, but their mothers nonetheless continued to use the dominant western mode of interaction with children, which requires adaptation to the child's topic. Furthermore, as suggested earlier, it is possible that our measure of semantic contingency confounds simpler semantically contingent responses, more relied upon in novel situations, with more complex ones used in routine situations.

Implications.   The nature of social interaction with and speech to young children, and their relation to language acquisition, are of especial interest to those with the responsibility of designing intervention programs for children with language disabilities or some handicap that leads to language delay. They search the literature for clues as to the optimal language environment, but find only the dilemmas sketched in the first section of this chapter. What must they conclude—that no language environment is better than any other and thus than no intervention program can be motivated?

We think the continuum sketched above can help shed light on their problem. The value of the language environment to the language learner cannot be assessed in a unidimensional way, as simply high (= good) versus low (= bad) on contingency or high (= good) versus low (= bad) on predictability. Predictability and contingency are both good, but they are also to some extent in conflict

TABLE 4.10
Percent Semantically Contingent Maternal Utterances While
Reading Familiar Vs. Unfamiliar Book

	Familiar Book	Unfamiliar Book
Josh I	11	11
Josh II	18	7
Jim	71	51
Alex I	53	40
Alex II	27	38

with one another. Speech that is highly contingent need not be high on predictability and speech that is highly predictable may (at least until the child has learned the routine) be noncontingent; thus, in any short session of interaction, it may appear that the mother is violating the canons of contingency, when in fact she is practicing a different model of interaction based on predictability. It may, practically speaking, be impossible for the unfamiliar observer even to score predictability in caretakers' speech—almost by definition, that requires a long history of familiarity with the speech patterns of the caretaker, not a one-off observation.

It might be more helpful, in assessing or designing optimal language environments, to take the child's point of view, and focus on the degree to which any caretaker behavior puts the child's utterances in context. This process, of creating discourse around the child speech, was proposed above as the crucial contribution of caretaker speech. It should be, then, the goal of any intervention in the child's linguistic environment. The manner of creating the context—by contingency or by predictability—may not make any difference to the desired outcome, a child who can extract from the caretaker's language information useful in developing an autonomous linguistic system.

The model proposed here, if accepted in its strongest form, makes the prediction that any child will fail to learn to talk if no embedding of the child's actions or utterances in discourse context occurs. It suggests, however, that the absence of such embedding is rather rare, given the variety of options available for ensuring the embedding. Either sensitive responsiveness to the child's utterances, on the model of the mother having conversations with her child in which she responds to child topics and focus of attention, or exposure to highly predictable utterances in recurrent routines, on the model of the mother reciting nursery rhymes with her child, will work. Thus, the highly buffered nature of language acquisition, its resistance to failure, and the wide variety of successful language-learning environments, need not push us into a position of concluding that the language input to the child is immaterial—only to the recognition that it can work in a variety of ways.

ACKNOWLEDGMENT

Thanks are due to the Spencer Foundation, which funded the collection of data reported in this paper, to Andrea Senkowski, Susan Bertram, Cheryl D'Amelio, Carol Johnson and Joan Test for their contributions as observors and transcribers, and to Amy, Jim, Josh, Alex and Ben and their mothers. Portions of the analysis reported here were carried out while the first author was a Fellow at the Institute for Advanced Studies, Hebrew University. Many fruitful discussions with other members of the Institute contributed to the ideas expressed in the paper.

REFERENCES

Baker, N., & Nelson, K. (1984). Recasting and related conversational techniques for triggering syntactic advances by young children. *First Language, 5,* 3–22.

Baker, N., Pemberton, E., & Nelson, K. (1985, October). *Facilitating young children's language development through stories: Reading and recasting.* Paper presented at Boston University Child Language Conference, Boston.

Barnes, S., Gutfreund, M., Satterly, D., & Wells, G. (1983). Characteristics of adult speech which predict children's language development. *Journal of Child Language, 10,* 65–84.

Bellinger, D. (1979). Changes in the explicitness of mother's directives as children age. *Journal of Child Language, 6,* 443–455.

Bellinger, D. (1980). Consistency in the pattern of change in mother's speech: Some discriminant analyses. *Journal of Child Language, 7,* 469–481.

Bohannon, J. N., & Marquis, A. (1977). Children's control of adult speech. *Child Development, 48,* 1002–1008.

Bohannon, J. N., Stine, E. L., & Ritzenberg, D. (1982). The "fine-tuning" hypothesis of adult speech to children: Effects of experience and feedback. *Bulletin of the Psychonomic Society, 19*(4), 201–204.

Brown, R. (1968). The development of WH questions in child speech. *Journal of Verbal Learning and Verbal Behavior, 7,* 279–290.

Brown, R. (1973). *A first language.* Cambridge, MA: Harvard University Press.

Brown, R. (1977). Introduction. In C. Snow & C. Ferguson (Eds.), *Talking to children: Language input and acquisition* (pp. 1–27). Cambridge, England: Cambridge University Press.

Bruck, M. (1978, September). *Teacher speech to the language disabled child.* Paper presented at the Third Boston University Conference on Language Development, Boston.

Bruner, J. (1977). Early social interaction and language acquisition. In H. R. Schaffer (Ed.), *Studies in mother infant interaction.* New York: Academic Press.

Bruner, J. (1983). *Child's talk: Learning to use language.* New York: Norton.

Bruner, J. S., & Sherwood, V. (1976). Peekaboo and the learning of rule structures. In J. S. Bruner, A. Jolly, & K. Sylva (Eds.), *Play: Its role in development and evolution* (pp. 277–285). Harmondsworth: Penguin.

Cazden, C. (1965). *Environmental assistance to the acquisition of grammar.* Unpublished doctoral dissertation. Harvard Graduate School of Education.

Chapman, R. (1981). Mother child interaction in the second year of life: Its role in language development. In R. Schiefelbusch & J. Bricker (Eds.), *Early language acquisition and intervention* (pp. 201–250). Baltimore, MD: University Park Press.

Clarke-Stewart, K. (1973). Interactions between mothers and their young children: characteristics and consequences. *Monographs of the Society for Research in Child Development, 38,* (6–7, Serial #153).

Clarke-Stewart, K., Vanderstoep, L., & Killian, G. (1979). Analyses and replication of mother-child relations at 2-years of age. *Child Development, 50,* 777–793.

Cohen, S., & Beckwith, L. (1976). Maternal language in infancy. *Developmental Psychology, 17,* 371–372.

Cross, T. (1977). Mothers' speech adjustments: The contribution of selected child listener variables. In C. Snow & C. Ferguson (Eds.), *Talking to children* (pp. 151–188). Cambridge, England: Cambridge University Press.

Cross, T. (1978). Motherese: Its association with the rate of syntactic acquisition in young children. In N. Waterson & C. Snow (Eds.), *The development of communication* (pp. 199–216). London: Wiley.

Cross, T. (1983). Habilitating the language-impaired child: Ideas from studies of parent-child interaction. *Topics in Language Disorders, 4,* 1–14.

Dickinson, D. (1985). Creating and using formal occasions in the classroom. *Anthropology and Education Quarterly, 16*, 47–62.

d'Odorico, L., & Franco, F. (1985). The determinants of baby talk: Relationship to context. *Journal of Child Language, 12*, 567–586.

Engle, M. (1979). *Do fathers speak motherese? An analysis of the language environments of young children.* Unpublished paper, University of California, San Diego.

Feld, S., & Schieffelin, B. B. (1981). Hard words: A functional basis for Kaluli discourse. In D. Tannen (Ed.), *Analyzing discourse: Text and talk.* Georgetown University Round Table on Language and Linguistics. Washington, D.C.: Georgetown University Press.

Fraser, C., & Roberts, A. (1975). Mothers' speech to children of four different ages. *Journal of Psycholinguistic Research, 4*, 9–16.

Furrow, D., Nelson, K., & Benedict, H. (1979). Mothers' speech to children and syntactic development: Some simple relationships. *Journal of Child Language, 6*, 423–442.

Gearhart, M. (1983). *Social plans and social episodes: The development of collaboration in role playing.* Unpublished doctoral dissertation, City University of New York.

Gleason, J. Berko (1977). Talking to children: Some notes on feedback. In C. Snow & C. Ferguson (Eds.), *Talking to children: Language input and acquisition* (pp. 199–205). Cambridge, England: Cambridge University Press.

Goldfield, B. (1985). *The contribution of child and caregiver to individual differences in language acquisition.* Unpublished doctoral dissertation, Harvard Graduate School of Education.

Goldfield, B., & Snow, C. (1985). Individual differences in language acquisition. In J. Berko Gleason (Ed.), *The development of language* (pp. 307–330). Columbus, OH: Merrill.

Heath, S. B. (1983). *Ways with words.* New York: Cambridge University Press.

Hirsch-Pasek, K., & Treiman, R. (1982). Doggerel: Motherese in a new context. *Journal of Child Language, 9*, 229–237.

Hovell, M., Schumaker, J., & Sherman, J. (1978). A comparison of parents' models and expansions in promoting children's acquisition of objectives. *Journal of Experimental Child Psychology, 25*, 41–57.

Kaye, K. (1980). Why we don't talk baby talk to babies? *Journal of Child Language, 7*, 489–507.

Kaye, K., & Charney, R. (1980). How mothers maintain "dialogue" with two-year olds. In D. Olson (Ed.), *The social foundations of language and thought: Essays in honor of Jerome S. Bruner* (pp. 211–230). New York: Norton.

Kaye, K., & Fogel, A. (1980). The temporal structure of face-to-face communication between mothers and infants. *Developmental Psychology, 16*, 454–464.

Landers, C. (1983). *Biological, social and cultural determinants of infant behavior in a South Indian community.* Unpublished doctoral dissertation, Harvard Graduate School of Education.

LeVine, R. (1977). Child rearing as cultural adaptation. In P. H. Liederman, S. Tulkin, & A. Rosenfeld (Eds.), *Culture and infancy: Variations in the human experience* (pp. 15–28). Orlando, FL: Academic Press.

Liederman, P. H., Tulkin, S., & Rosenfeld, A. (Eds.). (1977). *Culture and infancy: Variations in the human experience.* Orlando, FL: Academic Press.

Longhurst, T., & Stephanich, L. (1975). Mothers' speech addressed to one-, two-, and three-year-old normal children. *Child Study Journal, 5*, 3–11.

Nelson, K. (1981). Individual differences in language development: Implications for development and language. *Developmental Psychology, 17*, 170–187.

Nelson, K., & Gruendel, J. (1979). At morning it's lunchtime: A scriptal view of children's dialogues. *Discourse Processes, 2*, 73–94.

Nelson, K. E. (1977). Facilitating children's syntax acquisition. *Developmental Psychology, 13*, 101–107.

Nelson, K. E. (1981). Toward a rare-event cognitive comparison theory of syntax acquisition: Insights from work with recasts. In P. Dale & D. Ingram (Eds.), *Child language: An international perspective* (229–240). Baltimore, MD: University Park Press.

Nelson, K. E., Carskaddon, G., & Bonvillian, J. (1973). Syntax acquisition: Impact of experimental variation in adult verbal interaction with the child. *Child Development, 44,* 497–504.

Nelson, K. E., Bonvillian, J., Denninger, M., Kaplan, B., & Baker, N. (1984). Maternal input adjustments and nonadjustments as related to children's linguistic advances and to language acquisition theories. In A. Pellegrini & T. Yawkey (Eds.), *The development of oral and written language in social contexts* (pp. 31–56). Norwood, NJ: Ablex.

Newport, E., Gleitman, H., & Gleitman, L. (1977). Mother, I'd rather do it myself: Some effects and noneffects of maternal speech style. In C. Snow & C. Ferguson (Eds.), *Talking to children: Language input and acquisition* (pp. 109–149). Cambridge, England: Cambridge University Press.

Ochs, E., & Schieffelin, B. B. (1984). Language acquisition and socialization: Three developmental stories and their implications. In R. Schweder, & R. LeVine (Eds.), *Culture theory: Essays on mind, self, and emotion* (pp. 276–322). Cambridge, England: Cambridge University Press.

Ochs, E., Schieffelin, B., & Platt, M. (1979). Propositions across utterances and speakers. In E. Ochs & B. Schieffelin (Eds.), *Developmental pragmatics.* New York: Academic Press.

Phillips, J. (1973). Syntax and vocabulary of mothers' speech to young children: Age and sex comparisons. *Child Development, 44,* 182–185.

Retherford, K. S., Schwartz, B. C., & Chapman, R. S. (1981). Semantic roles and residual grammatical categories in mother and child speech: who tunes in to whom? *Journal of Child Language, 8,* 583–608.

Rondal, J. (1978). Maternal speech to normal and Down's syndrome children matched for mean utterance length. In C. Meyers (Ed.), *Quality of life in severely and profoundly mentally retarded people.* American Association on Mental Deficiency, Washington, DC.

Rondal, J. A. (1980). Fathers' and mothers' speech in early language development. *Journal of Child Language, 7,* 353–370.

Sachs, J. (1979). Topic selection in parent-child discourse. *Discourse Processes, 2,* 145–153.

Sachs, J. (1983). Talking about the there and then: The emergence of displaced reference in parent-child discourse. In K. E. Nelson (Ed.), *Children's language, Vol. 4* (pp. 1–28). Hillsdale, NJ: Lawrence Erlbaum Associates.

Schaffer, H. R., & Crook, C. K. (1979). Maternal control techniques in a directed play situation. *Child Development, 50,* 989–998.

Schieffelin, B. (1979). Getting it together: An ethnographic approach to the study of the development of communicative competence. In E. Ochs & B. Schieffelin (Eds.), *Developmental pragmatics.* New York: Academic Press.

Schieffelin, B. B. (1983). Talking like birds: Sound play in a cultural perspective. In E. Ochs, & B. B. Schieffelin (Eds.), *Acquiring conversational competence.* London: Routledge and Kegan Paul.

Schieffelin, B. B. (1984). *How Kaluli children learn what to say, what to do, and how to feel: An ethnographic study of the development of communicative competence.* Orlando, FL: Academic Press.

Schumaker, J. B. (1976). *Mothers' expansions: Their characteristics and effects on child language.* Unpublished doctoral dissertation, University of Kansas.

Sherrod, K., Friedman, S., Crowley, S., Drake, D., & Devieux, J. (1977). Maternal language to prelinguistic infants: Syntactic aspects. *Child Development, 48,* 1662–1665.

Snow, C. E. (1972). Mothers' speech to children learning language. *Child Development, 43,* 549–565.

Snow, C. E. (1977a). The development of conversation between mothers and babies. *Journal of Child Language, 4,* 1–22.

Snow, C. (1977b). Mothers' speech research: From input to interaction. In C. Snow & C. Ferguson (Eds.), *Talking to children* (pp. 31–49). Cambridge, England: Cambridge University Press.

Snow, C. E. (1979). The role of social interaction in language acquisition. In A. Collins (Ed.),

Children's language and communication: 12th Minnesota symposium on child psychology (pp. 157–182). Hillsdale, NJ: Lawrence Erlbaum Associates.

Snow, C. (1981). Social interaction and language acquisition. In P. Dale & D. Ingram (Eds.), *Child language: An international perspective* (pp. 195–214). Baltimore, MD: University Park Press.

Snow, C. (1982). Are parents language teachers? In K. Borman (Ed.), *The social life of children in a changing society*. Hillsdale, NJ: Lawrence Erlbaum Associates.

Snow, C., Arlman-Rupp, A., Hassing, Y., Jobse, J., Joosten, J., & Vorster, J. (1976). Mother's speech in three social classes. *Journal of Psycholinguistic Research, 5,* 1–20.

Snow, C., de Blauw, A., & van Roosmalen, G. (1979). Talking and playing with babies: The role of ideologies of childrearing. In M. Bullowa (Ed.), *Before speech*. Cambridge, England: Cambridge University Press.

Snow, C., Dubber, C., & de Blauw, A. (1982). Routines in parent-child interaction. In L. Feagans & D. Farran (Eds.), *The language of children reared in poverty: Implications for evaluation and intervention*. New York: Academic Press.

Snow, C. E., & Gilbreath, B. J. (1983). Explaining transitions. In R. M. Golinkoff (Ed.), *The transition from prelinguistic to linguistic communication*. Hillsdale, NJ: Lawrence Erlbaum Associates.

Snow, C. E., & Goldfield, B. A. (1982). Building stories: The emergence of information structures from conversation. In D. Tannen (Ed.), *Analyzing discourse: Text and talk*. Georgetown University Round Table on Languages and Linguistics, 1981. Washington, DC: Georgetown University Press.

Snow, C., Nathan, D., & Perlmann, R. (1985). Assessing children's knowledge about book-reading. In L. Galda & A. Pellegrini (Eds.), *Language in play*. Norwood, NJ: Ablex.

Stern, D. N., Spieker, S., Barnett, R. K., & MacKain, K. (1983). The prosody of maternal speech: Infant age and context related changes. *Journal of Child Language, 10,* 1–16.

Stine, E. L., & Bohannon, J. N. III. (1983). Imitations, interactions, and language acquisition. *Journal of Child Language, 10,* 589–604.

Van Kleeck, A., & Carpenter, R. (1980). The effect of children's language comprehension level on adults' child directed talk. *Journal of Speech and Hearing Research, 23,* 546–569.

Wagner, D. A. (1983). Islamic education: Traditional pedagogy and contemporary change. In T. Husen & T. N. Postlethwaite (Eds.), *International encyclopedia of education: Research and studies*. New York: Pergamon Press.

Wagner, D. A. (1985). Rediscovering "rote": some cognitive and pedagogical preliminaries. In R. Irvine & J. W. Berry (Eds.), *Human assessment and cultural factors*. New York: Plenum.

Wallat, C., & Green, C. (1982). Construction of social norms by teachers and children: The first year of school. In K. Borman (Ed.), *The social life of children in a changing society*. Hillsdale, NJ: Lawrence Erlbaum Associates.

Warren-Leubecker, A., & Bohannon, J. N. III. (1983). The effects of verbal feedback and listener type on the speech of preschool children. *Journal of Experimental Child Psychology, 35,* 540–548.

Ward, M. (1971). *Them children: A study in language learning*. New York: Holt, Rinehart, Winston.

Watson, J. (1972). Smiling, cooing and 'the game'. *Merril-Palmer Quarterly, 18,* 323–339.

Wells, G. (1980). Adjustments in adult-child conversation: Some effects of interaction. In H. Giles (Ed.), *Language: Social psychological perspectives*. London: Pergamon Press.

Whitehurst, G., & Novak, G. (1973). Modeling, imitation training, and the acquisition of sentence phrases. *Journal of Experimental Child Psychology, 16,* 332–345.

5 Conversation and Language Learning in the Classroom

Gisela E. Speidel
Center for Development of Early Education, Honolulu

Language can be learned through medium oriented talk or through message oriented talk (Dodson, 1984). In the medium oriented approach the focus is on learning the separate components of language, its grammatical forms and structures, and its lexicon. In the message oriented approach the focus is on understanding the messages of others and on putting one's thoughts into words. In our society our first language is learned through message oriented talk (e.g., Bates, 1976; Dore, 1979; Grimm, 1982; Halliday, 1975; Moerk, 1983a; Oksaar, 1977; Snow, 1977; Vygotsky, 1962; Wells, 1978). Medium oriented talk is rare in caregivers (Brown & Hanlon, 1970) but does occur (Schachter, 1979).

Language learning through medium oriented speech has been typical of second language instruction (see Krashen & Terrell, 1983, for a review). Some of the medium oriented methods developed for second language instruction have been adapted for language development in young children from low SES or dialect speaking backgrounds (Bereiter & Engelmann, 1966; Dunn, Horton, & Smith, 1968; Hawaii District Office, 1969).

Medium oriented methods can emphasize either learning grammatical rules and lists of vocabulary, or pattern drills without direct instruction of grammatical rules. The common denominator in these methods is that the learners are not free to put their own thoughts into words, that the lessons focus on learning features of the language and not on an interesting topic of discussion and on meaning exchange.

These medium oriented methods have recently come under some heavy fire by critics in the Head Start as well as in the second language acquisition field. Joan Tough writes about Head Start language development programs such as the Peabody Language Development Kits: "In the view of many these programs fail

99

to tackle the basic problems which some children have. Language is not best seen as a set of skills to be established by drilling; this is to neglect the essential character of language which is its potential for expressing meaning. For the child to learn to use language successfully he needs to have strong motivation for wanting to express his own ideas'' (Tough, 1977, p. 14). Hatch writes about second language learning: "It is assumed that one first learns how to manipulate structures, that one gradually builds up a repertoire of structures and then, somehow, learns to put the structures to use in discourse. We would like to consider the possibility that just the reverse happens. One learns how to do conversation, one learns how to interact verbally and out of this interaction syntactic structures are developed" (Hatch, 1978, p. 404).

In response to such dissatisfaction, a variety of different kinds of message oriented approaches have been developed. For the young "Head Start" child, who has difficulty in using school type language (e.g., Blank, Rose, & Berlin, 1978; McGinness, 1982; Tough, 1977), the emphasis has shifted from the direct teaching of grammar and vocabulary to developing a *language of learning*. For example, Tough's (1977) approach focuses on increasing the student's ability to use language for classifying, predicting, talking about nonpresent events, and so on. The vehicle for such language development is the dialogue between teacher and students. "When we intend to make our meanings clear and work toward effective communication, then our talk becomes more deliberate, reflecting the effort to exchange meanings intact" (p. 21). The approach taken by Blank and her colleagues (Blank et al., 1978) is to help children use language for abstract reasoning. Again dialogue is seen as a central feature by which such learning occurs.

In second language acquisition, the message oriented approach is seen in language immersion programs, where students are instructed in their regular school subjects using a second language. For instance in Canada, English-speaking students in French immersion programs receive their education in French (see Barik & Swain, 1975; Lambert & Tucker, 1972). In California English-speaking students in Spanish immersion programs receive their education in Spanish (see Cohen, Frier, & Flores, 1973; Snow, Galvan, & Campbell, 1983). A rather different message oriented approach is the Natural Approach (Krashen & Terrell, 1983; Terrell, 1977), which tries to recreate some of the learning conditions of first language acquisition.

That message oriented speech can be a powerful teacher of language, including grammar and vocabulary, is evident from first language acquisition. Yet, not all message oriented talk with older children lends itself to language learning. The kind of talk teachers typically use in the classroom does not appear to foster sufficient language learning in the dialect speaking student (Speidel, Tharp, & Kobayashi, 1985), the student from lower SES background, or some students in immersion classes (Dodson, 1984; Swain, 1985). If any kind of message oriented teacher talk were adequate, then there would not be the press for language development programs for children from poverty (Feagans & Farran, 1982), for dialect speaking children, or the special programs and language classrooms for immigrant children who speak no English.

If not all message oriented talk is equally beneficial, then what kind of talk in the classroom will foster language learning, particularly, the learning of grammar and vocabulary? Conversation has received a lot of attention, and is seen as a significant environment for first language learning in our culture (e.g., Dore, 1979; Howe, 1981; Moerk, 1983a, in press; Shatz, 1982; Wells, 1978). In conversation children are helped to put their thoughts into speech. The caregivers interpret the children's ambiguous utterances and adjust their speech so that the child can understand it.

In second language research, too, there has been a lot of interest in the variables in conversation that may help the language learner acquire the grammar and lexicon of the new language. For example, Hatch (1978) suggests that the following are important features: (1) cross-utterance buildups or vertical structures (Scollon, 1974) which come to be prototypes for longer horizontal constructions; (2) frequent paraphrasing and restatement of the learner's message by native speakers; and (3) the frequency with which certain structures are used during conversations (see also Peck, 1978, for similar analyses).

Long (1983a) observed that native speakers modify their language in many ways when speaking to second language learners. The function of many adjustments, Long (1983a, 1983b) suggests, is to provide comprehensible input to the language learner: If the native speakers do not get feedback on how well the nonnative speaker understands, they will not adjust their speech (Long, 1983b). He cautioned, however, that these adjustments "may be *necessary* for acquisition to take place . . . They may even be *sufficient* to guarantee that it occurs. Or they may be altogether *irrelevant*" (p. 188).

In an experimental study with Hawaiian-English speaking kindergarteners, I compared the effects of medium oriented instruction, emphasizing pattern drill, repetition, and nursery rhymes, with a conversational approach (Speidel, in press). The latter approach was clearly superior to the former in fostering a variety of expressive language skills; however, it did not significantly increase standard English grammatical speech. I argued there that the input from the teacher may not have been sufficiently finely tuned to the students' language. Since from the data base in that study a process analysis of the interaction could not be conducted, this hypothesis could not be verified.

The present study was, therefore, conducted to expand our knowledge of how the learning of grammar and vocabulary can take place during conversation between a teacher and a small group of students, and to see how such conversation might do its work as a facilitator of language learning. Conversations between a teacher and a small group of students is not a typical routine in most classrooms (e.g., Mehan, 1979). However, a central feature of the Kamehameha Early Education Program (KEEP), a successful reading program for students who speak Hawaiian English (Speidel, 1981a; Tharp et al., 1984), is the conversation between a small group of students and their teacher to prepare the students for better reading and understanding.

Earlier observations suggested that these reading lessons might promote language learning (Speidel, 1981b, 1982). In the present study, a series of analyses were conducted on transcripts of such lessons to answer the following questions:

1. Are the reading lessons characterized by a conversational style?

2. If they are conversational, how does the teacher give linguistic input, how does she provide linguistic information while talking with the students?

3. If the teacher provides usable linguistic input, is there evidence that the students make use of this input?

4. Finally, do the conversational reading lessons lead to measurable changes in the students' grammatical skills as measured by standardized tests?

METHOD

Subjects

Six Hawaiian first graders (two boys and four girls) were studied during their reading lessons from the beginning of November through the end of May. The children were predominantly Hawaiian-English speakers and had difficulties with standard English grammar. The students were of average intelligence as measured on the WISC-R, but were in the lowest reading group in their class.

The Dialect

The form of English spoken by these students is a creole that has English as its base. It has been called Hawaii Creole English (Day, 1972), Hawaiian Islands Dialect (Hawaii District Office, 1969), or Hawaiian English (Bickerton & Odo, 1976–77). It is a language in flux, encompassing a range of forms, a true speech continuum across time and social class. Therefore, a definitive description is not possible. Generally speaking, it differs from standard American English in pronunciation, and in grammar. Many bound morphemes are expressed syntactically, and free grammatical morphemes are deleted or their use is altered. The lexicon is based mainly on English, though there are differences in word usage between Hawaiian English and standard English. The dialect is becoming a source of pride for people in all walks of life, upper or lower SES, and from many ethnic backgrounds, Hawaiian, Japanese, Chinese, and so forth.

The only problem with Hawaiian English is that it is not the language of instruction in the schools; standard English is, and most parents want their children to learn this *school language*. This language difference may contribute to difficulties in school achievement for some Hawaiian children (Speidel, 1981b; Speidel et al, 1985; Tharp et al., 1984).

Setting

As a regular part of the KEEP language arts program, the six children were instructed daily for 20 minutes in a small group. The discussions were about "here-and-now" experiences, wordless books, sequencing, classifying and predicting events, and about their readings. The discussions were marked by an open participation structure in which the children could contribute whenever they wished and did not need to raise their hands to be called upon. The children were seated on one side of a semicircular table, with the teacher opposite them.

Recording and Transcribing

The lessons were audio-recorded. Each student wore a lavalier microphone, which lead into a separate tape-recorder. In this manner, 6 separate tapes were made during each taping session. These 6 recordings, including the teacher's speech, which was readily obtained from the tapes of the students, were compiled into a single transcript along with indications of overlapping speech.

The children spoke a considerable amount of Hawaiian English. Many of the features were captured in the verbatim transcriptions. Since we were not interested in pronunciation, their speech was transcribed using regular English spelling conventions.

The lessons were recorded a total of 27 times, in approximately weekly intervals. The subsequent analyses are based on 3 transcripts chosen randomly from recordings made during the middle of the school year—transcripts 9, 12, 19.

ARE THE READING LESSONS CONVERSATIONAL?

Teachers, we had said earlier, can talk to their students using different kinds of message oriented speech. They often use "talk and chalk methods," monologue-lectures, or they go through question-answer routines in which the purpose is to see what the students know and what they have learned. (According to a study by Long & Sato, 1983, this is also a predominant routine used by teachers of English as a second language.)

What makes conversation distinct from such other uses of language? In conversation, there is constant turn-taking among the conversational partners, there are usually no long monologues or extended explanations; the conversational partners respond to each other's statements and build upon them; there is talk on the same topic for several turns. Good conversation, then, is characterized by relatively equal speaking turns, by topic cohesion, and by meaning negotiation and meaning exchange leading to mutual understanding.

The beginning of transcript 12 shows the type of talk that dominated the reading lessons (brackets indicate simultaneous speech):

Teacher:
Now I'm going to say something to you and I want you to tell me all the reasons that you think this could happen. O.K. the boy hurt his knee. Why would the boy's knee be hurt?

John:
Cuz he was run . . . Because he was running too fast.

Jude:
Maybe he fall. He wen run and wen slip. Maybe have rocks.

Teacher:
Because he was running too fast. The boy's knee was hurt because he was running too fast.

John:
He fell . . . He fell.

Jude:
Maybe have, um . . . rocks and then he ranned and felled on it.

Teacher:
Maybe because he ran and fell down. He probably tripped.

Mileka:
Probably wen trip.

Lei:
But maybe . . .
Maybe he was riding his bike and then he wen go fall down.

John:
Probably fell off his bike and skin his knee.

Mileka:
Prob . . .
Probably he wen scrape and riding his skateboard and, um, he, um, he wen fall and wen scrape his knee.

Teacher:
You gave me about five different reasons why he might have hurt his knee.

John:
I think he don't know how to . . . Maybe he don't know how to ride his things yet.

Teacher:
>Maybe he fell down because he
>was just learning something.

The excerpt shows that not all features of the discourse during the reading lessons are conversational. For instance, the teacher is generally in command of the overall topic flow. Nevertheless, those features believed to be helpful for language learning, such as turn taking and responding to each others' messages are evident in the transcript. To obtain more formal evidence, however, codes were developed and were applied to the transcripts.

Teacher's Speech: Degree of Responsiveness (Analysis 1)

To study the frequency with which the teacher responded to the students' messages, all of her utterances were categorized as either responsive or nonresponsive (see Fig. 5.1 for the coding scheme; I am indebted to Grimm, 1982, for the concept of a hierarchical coding scheme for teacher utterances). Nonresponsive utterances were those in which the teacher did not respond to what a student had said or done. These utterances included giving instructions, talking continuously for more than three utterances in a row, changing the topic of discussion, or asking questions not directly related to a student's preceding comments. Utterances in which the teacher responded to a student's message or behaviors were categorized as responsive. Examples of responsive utterances are shown in the second and third teacher utterance below.

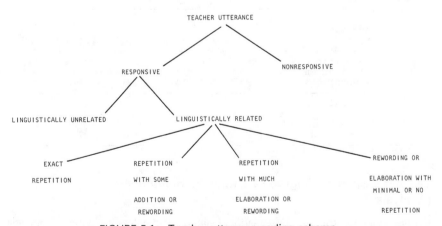

FIGURE 5.1. Teacher utterance coding scheme.

Teacher: Have you ever made anything at home by yourself?
Jerry: ´Cake.
Teacher: You've made a cake? Tell me about it?
Jerry: (no response)
Mileka: I made a cake with strawberries.
Teacher: You made a strawberry cake? With your mother?

Of the first 150 teacher utterances from each of the 3 transcripts, 87.6% on the average were responsive (see Table 5.1). Thus, most of her talk during these reading lessons was in response to what the students were saying or doing. Her few nonresponsive utterances were typically ones in which she either set the topic of discussion or shifted the topic. She rarely had long explanations, or didactic instructions.

TABLE 5.1
Percentage of Teacher Utterance Types   (Analyses 1, 2, and 4)

		Transcript			
		9	12	19	Mean
Analysis 1:					
Responsive		88.7	87.3	86.7	87.6
Nonresponsive		11.3	12.7	13.3	12.4
Analysis 2:					
Linguistically Related (all categories)		59.3	62.0	41.3	54.2
Analysis 4:					
Linguistically Related					
High	Exact repetition	7.3	4.0	12.7	8.0
	repetition with some addition or rewording	29.3	32.0	13.3	24.9
	repetition with much elaboration or rewording	14.0	14.7	12.0	13.6
Low	rewording and elaboration with minimal or no repetition	8.7	11.3	3.3	7.8

(Similarity — High to Low)

Note. Based on 150 utterances.

Teacher's Speech: Degree of Linguistic Relatedness (Analysis 2)

Further evidence for the conversational nature of the lessons comes from an analysis of the frequency with which the teacher's utterances were linguistically related to the students'. Linguistically related utterances are those responsive utterances in which all, or part, of what a student has just said is either repeated, reworded, or elaborated upon. For example:

Jude: They was inside the ice and they was freezing, and you know the stuff
          for take them up in the, um, plane, they was hanging on to 'om. The
          lady's leg was bleeding.
Teacher: Oh yes, it was a terrible crash, wasn't it?

The linguistically related teacher responses build upon what students say and help them put their ideas into words by providing linguistic models related to their messages.

Not all responsive teacher utterances, however, build upon the child's utterance linguistically. For example:

John: Maybe the, the guys that supposed to drive the plane . . .
Teacher: Just a second John. (attends to something else)

                              and

Milkea: Because the mother wen buy her toy.
Teacher: All right.

These responsive but linguistically unrelated utterances do not advance the conversation. In the section on modeling and feedback below, a more detailed description of linguistic relatedness is given.

Of the same 150 teacher utterances from each of the 3 transcripts, 54.2% on the average were linguistically related to the students' utterances (see Table 5.1, Analysis 2).

Students' Speech (Analysis 3)

For each student, the first 50 utterances from each of the three lessons (for a total of 150 utterances) were analyzed. These utterances were coded in a similar manner as the teacher's were for Analysis 1 and 2 above. This analysis showed that the students were highly responsive and their utterances were frequently linguistically related to those of the other speakers. The extent to which their utterances were both responsive and linguistically related ranged from 73.3% to 92% (see Table 5.2, Analysis 3). Also, like the teacher, the students frequently repeated other speakers' words and phrases. Nearly 53% of the words they used had just been spoken before.

Discussion

The high frequency of repetition of other speakers' words and phrases is reminiscent of talk with, and between, toddlers. Keenan, who has observed such talk in her 3-year-old twins, argues convincingly that these repetitions function to create

TABLE 5.2
Student Utterances (Analyses 3 and 6)

| | Analysis 3 | | Analysis 6 | |
Student	% Responsive/ Linguis- tically Related	% Words Repeated	Instances of 3 or More Words in Repeated Unit	% Utterances with Combi- nations of Repeated Units
1	84.7	54.5	24	16.0
2	92.0	50.4	32	18.6
3	86.7	55.5	29	14.0
4	85.3	49.0	24	16.6
5[a]	73.3	57.6	42	19.3
6	80.0	49.5	41	24.6
Mean	84.2	52.8	32	18.2

[a]This student had fewer than 50 utterances in one transcript. The results therefore were prorated for that transcript.

a cohesive conversation and function as "communication checks," that is, checks on whether one has understood the message. "What communication checks do is to precisely turn an utterance into shared knowledge" (Keenan, 1977). In other words, we can see the negotiation of meaning, which is considered so important for language acquisition, taking place in these partial repetitions of other speakers' utterances.

The high degree of responsiveness and linguistic relatedness of both teacher and student utterances show that these reading lessons are truly conversational in nature. We can now turn to the analysis of how, during this conversational interchange, the students can learn grammar and vocabulary, or, in Hatch's words, the analysis of how "language learning evolves out of learning how to carry on conversation" (Hatch, 1978, p. 404).

In the following sections, I describe and analyze the reading lessons from two perspectives: (1) How does the teacher provide linguistic information in talking with the students and what kind of information does she provide? (2) Do the students incorporate such information into their speech, and if so, how?

ARE THERE LANGUAGE LEARNING OPPORTUNITIES DURING THE READING LESSONS? PROCESS ANALYSES OF TEACHER TALK

The analyses of the teacher talk are based on two concepts which have received a lot of attention in the language learning literature—*input* and *feedback*. Each of these concepts and their related issues are briefly reviewed so that the subsequent process analyses will be better understood.

Input and Input Tuning

The kind of input to toddlers which is thought to help them acquire language has been described frequently and at length (e.g., Brown, Cazden, & Bellugi, 1969; Cross, 1977; Hoff-Ginsberg & Shatz, 1982; Grimm, 1982; Moerk, 1983a, 1983b, in press; Newport, Gleitman,& Gleitman, 1977; Shatz, 1982; Snow, 1977; Snow & Goldfield, 1983). From this literature the concept of input tuning has emerged and a debate has arisen on how finely tuned the caregiver's speech and input should be for efficient language learning. On the one hand, Brown (1977) writes, "It has turned out that parental speech is well-formed and finely tuned to the child's psycholinguistic capacity" (p. 20), and Cross (1977) concludes, "Input is closely tailored to the child's linguistic requirements" (p. 154). On the other hand, Newport et al. (1977) state, "Whatever syntactic simplifications occur are not finely tuned to the child's developing language" (p. 145). (See also Mannle & Tomasello, this volume, Nelson, Bonvillian, Denninger, Kaplan, & Baker, 1983; Shatz, 1982; Snow, Perlmann, & Nathan, this volume, for a discussion of input tuning.)

The fine-tuning hypothesis is also called into question by recent cross-cultural reports on how children learn language in societies that differ greatly from ours. Thus, in the Kaluli and Samoan society, according to Ochs and Schieffelin (1982), in many situations "the mother does not modify her language to fit the linguistic ability of the young child. Instead her language is shaped so as to be appropriate (in terms of form and content) for the child's intended addressees" (p. 32).

Although the nature of the mother-child interactions in these societies is clearly different from those found typically in middle-class American families, the striking differences may hide other forms of adjustment in the input to the child. For instance:

1. In the "elema" or "say like that" routine, in which the child is told how to speak in a socially appropriate, adult like fashion, the models which the toddlers are to repeat are rather short, 3- to 4-words in length on the average, so that the child is capable of imitating them at least partially. Relevant here is also Watson-Gegeo and Gegeo's (in press) very careful developmental analysis of a request-for-repetition routine among the Kwara'ae, a Melanesian people. She observed that the request for repetition was gradually built up, from simple listening to single word labeling, to complex social talk.

2. The Kaluli mothers give clear corrective feedback that models for the child how to say the phrase correctly. Such corrective input is by its very nature finely tuned to the child's linguistic performance.

3. Toddlers not only get language input from adults but also from siblings and other children (see Tomasello & Mannle, 1985, and Mannle & Tomasello, this volume, for a discussion of sibling input). The Kaluli toddlers may, there-

fore, be getting a rich source of language input from conversations with their siblings and other children.

In short, in these different cultures there probably is some kind of linguistic tuning, even though it may be quite different from that with which we are familiar.

These descriptions of how toddlers learn language in societies that differ greatly from our own help us to see more clearly the complex picture of language learning and its environmental supports. Thus, Snow et al., this volume, have presented an elegant and convincing model through which to understand these seemingly different ways to talk with a language learning child.

In second language learning, the importance of fine tuning of the native speaker's talk has also been questioned. Thus, in Krashen and Terrell's (1983) Natural Approach, rough tuning is the preferred strategy. Finely tuned input, according to Krashen and Terrell (1983), is "i + 1" input, that is, input that is just a little bit beyond the students' level of learning (which is at "i"). Roughly tuned input covers a much wider range of language skills and includes input that is at "i", "i + 1", "i + 2", . . . "i + n". Roughly tuned input has several advantages. "With rough tuning, we are always assured that 'i + 1' will be covered, while with finely tuned exercises, we are taking a guess as to where the student is. With roughly tuned input, we are assured of constant recycling and review; this is not the case with 'lock-step' exercises. Third, roughly tuned input will be good for more than one acquirer at a time, even when they are at slightly different levels" (p. 35).

Winitz (1981) also argues for rough tuning in second language acquisition, though for reasons somewhat different to those of Krashen and Terrell: "Full linguistic knowledge of a structure cannot be acquired by . . . experiences that do not involve a broad enough range of linguistic information . . . Experiences are broadened . . . by exposure to later appearing structures" (p. 7).

The issue of tuning in second language learning is, however, far from re-solved. A very recent review by Long (in press) and data by Sato (1986) suggest that natural conversation may not supply all the necessary input.

Discussions by Nelson et al. (1983), Mannle and Tomasello (this volume) and Snow et al. (this volume) in first language learning, and by Long in second language learning, make it clear that there are many different ways and many different dimensions on which caregivers or native speakers and teachers can modify and tune their language. They can tune their language semantically, pragmatically, or syntactically to that of the child's; they can make prosodic adjustments, speak more slowly, repeat themselves or repeat parts of the learn-er's speech, and so forth.

Given that there are so many different ways of rough and fine tuning, a logical hypothesis then is that some forms of adjustments may be more helpful to language learning than others. Furthermore, the need for adjustment may be a function of how predictable the discourse is, whether it is routine or novel, and so forth (Snow et al., this volume).

Feedback

The second concept that has received attention in both first and second language research is feedback. Feedback is a form of responsive or, in Snow's et al. (this volume) terminology, contingent input. For any theory of learning—be it behaviorism, cognitive development, information processing—feedback is important. Yet, some researchers in first language learning have argued that children do not use feedback for learning language (Cromer, 1984; Gleitman & Wanner, 1982; Wexler, 1982). This conclusion comes from two kinds of evidence. First, it is believed that parents give their children very little feedback on their language performance. The evidence for this belief comes mainly from a study by Brown & Hanlon (1970). Second, when parents do correct their child's language, the correction does not result in any immediately observable changes in the child's speech (McNeill, 1966).

The conclusion that feedback is not used by the children is based on an oversimplified conception of feedback. Feedback for language learning can take many forms (see Dulay, Burt, & Krashen, 1982; Moerk, 1983a, in press). The feedback Brown and Hanlon studied was restricted to praise, punishment, and communication pressure, that is, feedback that is not related in its response structure to the specific linguistic structure of the child's previous utterance. However, extensions, expansions, paraphrases and other strategies which are used as communication checks and topic continuations by parents can also serve as feedback, as *linguistically related* feedback, for the child. If a child says, ''Mommy sock,'' and the mother expands this to, ''Yes, that's mommy's sock,'' then the child gets confirmation that her use of mommy and sock was correct. She also gets (in the form of the mother's additions) feedback about what else she might have added to her message and how.

Although it is true that toddlers often do not understand corrections of their speech, and will not always repeat back correctly when explicitly asked to repeat, there are also instances when they do use the feedback given by the parent (Moerk, 1983b; Slobin, 1968). Not all linguistic feedback will have an immediate effect. For learning to occur, a child may need many instances of the kind of linguistic feedback just described. This kind of linguistic feedback is what the children frequently get according to Moerk (1983, in press) and Snow and Goldfield (1983).

The distinction between input, which serves as a speech model, and feedback (e.g., Gleitman & Wanner, 1982; Wexler, 1982) may be impossible to make in an ongoing conversation, where an utterance may serve simultaneously as feedback for the preceding utterance and as input, or as model, for the next utterance.

For example,

Teacher: Why else might she be crying?
Jude: Maybe her mother licked her.
Teacher: Because the mother gave her a spanking.
Lei: A spanking, spanking.

Thus, the teacher's feedback to Jude, the substitution of spanking for licking, is input in the form of a model for Lei who immediately repeats the word twice. Further examples of feedback, which functions also as a speech model, are found in the following section on how the students are influenced by the speech of the teacher and their peers when constructing their own utterances.

Such exchanges have also been noted in first language acquisition; the mother's feedback in the form of recasts or extensions serves as a model for the child's next utterance (Moerk, 1983a; Slobin, 1968). Utterances that potentially have such a dual function, I will call "model/feedback."

Incidentally, in conversation the same utterance may also have several pragmatic functions, in addition to providing linguistic information. Thus, expansions, paraphrases, focus functions, and so on, may pragmatically be communication checks, signals for attention, or approval, and acknowledgment, while at the same time they are linguistic input—models and feedback—to the learner.

The concepts of input tuning and model/feedback guided the analyses below for determining, from a language learning perspective, the instructional quality of the teacher's utterances during the reading lessons.

Amount of Linguistic Model/Feedback Provided by the Teacher

From the previous discussion it becomes clear that there are many different features to study in the input to the language learner during conversation. Some systems look at general characteristics of the input, for example, at mother's MLU, or syntactic modifications (see Cross, 1977); others look specifically at how the utterances of the caregiver are contingent upon the statements of the learning child (Nelson et al., 1983; Snow et al., this volume).

For the analyses of the teacher's talk that follow, I selected only responsive utterances, that is, only teacher's utterances that were contingent upon a student's utterance and that were also linguistically related to the students' utterances (see Fig. 5.1 for the category scheme applied). The reason for this selection is that these utterances provide the students with model/feedback. They model for the students how they can add to, or change their utterances.

A description of responsive, linguistically related utterances was already given earlier in the section on the conversational nature of the reading lessons. Here I briefly elaborate on the category "linguistically related." The feature that determined whether a responsive teacher utterance is also classified as a linguistically related utterance is whether the teacher's utterance could be considered to be a source of feedback for what the student said, or a model for how the student might have elaborated his message. For example:

Jude: Maybe have, um . . . rocks, and then he ranned and felled on it.
Teacher: Maybe because he ran and fell down.

and

Mileka: Probably wen scrape and riding his skateboard and um, he um, he wen fall and he wen scrape his knee.
Teacher: You gave me about five different reasons why he might have hurt his knee.

Both of the teacher's utterances above are linguistically related to those of the student.

Excluded from the linguistically related category are those responsive utterances in which the teacher comments about a child's language performance; for instance, "That was a good sentence"; or, "Maile, you used an excellent word." Such comments may have a motivating effect, but do not help children in putting their ideas into words and tell the children little about how language works. Also excluded are encouragements to a student to continue speaking, if such encouragements do not include thoughts presented by the student. For instance, not included are statements like, "Go on!" or, "Tell me more!"

The analysis of the teacher's model/feedback utterances is the same as the one presented previously on the linguistically related utterances, that is, Analysis 2, Table 5.1. The findings in that table show that the teacher frequently provided the students with linguistic model/feedback: on the average, over half of the teacher's utterances were linguistically related to the students' talk.

The Degree of Tuning of the Teacher's Model/Feedback (Analysis 4)

The concept of input tuning is assessed here only on a subset of teacher utterances, namely on the linguistically related utterances. The tuning of each of these utterances is assessed by rating their similarity to the student utterance upon which they build. Similarity between student-utterance and teacher-utterance is defined by the ratio of words incorporated from the student's utterance into the teacher's utterance to the number of words introduced by the teacher.

At the most similar level is exact repetition in which the teacher repeats everything or parts of what the student has said without adding any of her own words. When the teacher's reply goes beyond exact repetition, her feedback/model can vary to different degrees from the student's statement. At a slightly less similar level than exact repetition is an utterance in which she repeats parts or all of a student's words, but also adds or substitutes her own words. At the next level, the teacher repeats some of the student's words, but there is also extensive rewording or elaboration. At the level of least similarity between student-utterance and teacher-utterance are utterances in which the teacher rewords or elaborates a student's message with minimal or no repetition.

Nelson et al. (1983) also looked at the similarity between adult and child utterance. They distinguished between simple and complex recasts. According to Nelson (personal communication) simple recasts would be included in the present category of repetition with some additions and substitutions, while complex recasts would be included in the category of repetition with extensive additions and rewording.

The reasoning underlying this method of analyzing tuning is based on the following two considerations:

1. For input to advance language learning, it must be at least partially understood. Because understanding occurs in the listener's head, such a scheme will by its very nature be inferential, but some schemes are more inferential than others. In linguistically related teacher utterances—those utterances in which the teacher builds upon the student's utterance—one can judge with some degree of confidence the ease with which the utterance will be understood by a student: The more similar the teacher's utterance is to the student's utterance, the more likely it will be understood by the student; the easier it will be for the student to compare the two utterances and abstract the meaning and the linguistic rules contained in the teacher's utterance. The more the teacher varies a student's response, the harder it will be for the student to compare the utterances, to map the meaning onto his or her thoughts and knowledge base, and the harder it will be to induce new linguistic rules that extend beyond the student's current rules.

2. Similarity will help only up to a point. If the input is to foster advances in the children's language skills then it must include input that is beyond their present speaking skills. Moreover, children understand usually much more than is reflected in their grammar and in the words they use. A certain amount of rewording and elaboration is, therefore, necessary if modeling/feedback is to advance language skills. Indeed, Baker and Nelson (1984) found that children learn new rules from recasts that combine similarity with new information.

In basing the coding scheme of teacher's input on number of words repeated from the student and number of new words introduced by the teacher, we have a relatively concrete way of measuring similarity and dissimilarity. An analysis of the transcripts using this coding scheme will, therefore, show us how closely a teacher matches her speech to that of her students': how many utterances are completely matched, how many have close similarity to the students', how many are moderately similar and how many are dissimilar in their words, but elaborate upon the students' messages. By comparing changes in the six students' language over time with changes in a group of children that did not receive this kind of input, we can obtain some correlational estimate of the effectiveness of this type of input (see Analysis 7).

Illustrations of each kind of linguistically related utterance follow below, as well as the rate with which the teacher uses each type of feedback during her conversations with the students. The rate figures are again based on the first 150 utterances from each of transcripts 9, 12, and 19.

Exact Repetition.   In exact repetition, the teacher repeats all or part of a student's words exactly and does not add or substitute anything. This form of exact repetition gives the students not only the information that what they said was well-formed, but the actual repetition may help to fix in memory the well-formed parts of their speech. However, this kind of response by the teacher does not provide the students with any new linguistic information to stretch their linguistic knowledge, or in Krashen's terms, this is input at the "i" level and not the "i + 1" level. If the teacher uses this type of feedback extensively we would not expect the students' language to develop. Also one would expect the conversation to come to a boring halt.

The coding analysis shows that the teacher did not use exact repetition very frequently. In Table 5.1 (Analysis 4) we see that she used this type of model/feedback in 8% of her total utterances on the average (15% of her linguistically related utterances).

Repetition with Some Addition Or Rewording.   In this type of linguistically related utterance, the teacher repeats parts or everything of a student's message and adds or substitutes information, or rewords. This form simultaneously provides positive feedback to the student, letting the student know what was well formed, as well as giving information about what might be changed. For example:

Mileka: Probably wen trip.
Teacher: He probably tripped. (Acknowledges contribution)

In this example, the child receives the information that his words "probably" and "trip" were good choices and were in the correct sequence. Moreover, there is the additional information on how to use the pronoun "he" and that the past tense in standard English is marked by "ed" added to the verb-stem rather than by "wen" (the Hawaiian-English form). A more elaborate example is the following one:

Jude: Maybe they was going . . . maybe, maybe the wind. The wind wen go push 'om down. Maybe the wind wen push 'om down like inside the news.

Teacher: Oh, like on the news? Like maybe the wind was too strong and pushed the plane down?

Again, in repeating parts of what the student has said, the teacher provides positive feedback for words like "push," "wind," and "news." She also gives feedback about use of the preposition "on," the past tense marking in standard English, and provides the label "plane" for the Hawaiian English indefinite " 'om."

The coding analysis shows that this type of feedback and linguistic modeling is the one most frequently used by the teacher. As Table 5.1 shows, across the three sessions she used this in nearly 25% of her utterances (46% of her linguistically related utterances).

Repetition with Much Elaboration Or Rewording.   In this group of model/feedback utterances the emphasis is on rewording or elaborating a child's message. However, the teacher also repeats part or all of what a child has said. The difference between this category and the previous one is that here there is a higher ratio of added and substituted words to repeated words.

John: Probably, probably have snow on the . . . stuff and . . . thing, thing was heavy and thing fall.
Teacher: Oh, you mean there might be so much snow and ice on the plane that it couldn't fly.

This kind of responsive input is more complex than the previous types because in a cross-utterance comparison the linguistic information is less obvious to the learner. Yet, both positive and extending linguistic feedback is provided. "Snow on the,—" by being repeated, provides information that this part was well-formed. The substitution of "there might be" for "probably had" could inform the child that in standard English this is the way to express potential existence. The substitution of "plane" for "thing" provides a label for the child's concept. "It couldn't fly" provides an alternative way of saying "thing fall." And finally, by adding "so- - -that" to the child's utterance the teacher is showing how one can express linguistically two events which are in a cause-effect relationship. The above sequence also shows how mapping words to their referent might occur solely from linguistic input without the object present.

The results of the coding show that the teacher used this form of input with moderate frequency. In Table 5.1, we see that she used it on the average in nearly 14% of her total utterances (25% of her linguistically related utterances).

Rewording with Minimal Or No Repetition.   In rewording, the student's language is paraphrased. Sometimes this will mean clearer or more condensed language; at other times this will mean standard English or a mixture of these. The following is an example of rewording.

John: Maybe the guys that 'sposed to drive the plane went to look at some-
            thing and they, they felt the plane go down and then they just run to
            there and the plane was on the ground already.
Teacher: Oh, you mean perhaps the pilots weren't watching what they were
            doing?

Even though there is virtually no overlap between the student's and the
teacher's words, the student will probably be able to map the structure and the
lexicon of the teacher's rewording onto the internal image of the situation he was
trying to describe, because he already has the concept in his mind (given the
teacher paraphrased him correctly). This type of meaning induction is probably
typical for children who already have a fair amount of competence in the language. However, with children who are less knowledgeable, this form might be
too complex for rule or meaning induction.

Elaboration with Minimal or no Repetition.   At the least similar level is
elaboration. In elaboration the teacher adds information to the student's message
without using any of the student's words. For instance:

Teacher: What do we put in our mouth underneath our tongue?
Jude: A temperature.
Jason: A temperature.
Teacher: No that's what we find out. (Elaboration)
            Your temperature goes up. (Imitation with Elaboration)
            That means your body gets hot. (Elaboration)

This type of teacher utterance which extends beyond the student's response
without any resemblance to what the student had said would appear to require
more effort for semantic mapping and induction of linguistic rules than the
previous types, everything else held constant. However, within the context of the
discussion, it seems quite likely the students learned that the word temperature
had something to do with measuring heat.

The coding analysis shows that the teacher used rewording and elaboration
with minimal or no repetition with a fairly low frequency. We see in Table 5.1,
Analysis 4, that the two categories together make up not quite 8% of her utterances on the average (14% of the linguistically related utterances).

Linguistic Information Provided in the Model/Feedback (Analysis 5)

All of the teacher's model/feedback utterances, except simple exact repetition,
were also analyzed for the kind of linguistic information they provided: lexical,
morphological, and syntactic. This type of analysis is problematical simply

because language is not cleanly divisible into these categories (e.g., Bolinger & Sears, 1981; Hakuta, 1981; Peters, 1983). The view that the lexicon plays an essential part in syntactic development and that a unified account of semantic and syntactic development may be the proper description for language learning is supported by the difficulty we had in creating this category system, and I will not claim that the system is totally satisfactory. Nevertheless, the results of the analysis are shown here, because they do give a general indication about what was covered linguistically in the teacher's model/feedback.

Lexical Information. This category describes information contained in the teacher's utterance on the meaning of nouns, adjectives, verbs, and adverbs. Subcategories indicate whether the teacher supplied a referent (for example, "plane" for "thing"), a category term (for example, "fruit" for "orange"), a synonym (for example, "glad" for "happy", or "spread" for "rub"), or a more specific term (for example, "duty" for "job," or "race" for "run").

Grammatical Morpheme Information. This category includes information about grammatical or functional morphemes. Bolinger and Sears' definition of grammatical morphemes was used: "words and parts of words which signal relationships within language and meanings occurring with high frequency, such as number, tense, possession" (1981, p. 67). Below are a few examples of grammatical morpheme additions and substitutions.

Mileka: Probably wen trip.
Teacher: He probably tripped.
(Addition of "he" and substitution of "-ed" for "wen")

Jude: Like inside the news.
Teacher: Like on the news?
(Substitution of "on" for "inside")

Lei: I going school.
Teacher: You are going to school?
(Substitution of "you" for "I"; addition of "are" and "to")

The above examples show how much overlap there is between grammatical morpheme category and the lexical information category as well as the syntactic category. Thus, in the first and third examples the teacher also provides standard English syntactic information: the need for a subject, the need for a predicate, and the need for a preposition. This overlap between syntax and morphology is particularly evident in contrasting a creole language, in this case Hawaiian English, and the language upon which the creole is based, in this case English, because creoles tend to express syntactically what is expressed through bound morphemes in the base language (Hall, 1966).

Syntactic Information.   This category includes additions and substitutions of phrases, clauses, or transformations of clauses. Expanding a phrase into a sentence by just adding obligatory structures is included in the grammatical morpheme category and not here. Some examples of syntactic information are in the following transcript excerpts.

Lei: They all the same.
Teacher: If they were all the same, what would you do?
(Syntactic addition: what would you do?)

Jude: Maybe the wind wen push 'om down like inside the news.
Teacher: Like maybe the wind was too strong and pushed the plane down.
(Syntactic addition: was too strong)

Jerry: I saw him.
Teacher: Did you see him?
(Syntactic transformation)

Table 5.3 shows the number of instances of each type of linguistic feedback in the first 150 teacher utterances from transcripts 9, 12 and 19. From this we can conclude that the teacher's input covers the three linguistic dimensions well, but with greater emphasis on the syntactic and grammatical morpheme information than on lexical information.

Discussion

An obvious question is whether the teacher's naturally occurring input during the reading lessons is the most appropriate and effective one for language learning, particularly the learning of standard English grammar. This study cannot answer this question directly. There are, nevertheless, several kinds of indirect forms of evidence for the effectiveness of the model/feedback input described: (1) the strong face validity of the model/feedback analyses reported above; (2) the

TABLE 5.3
Type of Linguistic Information in Teacher's
Repetitions With Addition
Substitution, Rewording or Elaboration:
Instances/150 Utterances (Analysis 5)

	Transcript		
	9	12	19
Grammatical morpheme	48	47	20
Syntactical	38	46	28
Lexical	15	32	10

relationship between frequency of mother use of model/feedback and their toddler's language acquisition; (3) the effects of experimental manipulation of model/feedback on children's language; and (4) the process examples of language learning and the standardized test results described in the section below entitled "Are there effects on the students' language?" Here we discuss the effectiveness issue at two levels: the general question about the effects of model/feedback and the more specific question about the appropriateness of the tuning of the teacher's utterances.

Effects of Model/Feedback.   We saw from Analysis 4 that the teacher frequently gave linguistic input in the form of partial repetitions and paraphrases, and that she added or substituted information in the students' messages. In short, she often used extensions, expansions, recasts, focus functions, reformulations, and so on. The overlap in meaning between these terms is not perfect. What they have in common is that they are utterances in response to the learner's speech and that they keep part of the learner's message constant while varying other parts. This allows the learner to compare his or her utterances to those of the mother, native speaker, or the teacher. In the examples taken from the transcripts it was shown how these linguistically related utterances could be used by the student as feedback, and could provide the students with linguistic models closely related to the thoughts they wished to communicate.

This form of model/feedback has been found to be related to speed of first language acquisition. For instance, Brown, Cazden & Bellugi-Klima (1969) found among three children that the two whose mothers used expansions often acquired language more quickly than the child whose mother used expansions less often. Similarly, Cross (1978) found that mothers of fast language learners more frequently responded to their children's utterances with expansions and extensions and Wells (1978, 1980) found that children whose language developed more quickly had more exposure to utterances which incorporated and extended their previous utterances. In a study by Schachter (1979) middle- and upper-middle class mothers, both black and white, tended to repeat and expand what their children said, while a group of lower SES mothers tended to repeat their own speech; this difference between the mothers was also associated with differences in the MLU of the children. Because these studies are correlational, they do not prove that the speech modifications helped language learning; nevertheless, they are certainly consistent with the hypothesis.

There is, moreover, experimental evidence that these strategies facilitate language learning in the child. There are several studies which report that children acquired more quickly structures that were modelled in expanded or recast feedback than children who did not receive this model/feedback (Baker & Nelson, 1984; Nelson, 1977; Nelson, Carskaddon, & Bonvillian, 1973). Excellent discussions of why such linguistically related utterances are ideal for inducing the linguistic rules are found in Hoff-Ginsberg & Shatz (1982), Moerk (in press), and Shatz (1982).

Appropriateness of Input Tuning. A second consideration in judging whether the teacher's talk was helpful for language learning is its tuning to the students' speech. If we accept Krashen & Terrell's (1983) assumptions about language learning or Winitz' (1981) comprehension model of nonlinear language learning, then the best input should have a wide, flexible range of tuning.

A slightly different way of looking at appropriateness of input tuning is whether the input was understood, understanding being considered a necessary condition for language learning. This view suggests that the necessary degree of tuning may shift according to the appropriateness of the learner's response which shows whether the learner has understood (see Long, 1983a, for a discussion of this view). The findings of Snow et al. (this volume) supports this notion: The need for tuning, or semantic contingency in Snow's terminology, seems to be a function of the frequency with which the topic, or routine, has been discussed. The more often a topic is talked about, the more the caregiver or teacher can elaborate the learner's response.

Thus, the controversy about tuning in both first and second language learning is moving away from the view that specific forms of input are necessary. For example, Nelson et al. (1983) conclude, "There are components of input for most children that are not necessary" (p. 47). Snow et al. (this volume) suggest that the important variable is not specific input, but "providing a context for the child's utterance . . . The first and major task, then, of the caretaker interested in his child's successful acquisition of language is to create discourse around the child's utterances. If the child reliably hears her own utterances embedded in discourse, she will discover ways to create longer linguistic contexts for herself, instead of relying on the caretaker to do it."

In light of the above discussion, it seems fair to conclude that the range of tuning used by the teacher in the present study seems appropriate. First, Analysis 4 showed that the teacher's talk during the reading lessons had a broad range of tuning. She mainly used utterances of intermediate similarity to those of the students', but not to the exclusion of level "i" input in the form of exact repetitions or to the exclusion of level "i+n" input in the elaborations or rewordings of the students' messages. Second, the fact that over 50% of the teacher's utterances were linguistically related (Analysis 2) and nearly 90% were responsive to the students' actions or utterances (Analysis 1), suggests that a fair proportion of her talk must have been understood by the students. Third, the examples of teacher's model/feedback and their high frequency (Analyses 2 and 4) show that the teacher provided highly relevant and appropriate discourse context for the learners' utterances. Finally, Analysis 5 shows that the input covered lexical, grammatical, and syntactic information.

Emotional Climate of the Lessons.   A final point in discussing model/feed-back deals with the affect that it might call forth in the students. By presenting the model/feedback examples out of context, it might seem as if the students were overwhelmed by corrections. However, in listening to audiotapes of these reading lesson, one hardly notices the corrective nature of these statements. The students appear to be excited conversational participants. Actually, an important guideline for teachers in the KEEP reading program is to try to enlist as much participation as possible from the students during the conversations. Had these model/feedback utterances disrupted the conversation, the teacher would very likely have stopped using them. The quality of the teacher's voice—whether it is warm and interested, or stern and didactic—will probably determine whether the model/feedback is perceived as criticism or not.

A point to emphasize here, is that the teacher, like the mother (e.g., Newport et al., 1977), uses these repetitions, additions, paraphrases for reasons other than language teaching. She may wish to check whether she has understood the students, to show that she is listening and attending to their talk, to help them put their messages into words, to extend their thoughts, and so on. However, this in no way detracts from the linguistic input-feedback value which these utterances may have.

Summary.   The analyses have shown that in the process of talking with the students, in trying to understand them, in trying to help them put their thoughts into words, in showing interest in what they are saying, the teacher provided the students with input at different levels of tuning and with input that is broad-based, covering lexical, grammatical, and syntactic information. Though the teacher and the students may be mutually unaware that language teaching is happening, these reading lesson conversations are truly language learning opportunities.

ARE THERE EFFECTS ON THE STUDENT'S LANGUAGE?

There are many different language skills that the students are learning and practicing during these conversations. For instance, they are probably learning to understand the teacher's messages with greater ease, and are probably learning to put their thoughts into words. The focus here is on whether, during these reading lesson conversations, the students learn to use in speech unfamiliar standard English grammatical features and words. The effect of the conversations on these skills is studied by the process analysis described in Analysis 6 and by changes on standardized language measures described in Analysis 7.

Do the Students Make Use of the Language Learning Opportunities? (Analysis 6)

Analyses 4 and 5 show that in the conversational context of the reading lesson, the teacher provided the students with a lot of linguistic information, models, and feedback. The question now is whether this roughly tuned input is used by the students. This question can be studied in different ways. One way is to look at the degree to which the students incorporate the teacher's and each other's speech into their own messages (Speidel, 1983). Table 5.2, Analysis 3 shows that, of the words used by the students, on the average, 52.8% had been spoken before.

Not only did the students repeat many of the words already used in the conversation, but also frequently incorporated fairly large phrases of others' speech. For example:

Teacher: Do you think the monkey is going to run away?
Jude: I don't *think* it's *going to run away.*
          (repetition of six words)

The number of instances with which each child used chunks of speech containing three or more repeated words is shown in Table 5.2, Analysis 6, p. 108): There are between 24 and 42 such instances in the 150 utterances analyzed for each student.

Analysis 6, Table 5.2, also shows that the students combined these chunks creatively, using parts from one person and parts from another person. On the average, nearly one-fifth of the students' utterances were constructed of such combinations of two or more chunks.

For example:

Lei: But maybe . . .
          Maybe he was riding his bike and then he wen go fall down.
John: Probably fell off his bike and skin his knee.
Mileka: Prob . . . *Probably he wen* scrape and *riding his* skateboard and, um,
          he, um, *he wen fall* and *wen scrape his knee.*

Mileka's utterance here shows his creativity in combining the chunks of other people's speech as well as his own speech. "Probably," "riding his," and "he wen fall" were used by Lei, while "his knee" was used by John. "Wen scrape" is a self-repetition. From these repetitions or incorporations Mileka constructed a new message. Some of these words are clearly already in Mileka's speech. However, just having heard them may have helped him to use them and to produce a longer utterance. An analysis by Speidel and Herreshoff (1985) shows that, indeed, students were able to make longer utterances, the more words they incorporated from previous speech.

The example also shows that the students not only incorporated parts of the teacher's utterance but also parts of each others' speech. Furthermore, it shows that a clear separation of the source of an utterance is virtually impossible, since the parts are combined and recombined several times by different speakers. One analysis, which did attempt to trace the source, suggests that the students repeated words used by each other twice as many times as they repeated words used by the teacher (Speidel, 1983). This peer imitation can be both helpful and a drawback. At times it leads to the use of standard English forms, at other times to the use of Hawaiian-English forms, and at still other times to the imitation of developmentally immature forms.

Incorporations of others' speech have been frequently noted in toddlers acquiring their first language. Snow (1981) shows how, in the language-learning child, these incorporations are building blocks to elaborate and spontaneous speech and how, over time, the incorporations become indistinguishable from spontaneous speech (see also Kucjaz, 1982; Moerk, 1985).

A more fine-grained analysis than percentage of speech adopted from others is the examination of immediate influence of speech models upon the students' choice of words or grammatical forms. This notion of immediate influence of modeled speech is based on the following conception about production. Learning to use a word or grammatical structure is in part a memory problem. One must retrieve from memory the words or forms that are needed for the thought one wishes to express. Just hearing someone use a particular grammatical form will make its retrieval and its use easier. Such piggy-backing is probably of no help for the competent speaker; however, it should be particularly helpful if one has not yet had much practice in using the word or the form.

For this group of 6 Hawaiian children, such immediately preceding models should be particularly helpful in learning to use those grammatical forms that differ between Hawaiian English and standard English as well as those forms and lexical items that are infrequent in Hawaiian English. If a student is just beginning to use a particular standard English construction, the model predicts that this form will more likely be used just after having heard it. Therefore, we need to look for instances in which the students use standard English grammatical features that are difficult for them and to see whether the students are more likely to use them after they were just modeled. A few such examples follow.

In Hawaiian English " 'om" is used in the accusative case for third person pronouns. In the following excerpt, Mileka initially uses "that" and " 'om" instead of "it." However, after hearing the teacher and his peers use "it" several times, he also uses "it."

Mileka:	No, get the knife and put that in.	("That" refers to knife)
Teacher:	Oh, all right. I stuck it in the peanut butter.	(Replaced "that" by "it")
Mileka:	Then put 'om in on there.	(Referring to the knife)

Teacher:	You have to tell me what to do with the knife.	
Jude:	Put it in.	(Peer models "it")
Teacher:	I did put it in.	(Teacher models "it")
John:	Put it in.	(Another student models "it")
Mileka:	Now put it on the bread.	(Uses "it" to refer to the knife)

One minute later:

| Mileka: | Rub it on the bread. | (Uses "it" with a different verb and no immediate model) |

The next example is from a discussion about classifying objects. Jason initially adopts the wrong linguistic model. Both the teacher and another student then recast the utterance providing a model which Jason repeats spontaneously. During the conversation that preceded the example, the teacher had used "does" four times and "don't" twice as follows:

Who does it?
Now I'm gonna give you three things and one does not belong.
Why does a rooster not fit here?
You don't make music with a. . . . .
Why does a frog not belong?
and, You don't sit on a frog.

The conversation continues as follows:

Teacher:	Can you think of another way we could put these together?	
Jason:	We doesn't eat pencil and scissors.	(Uses "does" incorrectly)
Teacher:	Good for you, Jason, we don't eat pencils and scissors . . .	(Acknowledges his response; models correct form)
Jude:	Don't eat.	(Simultaneously with the teacher another child provides the correct form)
Teacher:	. . . and we usually don't eat turtles.	
Jason:	Don't eat pencils and scissors.	(Adopts correct form immediately)

In the next excerpt there is an example of how students learn vocabulary. The teacher is talking with the students about how to put peanut butter and jelly on a slice of bread (brackets indicate simultaneous speech):

| Mileka: | Rub it on the bread. | |
| Teacher: | Rub it on the bread. Or I could say, I | (Acknowledges Mileka; models |

would spread it on the bread. I am
spreading it on the bread.

(a synonym in the same linguistic context. Then models another form of spread)

A minute later:

Teacher: And then what'll I do with it?
Jude: Put it on top the bread.
Mileka: Rub it.
Teacher: O.K., you said rub it. Now what's the other word we were using for . . .   (Acknowledges answer; elicits new word)
Jude: Spread it on top the bread.
Mileka: Spread out.
Jerry: Spread it out.   (Three students respond with the new words simultaneously)

A little later, the teacher is asking the students to dictate sentences to her for writing a story about making peanut butter sandwiches:

Teacher: Lei, give me a sentence about that.
Lei: Put, the, peanut butter . .   (Dictates)
Jason: (Whispers) Spread.   (Prompts L)
Lei: . . . spread . . . on the bread.   (Picks up J's cue)

Learning to use a particular word or form is not a one-trial learning phenomenon. Typically, such learning goes on over a period of time and requires frequent input (Moerk, in press). An analysis presented in detail elsewhere (Speidel & Herreshoff, 1985), showed that, for example, the indefinite article, initially used mainly just after hearing it (i.e., in imitation) came to be used more spontaneously by the students over the 6-month observation period. This supports the conclusion that instances of immediate influence, such as those seen in the excerpts above, are one basis from which spontaneous use of grammatical forms emerge.

Changes on Standardized Language Measures (Analysis 7)

The previous analysis showed that the students incorporated units of the teacher's and their peers' speech and that this helped them use grammatical forms they were not accustomed to using. This next section reports on Fall to Spring changes in the performance of the 6 students on two standardized production measures of standard English grammar. The change for the 6 students is compared with that of a group of similar students who did not participate in such reading lesson conversations.

The Comparison Group.   A first-grade class was selected as a comparison group from a public school on Hawaiian Homestead Lands located in the same geographic rural area from which the 6 "experimental" students came. (Only students in this class who received first grade reading instruction were included.) The kind of instruction these students received was not monitored. However, given our knowledge of instruction in Hawaii's Public schools, it is highly unlikely that they participated extensively in small group discussions with their teacher. They did not receive any special language instruction. As the policy of the Hawaii Department of Education requires standard English as the language of instruction, we can assume that they received their instruction in standard English, that is, that they experienced a form of "immersion" in standard English.

Testing Procedures.   Both groups of students were tested individually in the Fall and in the Spring of first grade. They were given two tests of standard English grammar: a sentence repetition task, the *Carrow Elicited Language Inventory* (or CELI) (Carrow, 1974), and a cloze task, the Grammatic Closure Subtest of the *Illinois Test of Psycholinguistic Ability* (Kirk, McCarthy, & Kirk, 1968).

Results.   The various performance means for the two groups of students are shown in Table 5.4. Also shown are the percentile ranks of those means when compared to the performance of the standard English norm group. It is evident from the percentile ranks that the Hawaiian children in both groups were not very familiar with standard English grammar. The table shows that the groups were equivalent in performance on the Fall pretests.

The conversation group improved their percentile ranking by Spring on the Grammatic Closure test, while the comparison group did not. A two-way analy-

TABLE 5.4
Student Performance on Standardized Grammatical Measures (Analysis 7)

Group	Conversation		Comparison	
Time of Test	Fall	Spring	Fall	Spring
Grammatic closure:				
Mean standard score	25.5	30.2	24.7	24.9
SD	(4.9)	(5.1)	(6.7)	(6.2)
Mean percentile rank	< 5	≐ 16.7	< 5	< 5
CELI:				
Mean no. of errors	37.5	23.0	34.9	26.3
SD	(21.4)	(19.1)	(22.0)	(19.2)
Mean percentile rank	< 1	< 1	< 1	< 1

sis of variance on the standard scores, with one repeated measure (testing time) and one between-group measure (treatment condition) showed that this increase over the comparison group in Spring approached statistical significance (F = 3.41; df = 1/16; $p<.084$). On the CELI both groups improved in their error rate (F = 95.37; df = 1/16; $p<.0001$). However, the conversation group made significantly greater gains, the interaction effect being statistically significant (F = 6.05; df = 1/16; $p<.03$).

Vocabulary Learning.   As part of a larger test battery, the reading conversation group was also given a vocabulary test (a subtest from the Wechsler Intelligence Scale for Children) in the Fall and Spring of first grade. No increase in vocabulary performance above that expected by natural growth was found.

Discussion.   The conversational group clearly made greater gains on the standard English grammatical measures. However, we must be somewhat cautious in relying on these outcomes. The data from the two groups were not obtained from an experiment with random assignment of students into the two conditions. There are, therefore, factors other than the conversational reading instruction that could have produced the greater gains in the conversation group. Nevertheless, these findings on the standardized tests, taken together with the findings of the process analyses of the teacher talk and of the manner in which the students were influenced by the conversation in constructing their utterances, are (1) congruent with (though not proof of) our hypothesis that these reading lessons are language learning situations; and (2) congruent with the conclusion that the roughly tuned language input which the students receive from the teacher during the conversational reading lesson helps to develop language skills.

FINAL DISCUSSION AND CONCLUSION

This study draws upon findings and theories from first- and second-language learning to look at language learning in a very special kind of classroom setting, a small group, reading-comprehension lesson. We had begun by asking whether message oriented talk in the form of conversation could result in language learning in young dialect speakers who were extending their speaking skills in standard English. To answer this question by looking at naturally occurring speech events in school lessons, a whole series of analyses, mainly process analyses, had to be conducted. These analyses showed that:

1. The reading lessons could be characterized as conversational;
2. The teacher, in talking with the students, frequently gave linguistic input that was understandable and roughly tuned to the students' language and provided them with discourse context and models for their utterances;

3. The teacher's input contained lexical, grammatical morpheme and syntactic information;

4. The students incorporated elements of the teacher's and their peers' speech into the construction of their messages;

5. The students who had participated in the conversational approach showed a greater advance on standardized production tests of standard English grammar than a group who did not have this experience.

Taken together these findings suggest that the students extended their grammatical skills by participating in meaningful conversations with their teacher and a small group of peers. They did not require systematic instruction in the rules of grammar or drilling difficult grammatical patterns. The series of process analyses of how such learning can occur shows a remarkable similarity to how young children acquire their first language, namely through the analysis and use of responsive input in the form of repetitions, expansions, focus functions, recasts, and requests for clarification. Clearly there are also differences in the conversations between toddlers and their caregivers and between the students and their teacher. However, a description of such differences are beyond the scope of this chapter.

It should be emphasized, once again, that the nature of the message oriented talk in the conversational approach is different from message oriented talk in classrooms in which the teacher talks at length at the children or asks rounds of questions to find out what the children have learned. In such settings there is not much opportunity for meaning exchange, for model/feedback, for putting a child's utterance into longer syntactic frames, or all those features described above that are thought to be helpful for language learning during conversation.

This study is only a beginning. First, we need to research how easily such a conversational environment is replicated. Is the interaction observed with the present teacher and her group of students typical of reading lesson conversations using the KEEP approach or other comprehension approaches to reading? What other topics allow for conversations and discussions that will yield usable linguistic model/feedback for the language learner? For instance, how ammenable to a conversational approach are other school subjects, such as science, art, or social studies? Will such subject matter also allow conversations in which the students can put their thoughts into words and can get appropriately tuned linguistic feedback.

Studies comparing the effects of this approach to other ways of instruction are necessary. In the present study language learning took place. But, except for a comparison with an unanalyzed form of language immersion, there was no comparison with another approach to language learning to determine the efficiency of the present learning process.

We need to learn in more depth about factors in conversations that alter the efficacy of the approach: What factors foster, what factors hinder language learning in this group setting. For instance, one factor that needs close attention is that the students not only use the teacher's speech as models for their own speech, but also incorporate each other's speech (Speidel, 1983). We saw earlier that this imitation of peers can be both helpful and a drawback. The proportion of students that are already speakers of the target language will, therefore, in part, determine the degree of effectiveness of the conversational small group approach.

How does the degree of skill in the target language—understanding and speaking—alter the use of conversation? How must a teacher adjust instruction for children who hardly understand her? The dialect speaking children in the present study had some familiarity with standard English and therefore could understand within the context of the lesson a fair proportion of the teacher's talk. The nature of the conversation will clearly be different if children have less skill in the target language. Nevertheless, since the basic input strategies are the same as in first language learning, we would expect that with some adjustments in content and process, the conversational approach would still work.

How does the age of the student affect learning by this conversational approach? The present group of students, 6- and 7-year-olds, has probably not yet acquired formal operational thought in the Piagetian sense. For these students the present inductive approach to language learning, which uses meaningful message exchange, seems appropriate. However, older students, 11 years on up, who are capable of formal operational thought, may well respond better to a mixture of conversation and medium oriented instruction. (See Long, in press, and van Kleeck, 1984, for discussions of this point.)

Finally, there is the concept of "catalysts" for language learning (Nelson et al., 1983). Even though the research on input tuning suggests that no one specific modification is necessary for language learning (except perhaps that the input needs to be understood by the learners), there are also findings that certain kinds of input at certain stages of language learning may speed up learning considerably. Thus, Nelson concludes from a series of experimental studies he and his colleagues have conducted with first language learners (Baker & Nelson, 1984; Nelson, 1977; Nelson, Carskaddon, & Bonvillian, 1973), "A little of the right kind of evidence for the child's current level is often all that is required to induce an advance to the next level" (Nelson et al., 1983, p. 48.). In second language learning research, there is also a search for variables which will speed up learning.

For pedagogical reasons we must try to discover factors that create conversations which will be effective language learning situations; we must discover catalysts for language learning. The assessment and comparison of the effectiveness of catalysts can only be done in controlled experimental studies, such as those by K. E. Nelson and his colleagues. However, such catalysts cannot be automatically included into a conversational approach for they may destroy the very features that make conversation so potent: It may dampen the motivation of the learners to speak as well as their attention to the input language. The ultimate test of these catalysts must be conducted on quasi-naturalistic studies such as the present one.

Research which addresses these diverse questions may find that dialect-speaking children, children from poverty, and perhaps even children who are learning English as a second language in school may not need to spend time tediously reading lessons and for their help in coding and counting behaviors. Finally, I thank Ernst Moerk, Keith Nelson, Ann Peters, Michael Power, and Thomas White for their helpful comments on earlier versions of this manuscript.

ACKNOWLEDGMENTS

I am most grateful to Sarah Dowhower, the teacher of the reading lessons. The study was only possible because of her superior teaching skill, her patience, flexibility and openness to being taped, as well as her personal interest in the research. I thank Madeleen Herreshoff, Sherrie Ching and Joan Tagashira for their patience and hard work in transcribing the complex interactions of the reading lessons and for their help in coding and counting behaviors. Finally, I thank Ernst Moerk, Keith Nelson, Ann Peters, Michael Power, and Thomas White for their helpful comments on earlier versions of this manuscript.

REFERENCES

Baker, N. D., & Nelson, K. E. (1984). Recasting and related conversational techniques for triggering syntactic advances by young children. *First Language, 5,* 3–22.

Barik, H. C., & Swain, M. (1975). Three-year evaluation of a large scale early grade French Immersion Program: The Ottawa Study. *Language Learning, 25,* 1–29.

Bates, E. (1976). *Language and context: The acquisition of pragmatics.* New York: Academic Press.

Bereiter, C., & Engelmann, S. (1966). *Teaching disadvantaged children in preschool.* Englewood Cliffs, NJ: Prentice Hall.

Bickerton, D., & Odo, C. (1976–77). *Change and variation in Hawaiian English,* 1(3). (Final report on National Sciences Foundation Grant No. GS-39478.) University of Hawaii: Social Sciences and Linguistics Institute.

Blank, M., Rose, S. A., & Berlin, L. J. (1978). *The language of learning: The preschool years.* New York: Grune & Stratton.

Bolinger, D., & Sears, D. A. (1981). *Aspects of language* (3rd ed.). New York: Harcourt, Brace, Jovanovich.

Brown, R. (1977). Introduction. In C. E. Snow & C. A. Ferguson (Eds.), *Talking to children: Language input and language acquisition* (pp. 1–27). New York: Cambridge University Press.

Brown, R., Cazden, C., & Bellugi, U. (1969). The child's grammar from I to III. In J. P. Hill (Ed.), *Minnesota symposium on child psychology* (Vol. 2). Minneapolis: University of Minnesota Press.

Brown, R., & Hanlon, C. (1970). Derivational complexity and order of acquisition in child speech. In J. R. Hayes (Ed.) *Cognition and the development of language* (pp. 1–53). New York: Wiley.

Carrow, E. (1974). *Carrow Elicited Language Inventory*. Austin, Texas: Learning Concepts.

Cohen, A., Frier, V., & Flores, M. (1973). The Culver City Spanish Immersion Program—end of year no. 1 and year no. 2. *Working Papers in Teaching English as a Second Language, 7*, 65–74.

Cromer, R. (1984). *Language change with experience without feedback. Situational effects on children's and mother's speech*. Paper presented at the Third International Congress for the Study of Child Language, Austin, Texas.

Cross, T. G. (1977). Mother's speech: Role of child listener variables. In C. E. Snow & C. A. Ferguson (Eds.), *Talking to children: Language input and acquisition* (pp. 151–188). New York: Cambridge University Press.

Cross, T. (1978). Mothers' speech and its association with rate of linguistic development in young children. In N. Waterson & C. Snow (Eds.), *The development of communication* (pp. 199–216). London: Wiley.

Day, R. R. (1972). *Patterns of variation in copula and tense in the Hawaiian post-Creole continuum*. Unpublished doctoral dissertation, University of Hawaii, Honolulu, Hawaii.

Dodson, C. J. (1984). *Models for second language acquisition*. Paper presented at the Second International Conference on Language Acquisition-Language Contact-Language Conflict, Hamburg, Germany.

Dore, J. (1979). Conversation and preschool language development. In P. Fletcher & M. Garman (Eds.), *Language acquisition: Studies in first language development* (pp. 337–361). New York: Cambridge University Press.

Dulay, H., Burt, M., & Krashen, S. D. (1982). *Language 2*. New York: Oxford University Press.

Dunn, L. M., Horton, K. B., & Smith, J. O. (Eds.). (1968). *Peabody Language Development Kits: Level #P*. Circle Pines, MN: American Guidance Services, Inc.

Dunn, L. M., & Smith, J. O. (Eds.). (1965). *Peabody Language Development Kits: Level #1*. Circle Pines, MN: American Guidance Service, Inc.

Feagans, L., & Farran, D. C. (Eds.). (1982). *The language of children reared in poverty: Implications for evaluation*. New York: Academic Press.

Gleitman, L. R., & Wanner, E. (1982). Language acquisition: The state of the art. In E. Wanner & L. R. Gleitman (Eds.), *Language acquisition: The state of the art* (pp. 3–28). New York: Cambridge University Press.

Grimm, H. (1982). *On the interrelation of internal and external factors in the development of language structures in normal and dysphasic preschoolers: A longitudinal study*. (Occasional Paper No. 5) Honolulu: The Kamehameha Schools, Kamehameha Early Education Program.

Hakuta, K. (1981). Some common goals for second and first language acquisition research. In R. W. Anderson (Ed.), *New dimensions in second language acquisition research* (pp. 1–9). Rowley, MA: Newbury House.

Hall, R. A. (1966). *Pidgin and creole languages*. Ithaca, NY: Cornell University Press.

Halliday, M. A. K. (1975). Learning how to mean. In E. H. Lenneberg & E. Lenneberg (Eds.), *Foundations of language development: A multidisciplinary approach* (pp. 239–265). New York: Academic Press.

Hatch, E. (1978). Discourse analysis and second language acquisition. In E. M. Hatch (Ed.), *Second language acquisition* (pp. 401–435). Rowley, MA: Newbury House.

Hawaii District Office (1969). *Teacher's guide and lessons for teaching standard English as a second dialect to primary school children in Hawaii*. Hilo, Hawaii: Hawaii District Office, Department of Education, State of Hawaii.

Hoff-Ginsberg, E., & Shatz, M. (1982). Linguistic input and the child's acquisition of language. *Psychological Bulletin, 92*, 3–26.

Howe, C. (1981). *Acquiring language in a conversational context*. London: Academic Press.

Keenan, E. O. (1977). Making it last: Repetition in children's discourse. In S. Ervin-Tripp & C. Mitchell-Kernan (Eds.), *Child discourse* (pp. 125–128). New York: Academic Press.

Kirk, S. A., McCarthy, J. J., & Kirk, W. D. (1968). *Illinois Test of Psycholinguistic Abilities* (rev. ed.). Urbana: University of Illinois Press.

Krashen, S. D., & Terrell, T. D. (1983). *The Natural Approach: Language acquisition in the classroom.* New York: Pergamon Press.

Kucjaz, S. A. II (1982). Language play and language acquisition. In H. W. Reese (Ed.), *Advances in child development and behavior* (Vol. 17, pp. 197–232). Orlando, FL: Academic Pres.

Lambert, W. E., & Tucker, G. R. (1972). *Billingual education of children.* Rowley, MA: Newbury House.

Long, M. H. (1983a). Native speaker/non-native speaker conversation and the negotiation of comprehensible input. *Applied Linguistics, 4,* 126–141.

Long, M. H. (1983b). Linguistic and conversational adjustments to non-native speakers. *Studies in second language acquisition, 5,* 177–249.

Long, M. H. (in press). Instructed interlanguage development. In L. Beebe (Ed.), *Issues in second language acquisition: Multiple perspectives.* Rowley, MA: Newbury House.

Long, M. H., & Sato, C. J. (1983). Classroom foreigner talk discourse: Forms and functions of teachers' questions. In H. W. Seliger & M. H. Long (Eds.), *Classroom-oriented research in second language acquisition* (pp. 268–285). Rowley, MA: Newbury House.

McGinness, G. D. (1982). The language of the poverty child: Implications from center-based intervention and evaluation programs. In L. Feagans & D. C. Farran (Eds.), *The language of children reared in poverty: Implications for evaluation and intervention* (pp. 219–240). New York: Academic Press.

McNeill, D. (1966). Developmental psycholinguistics. In F. Smith & G. A. Miller (Eds.), *The genesis of language: A psycholinguistic approach* (pp. 15–84). Cambridge, MA: The MIT Press.

Mehan, H. (1979). *Learning lessons.* Cambridge, MA: Harvard University Press.

Moerk, E. L. (1983a). *The mother of Eve—as a first language teacher.* Norwood, NJ: Ablex.

Moerk, E. L. (1983b). A behavioral analysis of controversial topics in first language acquisition: Reinforcements, corrections, modeling, input frequencies and the three-term contingency pattern. *Journal of Psycholinguistic Research, 12,* 129–155.

Moerk, E. L. (1985). The fuzzy set called "imitations." In G. E. Speidel (Chair), *The many faces of imitation.* Symposium conducted at the Biennial Meeting of the Society for Research in Child Development, Toronto.

Moerk, E. L. (in press). Environmental factors in early language acquisition. In G. J. Whitehurst (Ed.), *Annals of child development,* (Vol. 3.) Greenich, CT: JAI Press.

Nelson, K. E. (1977). Facilitating children's syntax. *Developmental Psychology, 13,* 101–107.

Nelson, K. E., Bonvillian, J. D., Denninger, M. S., Kaplan, B. J., & Baker, N. D. (1983). Maternal input adjustments and non-adjustments as related to children's linguistic advances and to language acquisition theories. In A. D. Pelligrini & T. D. Yawkey (Eds.), *The development of oral and written languages: Readings in developmental and applied linguistics* (pp. 31–56). Norwood, NJ: Ablex.

Nelson, K. E., Carskaddon, G., & Bonvillian, J. D. (1973). Syntax acquisition: Impact of experimental variation in adult verbal interaction with the child. *Child Development, 44,* 497–504.

Newport, E. L., Gleitman, H., & Gleitman, L. R. (1977). Mother, I'd rather do it myself: Some effects and non-effects of maternal speech style. In C. E. Snow & C. A. Ferguson (Eds.), *Talking to children: Language input and acquisition* (pp. 109–149). Cambridge, MA: Cambridge University Press.

Ochs, E., & Schieffelin, B. B. (1982). Language acquisition and socialization: Three developmental stories and their implications. *Sociolinguistic Working Paper, No. 105.* Austin, Texas: Southwest Educational Development Laboratory.

Oksaar, E. (1977). *Language acquisition in the early years: An introduction to paedolinguistics.* Translated from German by Katherine Turfler. New York: St. Martin's Press.

Peck, S. (1978). Child-child discourse in second language acquisition. In E. M. Hatch (Ed.), *Second language acquisition* (pp. 383–400). Rowley, MA: Newbury House.

Peters, A. M. (1983). *The units of language acquisition.* Cambridge, England: Cambridge University Press.

Sato, C. J. (1986). Conversation and interlanguage development: Rethinking the connection. In R. R. Day (Ed.), *Conversation in second language acquisition.* Rowley, MA: Newbury House.

Schachter, F. F. (1979). *Everyday mother talk to toddlers.* New York: Academic Press.

Scollon, R. T. (1974). *One child's language from one to two: The origins of construction.* Doctoral dissertation University of Hawaii, Honolulu: Hawaii.

Shatz, M. (1982). On mechanisms of language acquisition: Can features of the communicative environment account for development. In E. Wanner & L. R. Gleitman (Eds.), *Language acquisition: The state of the art* (pp. 102–127). New York: Cambridge University Press.

Slobin, D. I. (1968). Imitation and grammatical development in children. In N. S. Endler, L. R. Boulter, & H. Osser (Eds.), *Contemporary issues in developmental psychology* (pp. 437–443). New York: Holt, Rinehart and Winston.

Snow, C. E. (1977). Mothers speech research: From input to interaction. In C. E. Snow & C. A. Ferguson (Eds.), *Talking to children: Language input and acquisition* (pp. 31–49). Cambridge, England: Cambridge University Press.

Snow, C. E. (1981). The uses of imitation. *Journal of Child Language, 8,* 205–212.

Snow, C. E., & Goldfield, B. A. (1983). Turn the page please: Situation specific language acquisition. *Journal of Child Language, 10,* 551–569.

Snow, M. A., Galvan, J. L., Campbell, R. N. (1983). The pilot class of the Culver City Spanish Immersion Program: A follow-up report, or whatever happened to the immersion class of '78? In K. M. Bailey, M. H. Long, & S. Peck (Eds.), *Second language acquisition studies* (pp. 115–125). Rowley, MA: Newbury House.

Speidel, G. E. (Ed.). (1981a). KEEP-The Kamahameha Early Education Program [Special issue]. *Educational Perspectives, 20.*

Speidel, G. E. (1981b). Language and reading: Bridging the language difference for children who speak Hawaiian English. *Educational Perspectives, 20,* 23–30.

Speidel, G. E. (1982). Responding to language differences. In *Oral language in a successful reading program for Hawaiian children* (Technical Report, No. 105). Honolulu: The Kamehameha Schools, Kamehameha Early Education Program.

Speidel, G. E. (1983). *Can findings from first language acquisition be useful for second dialect learning?* Paper presented to the Seventh Biennial Meeting of the International Society for the Study of Behavioral Development. Munich, West Germany.

Speidel, G. E. (in press). Language differences in the classroom: Two approaches for developing language skills in dialect speaking children. In E. Oksaar (Ed.), *Sociocultural perspectives of language acquisition and multilingualism.* Tubingen, Germany: Gunter Narr Verlag.

Speidel, G. E., & Herreshoff, M. (1985). Imitation and learning to speak standard English as a second dialect. In G. E. Speidel (Chair), *The many faces of imitation.* Symposium conducted at the Biennial Meeting of the Society for Research in Child Development, Toronto, Canada.

Speidel, G. E., Tharp, R. G., & Kobayashi, L. (1985). Is there a comprehension problem for nonstandard English speaking children? A study with children of Hawaiian English background. *Applied Psycholinguistics, 6,* 83–96.

Swain, M. (1985). Communicative competence: Some roles of comprehensible input and comprehensible output in its development. In S. Gass & C. Madden (eds.), *Input and second language acquisition* (pp. 225–253). Rowley, MA: Newbury House.

Terrell, T. D. (1977). A Natural approach to the acquisition and learning of a language. *Modern Language Journal, 61,* 325–336.

Tharp, R. G., Jordan, C., Speidel, G. E., Au, K. H., Klein, T. W., Calkins, R. P., Sloat, K. C. M., & Gallimore, R. (1984). Product and process in applied developmental research: Education and the children of a minority. In M. Lamb, A. L. Brown, & B. Rogoff (Eds.), *Advances in developmental psychology* (Vol. 3, pp. 91–141). Hillsdale, NJ: Lawrence Erlbaum Associates.

Tomasello, M., & Mannle, S. (1985). Pragmatics of sibling speech to one-year-olds. *Child Development, 56,* 911–917.

Tough, J. (1977). *Talking and learning.* London: Ward Lock Educational.

van Kleeck, A. (1984). Assessment and intervention: Does 'meta' matter? In G. Wallach & K. Butler (Eds.), *Language learning disabilities in school-age children* (pp. 179–197). Baltimore: William & Wilkins.

Vygotsky, L. S. (1962). *Thought and Language.* Cambridge, MA: The MIT Press.

Watson-Gegeo, K. A., & Gegeo, D. W. (in press). Some aspects of calling out and repeating routines in Kwara'ae children's language acquisition. In B. B. Schieffelin & E. Ochs (Eds.), *Language socialization across cultures.* New York: Cambridge University Press.

Wells, C. G. (1978). What makes for successful language development? In R. Campbell & P. Smith (Eds.), *Advances in the psychology of language* (Vol. 2). New York: Plenum.

Wells, C. G. (1980). Apprenticeship in meaning. In K. E. Nelson (Ed.), *Children's language Vol. 2,* pp. 45–126). Hillsdale, NJ: Larence Earlbaum Associates.

Wexler, K. (1982). A principle theory for language acquisition. In E. Wanner & L. R. Gleitman (Eds.), *Language acquisition: The state of the art* (pp. 288–315). New York: Cambridge University Press.

Winitz, H. (1981). Nonlinear learning and language teaching. In H. Winitz (Ed.) *The comprehension approach to foreign language instruction* (pp. 1–113). Rowley, MA: Newbury House.

6 Temporal Characteristics of Maternal Verbal Styles

Priscilla L. Roth
Harvard University Graduate School of Education

INTRODUCTION

The timing of a mother's verbal response to her infant's behavior may be a salient feature of the infant's environment and an important component of maternal linguistic responsiveness. For the infant, the temporal contingency of maternal verbal response may signify a responsive environment, or the lack of it, long before the infant understands the semantic content of the mother's utterances. Prompt, consistent verbal response to infant behavior may contribute to the infant's perception of the function of language, and may demonstrate for the infant when and how to use language. This chapter presents evidence to establish the infant's capacity to perceive temporal relationships, and to provide preliminary support for the main hypotheses of the present research: (1) that temporal characteristics of maternal speech (i.e., the contingent frequency and latency) are an important component of maternal speech input, and (2) that these temporal characteristics are related to other characteristics of maternal speech that are thought to facilitate language development, such as the mother's semantic expansions of the child's utterance or focus of attention.

Infants Perceive Temporal Patterns

There is now evidence to suggest that even young infants are sensitive to temporal regularity, can detect varying temporal patterns, and prefer certain temporal frequencies rather than others (see Miller & Byrne, 1984, and Stern & Gibbon, 1979, for reviews). Temporality is so salient a feature of stimuli for infants that infants often must habituate to the temporal dimension of a stimulus before they are able to attend to its other physical properties (Stern & Gibbon, 1979). Infants seem to prefer a generally regular pattern of stimulation with occasional limited variability (Stern & Gibbon, 1979). Minor violations of temporal expectancy, often used in games with young infants, tend to arouse the infant and heighten affect (Arco & McCluskey, 1981; Sroufe, 1979; Stern, 1974, 1977; Stern & Gibbon, 1979). Stimuli that are temporally predictable are soothing to infants, and infants prefer regular temporal frequencies of about 1 cycle per second (Brackbill, 1970; Byrne & Horowitz, 1981; Pederson & Ter Vrugt, 1973; Wolff, 1968). Infants rhythmically suck on a pacifier at a rate of about 1 cycle per second (Wolff, 1968), and repetitive rocking or other rhythmic stimulation is also most effective in soothing an infant when it occurs at this same frequency (Ambrose, 1969; Ter Vrugt & Pederson, 1973). Furthermore, studies of temporal estimation show that both infants and adults are very accurate at estimating temporal intervals of about 1 second (Demaney, McKenzie, & Vurpillot, 1977; Treisman, 1963; Woodrow, 1934). Recent research using micro-behavioral analysis suggests that intervals of approximately 1 second are especially meaningful in social interaction. Although it is no longer thought that infants coordinate their movements in synchrony with adult speech (cf. Dowd & Tronick, 1986), infants have been found to respond behaviorally within 1 second of maternal utterances (Beebe & Stern, 1977; Kato, Takahashi, Sawada, Kobayashi, Watanabe, & Ishii, 1983). Beebe (1982) found that the interval with the most positive affect for reciprocal turn-taking was just under 1 second. Finally, studies have shown that most maternal verbal responses to infant vocalizations occur within this interval (Beebe, Jaffe, Feldstein, Mays, & Alson, 1985; Schaffer, Collis, & Parsons, 1977; Stella-Prorok, 1983), although there can be considerable variation in responsiveness among individual mothers (cf. Schaffer et al., 1977). Given that much of the rhythm of social interaction regularly occurs within a 1-second interval, it may function as an optimum information-processing constant for the infant (Beebe, 1982) both because of its temporal regularity and its temporal contingency. When maternal speech is temporally predictable for the infant, as in familiar routines or in the repetitious "runs" of maternal speech to infants, the infant may be able to proceed to an analysis of the phonetic or semantic content of the recurring utterance (cf. Stern & Gibbon, 1979). That one second is an optimal interval for learning contingent relationships is supported by studies of infant conditioning (Millar, 1972; Millar & Watson, 1979).

Infants Perceive Temporal Contingency

Infants perceive temporally contingent relationships and form temporal expectancies based on responses to their own behavior. Research has shown that infants can acquire a variety of conditioned behavioral responses as a result of immediately contingent reinforcement (Millar, 1972; Watson, 1972, 1979). Infants also reliably increase their vocal responding rates as a result of immediate, contingent verbal stimulation (Lewis & Wilson, 1972; Ramey & Mills, 1977; Tulkin & Kagan, 1972). Furthermore, the temporal pattern of infant vocal behavior is differentially affected by contingent vs. noncontingent response (Bloom & Esposito, 1975; Bloom, 1975, 1977, 1979). With noncontingent stimulation, the infant produces a burst, or rapid series of vocalizations. In response to contingent stimulation, however, infants pause significantly longer between their vocalizations. This increased pausing reliably occurs following contingent responses that are either verbal or silent, and therefore is not due to the possibility that subsequent adult speech prevents or interrupts further infant vocalization (Bloom & Esposito, 1975). Bloom (1977) concludes that the infant's increased pausing following contingent stimulation demonstrates the infant's ability to detect the correlation between the adult's behavior and his own. The actual effect of the infant's pattern of vocalizing and pausing is to allow time for the adult to repeat his or her behavior, which may elicit a repetition of the infant's vocalization and pausing, and thus effectively furthers the reciprocal turn-taking of the interaction.

Temporal Delay Interferes With Infants' Learning

Temporal delays in response interfere with infants' perception of contingent relationships. Temporal delays in reinforcement of greater than 1 second are significantly less effective for infants' learning, even when infants are given prolonged exposure to the delayed reinforcement (Millar, 1972; Todd & Palmer, 1968). Moreover, Millar (1972) found that with a temporal delay of 3 seconds before contingent reinforcement, infants were completely unable to learn contingent relationships. Temporal delay interferes with the perception of contingency for both 3- and 9-month-olds (Millar & Watson, 1979; Ramey & Ourth, 1971), and for children 2-years-of-age as well (Stella-Prorok, 1983). Stella-Prorok (1983) found that experimentally introducing a 3-second delay interval into an adult's conversations with 2-year-olds completely disrupted the communication. During the delayed-response condition, the children stopped responding, even though the adult's responses were relevant and easily understood by young children. Temporal delay was more disruptive to the conversation than were contingent adult responses that were too difficult for the children to understand (Stella-Prorok, 1983). Temporal delays in response have been shown to be equally disruptive for children learning language. Whitehurst, Kedesdy, and White (1982) found that 2-year-olds acquired novel words easily when an adult labeled objects simultaneously with their presentation, but children had difficulty learning novel words if there was a 10-second latency between object presentation and labeling. Young children also notice when a usually responsive mother does not respond. Stella-Prorok (1983) found that mothers were much less likely to respond to their children's more primitive or unintelligible utterances. This disruption in the temporal structure of ongoing verbal interaction signals to the child that communication has failed, and perhaps prompts the child to make another attempt. If the mother is usually responsive, but selectively pauses in response to the child's unintelligible message, this omission of response may be functional for the child's linguistic development. However, as Tomasello and Mannle (1985; and Mannle & Tomasello this volume) conclude, if a young child's speech is ignored much of the time, the child's assessment of the efficacy of speech must be greatly diminished. Given the dramatic effect of temporal delay on infants' and young children's perception of contingent relationships, and the efficacy of immediate-response conditions, the timing of maternal responses may be an especially important feature of speech input during the first and second year of life when the child is learning language.

Contingent Maternal Responsiveness is Associated With the Infant's Cognitive and Language Development

It is not surprising, then, given the infant's capacity to perceive contingent relationships, that research assessing the quality of mother-infant interaction has found that maternal responsiveness is important for the infant's development. Research on mother-infant interaction suggests that a mother's prompt and contingent response to her infant's needs is related to the infant's later cognitive and language development (Ainsworth, 1973; Clarke-Stewart, 1973; Donovan & Leavitt, 1978; Schaffer et al., 1977). Prompt maternal responsiveness to the young infant's crying is associated subsequently with both less frequent crying and the development of noncrying modes of communication (Ainsworth, 1973; Bell & Ainsworth, 1972). Maternal verbal responsiveness is associated with more infant vocalization (Adams & Ramey, 1980; Ramey & Mills, 1977), and with the infant's later advanced cognitive performance (Donovan & Leavitt, 1978; Ramey, Sparling, & Wasik, 1981). Middle-class mothers interacting with their preverbal infants have been found to vocalize more frequently (Cohen & Beckwith, 1976; Tulkin & Kagan, 1972) and engage in more contingent, reciprocal vocalizing with their infants (Lewis & Wilson, 1972; Tulkin & Kagan, 1972). In contrast, mothers of low socioeconomic status (SES) talk less to their infants, and have infants who vocalize less (Adams & Ramey, 1980; Ramey & Mills, 1977). Thus, prompt maternal response and contingent verbal response seem to be styles that are established early in infancy and are associated with later language and cognitive competence.

The latency of the mother's verbal responses to her child may be especially important when the child first begins to comprehend language. A prompt maternal response allows the child to hear a word while he or she is still attending to the object or event being named (Bruner, 1975; Chapman, 1981; Ratner & Bruner, 1978). This makes it more likely for the child to associate words with their appropriate referents, and facilitates vocabulary development (Chapman, 1981; Whitehurst et al., 1982). Contingent response at such times in the interaction also demonstrates to the child when and how to use language effectively. Mothers who respond contingently, commenting on the child's focus of attention or activity, have children who use language for a greater variety of referential and symbolic purposes (Rescorla, 1984; Tomasello & Mannle, 1985).

Characteristics of Maternal Speech Input Influence Language Development

It is generally assumed that certain characteristics of maternal speech input to young children enable children to learn language. Mothers talking to their young children speak more clearly than they do to adults, use simple words and short sentences, and frequently repeat their message (Bendict, 1975; Broen, 1972; Newport, 1976; Phillips, 1973; Snow, 1972, 1977). Compared with adult speech, mothers also use fewer words per utterance, fewer utterances per speaking turn, and longer pauses between utterances (Broen, 1972; Snow, 1977). It has been suggested that this is especially appropriate for young children, because children in the one-word stage of language production may only comprehend one or two words in an utterance (Chapman, 1981; Shipley, Smith, & Gleitman, 1969). Cross (1977) found that the use of fewer utterances per speaking turn was associated with accelerated language acquisition, and suggests that both the slower rate and high intelligibility of the mother's speech increase its usefulness for the child.

However, there is considerable variation in the rate at which children acquire language (Howe, 1975; Cross, 1978; Demos, 1982; Ninio, 1980), and research suggests that children also vary significantly in their communicative competence, or the variety of functions for which they can use language effectively (Rescorla, 1984; Tomasello & Mannle, 1985; Tomasello & Todd, 1983). Recent investigations have begun to identify individual differences in maternal speech input that might account for these differences in child language outcome. Individual differences have been found in certain characteristics of maternal verbal style, such as the communicative intent, or discourse function, of maternal speech (Cross, 1978; Demos, 1982; McDonald & Pien, 1982; Olsen-Fulero, 1982). For example, some mothers talk to their children primarily to direct or control the child's behavior, whereas other mothers respond to the child's verbal behavior as though the child were contributing to the conversation. In this latter style, the mother focuses on the child's topic of interest, comments on that topic, and then passes the speaking turn, which encourages the child to participate in the conversation (McDonald & Pien, 1982; Olsen-Fulero, 1982). Maternal speech that is used primarily to direct the child's behavior has been associated with a slower rate of language acquisition (Cross, 1978; Demos, 1982; Furrow, Nelson, & Benedict, 1979; Newport, Gleitman, & Gleitman, 1977; Ninio,

1980), while maternal speech that effectively elicits the child's conversational participation is thought to facilitate language acquisition (Demos, 1982; McDonald & Pien, 1982; Ninio, 1980; Olsen-Fulero, 1982).

A Conversation-Eliciting Maternal Speech Style is Positively Related to Language Development

One aspect of maternal speech style that may encourage the child's conversational participation and facilitate language development is the mother's continuing the child's topic of conversation by repeating, expanding, or extending the semantic content of the child's utterance. Mothers who imitate the child's utterances, use expansions (completed phrases repeating all of the child's words), and use extensions (completed phrases repeating some of the child's words and adding new content) are more likely to have children who are linguistically advanced (Cross, 1978; Lieven, 1978; Nelson, 1980; Nelson, Carskaddon, & Bonvillian, 1973; Snow, 1977; Stella-Prorok, 1983). Middle-class mothers use twice as many repetitions and expansions of the child's utterances as working-class mothers (Snow, Arlman-Rupp, Hassing, Jobse, Joosten, & Vorster, 1976) and middle-class children are linguistically more advanced than low-SES children by the age of 3 (Clarke-Stewart, 1973; Howe, 1975; McCall, 1981; Ninio, 1980; Ramey et al., 1981). Maternal expansions are more effective than other responses in maintaining the child's conversational response, and children are more likely to learn new words that are contained within maternal expansions (Folger & Chapman, 1978; Schumaker, 1976). Chapman (1981) suggests that the accelerating effects of expansion are the result of modeling for the child how to add semantic and syntactic elements to his or her utterance, as well as confirming for the child that he or she has been understood, and encouraging the child to continue his or her topic of conversation. Other researchers suggest that expansions facilitate language development because mothers who expand and extend their children's utterances are more likely to be matching their input to their children's semantic ability (Snow, 1977), or matching the child's own communicative intent (Cross, 1978).

It also could be suggested that maternal expansions and extensions are effective in facilitating language development because they provide language modeling within an optimal temporal interval for learning. By expanding those semantic relations that the child has just produced the mother is more likely to be commenting on the child's current focus of attention. The mother thus would provide words that the child might need to articulate his or her own experience at a time when the words are very salient for the child. Research suggests that mother-infant dyads who frequently share attentional focus have children with a larger vocabulary and a greater MLU (Rocissano & Yatchmink, 1983; Tomasello & Todd, 1983). For the preverbal infant, the mother's temporally contingent comments on the infant's focus of attention would provide semantic information within an optimal temporal interval for the infant to perceive the relationship between words and their referents. Indeed, research indicates that young children have difficulty comprehending the subject of an utterance if it refers to an object other than the one they are holding (Bem, 1970; Huttenlocher, Eisenberg, & Strauss, 1968), and mothers more frequently refer to a toy when it is being manipulated by the infant than at other times during their interaction (Messer, 1978). It is thought that the infant uses such contextual cues to associate language with specific referents (Messer, 1978; Ninio & Bruner, 1978; Ratner & Bruner, 1978). Thus, maternal speech that is temporally contingent and semantically relevant to the child's focus of attention may be particularly useful for the child's language learning.

A Directive Maternal Speech Style is Negatively Associated with Language Development

Maternal speech that is used primarily to direct or control the child's behavior (including the use of grammatical imperatives) has been associated with a slower rate of language acquisition (Cross, 1978; Demos, 1982; Furrow et al., 1979; Newport et al., 1977; Rescorla, 1984). Research indicates that a directive maternal speech style is used more often in low-SES mother-infant dyads (Adams & Ramey, 1980; Bronson, 1974; Ramey et al., 1981; Snow et al., 1976), and its use is inversely related to maternal education and IQ (Adams & Ramey, 1980). Children of directive mothers often have a more *expressive* (i.e., self-oriented) style of language, and are more likely to use language primarily to express desires or refusals and to control the behavior of others. These children have been reported to have slower early vocabulary growth, and a less varied vocabulary (Della Corte, Benedict, & Klein, 1983; Nelson, 1973; Rescorla, 1984; Tomasello & Todd, 1983). In contrast, mothers who use more description of their own and their child's activity have children with a *referential* language style (i.e., with a greater variety of object labels in their early vocabulary). Referential children use language for a variety of purposes, including the communication of more abstract ideas and concepts (Rescorla, 1984). This research suggests that differences in maternal verbal interaction style are related to differences in the rate and style of the child's language acquisition.

THE PRESENT RESEARCH

The present research examined the timing and content of maternal speech to preverbal infants. This research was designed to measure maternal speech input in the temporal and behavioral context in which it occurs. It is now recognized that methodologies are needed to measure the behavior of mother-infant dyads as being interactive, behavioral *patterns over time,* and not as frequencies of specific behaviors (DeMeis, Francis, Arco, & Self, in press; Gottman & Ringland, 1981; Schaffer, 1979). Measuring the temporal characteristics of maternal speech input in relation to the infant's behavior may assess the extent to which the mother's communication is likely to be attended to and understood, in that a temporally contingent verbal response is more likely to refer to what the infant is looking at or doing, and thus allows the child to more easily associate the mother's words with their intended referents. Accordingly, in this research three aspects of maternal speech were expected to reflect differences in maternal interaction style, and to be important for facilitating language development: (1) how promptly and frequently the mother responds to infant vocalizations, (2) how frequently the mother describes events to which the infant is currently attending, and (3) how frequently the mother uses language to elicit the infant's conversational participation rather than directing the infant's behavior.

Study 1: Two 12-Month-Olds and Their Mothers

Subjects and Procedure. The initial subjects were two 12-month-old male infants and their mothers. Data from four additional mother-infant dyads are reported in Study 2. The initial two infants were from middle-class families, and were recruited from birth announcements that had appeared in local newspapers. Neither infant showed evidence of referential language production at the time of testing. Each mother-infant dyad had been videotaped in the home for one 30-minute free-play session with a set of toys provided by the experimenter. These two mother-infant dyads were chosen from among six mother-infant dyads who had been videotaped as part of a study by other investigators (Koenig & Mervis, in press). These particular dyads were chosen because in informal viewing of the videotapes, these two mothers seemed to have contrasting interaction styles. One mother seemed to be responsive to her infant's vocalizations and activity, whereas the other mother seemed to miss many opportunities for interaction and conversation with her infant.

Data-Coding. Data-coding included making written transcripts of all mother and infant vocalizations from the audio portion of the videotape. In addition, transcripts of all mother and infant actions were made from the same videotape segments played back in slow motion. Time-coding of these events was accomplished using a Commodore 64 computer and its internal clock, and a Cipher Digital standard Society of Motion Picture and Television Engineers (SMPTE) time-code reader/generator. During videotaping, the time-code reader/generator dubbed a permanent time address onto each frame of the videotape, measuring time in minutes, seconds, and frames, with 30 frames per second. During data coding, the time-code reader/generator was used to identify and play back exact segments of each videotape. To begin each time-coding, the computer clock was re-set to zero and was aligned with the first still-frame of the videotape. A computer record of the time of onset of each vocalization and action was made by depressing a key on the computer keyboard while the videotape was played in slow motion (1/2 speed). Thus, the same videotape segment was time-coded in four separate passes (one each for the infant's and mother's actions and vocalizations). While time-coding the vocalizations, the monitor screen was darkened, so that only the clock readout remained visible. Conversely, while the actions were being time-coded, the sound was turned off. Calculations of interrater reliability for time-coding of the same videotape segments showed that the rater's mean latencies differed by only 69 milliseconds, with a standard deviation of 100 milleseconds.

In order to measure the temporal relationship between individual events on the videotape, the computer integrated the four separate time-coded files into one file that depicted the actual sequence of mother's and infant's actions and vocalizations. This made it possible to calculate the latency between the onsets of any two types of event (e.g., between the infant's action and the mother's subsequent utterance, or between the infant's vocalization and the mother's subsequent utterance). A contingency analysis was then conducted, which included the conditional probability of one type of event given the occurrence of another event for responses within 1 second of the previous event. The 1-second response criterion was chosen as defining a prompt response because studies of infant conditioning show that reinforcement latencies greater than 1 second are significantly less effective for learning contingent relationships (Millar, 1972; Ramey & Ourth, 1971), and studies of infant social interaction and studies of infant temporal perception show that infants prefer this temporal frequency of response (Beebe, 1982; Ter Vrugt & Pederson, 1973).

In addition to the contingency analysis, a discourse analysis of the mother's verbal responses to infant vocalizations was carried out, using an adaptation of the categorization scheme described by McDonald and Pien (1982), as shown is Table 6.1. The maternal speech data were summarized according to discourse categories that indicated a high level of maternal directiveness or control (Categories 1–5) vs. categories of low constraint (Categories 6–14), in which the mother encouraged the infant's conversational participation. The conversation-eliciting categories were further divided into utterances that functioned specifically to semantically encode the infant's actions or focus of attention at the time of the infant's vocalization (Categories 5–8) vs. other utterances that functioned to contribute to the conversation without providing additional semantic information about the infant's actions or focus of attention (Categories 9–14). Interrater reliability for this categorization scheme, calculated as the number of agreements between two independent raters divided by the total of both agreements and disagreements, was 92%.

Results. There were two main findings. First, of all maternal responses contingent on infant actions and vocalizations, only maternal verbal responses to

TABLE 6.1
DISCOURSE ANALYSIS[a]

Directive Categories	Examples[b]
1. <u>Directives</u>. Utterances which elicit and constrain the physical behavior of the hearer (including both direct and indirect commands).	"Pick up the blue one." "Bounce it!" "Can you sit down for a minute?"
2. <u>Attention Devices</u>. Utterances eliciting or directing the hearer's attention	"Tony!" "Watch mommy!" "Come on, look at this."
3. <u>Prompts</u>. An utterance which elicits or makes obligatory a response from the hearer.	"Huh?' "Okay?" "Please."
4. <u>Test Questions</u>. Questions requiring the hearer to provide a specific answer demonstrating his knowledge.	"What color is this block?" "What is that?" "Where's his eyes?"
5. <u>Negations/Corrections</u>. Utterances specifically rejecting or correcting a child's previous utterance or action.	"No, you gotta pull to make it work, honey." "No, hold it with your thumb." "You don't want to eat that, no."

Conversation-Eliciting Categories	Examples
6. <u>Semantic Encoding Comments</u>. Utterances which articulate or describe the child's action, or focus of attention commenting on it or adding new information about it.	"That spins around fast." "Yeah, she sees you making music, too." "Yeah, that's a bright picture."
7. <u>Semantic Encoding Questions</u>. Questions that describe the child's action or focus of attention while passing the speaking turn.	"Making your own music now?" "Are you watching people, too?" "Yeah, you hugging?"
8. <u>Labeling</u>. Utterances whose essential function is to identify an object.	"Car." "That's a car." "Is that an airplane?"
9. <u>Verbal Acknowledgments</u>.Utterances which acknowledge the child's previous action or utterance.	"Yeah." "Uh-huh." "Oh boy."
10. <u>Permission Requests/Offers of Help</u>. Questions which seek permission or acceptance for an action of the speaker.	"Can mommy do it now, too?" "Want some help?" "Want me to help you-- little bit?"
11. <u>Real Questions</u>. Questions seeking information which only the hearer could know or decide.	"What did you find?" "You like that?" "You wanna play peek-a-boo?"
12. <u>Positive Evaluations</u>. Utterances praising or encouraging the child's actions.	"Good boy." "Hooray!"
13. <u>Comments on Completed Actions</u>. Utterances that mark the end of an action without semantically encoding it.	"There!" "Oops." "Boom!"
14. <u>Comments Accompanying Actions</u>. Utterances made simultaneously with an action that mark or imitate the sound of the action or object without semantically encoding it.	"Brmmm." "Boop-boop-boop." "Wuf, wuf."

[a]Adapted from McDonald & Pien, 1982.
[b]Examples are from the present data.

TABLE 6.2
Conditional Probability of a Mother Event Following an Infant
Event for Two Mother-Infant Dyads

Contingent Events	Dyad 1	Dyad 2
p (Mother Action|Infant Action)	.32	.34
p (Mother Vocalization|Infant Action)	.28	.30
p (Mother Action|Infant Vocalization)	.31	.30
p (Mother Vocalization|Infant Vocalization)	.64[a]	.36[a]

Note: Events whose onsets occurred within a 1-second observation interval were counted in this contingency analysis.
[a] $p < .001$.

infant vocalizations were significantly different for the two dyads, as shown in
Table 6.2. All other event relationships, such as the timing of a mother's action
in response to her infant's action, were very similar for the two mothers. Thus,
maternal verbal responses to infant vocalizations revealed the most information
about the two interaction styles. Second, several of the discourse measures
distinguished between the two mothers and confirmed that the mothers had
different speech styles, as shown in Table 6.3. The measures were converted to
proportions for each mother, and were compared statistically with z tests for
proportions. In all comparisons, Mother 1 was found to be more verbally responsive. Her proportion of verbal responses within 1 second of an infant vocalization
(.64) was significantly higher than that of Mother 2 (.36): $z = 3.32, p < .001$. In
the discourse analysis of the mothers' contingent responses, it was found that the
proportion of conversation-eliciting responses for Mother 1 was .81, compared
with only .36 for Mother 2 ($z = 5.43, p < .001$). When examining the semantic-
encoding conversation-eliciting responses vs. the other conversation-eliciting
responses, it was found that only the semantic-encoding responses differentiated

TABLE 6.3
Proportions of Maternal Response to Infant Vocalizations for
Two Mother-Infant Dyads

Measure	Dyad	
	1	2
Number of infant vocalizations	84	56
Responses within 1 second of infant vocalizations	.64[e]	.36[e]
Directive responses[a]	.07[e]	.43[e]
Conversation-eliciting responses[b]	.81[e]	.36[e]
Semantic encoding responses[c]	.56[e]	.13[e]
Other conversational responses[d]	.25	.23

Note. Proportions are based on the total number of infant vocalizations to which
the mother responded verbally.
[a] Categories 1-5
[b] Categories 6-14
[c] Categories 6-8
[d] Categories 9-14
[e] Significant difference between mothers, $p < .001$.

between the two mothers. Mother 1 had proportionately more semantic-encoding responses than Mother 2 (.56 vs. .13, $z = 5.18$, $p<.001$); however, Mother 1 did not differ from Mother 2 in other conversational responses (.25 vs. .17, $z = 0.24$). Finally, Mother 1 used proportionately very few directive responses, while almost half of Mother 2's responses consisted of directives, (.07 vs. .43, $z = 5.05$, $p<.001$). Thus, the mother who made proportionately more conversation-eliciting responses and proportionately fewer directive responses also provided more useful semantic information for the child.

In summary, one mother consistently was more responsive than the other mother according to all measures. The responsive mother was more prompt in her verbal responses to her infant, thus making it more likely that the infant would perceive the mother's utterance as contingent on the infant's own speech. The responsive mother also was more likely to acknowledge the infant's vocalization by responding with utterances that functioned to elicit the infant's further conversational participation. Moreover, the responsive mother was more likely to provide useful linguistic information for the infant by semantically elaborating the infant's focus of attention or activity. In contrast, the less responsive mother, who made fewer temporally contingent verbal responses to her infant's vocalizations, used speech primarily to direct or control the infant's behavior. Her speech was neither temporally contingent nor semantically relevant to her infant's activity at the time of the infant's vocalization. Thus, her speech rarely functioned to acknowledge or encourage her infant's vocalizations or activity.

Study 2: A Comparison of Six Mother-Infant Dyads

To test the generalizability of the results obtained from the initial two subjects, data from four additional mother-infant dyads were examined. The purpose of this second study was to examine whether the temporal pattern of maternal speech consistently is related to particular discourse functions, and whether the maternal speech of randomly selected dyads would vary according to characteristics of the two speech styles identified in Study 1.

Subjects and Procedure.   Two male and two female 12-month-old firstborn infants from middle-class families were recruited from birth announcements that had appeared in local newspapers. Each mother-infant dyad was videotaped for 30 minutes in a laboratory playroom equipped with toys similar to those available to the first two dyads. The time-coding of mother and infant vocalizations and the discourse analysis of maternal speech were performed according to the procedure for Study 1.

Results.   Analysis of the data obtained from these four dyads was generally consistent with the results from the first two dyads. This analysis indicated that

TABLE 6.4
Proportions of Maternal Verbal Response to Infant Vocalizations
for Six Mother-Infant Dyads

				Dyad				
Measure	1	2	3	Mean (SD)	4	5	6	Mean (SD)
Number of infant vocalizations	84	41	66	64 (22)	56	63	63	61 (4)
Responses within 1 second	.64	.49	.41	.51[e] (.12)	.36	.29	.21	.29[e] (.08)
Directive responses[a]	.07	.20	.18	.15 (.07)	.43	.35	.14	.31 (.15)
Conversation-eliciting responses[b]	.81	.76	.71	.76[f] (.05)	.36	.40	.57	.44[f] (.11)
Semantic-encoding responses[c]	.56	.46	.41	.48[f] (.08)	.13	.27	.17	.19[f] (.08)
Other conversational responses[d]	.25	.29	.30	.28 (.03)	.23	.13	.40	.25 (.14)

Note. Proportions are based on the number of infant vocalizations to which the mother responded verbally.

[a] Categories 1-5
[b] Categories 6-14
[c] Categories 6-8
[d] Categories 9-14
[e] $p < .05$
[f] $p < .025$

there is variation in maternal verbal responsiveness to infants' vocalizations, and that prompt maternal response is related to the function of the mother's utterance, especially to the mother's semantic encoding of the child's activity. In Table 6.4, the data from all six dyads are presented in an order based on the proportion of maternal verbal responses to infant vocalizations, with the dyads from Study 1 included in columns 1 and 4. The proportion of infant vocalizations to which a mother responded verbally within 1 second ranged from .21 to .49 for the four new dyads, compared with response probabilities of .36 and .64 for the first two mothers. To test whether mothers who responded with a higher proportion of utterances within 1 second of the infant's vocalization also responded consistently more frequently to infant vocalizations, the frequency of maternal verbal response within 1 second of the infant's vocalization was compared to all maternal verbal responses to infant vocalizations. It was found that the frequency of maternal verbal response is stable over time ($r = .79$, $p < .05$). Thus, mothers who responded most promptly also responded consistently most frequently to infant vocalizations.

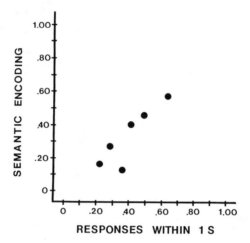

FIGURE 6.1. The proportion of maternal verbal responses within 1 second of an infant vocalization correlated with the proportion of maternal semantic-encoding responses.

To examine how temporal characteristics of maternal speech are related to the discourse function of maternal speech, correlations were calculated between the proportion of prompt maternal verbal responses and the proportion of maternal speech for each of the discourse measures. As depicted in Fig. 6.1, the proportion of maternal verbal responses within 1 second of the infant's vocalization was significantly correlated with the proportion of maternal responses that were semantic-encoding responses: $r = .87$, $p<.05$. This correlation suggests that mothers who responded most promptly to infant vocalizations also were most likely to semantically encode their infant's focus of attention or activity. However, the proportion of prompt maternal responses to infant vocalizations was not found to be significantly related to the proportion of maternal responses in the more general conversation-eliciting category ($r = .71$). This finding is consistent with results obtained from the first two dyads that suggest that of all the conversational responses, the semantic-encoding conversational responses are most likely to differentiate maternal verbal styles. Finally, as expected, the proportion of prompt maternal verbal responses was not related to the proportion of directive maternal utterances, ($r = -.44$). Maternal directives, which express mother-initiated activity or intentions, thus prove not to be temporally related to infant-initiated activity or speech.

The data were also examined to determine whether the strong correlation between the proportion of prompt maternal responses to infant vocalizations and the proportion of maternal semantic-encoding responses might have occurred simply because there is a shorter latency for those maternal utterances categorized as semantic-encoding responses. To address this possibility, a comparison was made between the mean latency of the mothers' semantic encoding responses ($\bar{X} = 0.62$ seconds) and the mean latency of the mothers' other responses ($\bar{X} = 0.60$ seconds); this difference was not significant ($t(4) = 0.53$). Thus, the correlation between the proportion of temporally contingent maternal verbal responses and the proportion of semantic-encoding responses reflects a distinct maternal speech style. The linguistically responsive mother responds contingently to her infant's vocalizations and continues her preverbal infant's *topic* of conversation by semantically elaborating whatever the infant was attending to at the time of the infant's vocalization.

In order to further investigate whether the temporal pattern of maternal speech provides a reliable index of two different maternal verbal styles, the maternal response data were divided at the median into two groups: (1) a high-response group of mothers who responded contingently more frequently to infant vocalizations, and (2) a low-response group of mothers who responded contingently less frequently. Mothers in the high-response group responded within 1 second of infant vocalizations significantly more frequently than mothers in the low-response group, $t(2) = 3.33$, $p<.05$, one-tailed. Mothers in the high-response group also had a higher proportion of semantic-encoding responses ($t(2) = 6.00$, $p<.025$, one-tailed) and a higher proportion of conversation-eliciting responses ($t(2) = 5.54$, p .025, one-tailed). Finally, mothers in the high-response group had proportionately fewer directive utterances than mothers in the low-response group, although this difference was not significant ($t(2) = 2.07$, $p<.1$, one-tailed). These results suggest that the temporal pattern of maternal speech consistently was related to the purposes for which a mother used language with her infant, and suggest two distinct maternal speech styles. Mothers who respond promptly provide their infants with contextually relevant linguistic information, whereas mothers whose utterances are less frequently temporally contingent on infant vocalizations provide less linguistic information for their infants. Mothers in the low-response group had fewer semantic-encoding responses, and instead used either proportionately more directive utterances (e.g., "Bounce it" "Pick it up"), as in Dyads 4 and 5, or used proportionately more simple conversational responses (e.g., "Yeah", "Good boy!"), as in Dyad 6. Whether low-response mothers typically show one of these two profiles, a directive style vs. a more passive, uninvolved style, needs to be investigated with a larger subject sample. However, neither of these verbal styles contain temporally contingent linguistic information.

DISCUSSION

The present research suggests that the temporal organization of maternal speech is indicative of the purposes for which a mother uses language with her infant and reflects her perception of her infant as a conversational partner. The temporal pattern of a responsive, contingent maternal verbal style consists of a high proportion of utterances that are temporally contingent on infant vocalizations. Prompt maternal verbal responses to the child's vocalizations may allow the child to experience his or her vocalizations as communication, encouraging the child to continue the verbal interaction and consequently promoting the child's communicative competence. A prompt verbal response, as well as signifying a responsive environment, provides optimal learning conditions for the young child, while delays in response of greater than 1 second may interfere with learning. In the present research with preverbal infants, maternal utterances that occurred within 1 second of the infant's vocalization not only seemed the most appropriately timed in the interaction, but also provided an index of whether the mother was attending to her infant's activity. Responses with latencies greater than 1 second seemed more like pauses in the interaction and were characteristic of responses that were not related to the behavior of the infant. The present research suggests that the defining characteristic of a linguistically responsive verbal style is the mother's semantically encoding or elaborating the child's current focus of attention or activity. A mother with a contingent style attends to the child's activity, and participates in the child's activity by encouraging or commenting on that activity. Previous research suggests that mother-infant dyads who frequently share joint attentional focus have children with better vocabularies (Tomasello & Mannle, 1985; Tomasello & Todd, 1983). The present research suggests that an important component of verbal reference made during joint attention is the temporal contingency of this linguistic information. By already attending to the infant's attentional focus, the mother can provide language modeling within an optimal temporal interval for learning. With prompt and useful semantic information, the child would be more likely to associate words with their appropriate referents. This should make language more transparent for the child and facilitate vocabulary development.

In contrast, a highly directive mother uses language primarily to control the infant's attention and behavior, rather than using language as a reciprocal conversational exchange. When a directive mother interacts with her child it is often to elicit the child's attention toward the mother's activity. A directive mother is more likely to interrupt or intervene in the child's ongoing activity, as though she does not recognize the child's self-initiated behavior, or does not value it. The present research suggests that a highly directive verbal style significantly alters the temporal organization of the interaction. A temporal analysis of a directive mother's speech shows that very few of her utterances are temporally contingent on her infant's vocalizations or activity. Although a directive mother may speak just as often as, or more frequently than, mothers with a more contingent conversational style, a directive mother's utterances are not temporally contingent on her infant's behavior. Furthermore, directive statements do not invite a verbal response from the child, and thus allow little opportunity for a reciprocal, contingent verbal exchange to develop.

CONCLUSION

Given the dramatic effect of temporal delay on infants' and young children's perception of contingent relationships, and the efficacy of contingent response, the timing of maternal verbal response may be an especially important feature of speech input during the first and second year of life when the child is learning language. Developmental theorists such as McCall (1981) consider the development of language in the second year of life to be a crucial time for the emergence of important and enduring individual differences. The present research clearly indicated that there is individual variation in the language environments experienced by 12-month-old infants. Some mothers attended to infant-initiated behavior and responded promptly to the infant's vocalizations. In contrast, other mothers talked to their infants primarily to control the infant's behavior and to direct the infant's attention to mother-initiated activity, while missing many opportunities to respond to infant-initiated activity. These results suggest that some infants may be experiencing language under conditions that optimize learning, while other infants hear less linguistic information, and information that is neither temporally contingent nor semantically relevant to their behavior.

The use of microbehavioral analysis techniques in the present research made it possible to measure very small intervals of time so that the temporal relationship between maternal and child speech could be examined. This temporal analysis also differentiated between the total amount of speech directed toward the child and the actual temporal pattern of maternal speech in relation to the child's vocalizations and behavior. Mothers with a contingent verbal style responded promptly to child speech and activity. However, mothers with a directive verbal style had few utterances that were temporally contingent on child speech or child-initiated activity. Such differences in maternal verbal style may be related to reported differences in the child's verbal styles or language acquisition strategies. Research suggests that mothers of referential children frequently repeat or expand child utterances (Nelson, 1973; K. E. Nelson, Baker, Denninger, Bonvillian, & Kaplan, 1985). Mothers of expressive children, however, are more likely to use directive utterances, use relatively more pronouns than nouns, and have both less education and lower income (Nelson, 1973; Tomasello & Todd, 1983). Although child language style or strategy differences may be multiply determined, as Nelson (1981) suggests, the kind of temporal analysis used in the present research could measure the language-learning environment provided by individual mothers and thus differentiate between variation in maternal verbal style and the non-optimal maternal speech input that might interfere with language learning and influence the child's language competence as well as style of language acquisition.

Temporal analysis of verbal interaction also may provide insight into the mechanisms that allow children to learn language. Mothers who attend to child-initiated behavior, and thus already share the child's attentional focus, are able to respond to infant vocalizations within approximately 1 second. Events that occur wihin a 1-second interval are most easily perceived as being contingently related. Thus, mothers who provide semantically relevant linguistic information within an optimal temporal interval for the infant to perceive the relationship between words and their referents may facilitate the infant's language acquisition.

Future research using temporal analysis is needed to measure variation in the language environments of a larger sample of mother-infant dyads (e.g., Roth, 1985), to follow these dyads longitudinally in order to study the stability of maternal verbal styles as the child learns language, and to assess the effects of these different maternal verbal styles on the child's speech style and the child's later language competence.

ACKNOWLEDGMENTS

The research reported in this paper was presented at the Third International Congress for the Study of Child Language, Austin, 1984. The author is grateful to the mothers and infants who participated in the study, to Mareile Koenig for use of two of her subject videotapes, to Carolyn Mervis for generously sharing her video equipment, to Nelson Cowan for advice and assistance computer programming, and to Linda Kenyon for assistance data coding.

Address for correspondence: Dr. Priscilla L. Roth, Harvard University, Graduate School of Education, Larsen 712, Cambridge, MA 02138.

REFERENCES

Adams, J. L., & Ramey, C. T. (1980). Structural aspects of maternal speech to infants reared in poverty. *Child Development, 51,* 1280–1284.

Ainsworth, M. D. (1973). The development of infant-mother attachment. In B. Caldwell & H. Riccuiti (Eds.), *Review of child development research, Vol. 3,* pp. 1–94). Chicago: University of Chicago Press.

Ambrose, A. (Ed.). (1969). *Stimulation in early infancy.* Orlando, FL: Academic Press.

Arco, C. M. B., & McCluskey, K. A. (1981). "A change of pace:" An investigation of the salience of maternal temporal style in mother-infant play. *Child Development, 52,* 941–949.

Beebe, B. (1982). Micro-timing in mother-infant communication. In M. Key (Ed.), *Nonverbal communication today: Current research* (pp. 169–195). New York: Mouton.

Beebe, B., & Stern, D. (1977). Engagement-disengagement and early object experience. In N. Freedman & S. Grand (Eds.), *Communicative structures and psychic structures* (pp. 35–55). New York: Plenum.

Beebe, B., Jaffe, J., Feldstein, S., Mays, K., & Alson, D. (1985). Matching of timing: The application of an adult dialogue model to mother-infant vocal and kinesic interactions. In T. Field (Ed.), *Infant social perception* (pp. 217–247). Norwood, NJ: Ablex.

Bell, S. M., & Ainsworth, M. D. (1972). Infant crying and maternal responsiveness. *Child Development, 43,* 1171–1190.

Bem, S. L. (1970). The role of comprehension in children's problem solving. *Developmental Psychology, 2,* 351–358.

Benedict, H. (1975, April). *The role of repetition in early language comprehension*. Paper presented at the Society for Research in Child Development Biennial Meeting, Denver.

Bloom, K. (1975). Social elicitation of infant vocal behavior. *Journal of Experimental Child Psychology, 20*, 51–58.

Bloom, K. (1977). Patterning of infant vocal behavior. *Journal of Experimental Child Psychology, 23*, 367–377.

Bloom, K. (1979). Evaluation of infant vocal conditioning. *Journal of Experimental Child Psychology, 27*, 60–70.

Bloom, K., & Esposito, A. (1975). Social conditioning and its proper control procedures. *Journal of Experimental Child Psychology, 19*, 209–222.

Brackbill, Y. (1970). Acoustic variation and arousal level in infants. *Psychophysiology, 6*, 517–526.

Broen, P. A. (1972). The verbal environment of the language-learning child. *American Speech and Hearing Association Monograph*, No. 17. Washington, DC: American Speech and Hearing Association.

Bronson, W. (1974). Mother-toddler interaction: A perspective on studying the development of competence. *Merrill-Palmer Quarterly of Behavior and Development, 20*, 275–301.

Bruner, J. S. (1975). From communication to language—a psychological perspective. *Cognition, 3*, 255–287.

Byrne, J. M., & Horowitz, F. D. (1981). Rocking and soothing intervention: The influence of direction and type of movement. *Infant Behavior and Development, 4*, 207–218.

Chapman, R. S. (1981). Mother-child interaction in the second year of life: Its role in language development. In R. Schiefelbusch & D. Bricker (Eds.), *Early language: Acquisition and intervention* (pp. 203–250). Baltimore, MD: University Park Press.

Clarke-Stewart, K. A. (1973). Interactions between mothers and their young children: Characteristics and consequences. *Monographs of the Society for Research in Child Development, 38*, (6–7 Serial No. 153).

Cohen, S., & Beckwith, L. (1976). Maternal language in infancy. *Developmental Psychology, 12*, 371–372.

Cross, T. (1977). Mothers' speech adjustments: The contributions of selected child listener variables. In C. E. Snow & C. A. Ferguson (Eds.), *Talking to children: Language input and acquisition* (pp. 151–188). Cambridge, England: Cambridge University Press.

Cross, T. G. (1978). Mothers' speech and its association with rate of linguistic development in young children. In N. Waterson & C. Snow (Eds.), *The development of communication* (pp. 199–216). New York: Wiley.

Della Corte, M., Benedict, H., & Klein, D. (1983). The relationship of pragmatic dimensions of mothers' speech to the referential-expressive distinction. *Journal of Child Language, 10*, 33–44.

Demany, K., McKenzie, B., & Vurpillot, E. (1977). Rhythm perception in early infancy. *Nature, 266*, 718–719.

DeMeis, D. K., Francis, P. L., Arco, C. M., & Self, P. A. (in press). Context, reciprocity, and temporality in mother-infant interaction. *Psychology Today*.

Demos, V. (1982). The role of affect in early childhood: An exploratory study. In E. Tronick (Ed.), *Social interchange in infancy: Affect, cognition, and communication* (pp. 79–123). Baltimore, MD: University Park Press.

Donovan, W., & Leavitt, L. (1978). Early cognitive development and its relation to maternal physiologic and behavioral response. *Child Development, 49*, 1251–1254.

Dowd, J. M., & Tronick, E. Z. (1986). Temporal coordination of arm movements in early infancy: Do infants move in synchrony with adult speech? *Child Development, 57*, 762–776.

Folger, J. P., & Chapman, R. S. (1978). A pragmatic analysis of spontaneous imitations. *Journal of Child Language, 5*, 25–38.

Furrow, D., Nelson, K., & Benedict, H. (1979). Mothers' speech to children and syntactic development: Some simple relationships. *Journal of Child Language, 6*, 423–442.

Gottman, J. M., & Ringland, J. T. (1981). The analysis of dominance and bidirectionality in social development. *Child Development, 52*, 393–412.

Howe, C. (1975). *The nature and origin of social class—differences in the propositions expressed by young children.* Unpublished doctoral dissertation, University of Cambridge.

Huttenlocher, J., Eisenberg, K., & Strauss, S. (1968). Comprehension: Relation between perceived actor and logical subject. *Journal of Verbal Learning and Verbal Behavior, 7*, 527–530.

Kato, T., Takahashi, E., Sawada, K., Kobayashi, N., Watanabe, T., & Ishii, T. (1983). A computer analysis of infant movements synchronized with adult speech. *Pediatric Research, 17*, 625–628.

Koenig, M. A., & Mervis, C. B. (in press). The interactive bases of severely handicapped and normal children's initial language development. *Journal of Speech and Hearing Research.*

Lewis, M., & Wilson, C. D. (1972). Infant development in lower-class American families. *Human Development, 15*, 112–127.

Lieven, E. V. M. (1978). Conversations between mothers and young children: Individual differences and their possible implication for the study of language learning. In N. Waterson & C. Snow (Eds.), *The development of communication* (pp. 173–187). New York: Wiley.

McCall, R. B. (1981). Nature-nurture and the two realms of development: A proposed integration with respect to mental development. *Child Development, 52*, 1–12.

McDonald, L., & Pien, D. (1982). Mother conversational behavior as a function of interactional intent. *Journal of Child Language, 9*, 337–358.

Messer, D. (1978). The integration of mothers' referential speech with joint play. *Child Development, 49*, 781–787.

Millar, W. S. (1972). A study of operant conditioning under delayed reinforcement in early infancy. *Monographs of the Society for Research in Child Development, 37*, (2, Serial No. 147).

Millar, W. S., & Watson, J. S. (1979). The effect of delayed feedback on infant learning reexamined. *Child Development, 50*, 747–751.

Miller, C. L., & Byrne, J. M. (1984). The role of temporal cues in the development of language and communication. In L. Feagans, C. Garvey, & R. Golinkoff (Eds.), *The origins and growth of communication* (pp. 77–101) Norwood, NJ: Ablex.

Nelson, K. (1973). Structure and strategy in learning to talk. *Monographs of the Society for Research in Child Development, 38*, (Serial No. 149).

Nelson, K. (1981). Individual differences in language development. *Developmental Psychology, 17*, 170–187.

Nelson, K. E. (1980). Theories of the child's acquisition of syntax: A look at rare events and at necessary, catalytic, and irrelevant components of mother-infant conversation. *Annals of the New York Academy of Sciences, 345*, 45–67.

Nelson K. E., Baker, N., Denninger, M., Bonvillian, J., & Kaplan, B. (1985). *Cookie* versus Do-it-again: imitative-referential and personal-social-syntactic-initiating language styles in young children. *Linguistics, 23*, 433–454.

Nelson, K. E., Carskaddon, G., & Bonvillian, J. D. (1973). Syntax acquisition: Impact of experimental variation in adult verbal interaction with the child. *Child Development, 44*, 497–504.

Newport, E. (1976). Motherese: The speech of mothers to young children. In N. Castellan, D. Pisoni, & G. Potts (Eds.), *Cognitive theory, Vol. 2* (pp. 177–218). Hillsdale, NJ: Lawrence Erlbaum Associates.

Newport, E., Gleitman, H., & Gleitman, C. (1977). Mother, I'd rather do it myself: Some effects and non-effects of maternal speech style. In C. C. Snow & C. Ferguson (Eds.), *Talking to children* (pp. 109–149). Cambridge, England: Cambridge University Press.

Ninio, A. (1980). Picture-book reading in mother-infant dyads belonging to two subgroups in Israel. *Child Development, 51*, 587–590.

Ninio, A., & Bruner, J. (1978). The achievements and antecedents of labeling. *Journal of Child Language, 5*, 1–16.

Olsen-Fulero, L. (1982). Style and stability in mother conversational behaviour: A study of individual differences. *Journal of Child Language, 9,* 543–564.

Pederson, D. R., & Ter Vrugt, D. (1973). The influence of amplitude and frequency of vestibular stimulation on the activity of two-month-old infants. *Child Development, 44,* 122–128.

Phillips, J. R. (1973). Syntax and vocabulary of mother's speech to young children: Age and sex comparisons. *Child Development, 44,* 192–195.

Ramey, T., & Mills, P. J. (1977). Social and intellectual consequences of day care for high-risk infants. In R. Webb (Ed.), *Social development in childhood: Day care programs and research* (pp. 79–110). Baltimore, MD: Johns Hopkins University Press.

Ramey, C. T., & Ourth, L. L. (1971). Delayed reinforcement of vocalization rates in infants. *Child Development, 42,* 291–297.

Ramey, C. T., Sparling, J. J., & Wasik, B. H. (1981). Creating social environments to facilitate language development. In R. Schiefelbusch & D. Bricker (Eds.), *Early language: Acquisition and intervention* (pp. 449–471). Baltimore, MD: University Park Press.

Ratner, N., & Bruner, J. (1978). Games, social exchange, and the acquisition of language. *Journal of Child Language, 5,* 391–402.

Rescorla, L. (1984). Individual differences in early language development and their predictive significance. *Acta Paedologica, Vol. 1,* pp. 97–116.

Rocissano, L., & Yatchmink, Y. (1983). Language skill and interactive patterns in prematurely born toddlers. *Child Development, 54,* 1229–1241.

Roth, P. L. (1985, April). *Temporal characteristics of maternal verbal interaction styles.* Paper presented at the Biennial Meeting of the Society for Research in Child Development, Toronto.

Schaffer, H. R. (1979). Acquiring the concept of dialogue. In M. H. Bornstein & W. Kessen (Eds.), *Psychological development from infancy: Image to intention* (pp. 279–306). Hillsdale, NJ: Lawrence Erlbaum Associates.

Schaffer, H. R., Collis, G., & Parsons, G. (1977). Vocal interchange and visual regard in verbal and pre-verbal children. In H. R. Schaffer (Ed.), *Studies in mother-infant interaction* (pp. 291–324). London: Academic Press.

Schumaker, J. B. (1976). *Mothers' expansions: Their characteristics and effects on child language.* Unpublished doctoral dissertation, University of Kansas, Lawrence.

Shipley, E., Smith, C., & Gleitman, L. (1969). A study on the acquisition of language: Free responses to commands. *Language, 45,* 322–342.

Snow, C. (1972). Mothers' speech to children learning language. *Child Development, 43,* 549–565.

Snow, C. (1977). Mothers' speech research: From input to interaction. In C. E. Snow & C. A. Ferguson (Eds.), *Talking to children: Language input and acquisition* (pp. 31–50). Cambridge, England: Cambridge University Press.

Snow, C. E., Arlman-Rupp, R., Hassing, Y., Jobse, J., Joosten, J., & Vorster, J. (1976). Mothers' speech in three social classes. *Journal of Psycholinguistic Research, 5,* 1–20.

Sroufe, A. L. (1979). Socioemotional development. In J. D. Osofsky (Ed.), *Handbook of infant development* (pp. 462–516). New York: Wiley.

Stella-Prorok, E. M. (1983). Mother-child language in the natural environment. In K. Nelson (Ed.), *Children's language, Vol. 4* (pp. 187–230). New York: Gardner Press.

Stern, D. N. (1974). Mother and infant at play: Dyadic interaction involving facial, vocal, and gaze behavior. In M. Lewis & L. A. Rosenblum (Eds.), *The effect of the infant on its caregiver* (pp. 187–214). New York: Wiley.

Stern, D. N. (1977). *The first relationship: Infant and mother.* Cambridge, MA: Harvard University Press.

Stern, D. N., & Gibbon, J. (1979). Temporal expectancies of social behaviors in mother infant play. In E. Thoman (Ed.), *Origins of the infant's social responsiveness* (pp. 409–429). Hillsdale, NJ: Lawrence Erlbaum Associates.

Ter Vrugt, D., & Pederson, D. R. (1973). The effects of vertical rocking frequencies on the arousal level in two-month-old infants. *Child Development, 44,* 205–209.

Todd, G., & Palmer, B. (1968). Social reinforcement of infant babbling. *Child Development, 39,* 591–596.

Tomasello, M., & Mannle, S. (1985). Pragmatics of sibling speech to one-year-olds. *Child Development, 56,* 911–917.

Tomasello, M., & Todd, J. (1983). Joint attention and lexical acquisition style. *First Language, 4,* 197–212.

Treisman, M. (1963). Temporal discrimination and the indifference interval: Implications for a model of the "internal clock." *Psychological Monographs, 77,* no. 13.

Tulkin, S., & Kagan, J. (1972). Mother-child interaction in the first year of life. *Child Development, 43,* 31.

Watson, J. S. (1972). Smiling, cooing, and "The Game." *Merrill-Palmer Quarterly, 18,* 323–339.

Watson, J. S. (1979). Perception of contingency as a determinant of social responsiveness. In E. Thoman (Ed.), *Origins of the infant's social responsiveness* (pp. 33–64). Hillsdale, NJ: Lawrence Erlbaum Associates.

Whitehurst, G. J., Kedesdy, J., & White, T. G. (1982). A functional analysis of meaning. In S. Kuczaj, II (Ed.), *Language development: Syntax and semantics, Vol. 1* (pp. 397–427). Hillsdale, NJ: Lawrence Erlbaum Associates.

Wolff, P. H. (1968). The serial organization of sucking in the young infant. *Pediatrics, 42,* 943–956.

Woodrow, H. (1934). The temporal indifference interval determined by the method of mean error. *Journal of Experimental Psychology, 17,* 167–188.

7

The Phonology of Parent-Child Speech

Nan Bernstein-Ratner
The University of Maryland at College Park

Researchers in child language have long recognized that one of the most formidable challenges which confronts the infant language learner is the isolation of individual words and morphemes within the fluid, concatenated speech stream he or she hears (cf. the debate between Braine (1963) and Bever, Fodor, & Weksel (1965)). Though Brown, Cazden, and Bellugi-Klima (1968) suggested that children learn to correctly segment language data by identifying recurrent forms, the power of such an explanation is weakened by our growing awareness of the extreme imprecision and variability with which words are produced in conversational speech. That is, recurrent lexical forms in the language are not produced with invariant phonetic characteristics, yet variants such as those seen in the utterances "What are you doing?", "Whacha doin'?", "Whadaya doing?", and "Whaya doing?" are easily classified by adult listeners as instances of the same words (Cole & Jakimik, 1980, p. 137). As this example shows, varying cues to word boundaries, articulatory undershoot of intended targets, and the utilization of optional phonological rules operate freely within conversation to vary the acoustic realization of words.

In fact, experimental results suggest that words embedded in conversational speech are so degraded by such processes that, presented in isolation and devoid of context, they cannot reliably be identified by listeners (Pollack & Pickett, 1963, 1964). Rather, competent adults must rely upon the insights provided by their knowledge of the language's syntax and lexicon to impose meaning on the speech signal. Cole and Jakimik (1980) suggest specific strategies for decoding speech input:

(1) . . . words are recognized by the interaction of sound and knowledge; (2) . . . speech is processed . . . word by word; (3) . . . each word's recognition (both) locates the onset of the . . . (next) word; and provides syntactic and semantic constraints that are used to recognize (it) . . . and (4) . . . a word is recognized when . . . analysis of its acoustic structure eliminates all candidates but one. (p. 134)

Although this model may account for adult speech understanding (and impose important constraints on machine speech recognition), it is, at some level, a theory of competent functioning which poses problems for accounts of language learning. That is, if speech is understood by resort to linguistic knowledge of possible syntactic, lexical, and phonological candidates, then naive listeners should be quite handicapped in their ability to decode spoken language. By the same analysis, if the language-learning infant cannot successfully segment and decode large amounts of the input to which he or she is exposed, his or her ability to make progress in language learning and use linguistic insight to resolve future ambiguous signals is reduced.

Most would agree that very young children probably do not attend to or comprehend all aspects of the input signal. However, their relatively rapid success in identifying and acquiring words and morphemes can be viewed as somewhat surprising if estimates of the relative unintelligibility of conversational speech are taken as accurate. Pollack and Pickett estimated that as much as half of all words embedded in conversational speech are not decodable without resort to linguistic and extra-linguistic hypotheses.

The fact that children may demonstrate language-learning patterns which suggest that they "pay particular attention" to certain types of linguistic units, or certain portions of words or utterances, has, in the past, been linked to the possibility that such segments may be more acoustically salient to the child than others. For instance, Slobin (1973) cites evidence on the existence of final-syllable lengthening across languages to support a rational basis for the operating principle "pay attention to the ends of words," and suggests that "a child will begin to mark a semantic notion earlier if its morphological realization is more salient perceptually" (p. 202).

However, in much the same way that developmental psycholinguists began to suspect that adult conversational syntax should probably not be viewed as the child's data base for computing the grammar of his language, some researchers have recently questioned the wisdom of relying upon either idealized or extrapolated notions of the acoustic characteristics of the spoken signal in attempting to explain the child's acquisition of language. In fact, one might argue that research into the phonological attributes of adult-child speech may greatly enhance our understanding of constraints on infant language-learning and/or constraints on the nature of readily learnable language input.

ACOUSTIC CHARACTERISTICS OF PARENT-CHILD
SPEECH: SOME PRELIMINARY FINDINGS

Within the last 10 years, some researchers have attempted to evaluate the possibility that parent-child input registers are characterized by a more precise articulatory style than that commonly seen in the types of adult-adult interactions studied by Pollack and Pickett (1963, 1964). Investigations have produced conflicting results. A number of researchers have chosen to study Voice-Onset-Time (VOT) characteristics of adult-child speech. VOT is a characteristic which distinguishes between voiced and voiceless phoneme cognates. While stop consonants in words spoken in isolation are usually well delineated in terms of VOT, VOT values for stops in conversational speech are often rather ambiguous. That is, a speaker may produce the /p/ in *pear* with VOT characteristics which are actually appropriate, not to /p/, but to /b/ (Lisker & Abramson, 1967). The adult listener is relatively untroubled by such a "slip": conversational context usually biases an appropriate interpretation of the poorly formed item (Warren & Sherman, 1974). However, because such articulatory imprecision might be presumed to hamper the infant's ability to compute accurate acoustic representations for words, Malsheen (1980), Baran, Laufer, and Daniloff (1977), Kubaska (1982), and Luberoff (1985) all surveyed VOT values in adult-adult and adult-child speech. Malsheen examined five women's speech to six children ranging from preverbal to multiword expressive linguistic capacity; Baran et al.'s subjects were three women who were recorded while speaking to children who were at a stage "which preceded emergence of the child's first meaningful words" (p. 349); Kubaska analyzed the speech of two mothers to ascertain whether VOT characteristics changed after their children had begun to use single words; and Luberoff examined the VOT characteristics of nine women's speech to three children who were preverbal, three children who had begun to use single words, and three children who used 2 to 3-word expressive utterances. While Baran et al. and Kubaska found no differences between VOT characteristics of adult-adult and mother-child speech, Malsheen and Luberoff noted a tendency for some voiceless consonants to be more carefully distinguished from their voiced cognates in mother-child than in adult-adult speech. This tendency was particularly marked when women spoke to children at the 1-word stage in Malsheen's study, and was not limited to careful production of content words, such as object names. Rather, all classes of words appeared to be characterized by more canonical articulation. Interestingly, Baran's dissertation (1979), which followed her subjects until the children *had* begun to produce recognizable words, noted a tendency for VOT in mother-child speech to be characterized by more canonical values at that time. These additional observations do not appear to have been published. Luberoff (1985), while noting maternal clarification of VOT in speech to children, found that it was primarily confined to the speech of women addressing infants who were beginning to use combinatorial language, a some-what later stage than that reported by Malsheen and Baran. Thus, it appears that some mothers make an effort to produce discrete VOT values for English stops when talking to their young children, while demonstrating typically imprecise versions of initial stops in their adult-directed speech.

Cues to postvocalic voicing were examined in Bernstein-Ratner and Luberoff (1984). Mother-child speech was found to significantly exaggerate the vowel duration characteristics which typically signal the presence of voiced final conso-nants in adult-adult conversation. This is an interesting phenomenon, because final stops are often checked (unreleased) or glottalized in running speech. Many mothers appear to "compensate" for this fact by exaggerating secondary cues to the nature of the underarticulated consonant. The fact that some normal and some misarticulating children produce words with similar characteristics (final conso-nant deletion and exaggerated vowel length alternation) may suggest that this maternal habit can lead children to compute inaccurate representations of items in the language.

Vowel articulation characteristics of mother-child speech have also been stud-ied. Vowels in conversational adult speech are often quite ambiguous in their formant frequency characteristics. In a fashion similar to that illustrated earlier, the intended target is produced with vowel formants appropriate to an entirely different lexical item in the language (perhaps /pir/ (*peer*) for /per/ (*pear*)). Again, while such behaviors do not trouble adults, they may be interpreted as substantial stumbling blocks to the naive learner's attempts to process the lan-guage. Bernstein-Ratner (1984a) recorded nine mothers speaking to their chil-dren and an adult listener. Children in the study ranged in language ability from preverbal to expressive multiword utterances. Overall, vowels were not articu-lated very differently when mothers spoke to adults or preverbal children. Vowels addressed to holophrastic children were somewhat more canonical in formant frequency characteristics, and vowels addressed to children who were just beginning to produce expressive multiword utterances were quite carefully delineated. As in the Malsheen investigation, vowels appeared to be clarified in both content and function words addressed to children. It should also be noted that the increased accuracy in achieving vowel targets was not merely artifactual of the slow rate often observed when adults speak to children. Rather, mothers appeared to be able to produce clear and unambiguous vowels in speech to children without increasing segmental length (Bernstein-Ratner, 1985).

Two studies, however, have suggested that parent-child speech is even *less* carefully articulated than adult-adult speech. Shockey & Bond (1980) examined the incidence of phonological rules such as palatalization (did you → /dɪdʒu/), dental deletion (want it → /wan ɪt/), /ð/ deletion (throw them → θrou ṃ/), and substitution of /s/ for /ts/ (that's nice → /ðæs nais/) in speech of eight British mothers conversing with their children and with an adult. They discovered that all four rules had a higher incidence in the speech of mothers to children than in

A-A speech, despite the fact that usage of such optional rules distorts the citation forms of words. The authors did not specify the ages or language abilities of the children in their study. Bernstein-Ratner (1984b) applied their protocol to data from her earlier (1984a) study; the American mothers demonstrated almost completely inverse behaviors. The latter group of women had significantly reduced incidences of all rules save palatalization when speaking to their children. Possible reasons for such directly conflicting findings are discussed later in this paper.

Recently, Gurman Bard, and Anderson (1983) also questioned whether parent-child speech was phonetically clarified. Their study examined the relative intelligibility of parent-child speech when compared to adult-adult speech. Their relatively surprising conclusion was that, even when matched words were compared across the two addressee conditions, adult-child speech was significantly *less* intelligible than was A-A speech, as measured by correct identification of excerpted words.

It is my contention that the parent-child, or babytalk, register *does* possess properties which make it acoustically easier to process than adult-adult conversational speech. Further, evidence to the contrary, such as that advanced by Baran et al., Shockey and Bond, and Gurman Bard and Anderson, can be accomodated within a view of the parent-child register which recognizes the child listener's linguistic abilities in prompting particular registral modifications. Additionally, descriptions of parent-child registers very different from those seen in Western societies can also be taken as support for a stage at which adults seek to make phonological input more easily processable by infants.

I shall propose some hypothetical strategies which govern the way in which adults address young language-learning children. By strategy, I do not mean to imply conscious behavior; our interviews with study parents would seem to indicate that adults are unaware of particular speech modifications they employ when conversing with their children. I view these strategies as empirically testable hypotheses about the general nature of input language to language-learning children, and believe that evaluation of such hypotheses can contribute to our understanding of the relative contributions of the child's innate strategies and the verbal environment to the acquisition of linguistic competence.

HOW TO TALK TO CHILDREN: SOME POSSIBLE STRATEGIES

Strategy 1: Make Phonological Modifications Responsive to Children's Linguistic Abilities

Evaluation of the small amounts of research literature currently available should make us suspect that, if phonological modifications are to be made in a caretaker register, they will not be made at all stages of child language learning. Rather, the literature should encourage the belief that an adult strategy is to clarify the acoustic signal primarily to children at the 1- and 2-word stages of language learning. Both of these are relatively early stages in the child's acquisition of language.

In the Malsheen, Luberoff, and Bernstein-Ratner studies, the children were fairly young and utilizing single words or very short combinatorial utterances when their mothers' speech underwent relative phonetic clarification (VOT delineation. vowel modification, decreased phonological rule usage). Baran's study children did not receive clarified VOT values when they were prelinguistic (Baran, Laufer, & Daniloff, 1977), but did when they had begun to produce expressive 1-word utterances (Baran, 1979). Both Shockey and Bond, and Gurman Bard and Anderson, who found no evidence of parental speech clarifications, utilized a rather mature sample of child addressees, (2–4 years, and 1;10–3;0, respectively), and neither specified the children's linguistic maturity.

Such data imply that phonetic modifications in input language may occur within a very short and finite time frame. That they do not occur before the child has begun to speak, and that they do not persist after the child has demonstrated the capacity to produce 3- to 4-word utterances is not necessarily surprising. One might hypothesize that children can profit best from clarified input when they are beginning to form notions of what constitute the minimal units of language. It is also interesting to note that in both the Malsheen and Bernstein-Ratner studies, speech was phonetically clarified across word classes. In fact, in the Bernstein-Ratner study (1984a), it was principally the clarification of vowels in function words such as pronouns, auxiliaries, deictics, and prepositions which contributed to the overall picture of clarified speech observed when mothers spoke to children at the 2- to 3-word stage. This was viewed as interesting in light of such children's emerging awareness and inclusion of such function words in their own expressive speech.

While the data from Western societies suggest that parents are most likely to clarify input to children at these early stages, it is probable that societal views of children's language competence could affect the timing of such modifications. For instance, the Kaluli (Schieffelin, 1979) do not believe children capable of speech until they have begun to use the Kaluli words for *breast* and *mother,* regardless of any other recognizable words the child may have begun to use. One can hypothesize that any adult attempts to modify speech input in this society (an as-yet unverified phenomenon) would be flavored by this differing view of what constitutes the child's progress in acquiring language.

Strategy 2: Modify Phonology for Relatively Short Periods of Time; Progressively Increase the Degree to Which Input Strings Resemble Adult-Addressed Phonological Tendencies

The findings of the studies discussed thus far should also prompt the hypothesis that any phonological modifications made by adults when speaking to children should decline rapidly to levels and styles commensurate with normal adult-adult speech, as the children's linguistic abilities mature.

Such a notion is premised on concern for the developing child's acquisition of speech processing abilities. Failure for phonological modifications in the input signal to fade should result in the child's inability to make rapid progress in learning to process normal conversational speech. It is also the case that, as children become more linguistically proficient, the nature of the syntax to which they are exposed becomes lengthier and more complex. Such structural modifications should make phonological clarification of the individual elements in the message more difficult.

Strategy 3: Expose the Child to Phonological Variability Through Repetitive, Varying Realizations of Words and Phrases

Additional analysis of reports of phonological modification in adult-child speech should make us suspicious of the need for phonological modifications to be uniform or all-pervasive. Statistical trends, not absolute strategies, are reported. Thus, it is probable that phonologically clarified elements alternate with less canonical versions of words to acquaint children with the acceptable variability in pronunciation of lexical units. Two well-noted features of the Western parent-child register would appear to contribute to the child's ability to segment words out of running input speech, and to store acceptable phonetic variants of words.

The first of these is the tendency for Western parents to embed certain lexical items in repetitive carrier phrases (Peters, 1982), such as the following: "Look, a *ball*," or "Say *ball*," or "Gimme the *ball*." Use of repetitive sentence frames may be viewed as one vehicle for the child's discovery of word boundaries, since the novel information is readily segmented out of familiar routines in such cases. Once the child has identified the lexical item *ball* out of such frames, it may be easier for him to recognize the word in more complex and unfamiliar contexts.

In addition to repetitive frames or carrier phrases, Western parents also appear to systematically alternate phonological forms in speech to children. In a study of phonological rule usage in mother-child speech (Bernstein-Ratner, 1984b), I observed, for example, that a phrase such as /putʃyɔrhænd/, on which a palatalization rule had operated to vary the articulation of /t/ and /y/ from their possible realizations in the phrase "You put" (/y/, /t/) to /tʃy/, would be followed, often directly, by the unpalatalized command, "Put your hand in there." Alternation of phonological rule-distorted and canonical forms was seen for all rule environments and for all mothers observed. The child's failure to respond to adult conversation often appeared to prompt the use of more canonical phonological formats by the adult. Conversely, it was also the case that strings of repetitive questions or commands often started out as rather carefully articulated versions, but soon "deteriorated" as the adult engaged in repetitive attempts to

get the child to respond. The following example is illustrative of such alterna-
tions:

(numbers refer to transcript lines):

To Cindy 1–5:	What's your name, Cindy?'' (absence of palatalization)	Cindy does not respond
1–12:	What's *your* name?'' (no palatalization)	No response
1–13:	"What's your /wʌtʃyɚ/ name?''	/tzi mi/
1–97:	Look at the dragon! oops! /gatʃya/! He's /gatʃya/. He's got you. He's got you.'' (absence of palatization)	(Bernstein-Ratner, 1984b, p. 253)

Stoel-Gammon (1984) also reports such behaviors on the part of mothers speaking to young children.

Is there a possible tradeoff between articulatory precision in the input, the
lexical tendencies of parents, and the linguistic abilities of young children? At
some level it can be argued that adult-child speech can very easily be *less* well-
articulated than adult-adult speech without sacrificing the child's comprehension. Because we do, in fact, identify words by use of phonological, lexical, and
syntactic knowledge, and because the child has relatively fewer possible candidates to fit to particular phonetic strings, he may well be somewhat more tolerant
of deformed input than are experimentally manipulated adults. After all, an adult
who hears the phonetic string /mæ/ may evaluate the hypotheses *man, map, mat,
mad,* etc.; the child may only, given his lexicon, hypothesize that he heard *man.*
William Safire's (1980) account of children who recite "I led the pidegeons to
the flag," and Marilyn Shatz's anecdote during the Third IASCL Conference's
keynote address of her daughter's query during a fairy-tale reading, "What's
supona mean?'' provide evidence of occasional spurious conclusions reached
from limited available data. Thus, models of input language which incorporate
stages of phonetic clarification should only need to posit that adults are likely to
clarify relatively *new* lexical or grammatical elements, or elements which the
child has either failed to attend to, or actively misunderstood.

Strategy 4: Clarify Phonological Strings Which Carry
New Linguistic Information

The Malsheen, Bernstein-Ratner, and Luberoff findings of clarification primarily
to children just acquiring basic lexical and syntactic skills are suggestive of
limited parental clarification of new lexical and grammatical forms; arguably,
Shockey and Bond, and Gurman Bard and Anderson's children were too ad-

vanced to present their parents with the challenge of clarifying basic vocabulary and sentence structure. Additionally, the finding that function word articulation was improved in speech to children just beginning to acquire syntactic knowledge (Bernstein-Ratner, 1984a), but not to children incapable of producing more than single word utterances, is supportive of such a view of parent-child speech.

What constitutes a new lexical or grammatical element? One possible way of considering this issue is to examine the effect of conversational redundancy on the way in which parents articulate words to children. That is, one might say that a given vocabulary item can be considered "new" for an 18-month-old child when it constitutes the first mention in the current conversation between the child and the adult. That is, when child and parent engage in block play, and the adult initially names or calls attention to the blocks, one may presume either that the parent is supplying a new name for a concept, or reminding the child of the name for these particular toys. However, as they continue to play with the blocks, the label becomes "old information" for the child. To what extent will the adult modify either the first or successive mention of a word such as *block?*

One researcher has examined this question in the speech and play behaviors of nine mother-child dyads (Luberoff, 1985). Parent-child speech is typically characterized by a rather small type-token ratio and a high degree of lexical redundancy. It is already known that there is a tradeoff between articulatory effort and the predictability of a message in speech shared between adults (Lieberman, 1970); when repetition or context play a large role in verbal interaction, articulatory precision suffers. This "redundancy" effect does not appear to be maintained or amplified in conversations between adults and very young children. Using measurement variables such as VOT, preliminary data suggest that one cannot make clear predictions about the acoustic characteristics of successive mentions of a given lexical item. There appears to be a general tendency for voiced initial stops to be less well articulated when mothers repeat words to children; that is, they tend to take on the characteristics of voiceless stops, with increased voicing onset time. This is true regardless of whether one examines the speech behaviors of the mothers as a single group, or separates the mothers into subgroupings of women who clarify VOT to children and mothers who do not. We are currently examining other articulatory parameters of repeated words in adult-child conversation; however, we are finding it likely that simple comparisons between words based solely upon order and frequency of occurence within conversations will be relatively uninformative. Mothers do not emphasize, or focus upon, the same words or even segments within the same word, when repeating phrases to their children. Rather, it becomes apparent that mothers' desires to highlight new information, or to clarify particular items which they want the child to attend to may alter the degree to which they emphasize or carefully articulate given lexical items. One of our mothers, for example, responded to her daughter's labeling of a cat as /ræp/, by saying, "It's not a *rat*, it's a *kitty*," with emphasis on and clear articulation of the words *rat* and *kitty*.

When the child persisted in renaming the picture incorrectly, the mother repeated the same utterance, but instead chose to emphasize the word *not,* with elongation of the vowel and precise, released articulation of the final consonant. When analyzed statistically, the interchange will be uninformative, as an emphasized item in its first presentation is an object of less focus in its second appearance, while another word, not given what the mother feels to be appropriate attention by the child, is now highlighted in the repetition of the phrase.

Adaptation of a taxonomy similar to that employed by Greenfield and Zukow (1978) in their analysis of child language focus may be fruitful in further attempts to analyze the degree to which parents use prosodic and articulatory processes in conveying information to their children during conversational interchanges. One may observe that there is a wider standard deviation in the values for certain variables in adult-child speech than in adult-adult speech. Our research has found much greater variability in VOT and vowel duration in child-addressed speech than in adult-adult conversation. This increase in variability is sometimes almost twice that seen when adults converse with each other. Because we do find overall effects suggestive of articulatory precision when adults speak to their children, this variability leads us to believe that caretakers employ a decision-making rubric not unlike that posited for children by Greenfield and Zukow (1978). That is, given their awareness of the child's processing limitations, adults will *selectively* exaggerate and underarticulate various phonological components of conversational elements. Greenfield and Zukow (1978) did address one aspect of this behavior, when they attempted to correlate parental lexical stress with children's repetitions following such stressed words. Although they argued that *stress* in conversational interchanges did not predict their study children's subsequent verbalizations, this does not mean that adults do not highlight phonological strings for purposes other than elicitation of a given element in the child's speech.

Gurman Bard and Anderson's (1983) finding of relatively unintelligible adult-child speech in their study sample is not necessarily an embarrassment for either models of adult speech to children or accounts of the child's acquisition of the ability to process speech. Given the high degree of redundancy of words and phrases in child-addressed speech, and the high degree of articulatory variability that we have observed, it may well be that sampling it for a word (such as *cat*), and then sampling the adult-adult corpus for its match (where it is probably less common) will yield a version which is underarticulated, or produced with dental deletion in the adult-child sample. In conclusion, the small type-token ratio of adult-child speech, and the tendency of speakers to selectively emphasize certain words and information may predict great *unevenness* in the articulatory description of speech to young children which bears closer and more focused scrutiny.

I would like to address one last strategy which would appear to characterize input language registers. While infants may be able to rely upon recurrent forms and repetitive frames to locate word, phrase, and utterance boundaries for analysis, examination of input register behaviors does not suggest that they are limited to only these mechanisms. Rather, the data suggest that adults do make efforts to *parse* the signal for young children in additional ways.

Strategy 5: Provide the Child with Parsing Cues

Itwouldseemtobedifficultforchildrentofindtheboundariesofwordsespeciallyiftheyd idnotknowmanypossiblewordsofthelanguage.

It is essential not to take language segmentation for granted. The parsing or segmentation of speech by young infants has attracted a great deal of interest lately. Ann Peters (1982) has alluded both to the problems of speech segmentation and hypothetical strategies used by children when faced with concatenated elements in running conversational speech. From the speech scientist's point of view, speech segmentation, either by man or machine, is not a trivial issue. It would appear that, for English, fewer than 40% of word boundaries are acoustically marked in conversational speech (Cole & Jakimik, 1980). Thus, it would seem that the use of isolated words, or of some strategies to delineate words from their phonetic surroundings would be necessary for the child's progression in language analysis. Differential stress, prolongation of segmental durations, and repetitions of specific lexical items following their embedded presentation have all been described in the literature (Blount & Padgug, 1977; Garnica, 1977). Such strategies would help the child to locate the boundaries of new lexical items. Additional cues for English would be a greater incidence in the release of final consonants (noted in Bernstein-Ratner, 1984b), and glottal stopping and the actual insertion of silence between words in utterances, neither of which have as yet been investigated to my knowledge. It is, however, notable that Broen (1972) found utterance boundaries to be more carefully demarcated in adult-child than in adult-adult speech. Additionally, Bernstein-Ratner (1986) found prominant secondary cues to clause termination (such as exaggerated prepausal lengthening) in adult-child speech. Such changes in boundary marking were significant in the speech of mothers addressing children who were on the verge of learning first words, and decreased in an almost perfect linear fashion as the children began to demonstrate that they understood word and phrase boundaries by incorporating appropriate lexical items in their expressive language.

It is interesting to observe an input register such as that seen in Kaluli communities (Schieffelin, 1979), whose adult speakers profess that infants need to be exposed to " 'hard speech' . . . as spoken by adults if they are to learn" (p. 86). Here, segmentation of linguistic units for the child appears to be accomplished at some level by the length of units which children are asked to repeat in ɛlɛma ("say like that") routines. Schieffelin provides examples of conversations between Kaluli mothers and their children, who range between 2- and 2½-years-of-age. In these examples, ɛlɛma appears to be used exclusively in conjunction with single-clause utterances. In cases where the mother asks the child to repeat more than one clause, she suffixes ɛlɛma to *each* of them: e.g., "It's mine, ɛlɛma Is it yours?!ɛlɛma" (p. 97).

Likewise, Pye's (1986) account of -tʃaʔ ("to say") usage among Quiche Mayan-speaking mothers is accompanied by similar examples. Although Pye argues that use of -tʃaʔ increases syntactic complexity, it is perhaps arguable that this affix is not processed as an independent lexical or syntactic unit by the child at all. Rather, it may be viewed as a syntactic boundary marker by the language-learning infant.

There are a number of issues to be considered when evaluating the potential contribution of studies of parental phonology to our understanding of child language acquisition.

First of these is whether any study of input language registral style enlightens our appreciation of the relative contributions of the environment and children's innate abilities to the language acquisition process. While avid argumentation continues to be generated regarding the relative contributions of the data and child strategies to the acquisition of grammar (cf. Wexler & Culicover, 1980), these authors admit that

> There are basic learnability problems in aspects of linguistic competence other than syntax. In phonology, for example, it is impossible to construct a learning context that is analogous to that for syntax. . . . The learner is presented with only superficial phonetic information, on the basis of which he must infer both the underlying phonological representations, and the rules relating them to the phonetic forms. (p. 492)

To this observation, I would add the personal belief that to construct theories of grammatical acquisition on the part of infants, without an account of the child's ability to segment and tolerate variance in the speech signal which carries the syntactic and semantic information, is to premise a theory of acquisition on a precarious foundation.

That a great deal of attention has been devoted to examining and describing infants' apparently innate abilities to discriminate and categorize speech stimuli does not necessarily obviate the need for further examination of the acoustic characteristics of the language to which they are actually exposed. Jusczyk (1981) surveyed well over 100 studies of infant speech perception. He concluded that

> For a child to learn a word and its meaning, he or she must first be able to recognize the word. Ten years ago, there was little comprehension of how the child came to distinguish between different utterances. In the interim, much has been learned about the perceptual abilities that the infant possesses for speech. Our knowledge of these capacities has given us a foothold toward understanding one critical aspect of language acquisition—how the child is able to decode the stream of speech into usable segments. (p. 156)

How great a *foothold* such data provide may be debatable, as MacKain and Stern (1985) have pointed out. That is, it is not necessarily of value to know that infants demonstrate adult-like categorical perception and discrimination of VOT in laboratory settings when study of adult interaction suggests that over *half* (53%) of initial stops in casual conversational contexts are ambiguous (overlap) in their VOT characteristics (Malsheen, 1980). That this degree of overlap can be reduced to approximately 10% when adults address young children would appear to make this perceptual skill on the part of infants of more utilitarian value. The same would seem to hold true for vowels as well as consonants; though infants show good ability to discriminate among them in the lab, researchers such as (Lindblom, 1963) have long recognized that vowel targets are often reduced, undershot, and highly coarticulated in conversational speech. Bernstein (1982) provides graphic illustration of the resulting overlap in formant frequency characteristics, and subsequent phonemic ambiguity which results in adult-adult conversation. The fact that many study infants did *not* receive such degraded vowels makes their ability to categorize and discriminate these speech stimuli useful, rather than confusing to them.

MacKain and Stern (1985) are additionally concerned about the use of laboratory speech perception tasks in appraising the effects of linguistic experience upon infant speech categorization and discrimination. They argue that infants must be aware of *meaningful* phonological contrasts before their performance on such tasks can be attributed to experience with a particular phonological system. I would agree. Researchers desirous of exploring either the innate speech processing abilities of children or the role of experience in shaping infant speech perception need to carefully examine the verbal environment of language-learning infants in order to justify cause-and-effect assertions. It is also interesting to note that parental speech appears to undergo particular changes at around the time that infants are beginning to demonstrate ability to make certain meaningful linguistic contrasts in their expressive language. Thus, it can be argued, as with other dimensions of child language acquisition, that phonological development is highly reciprocal in nature. In this case, the infant's natural abilities to perform certain discrimination tasks may be reinforced and aided by an environment which provides optimal input for generating and testing linguistic hypotheses.

CONCLUSION

There are a number of constraints which limit the gathering and interpretation of data on the acoustic characteristics of input registers. First, we would suggest after evaluating the limited available literature, that phonetic alterations in input language are highly transitory and associated with changes in infant language ability, not age. This is a notion highly congruent with a view of input language in general as responsive to, and fostering of, child language acquisition, not merely children's chronological maturation.

The need for cross-linguistic data in this area is great, and may be difficult to obtain. That is, for societies which present some of the most interesting questions about the nature, role and universality of input language registers because they differ so dramatically from descriptions of Western parent-child registers, data collection which is anthropologically sensitive may impede the ability to perform subsequent acoustic analyses (Bernstein-Ratner & Pye, 1984).

As a final observation, it is interesting to note that studies of modifications made by speakers to older, nonlinguistically proficient listeners, such as second-language learners and the hearing impaired, often show quantifiable evidence of the kinds of phonetic clarification described for adult-child speech (cf. Hatch, 1983; Picheny, 1981). A rather automatic speaker strategy which attempts to aid naive listeners in parsing and identifying units in the speech input appears to be part of what we might describe as capable language-users' linguistic competence. As such, it would appear that analysis of the nature and scope of phonological modifications made in speech to limited language processors, and their possible effects or noneffects (Fletcher, 1984) merit continued evaluation.

REFERENCES

Baran, J. (1979). *The mutual regulation of mother-child phonological behavior*. Unpublished doctoral dissertation, Purdue University, West Lafayette, Indiana.

Baran, J., Laufer, M. & Daniloff, R. (1977). Phonological contrastivity in conversation: A comparative study of VOT. *Journal of Phonetics, 5*, 339–350.

Bever, T., Fodor, J. & Weksel, W. (1965). Theoretical notes on the acquisition of syntax: a critique of "Contextual generalization." *Psychological Review, 72*, 467–482.

Bernstein, N. (1982). *An acoustic study of mothers' speech to language-learning children*. Unpublished doctoral dissertation, Boston University.

Bernstein-Ratner, N. (1984a). Patterns of vowel modification in mother-child speech. *Journal of Child Language, 11*(3), 557–578.

Bernstein-Ratner, N. (1984b). Phonological rule usage in mother-child speech. *Journal of Phonetics, 12*(3), 245–254.

Bernstein-Ratner, N. (1986). Durational cues which mark clause boundaries in mother-child speech. *Journal of Phonetics, 14*(2), 303–309.

Bernstein-Ratner, N. & Luberoff, A. (1984). Cues to post-vocalic voicing in mother-child speech. *Journal of Phonetics, 12*(3), 285–289.

Bernstein-Ratner, N., & Pye, C. (1984). Higher pitch in BT is *not* universal: Acoustic evidence from Quiche Mayan. *Journal of Child Language, 11*(3), 515–522.

Blount, B. & Padgug, E. (1977). Prosodic, paralinguistic and interactional features of parent-child speech: English and Spanish. *Journal of Child Language, 4*, 67–86.

Braine, M. (1963). On learning the grammatical order of words. *Psychological Review, 70*, 323–348.

Broen, P. (1972). *The verbal environment of the language-learning child*. ASHA Monographs.

Brown, R., Cazden, C., & Bellugi-Klima, U. (1968). The child's grammar from I to III. In J. Hill

(Ed.), *Minnesota symposia on child development, Volume 2* pp. 28–73). Minneapolis: University of Minnesota Press.

Cole, R. & Jakimik, J. (1980). A model of speech perception. In R. Cole (Ed.), *Perception and production of fluent speech*. Hillsdale, NJ: Lawrence Erlbaum Associates.

Fletcher, P. (1984). Clarification and the child's learning of grammar. *Language Sciences, 6*(1), 93–106.

Garnica, O. (1977). Some prosodic and paralinguistic features of speech to young children. In C. Snow & C. Ferguson (Eds.), *Talking to children: language input and acquisition* (pp. 63–88). Cambridge, England: Cambridge University Press.

Greenfield, P., & Zukow, P. (1978). Why do children say what they say when they say it:? An experimental approach to the psychogenesis of presupposition. In K. Nelson (Ed.), *Children's Language, Volume 1* (pp. 287–336), New York: Gardner Press.

Gurman Bard, E., & Anderson, A. (1983). The unintelligibility of speech to children. *Journal of Child Language, 10*(2), 265–292.

Hatch, E. (1983). *Psycholinguistics: a second language perspective*. Rowley, MA: Newbury House Publishers.

Jusczyk, P. (1981). Infant speech perception: a critical appraisal. In P. Eimas & J. Miller (Eds.), *Perspectives on the study of speech*. Hillsdale, NJ: Lawrence Erlbaum Associates.

Kubaska, C. (1982). *A longitudinal study of mothers' speech characteristics*. Unpublished doctoral dissertation, Brown University.

Lieberman, P. (1970). *Intonation, perception and language*. Cambridge, MA: MIT Press.

Lindblom, B. (1963). Spectrographic study of vowel reduction. *Journal of the Acoustical Society of America, 35,* 1773–1781.

Lisker, L., & Abramson, A. (1967). Some effects of context on voice-onset time in English stops. *Language and Speech, 10,* 1–28.

Luberoff, A. (1985). *VOT distinctions in mother-child speech*. Unpublished master's thesis, University of Maryland at College Park.

MacKain, K., & Stern, D. (1985). The concept of experience in speech development. In K. Nelson (Ed.) *Children's Language, Volume 5* (pp. 1–33). Hillsdale, NJ: Lawrence Erlbaum Associates.

Malsheen, B. (1980). Two hypotheses for phonetic clarification in the speech of mothers to children. In G. Yeni-Komshian, J. Kavanagh, & C. Ferguson (Eds.), *Child phonology, Volume 2*. New York: Academic Press.

Peters, A. (1982). *The units of language acquisition*. Cambridge, England: Cambridge University Press.

Picheny, M. (1981). Speaking clearly for the hard of hearing. Unpublished doctoral dissertation, MIT.

Pollack, I., & Pickett, J. M. (1963). The intelligibility of excerpts from conversational speech. *Language and Speech, 6,* 165–171.

Pollack, I., & Pickett, J. M. (1964). The intelligibility of excerpts from conversational speech: auditory vs. structural context. *Journal of Verbal Learning and Verbal Behavior. 3,* 79–84.

Pye, C. (1986). Quiche Mayan speech to children. *Journal of Child Language, 13*(1), 85–100.

Safire, W. (1980). *On language*. New York: Times Books.

Schieffelin, B. (1979). Getting it together: An ethnographic approach to the study of the development of communicative competence. In E. Ochs & B. Schieffelin (Eds.) *Developmental pragmatics*. Orlando, FL: Academic Press.

Shockey, L., & Bond, Z. (1980). Phonological processes in speech addressed to children. *Phonetica, 37,* 267–274.

Slobin, D. (1973). Cognitive prerequisites for the development of grammar. In C. Ferguson & D. Slobin (Eds.), *Studies of Child language development* (pp. 175–208). New York: Holt, Rinehart & Winston.

Stoel-Gammon, C. (1984). Phonological variability in mother-child speech. *Phonetica, 48,* 208–214.

Warren, R., & Sherman, G. (1974). Phonemic restorations based on subsequent context. *Perception & Psychophysics, 16*(1), 150–156.

Wexler, K., & Culicover, P. (1980). *Formal principles of language acquisition.* Cambridge, MA: MIT Press.

8 A Comparison of Initial Consonant Acquisition in English and Quiché

Clifton Pye
University of Kansas

David Ingram
Helen List
The University of British Columbia

Recent work on phonological development has emphasized individual variation and downplayed the effect of phonological organization in children's language. Jakobson's (1941/1968) theory, in particular, has been criticized for failing to capture the differences between children acquiring the same language (Ferguson & Farwell, 1975; Macken & Ferguson, 1983; Menn, 1983) and different language (Macken, 1980). To the extent that some constancies may remain across children, they are usually attributed to "universal phonetic tendencies which result from the physiology of the human vocal tract and central nervous system" (Ferguson & Farwell, 1975, p. 437). In this paper, we present data from the phonological development of five Quiché Mayan children which demonstrates the effect of internal phonological organization on phonological development. This is done through a comparison of initial consonant acquisition in Quiché with known results from English. The results show consistent differences that cannot be accounted for by ease of articulation. We present a version of Jakobson's theory which retains a universalist perspective at an abstract level, but which allows for interlinguistic and intralinguistic variations. Our model has an advantage over previous interpretations of Jakobson's theory and current cognitive models in that it makes specific predictions about the course of children's phonological development.

QUICHÉ INITIAL CONSONANTS

Quiché is a Mayan language spoken by a half-million people in the western highland region of Guatemala. It has an initial consonant inventory shown in Table 8.1. The plain stops /p t k q/ are unaspirated before vowels and aspirated

TABLE 8.1
The Word-Initial Consonants of Adult Quiché

	Bilabial	Alveolar		Palatal	Velar	Uvular	Glottal
Plosives	p	t	ts	tʃ	k	q	?
Ejectives	b'	t'	ts'	tʃ'	k'	q'	
Fricatives		s		ʃ	x		
Nasals	m	n					
Liquids		r,l					
Glides	w			j			

elsewhere. The affricates /ts tʃ/ are also produced with noncontrastive aspiration. The apostrophe (') indicates glottalization for the voiceless obstruents. All of the glottalized sounds except /b'/ are ejectives in the dialect studied. The /b'/ is a voiced implosive in syllable-initial position and a voiced unreleased stop in syllable-final position. The /r/ is a voiced apicoalveolar trill in word-initial position and a voiced apicoalveolar flap intervocalically. /l/ is a voiced apicodental lateral continuant. /r l w j/ are devoiced in word-final position and before consonants. Quiché has five vowels: /a/, /e/, /i/, /o/, /u/ and two degrees of vowel length: long and short (see Norman, 1976, and Mondloch, 1978 for further discussion of Quiché phonology).

METHOD

Subjects and Data. The Quiché data were collected during a longitudinal field study by the first author (Pye, 1980). Five children, aged 1;7 to 3;0, were visited in their homes over a 9-month period, approximately every 2 weeks, for a 1-hour session. Table 8.2 provides details of the ages and vocabulary. Quiché was the predominant language in all the households, although a few Spanish words occasionally appear in the children's speech. The tapes were transcribed phonemically with the help of two native Quiché speakers. A more narrow phonetic transcription was used to capture the children's sounds that were outside the adult Quiché phonology.

TABLE 8.2
Names, Ages, Sample Sizes, and Criterions of Frequency for Five Quiché Children

Child	Age	Number of Lexical Types	Criterion of Frequency		
			Marginal	Used	Frequent
A Tu:n	1;7	23	1	2,3	4+
A Li:n	2;0	85	2	3-5	6+
Al Tiya:n	2;1	52	1	2,3	4+
Al Cha:y	2;9	115	3,4	5-9	10+
A Carlos	3;0	68	2	3-5	6+

The first Quiché subject, A Tu:n, was an only son. We used his second language sample which contains 23 distinct words or lexical types. (Here we follow the terminology in Ingram (1981) where distinct words of the adult language are referred to as lexical types.) The second subject, A Li:n, was the oldest son of a neighboring family. He had a younger sister, but spent most of his time with his aunts (aged 7 and 12) and grandmother. A Li:n's language sample contains 85 lexical types. Al Tiya:n, our third subject, was the youngest daughter of a family of five children. She spent most of her time with an older sister (aged 4) and her mother. Al Tiya:n's language sample contains 52 monosyllabic lexical items. Al Cha:y was the youngest daughter of a family of four children. Her sample is based on 115 monosyllabic lexical types. Our fifth Quiché subject, A Carlos, was the first son in his family. Another baby, a girl, arrived during the study. A Carlos' family lived with his grandparents throughout most of the study, and he spent most of his time in the company of his 10-year-old cousin. A Carlos' sample contains 68 monosyllabic lexical items.

Analysis.   The resulting samples were subjected to a phonetic analysis described in Ingram (1981), which requires sounds to occur at a minimum frequency before being considered part of the child's phonetic inventory. This results in a conservative estimate of the child's phonology, but eliminates many of the arbitrary decisions about the category to which a particular segment belongs.

The sounds that a child uses are divided into three categories—Marginal, Used, or Frequent. These three categories are determined by comparing the frequency in which a sound occurs against a Criterion of Frequency (CF). The CF for any sample is determined by dividing the sample size by 25. This is done with the arbitrary assumption that a sound, if acquired, should occur at least once in every 25 words. For example, a sample size of 100 lexical types would have a CF of 4. This measure means that an ''acquired'' sound should occur in at least four words. Marginal sounds are ones which do not meet the CF, but occur at least one-half the CF. In this example, this would be sounds which occur 2 or 3 times. Used sounds are ones which meet the CF. Frequent sounds are ones that occur twice the CF, or in this example, at least 8 times. (See Ingram, 1981, for a discussion of the rationale for this methodology, and Ingram, 1983, for a discussion of its adaptation for crosslinguistic use.)

RESULTS AND DISCUSSION

Table 8.3 presents the Marginal, Used, and Frequent initial consonants for each of the five Quiché subjects. Marginal sounds are enclosed in parentheses, while Frequent sounds are marked with an asterisk for each time the sound doubles the CF. Used sounds are given without any notation. If the inventories are combined by taking those sounds appearing in the samples of at least four subjects, the result is the composite shown at the right of Table 8.3.

TABLE 8.3
Phonetic Inventories of Five Quiché Children

Quiché Consonants		A Tu:n	A Li:n	Al Tiya:n	Al Cha:y	A Carlos	Composite
				Children			
Nasals	/m/		m		m	(m)	(m)
	/n/	n	n**	n*	n	n	n
Stops	/p/	(p)	p	p	p*	(p)	p
	/t/		t	t*	t	t*	t
	/ts/					(t̪s)	
	/tʃ/	tʃ	tʃ*	tʃ	tʃ*	tʃ*	tʃ*
	/k/	(k)	k*	k*	k	k	k
Glottal	/q/		q				
Stops	/ʔ/	ʔ**	ʔ**	ʔ***	ʔ*	ʔ*	ʔ*
	/bʼ/		(bʼ)	(bʼ)		(bʼ)	(bʼ)
	/tʼ/						
	/tsʼ/						
	/tʃʼ/						
	/kʼ/					kʼ	
	/qʼ/						
Fricatives							
	/s/					s*	
	/ʃ/				ʃ*	(ʃ)	
	/x/		x*	x*	x	x*	x*
Liquid	/l/	l*	l**	l***	l***	l	l*
	/r/						
Glides	/w/	w*	w*	w**	w*	w	w*
	/j/		(j)				

The initial consonant inventories show a remarkable consistency, given their origin in samples of the children's spontaneous speech. There also seem to be well-defined cross-sectional trends in the acquisition orders, especially among the fricatives. There are a few anomalies, e.g., A Li:n's early [q] and [j] and A Carlos' marginal [p]. Overall, these data indicate that this analytic procedure produces a reasonable picture of the children's phonetic inventories. The composite appears to be the basic starter set of initial consonants for Quiché children.

Ingram (1981), using a comparable procedure for English, found a basic inventory for English-speaking children shown in Table 8.4. The subjects were

TABLE 8.4
Average Initial Consonant Inventory for Children Acquiring English[a]

	Labial	Alveolar	Velar	Glottal
Voiceless Stops	p	t	k	
Voiced Stops	b	d	(g)	
Nasals	(m)	n		
Fricatives	(f)	(s)		h
Glides	w			

[a]Based on Ingram (1981)

15 normally developing children between the ages of 1;5 and 2;2. Their lexicons contained between 30 and 333 lexical types.

These data allow a comparison with the results found for the five Quiché subjects. Both English and Quiché-speaking children show an early three-place voiceless stop series. Both have an early dental nasal and bilabial glide. Since Quiché lacks a voiced stop series, it is not too surprising that it does not appear in the children's speech. Quiché does have two Baby Talk items which begin with a /d/ and which the children acquire early, e.g., A Tu:n by 1;10. The Quiché children, however, tended to delete /d/ from Spanish words or substitute an /l/ in its place. Macken (1980) found that initial voiced stops were acquired later in Spanish due to their frequent alternation with spirant allophones. The Spanish subjects, however, substituted a spirant rather than /l/ for the voiced stops in their productions.

The fricative series is one point where the Quiché and English-speaking children look very different. Although the Quiché children did acquire an early /h/, it only occurs in word-final position where it was produced in opposition to the /ʔ/ and /x/. The Quiché children experienced a good deal of difficulty producing /s/, most often substituting /ʃ/ in its place. Al Cha:y produced ten lexical types with /s/ word initially. /ʃ/ was substituted for initial /s/ in seven of them, with /s/ deleted in one, and /s/ correct in two. A Li:n produced four lexical types with initial /s/. The substitutes were /ʃ/ in one and /tʃ/ in another. /s/ was produced correctly in the other two.

Another surprise of the early Quiché phonology is the affricate /tʃ/. Its presence may be a reflection of its heavy use in several Quiché Baby Talk items (e.g., /tʃiʃ/ 'yuck', /tʃuʃ/ 'sit'). A Li:n produced seven of nine lexical types correctly with initial /tʃ/. The two others lost the /tʃ/ due to the process of initial syllable deletion. Al Cha:y produced eight of ten lexical types correctly with initial /tʃ/. One was lost in initial syllable deletion, and the other was deleted. Al Tiya:n produced five of six lexical types correctly, losing one /tʃ/ in initial syllable deletion. It is interesting that the affricate appears in the children's speech before the homorganic fricative /ʃ/.

Finally, the early /l/ in Quiché marks a real difference with English. Al Tiya:n correctly produced all five lexical types with an initial /l/, Al Cha:y correctly produced nine of eleven lexical types, substituting /d/ for /l/ in a Spanish loan and /p/ for /l/ in a Quiché word. A Li:n correctly produced all six of his lexical types beginning with /l/.

John Locke (1983) has proposed another method for comparing phonological acquisition cross-linguistically. His method is based on a division of sounds between repertoire sounds, a "collection of readily available articulations" (p. 83), and nonrepertoire sounds which are the result of articulatory development under environmental pressure. Locke's repertoire sounds include all but one of the sounds in Ingram's basic inventory for English (/m,n,p,t,k,b,d,g,f,h,w,j/). Locke's sound classification reflects a low level phonological universal, but misses important phonetic and structural details. For example, he does not provide evidence that is independent of the children's production data to substantiate the claim that /f/ is a more readily available articulation than /v/. It is impossible to tell from the data that Locke provides whether any of the repertoire sounds being acquired in languages as diverse as Japanese, Russian and Swedish have any phonetic features in common. His method of comparison also overemphasizes the mere presence of repertoire sounds at the expense of details of the variation among the repertoire sounds and the significance of nonrepertoire sounds (such as the early Italian /tʃ/, Russian /z/, and Swedish /v/). Even by Locke's standards, however, the composite Quiché phonology remains peculiar. Only five (/n,p,t,k,w/) of its nine acquired sounds are repertoire while four (/tʃ,ʔ,x,l/) are not. Thus, the Quiché data would seem to be counterevidence to Locke's early repetoire hypothesis.

The systematic differences between the Quiché and English data challenge other theories of phonological acquisition as well. Current models of phonological development emphasize individual strategies based on "preferences for certain sounds, sound classes, or features . . ." (Ferguson & Farwell, 1975, p. 436; see also Kiparsky & Menn, 1977, p. 75; Locke, 1983). Such preferences are supposed to derive from a combination of articulatory and input factors. Menn (1983, p. 22) cites a combination of "external" factors "such as the frequency and salience of the sound in the speech of others" and "internal" factors such as "the probability of accidentally hitting on an acceptable way to produce it and the salience of the sound in one's own speech." The models emphasize individual strategies in order to explain the observed variation between children acquiring the same language and rely upon articulatory factors to explain the many aspects of phonological acquisition that children have in common. None of these models has attempted to operationalize these factors by measuring the frequency of the sounds in adult speech or the degrees of freedom of children's articulatory organs. Menn (1983, p. 23), for example, subscribes to the view that the probability of producing sounds correctly is physiologically governed.

Ignoring external factors (since they are not specified very clearly in any of the current models), one would expect children acquiring different languages to exhibit similar ranges of physiologically governed sounds. The differences between the early sounds of children learning Quiché and English, especially the early Quiché [tʃ] and [l] contradict this. There is the possibility that the Quiché [tʃ] and [l] are phonetically distinct from their English counterparts and therefore easier to articulate. The only distinction that we are aware of is the tongue placement for the [l]. A physiological model would have to show that the apicodental placement in Quiché was easier to produce than the apicoalveolar placement of the English [l]. It seems that children can produce a wider range of sounds than those that are frequent in English. Locke (p. 46) cites Crelin (personal communication to Locke, October 5, 1981) who states that "as far as the vocal tract anatomy is concerned an infant can make all three of the above sounds [b̪,d, f] when he can make the d-like sound.'' Some other factor must limit children to the sounds which are prevalent in the language they are acquiring.

We believe this factor is the pressure that the adult phonological system exerts on children's phonological development. Children must be specially adapted to search out the phonological contrasts which predominate in a language and attempt to capture those. MacKain and Stern (1985, p. 30) argue that infants must have a strategy that involves ''the discovery of those contrasts that convey differences in meaning.'' Children are, after all, attempting to produce meaningful forms. They are not attempting to hit an identical phonetic target every time they utter a word with the same sound. The way around such a humanly impossible task is to establish phonological categories of sounds and be content hitting targets that are within those categories.

Children must monitor the speech of others for forms with detectable meanings. Once these are found the forms can be stored by reference to their meanings. At this point, the children's lexical system can perform some type of abstraction process in order to subtract all of the variability from the various phonetic renditions given for the same meaning. Some meaningful signals may also be subtracted during this phase, such as plural /-s/ or past tense /-ed/. Such a process could not be carried out without also comparing the forms with different meanings since this vastly simplifies the search for meaningful contrasts. A child's phonological system results from a convergence of these two procedures, one across lexical types and one within each lexical type. The adult phonological system exerts its influence during a child's search across the different lexical types since the more frequent phonological contrasts should be the easiest to find.

Substitution patterns provide the clearest evidence of the effect of an adult system on children's phonological development. Physiologically based models only predict that children will select a substitution at random from similar sounds that are already in their articulatory repertoire (cf. Menn 1983, p. 21). They can not explain why so many children consistently display the same substitution patterns such as fronting, gliding, stopping, and so forth (cf. Ingram, 1974). Natural phonology is an improvement over physiological models in that it at least attempts to explain wide-spread substitution patterns (cf. Stampe, 1969). However, it predicts that all children will exhibit the same substitution patterns regardless of the language they are acquiring. A phonological model predicts that children will make use of the maximal oppositions in the language they are acquiring. This has the corollary that children acquiring the same language should exhibit the same patterns of substitution, whereas children acquiring different languages may show different patterns of substitution for the same sounds.

Some evidence already exists that children acquiring languages other than English will make different types of substitutions. Macken (citing Stoel, 1974) states that "in Spanish, [ð] frequently patterns with the liquids and is substituted for by [l] and in some cases [r]" (Macken, 1980, p. 149). The use of [l] for [ð] may also be common among children acquiring Greek (Hinofotis, 1976; Drachman & Malkouti-Drachman, 1973). Among children acquiring English, the usual substitute for [ð] is [d] or [t] (Macken, 1980).

The Quiché children produced substitution patterns that were very different from those produced by children learning English. The early appearance of [l] in the Quiché children's speech is underlined by its use as a substitute for /r/. This was the most frequent substitution for all the Quiché children. By comparison, English-speaking children frequently change /l/ to [j] and /r/ to [w], while French children prefer to delete an initial /l/ (Ingram, 1979, p. 135). Again, [j] and [w] were present in the Quiché children's speech and presumably available as substitutes. There is even a case in Al Tiya:n's speech of an [l] being used for /j/; /krajon/ "crayon" was produced as /lon/.

The fricatives are strikingly different in the speech of Quiché and English-speaking children. The /tʃ/ was always present as [tʃ] in the Quiché children's speech (with the minor exceptions noted earlier). But /tʃ/ is frequently replaced by a stop (e.g., Smith, 1973) or by another fricative (Ingram, Christensen, Veach, & Webster, 1980) in the speech of children learning English. Both English- and French-speaking children frequently substitute [s] for /ʃ/ (Ingram, 1979; Ingram et al., 1980) while Quiché children may go either way. Al Tiya:n changed /ʃ/ to [s] while A Li:n and Al Cha:y changed /s/ to [ʃ] (a Yucatec Mayan child 3;8 also changed /s/ to [ʃ], Straight, 1976). Again, we would emphasize the fact that English-type substitutions are possible for Quiché children, but typically they chose not to make them. There is some evidence that syllabic processes may have played a role in some of these substitutions, more often determining when a substitution took place rather than what was substituted. We also examined the data for evidence of consonant assimilation and cooccurrence restrictions, but did not find any evidence for these processes.

Given this evidence, we conclude that children exposed to different types of linguistic input, proceed along substantially different paths of phonological development. Ease of articulation seems to play only a partial role in determining the overall developmental route. Individual strategies seem similarly restricted when viewed from a cross-linguistic perspective. We believe the results are best explained by reference to the children's emerging phonological system. Here the emphasis is on system to underline the point that children are not acquiring isolated phonetic segments, but rather a set of systematically related phonological categories. The notion of phonemic opposition plays such a central role in the adult system that it is difficult to see how children could be successful language learners without it. It would also be difficult to construct a learning theory which would rely solely on positive evidence to establish the role of phonemic opposition in the phonology. However, children have to work out the particular system of phonemic oppositions that is relevant to the language they are learning.

Ingram (1983) discusses this notion in relation to Jakobson's theory of phonological development, showing that Jakobson makes certain allowances for the role of the adult surface forms of words. Accordingly, we suggest revising Jakobson by restricting the notion "maximal opposition" to hold just within the particular language the child is acquiring. Children acquiring different languages should exhibit common patterns of phonological development to the extent that the sounds within those languages enter corresponding sets of relationships. One would no longer expect children to follow a single, universal sequence in acquiring the sounds of their language. Their development would, however, remain unified at the more abstract level of maximal opposition within the language.

The early Quiché [tʃ], for example, is quite counter-Jakobsonian under previous interpretations. Jakobson explicitly predicts that affricates will be produced first as homorganic fricatives (1941/1968, p. 55). However, by placing priority on the maximal oppositions within Quiché we would predict the early appearance of [tʃ]. We preserve Jakobson's essential insight regarding the importance of phonemic contrasts by stipulating that the contrasts must be relative to the particular language being acquired. Since /tʃ/ provides a maximal opposition to the other Quiché consonants, children learning Quiché acquire it early.

One can gain a rough measure of the importance of various oppositions within different languages by determining the frequencies with which the different sounds occur. There are certain reservations about the frequency data which need to be explored. First, the average frequency with which a sound appears is fairly uninformative. In English, for example, /z/ is the eleventh most frequent consonant overall, but twenty-fifth most frequent in word-initial position, while /r/ is the fourth most frequent overall, but sixteenth in word-initial position (Mines, Hanson, & Shoup, 1978). We can expect a large difference between word-initial and word-final consonants in children's speech. Second, we need to make allowance for the fact that children's phonology is a reflection of their lexical organization, not just the frequency with which a sound occurs in adult conversations. There is ample room for individual differences to arise from the child's selection of which words or which part of words need to be subjected to phonological analysis (Ferguson & Farwell, 1975; Menn, 1978; Schwartz & Leonard, 1982). The phonological distinctions are most likely worked out from the child's lexicon, not the immediate speech. Thus, the relative frequency of sounds across lexical types, not tokens, is the measure we seek.

Unfortunately, the relative frequency of sounds in children's word types is not readily available from published sources. We made an estimate based on data reported by Moe, Hopkins, and Rush (1982). This provided us with the 500 most frequently used words of 329 children aged 5;10 to 8;4 living in north-central Indiana. We then counted the frequency with which the different consonants occurred in initial position in this lexicon. This second estimate again affects the relative frequencies of the initial consonants. The Mines et al. study (1978) gives /ð/ as the most frequently occurring word-initial consonant, while by our estimate it is fourteenth across word types.

Using this set of procedures, we examined the frequency of the sounds which are common to both Quiché and English in the speech of four Quiché children and the children reported on by Prather, Hedrick, and Kern (1975). For the Quiché subjects, we counted the frequency of the initial consonants in the adult word types the children attempted, not the sounds the children actually produced or the sounds in the adult input. We used the data from Moe et al. (1982) to establish the frequencies of the initial consonants in the speech of children learning English. The results appear in Table 8.5.

It is surprising how close the frequency of the sounds the children attempted is to the order in which they acquired those sounds. The Spearman rank-order correlation between the frequency and acquisition orders in Quiché is .76 (p < .01, one-tailed), and in English .55 (p < .05, one-tailed). The most frequent sounds in both Quiché and English are the sounds which appeared the earliest in the children's speech. The /tʃ/ and /l/ which appeared earlier in Quiché than in English are also much more frequent in Quiché than in English. Equally, the /s/ and /d/ are more frequent in English and appeared earlier in the speech of children learning English. However, there are also certain discrepancies: /r/ occurs with greater frequency in both Quiché and English than its late acquisition would warrant while /n/ and /d/ occur comparatively infrequently in English. The full list of frequency data for all the initial consonants in Quiché and English is also very similar to the children's acquisition orders in the respective languages. In Quiché, for example, the plain stops are much more frequent than their glottalized counterparts, while the back sounds (/tʃ/, /k/ and /x/) are more frequent than the labials and dentals. In English, the labial voiced stop is more frequent than its voiceless counterpart, but /k/ is much more frequent than /g/. The voiceless fricatives are also more frequent than their voiced counterparts with the exception of /ð/.

It might be the case that similarities between the children's phonological acquisition orders and frequency orders are the result of selection constraints operating on the children's lexicons. Some children actively avoid attempting to produce words that have sounds not under their control (Ferguson & Farwell,

TABLE 8.5
Frequency and Acquisition Rank Orders for Initial Consonants Common to Quiché and English

	Sounds												
Language	/tʃ/	/w/	/k/	/p/	/t/	/l/	/n/	/s/	/m/	/r/	/ʃ/	/j/	/d/
Quiché[a]													
frequency	1	2	3	4	5	6	7.5	7.5	9.5	9.5	11	12	13
acquisition	2.5	2.5	5.5	5.5	7.5	2.5	2.5	10	7.5	12.5	9	11	12.5
English[b]													
frequency	13	1	3	6	4	7.5	9.5	2	5	9.5	12	11	7.5
acquisition	12.5	6	4.5	2.5	4.5	10.5	1	7	2.5	10.5	12.5	8.5	8.5

[a] rho = .77, p < .01 (one-tailed)
[b] rho = .55, p < .05 (one-tailed)

1975; Ingram, 1974; Kiparsky & Menn, 1977). This does not present a problem for our analysis since the sounds we chose all occur within the children's productions. Moreover, such selection constraints may only apply to children's early lexicons (Schwartz & Leonard, 1982), while most of the children reported on here have productive vocabularies with more than 50 lexical types. Avoidance phenomena such as this might provide additional evidence for a phonological model if convincing data could be found showing that children acquiring different languages avoided words with different types of sounds. However, in order to be truly convincing such a demonstration would have to show that the children were actively avoiding certain sounds rather than simply responding to the frequency of the sounds in the input (cf. Macken, 1980).

It is necessary to emphasize that frequency data can only provide a rough guide to phonological organization in children since children are developing a set of relations between segments, not the segments per se. The discrepancy we noted earlier involving /r/ may be due to this difference. /r/ may play a less important phonological role in Quiché and English than its frequency suggests. Children do not have the luxury of working out these relations in a single environment at a time, although there is plenty of evidence that some children prefer to concentrate more on the beginnings or ends of words (Branigan, 1976; Menn, 1978). It is all too easy to envision a child working out a pattern of oppositions initially in word-final position and then applying the result to word-initial position, or showing a continuous feedback effect between both positions.

Given the differences in the organization of the adult phonologies of Quiché and English (as partially reflected in relative frequencies of appearance), we can start to see why children learning these languages might begin differently. Children learning English face the task of sorting out the voiced-voiceless distinction. They may apply this distinction the way adults do and produce an initial voiced or voiceless series of stops. Until the opposition is controlled, they may equally have an initial /b/, /d/, /k/ series (Menn, 1978, p. 14). Quiché lacks a voiced-voiceless opposition so children learning it may initially oppose some other category to the voiceless stops, most likely the continuous category (since the Quiché children show an early /w/, /l/, /x/ series). Quiché children appear to incorporate /tʃ/ directly into their stop series, whereas English-speaking children treat it as an affricate and merge it with a stop or fricative. Nasals seem to operate independently of the other dimensions in both languages, although the children seem to prefer a dental nasal. Finally, place appears to play an important role in the children's phonologies. All the Quiché children substituted a homorganic stop for their glottalized counterparts.

REFINING THE PHONOLOGICAL MODEL

We have sketched a phonological model to account for the differences between the phonological development of children learning Quiché and English. The obvious strengths of the model are that it focuses attention on children's attempts to resolve which contrasts are phonemic in the adult language. It predicts the presence of some organization in children's phonologies rather than a random assortment of isolated articulations. The model also predicts that children will attempt to build phonemic contrasts on the basis of maximal opposition within the language. It follows that children learning the same language should follow roughly similar paths of phonological development. However, children learning different languages should show similarities in their phonological development only to the extent that segments in the languages possess similar sets of oppositions. This model explains why children learning the same language exhibit similar substitution patterns while children learning different languages may produce very different substitutions for the same sounds.

The model is compatible with evidence commonly cited in favor of *cognitive* explanations of phonological development. First, there is the variation between children acquiring the same phonological systems. The extent of variation is partly a reflection of the methods used to document children's phonologies. Thus, the "phone trees" of Ferguson & Farwell (1975) exaggerate the amount of phonetic variation by grouping together all the sounds a child might have used to produce a set of words. Children who happen to produce the same word once or twice with different sounds would have different phone trees. Still, some variation exists in the way children acquire the sounds of a particular language. Cognitive models explain this variation by assuming that children may discover different aspects of the adult phonological system at different stages of development. There is no reason to deny the role of discovery in a phonological model or any reason to think that all the children acquiring some language would discover its set of oppositions in exactly the same sequence. We predict, instead, that there will be limits to the amount of variation that children display. These limits are set by the status of the oppositions in the adult language.

Children's selectivity about the words they chose to produce is also cited as evidence for the cognitive model. The evidence typically comes from observed asymmetries in the number of words in a child's lexicon beginning with particular sounds. Menn (1978), for example, refers to the case of Jacob who avoided words beginning with /p/ and /g/. Macken (1980, p. 162) showed that Jacob's selectivity could be explained by the uneven distribution of English words beginning with these sounds, the number of syllables in the words, and their syntactic role (noun or verb). Schwartz & Leonard (1982) found that selectivity may not be just an artifact of the frequency of the sounds in the language, but that it was limited to a time when children produced fewer than 50 words. It does not seem to be a factor in children's comprehension (Leonard & Schwartz, 1985). A phonological model could tolerate some selectivity in the initial period of development since children would need to accumulate some number of words before they could begin phonological analysis. During this initial period, children would collect a set of word-based articulations, forming what Menn (1983) calls an "output lexicon." At or about the fiftieth word children would begin the process of extracting phonological contrasts, depending on the child's nature and the sample of lexical articulations collected.

This initial period would also explain the existence of what Moskowitz (1970) labeled "phonological idioms." These are lexical exceptions to rules that otherwise operate across the board in a child's lexicon. The most famous example is Hildegard Leopold's early and accurate production of "pretty." For many months, this was her only word that contained a consonant cluster. When she eventually incorporated the word into her system, she produced it as [bIdi]. In our version of Jakobson's model lexical exceptions would be just that—lexical exceptions. These would be lexical articulations that a child had not yet incorporated into a system of phonological oppositions. They should be highly idiosyncratic in nature and could remain in production for variable lengths of time. The existence of lexical exceptions makes it all the more necessary to base analyses of children's phonologies on sound productions that occur in several lexical types rather than in an isolated example.

No model that attempts to account for all of the intricacies of phonological development is wholly without difficulties, including our own. First, the matter of maximal opposition within a language needs clarification. Jakobson's original proposal has the merit that a single universal hierarchy of features explained the phonological development of all children. Children did not have to deduce the hierarchy from the languages they were acquiring. By restricting the application of maximal oppositions to individual languages we face the problem of specifying how children make use of phonetic information to uncover phonological features. We are, in effect, redefining the term maximal opposition from the universal reference frame that Jakobson envisioned to a scale that is relative to a child's emerging lexicon. Within this framework the frequency and distribution of phonological oppositions play a larger role than Jakobson realized. Thus, the /t/-/tʃ/ opposition is very different in Quiché and English despite the fact that the sounds are very similar. At this point we can not say whether the difference is only a matter of frequency or whether the opposition is more *marked* in some fashion in English. We need a rigorous definition of maximal oppositions that specifies the relative strengths of different features within any language.

A second problem is common to all versions of Jakobson's model, the problem of relating surface phonetics to the underlying set of oppositions in children's language. For example, it is not clear why a child learning Quiché would produce an apicodental [l] while a child learning English would aim for an apicoalveolar. Would not either of these serve the same set of oppositions in Quiché and English? If children recover oppositions from their own lexicons then the answer to our question must lie in a careful specification of children's recovery procedures. The Quiché children may just be stuck with their apicodental articulation. This raises a further problem, however, of how children acquire such remarkably accurate articulations in the absence of a phonological system.

We might appeal to some type of Gestalt processing, but this is obviously an area that demands further research.

A related problem is the task of demonstrating that children are using phonological oppositions in their speech. In this paper we were only able to resort to evidence from the chilren's spontaneous productions. This produced two types of evidence: different initial sounds and different patterns of substitution. Other revealing sources of evidence might come from experimental paradigms such as Braine's (1974) in which a child is taught a nonce form that can take various forms, depending on the child's phonological system.

SUMMARY

In this paper we have shown that Quiché children have a pattern of phonological development that is substantially different from that of children learning English. The Quiché children's early /ʔ tʃ x l/ are particularly noteworthy. We claimed that such differences invalidate models which appeal to ease of articulation for an explanation of children's phonological development. We argue, instead, for a version of Jakobson's theory which makes the notion "maximal opposition" relative to the child's emerging lexicon. This model predicts that children will learn the same language in a fairly unified fashion, but that there may be large differences in the way children approach the phonologies of different languages. The model also predicts that children will quickly develop an organization in their phonologies. Sound substitutions provide some evidence that children acquiring different languages develop different phonological systems. The Quiché children produced substitutions that were very different from those produced by children learning English. They used [l] as a substitute for /r/, [ʃ] for /s/, and produced an accurate [tʃ] from the beginning. English-type substitutions were possible for the Quiché children, but they did not make them.

We attempted to operationalize the idea of maximal opposition within a language by measuring the frequency of initial consonants in children's vocabularies. We then compared this measure to the children's order of phonological acquisition and found a statistically significant correlation for both Quiché and English. The frequency of consonants across lexical types is an imperfect guide to children's phonological systems because it refers to isolated segments rather than oppositions. Some children may develop an opposition more fully before moving on to the next most frequent segment.

We emphasize that the model of phonological development we present is preliminary. However, it does have the advantage of focusing attention on the organization of children's phonologies. To quote Jakobson (1941/1968, p. 67), "the appearance of single sounds must not be treated in an isolated fashion without regard for their place in the sound system." A central aspect of searching for organization is the development of techniques such as those of Ingram (1981) which provide a principled means for separating phonological systems from lexical exceptions. The Quiché results make clear the necessity of documenting how children cope with non-English phonologies. Jakobson's familiarity with the rich literature on the acquisition of Slavic phonologies may have been responsible for his initial insight into the problem of explaining children's acquisition. We trust that additional cross-linguistic work on this problem will be equally rewarding.

REFERENCES

Braine, M. D. S. (1974). On what might constitute a learnable phonology. *Language, 50,* 270–299.

Branigan, G. (1976). Syllabic structure and the acquisition of consonants: The great conspiracy in word formation. *Journal of Psycholinquistic Research, 5,* 117–133.

Drachman, G., & Malkouti-Drachman, A. (1973). Studies in the acquisition of Greek as a native language: I. Some preliminary findings on phonology. *Ohio State University Working Papers on Linguistics, 15,* 99–114.

Ferguson, C. A., & Farwell, C. B. (1975). Words and sounds in early language acquisition. *Language, 51,* 419–439.

Hinofotis, F. B. (1976). An initial stage in a child's acquisition of Greek as his native language. *Workpapers in teaching English as a second language, (University of California, Los Angeles) 11,* 85–96.

Ingram, D. (1974). Phonological rules in young children. *Journal of Child Language. 1,* 49–64.

Ingram, D. (1979). Phonological patterns in the speech of young children. In P. Fletcher & M. Garman (Eds.), *Language acquisition* (pp. 133–148). Cambridge, England: Cambridge University Press.

Ingram, D. (1981). *Procedures for the phonological analysis of children's language.* Baltimore, MD: University Park Press.

Ingram, D. (1983, December). Jakobson revisited: Some evidence from the acquisition of Polish phonology. Presented to the annual meeting of the Linguistic Society of America, Minneapolis.

Ingram, D., Christensen, L., Veach, S. & Webster, B. (1980). The acquisition of word-initial fricatives and affricates in English by children between 2 and 6 years. In G. H. Yeni-Komshian, J. F. Kavanagh, & C. A. Ferguson (Eds.), *Child phonology (Vol. 1)* (pp. 169–192). New York: Academic Press.

Jakobson, R. (1941/1968). *Kindersprache, Aphasie und allgemeine Lautgesetze.* [Translated by A. R. Keiler. (1968) *Child language, aphasia* and *phonological universals.* The Hague: Mouton.

Kiparsky, P., & Menn, L. (1977). On the acquisition of phonology. In J. MacNamara (Ed.), *Language, learning and thought* (pp. 47–78). New York: Academic Press.

Leonard, L. B., & Schwartz, R. G. (1985). Early linguistic development of children with specific language impairment. In K. E. Nelson (Eds.), *Children's language, Vol. 5 (pp. 291–318). Hillsdale, NJ: Lawrence Erlbaum Associates.*

Locke, J. L. (1983). *Phonological acquisition and change.* New York: Academic Press.

MacKain, K. S., & Stern, D. N. (1985). The concept of experience in speech development. In K. E. Nelson (Ed.), *Children's language, Vol. 5* (pp. 1–33). Hillsdale, NJ: Lawrence Erlbaum Associates.

Macken, M. A. (1980). Aspects of the acquisition of stop systems: a cross-linguistic perspective. In G. H. Yeni-Komshian, J. F. Kavanagh, & C. A. Ferguson (Eds.), *Child phonology: Production, Vol. 1* (pp. 143–168). New York: Academic Press.

Macken, M. A., & Ferguson, C. A. (1983). Cognitive aspects of phonological development: Model, evidence, and issues. In K. E. Nelson (Ed.), *Children's language, Vol. 4* (pp. 256–282). Hillsdale, NJ: Lawrence Erlbaum Associates.

Menn, L. (1978). *Pattern, control and contrast in beginning speech, a case study in the development of word form and word function.* Bloomington: Indiana University Linguistics Club.

Menn, L. (1983). Development of articulatory, phonetic, and phonological capabilities. In B. Butterworth (Ed.), *Language production: Development, writing and other language processes, Vol. 2* (pp. 3–50). New York: Academic Press.

Mines, M. A., Hanson, B. F., & Shoup, J. E. (1978). Frequency of occurrence of phonemes in conversational English. *Language and Speech, 21*, 221–241.

Moe, A. J., Hopkins, C. J., & Rush, R. T. (1982). *The vocabulary of first-grade children.* Springfield, IL: Charles C. Thomas.

Mondloch, J. L. (1978). *Basic Quiché grammar.* (Institute for Mesoamerican Studies, publication 2.) Albany: State University of New York.

Moskowitz, A. (1970). The two-year-old stage in the acquisition of English phonology. *Language, 46*, 426–441.

Norman, W. (1976). Quiché text. In L. Furbee-Losee (Ed.), *Mayan texts I (IJAL-NATS 1:1).* Chicago: University of Chicago Press.

Prather, E. M., Hedrick, D. L., & Kern, C. A. (1975). Articulation development in children aged two to four years. *Journal of Speech and Hearing Disorders, 40*, 179–191.

Pye, C. (1980). *The acquisition of grammatical morphemes in Quiché Mayan.* Unpublished doctoral dissertation, University of Pittsburgh.

Schwartz, R. G., & Leonard, L. B. (1982). Do children pick and choose? An examination of phonological selection and avoidance in early lexical acquisition. *Journal of Child Language, 9*, 319–336.

Smith, N. V. (1973). *The acquisition of phonology.* Cambridge, England: Cambridge University Press.

Stampe, D. (1969). The acquisition of phonemic representation. *Proceedings of the Fifth Regional Meeting of the Chicago Linguistic Society*, pp. 433–444.

Stoel, C. M. (1974). *The acquisition of liquids in Spanish.* Unpublished doctoral dissertation, Stanford University.

Straight, H. S. (1976). *The acquisition of Maya phonology: Variation in Yucatec child language.* New York: Garland.

9

Early Semantic Developments and Their Relationship to Object Permanence, Means-Ends Understanding, and Categorization

Alison Gopnik
Scarborough College, University of Toronto

Andrew N. Meltzoff
University of Washington

Children typically begin to use their first words when they are between 15- and 21-months-old. At about this time there are other significant changes in children's cognitive abilities, which has led many investigators to suggest that there might be some relationship between these two developments.

Piaget proposed one theory of the relationship between early language and cognition over 50 years ago, and this theory is still highly influential. Piaget (1962) and his followers (Morehead & Morehead, 1974; Sinclair, 1970), claimed that "symbolic" or "stage 6" intelligence was a prerequisite for the use of language. The logic of this argument is clear. In order to use language the child must represent the world in an abstract, symbolic way. If the child's cognition were limited to the action-based sensorimotor schemes of infancy, true language would be impossible.

This hypothesis has three important aspects. First, it is a claim about the formal aspects of language, rather than about its content or meaning. Piaget is making a claim about the ability to use words productively, not the ability to use words to talk about particular things. Second, it is a claim about the sequencing of linguistic and cognitive development. The Piagetian hypothesis argues that cognition is a prerequisite to language. You couldn't use language unless you had "stage 6" problem-solving abilities. Finally, it is a claim about very general characteristics of the child's cognition. According to Piaget, the advent of symbolic representation is reflected in many different kinds of cognitive abilities, including object permanence, the ability to use insight, certain spatial and causal abilities, and the ability to produce symbolic play and deferred imitation. Therefore, all these "stage 6" cognitive developments should be related to the general emergence of language.

191

In the past 10 years many researchers have investigated these hypotheses. The studies have yielded rather little empirical support for Piaget's view. There are few demonstrated correlations between general measures of language development, such as the emergence of the first words, M.L.U., or productive or receptive vocabulary size, and general measures of cognitive development (see Corrigan, 1979; Harris, 1982 for reviews). Moreover, there is evidence that children can use words before they show signs of "stage 6" cognitive abilities (Bates, Benigni, Bretherton, Camaioni, & Volterra, 1979; Dihoff & Chapman, 1977; Gopnik & Meltzoff 1985a; Tomasello & Farrar, 1984). Some researchers also suggest that deaf children may begin to sign earlier than 18 months (e.g., Bonvillian, Orlansky, & Novack, 1983), but the implications of such findings are still unclear.

Various attempts have been made to salvage Piaget's thesis. In a recent paper Smolak and Levine (1984) redefine the onset of language to mean the onset of reference to events that are distant in time and space. Not surprisingly, they find that on this definition, "stage 6" cognitive abilities do precede language. The problem is that by redefining language in this way the claim loses much of its interest. If we defined language as the ability to use complex syntax, as a Chomskyan might, we would certainly find that language follows after "stage 6" abilities, but this would hardly justify the claim that there is some deep and significant relationship between these linguistic and cognitive developments.

Similarly, Smolak and Levine have also tried to redefine "stage 6" abilities, arguing, for example, that children who recover an object in a basic object-permanence task, solving a single invisible displacement with a single cloth, should be counted as having entered "stage 6." Children can typically recover an object in this situation at a very early age, by using some form of magical procedure; for example, they may assume that pulling cloths off the table top always leads to the obects' reappearance. So, if we define "stage 6" cognitive abilities in this way, they will precede language. But redefining "stage 6." like redefining language, robs the hypothesis of much of its force.

Other authors have pointed out some of the methodological difficulties that are involved in assessing children's cognition and language in this period (Bloom, Lifter, & Broughton, 1981, 1985). In particular, they have criticized the Uzgiris and Hunt (1975) assessment scales, and pointed out the difficulty of assessing cognitive development accurately with this kind of instrument, and have also pointed out weaknesses in the usual linguistic measures. They suggest that the weakness of the measurement instrument might obscure links between cognition and language. While these criticisms may be well-placed, the fact remains that if there is a strong relationship between cognition and language it should show up *somewhere*. While the inadequacies of testing instruments may keep us from despairing of the Piagetian hypothesis altogether, they are hardly arguments in support of the hypothesis.

A number of other authors have suggested modifications of Piaget's view. Bates (Bates et al., 1979) has suggested that "stage 6" cognitive abilities may not be a prerequisite for language, but that the emergence of language and the development of "stage 6" cognitive abilities reflect the same underlying cognitive change, something she calls the "homologies" view. If this were true, we would expect that children would begin to use their first words at the same time that they began to solve "stage 6" tasks. There is, however, rather little evidence to support this view. If there can be gaps of up to several months between the relevant linguistic and cognitive developments, and if there is no correlation between them, it seems more parsimonious to conclude that there is no relationship between them than that there is some common development that underlies them both.

Similarly, Fischer and Corrigan (1981) have suggested a modification of the general Piagetian view. They have proposed that using language requires certain general skills that are also required for other cognitive developments in this period, though they do not define these skills in Piagetian terms. Like Piaget, however, both Bates and Fischer and Corrigan emphasize the general, formal, ability to use language, that is, the ability to use symbols at all, or to combine symbols into strings. And there is as yet little evidence to support the notion that "stage 6" cognitive developments are related to this general ability. Although these views may seem plausible, there just is no strong empirical evidence that there are interesting cognitive prerequisites or cognitive homologies to the development of general, formal linguistic abilities.

The failure to find evidence to support Piaget's hypothesis and similar hypotheses might lead us to conclude that there are no significant relationships between linguistic and cognitive development. This option is particularly tempting since two of the more influential recent theories of language acquisition deny or at least minimize the relationship between linguistic and cognitive development.

Recently, a number of authors have stressed the social and communicative aspects of language and the continuity between linguistic and prelinguistic communication (Bruner 1975, 1983; Lock, 1980; Snow, 1979). On this view, early words grow out of earlier nonlinguistic interactions between children and their caregivers. Cognitive factors might play a subsidiary role in this development but individual patterns of interaction and communication would be more important.

Chomsky's (1968, 1980) nativist theory of language acquisition also minimizes the general contribution of other cognitive developments to linguistic development. This view has recently made something of a comeback with the rise of learnability theories such as the theories of Wexler and Culicover (1980). According to Chomsky and the learnability theorists, language acquisition is the result of the maturation of an innate language learning capacity, which is a highly specific "module" (Fodor, 1983) and is not related to more general cognitive abilities.

While the social-interactionists and Chomskyans seem like strange bedfellows, both these schools might take heart at the failure of the Piagetian theory, and more generally the failure to find strong empirical relationships between general measures of linguistic and cognitive development. But while there is as yet little evidence for the Piagetian thesis, there *is* evidence suggesting that there are rather different relationships between language and cognition in the one-word stage.

A number of authors have noted the similarity between the kinds of concepts encoded by early words and the kinds of concepts that are developed in the 15- to 21-month period (Bloom, 1973; Brown, 1973; Gopnik, 1981, 1982, 1984a, 1984b; McCune-Nicolich, 1981). In particular, we have noted similarities between: (a) the kinds of concepts encoded by disappearance words like "gone" and the kinds of concepts required for an understanding of object permanence (Gopnik, 1984a), (b) the concepts encoded by success and failure words, like "there" and "uh-oh," and the concepts that are required to use insight to solve means-ends problems (Gopnik, 1982), (c) the concepts encoded by locative terms and spatial concepts, and (d) the concepts encoded by names and the concepts that underlie categorization (Gopnik & Meltzoff, 1985b, in press).

More significantly, we and others have shown that there are empirical relationships between object permanence skills and disappearance words (Corrigan, 1978; Gopnik, 1984a; Gopnik & Meltzoff, 1984, 1986; McCune-Nicolich, 1981; Tomasello & Farrar, 1984). Disappearance words are acquired at a very specific point in the development of the object concept, during "stage 6." Moreover, we have shown (Gopnik & Meltzoff, 1984, 1986) that there are also relationships between the development of "stage 6" means-ends abilities and the acquisition of words that encode success and failure. These words emerge during "stage 6" of means-ends development. However, the cross-relationships do not hold: Disappearance words do not seem to be this closely related to means-ends abilities, and success/failure words do not seem to be this closely related to object permanence abilities.

These studies suggest that there *are* relationships between language and cognition during the one-word stage but these relationships are very different from the relationships that Piaget suggested or that the more recent, revisionist theories have postulated. These relationships are different in three ways. First, they do not involve formal aspects of language, rather they involve the specific content of language, the acquisition of specific types of *meanings*. Second, these relationships appear to involve *concurrent* developments rather than involving prerequisites. In our studies, children consistently acquired words within a few weeks of their acquisition of the related problem-solving abilities, but the two developments could occur in either order. Finally, rather than being general relationships these relationships appear to be very *specific*. Disappearance words are related to object permanence, but are not closely related to means-ends skills. Success/failure words are related to means-ends skills, but are not closely related to object permanence. The earlier theories proposed that "stage 6" cognitive abilities are prerequisites or homologies to general linguistic developments. We disagree. Instead, we propose that very particular cognitive achievements are closely tied to certain very particular semantic developments but not others, a position we have called "the specific hypothesis" (Gopnik & Meltzoff, 1986).

In this chapter we present the results of further studies investigating this hypothesis. First, we describe a study which suggests that formal aspects of the emergence of language are not related to the development of general "stage 6" abilities. Children can use words productively well before they show signs of "stage 6" cognitive abilities in other areas, and there are no apparent formal differences between these pre-stage-6 words and later words. However, the results of this study also suggest that there are changes in the content of language during the transition from sensorimotor "stage 5" to "stage 6." Second, we present the results of studies investigating the sequencing of semantic and cognitive developments in the one-word stage. The results of these studies suggest that semantic developments and related cognitive developments occur concurrently. We discuss how the results of these studies bear on the specificity hypothesis, the notion that there are specific relationships between particular semantic and cognitive developments, rather than more general relationships between language and cognition.

Third, we present evidence which extends the specificity hypothesis to new domains. This evidence suggests that, in addition to the relationships between disappearance words and object permanence skills, and between success/failure words and means-ends skills, there is also a relationship between the naming explosion and categorization skills.

Finally, we consider the theoretical implications of these findings. We outline a general picture of the relationship between language and cognition in this period which could explain the existence of these several specific relationships. We further suggest that there is a functional rather than formal change in children's language at about the same time that they begin to solve "stage 6" problems. Even before this point children can use words in arbitrary, symbolic ways. At this point, however, children begin to apply language to the cognitive problems they are trying to solve at the moment. Language takes on an intrapersonal regulatory function, as well as the more obvious interpersonal communicative one. This change in the function of children's language results in a great expansion of their linguistic structures and may also facilitate changes in their cognitive abilities.

LANGUAGE BEFORE "STAGE 6"

Our recent research suggests that children begin to use language productively before they reach sensorimotor "stage 6." The results we focus on here come from a longitudinal study of eight children. The children were 13–14 months-old

TABLE 9.1
Description of the Object-Permanence and Means-Ends Tasks

Uzgiris and Hunt (1975)

Task Number	Task Description

Object Concept Tasks

13. Finding an object following one invisible displacement with three screens (7 trials)

   Object is hidden in hand, hand is placed under A, B, or C, object is left under A, B, or C.
   Child must search at correct cloth.

14. Finding an object following a series of invisible displacements (7 trials)

   Object is hidden in hand, hand is placed under A, then B, then C.
   Object is left under C.
   Child must search under A, then B, then C, or directly under C.

15. Finding an object following a series of invisible displacements by searching in reverse order

   After child has searched at C three times on Task 14, object is hidden in hand, hand is placed under A, then B, then C; object is left under A.
   Child must search under C, then B, then A.

Means-Ends Tasks

9. Use of string vertically to obtain object.

10. Use of stick to obtain object.

11. Placing a necklace in a bottle.

12. Stacking a set of rings on a post, avoiding one solid ring.

at the start of the study and were observed in the laboratory once every 3 weeks for approximately 6 months. The children received the tasks listed in Table 9.1 which were adapted from Uzgiris and Hunt (1975), and their performance on these tasks was recorded on videotape. Children were counted as having passed a particular object-permanence task if they searched for the object appropriately on more than half the trials. They were counted as having passed a particular means-ends task if they used insight to solve the problem, that is they solved the problem immediately without an intervening period of trial and error.

The language assessment was primarily based on mother's reports. The children's mothers were asked to record their language development on a detailed questionnaire. The questionnaire concentrated on recording object names and relational words encoding success, failure, disappearance, and location. Mothers were also asked to record any other early word uses. At the start of each recording session, mothers handed in the questionnaire to a language scorer, who was not involved in the cognitive testing in any way. This language scorer then listed all the children's words and assessed the contexts in which these words occurred. Thus, this scorer was blind to the children's cognitive level. Similarly, the cognitive scorer did not have access to the questionnaire data.

There are several measures which may be taken to indicate the development of "stage 6" cognitive abilities. In particular, however, Piaget (1952, 1954) suggests that the hallmarks of "stage 6" are the ability to solve a simple invisible displacement task, with suitable controls to ensure that magical procedures are not used (object-permanence task 13) and the ability to use insight to solve means-ends tasks. We therefore counted children as being in "stage 5" if they were unable to solve object permanence tasks 13–15, and did not use insight to solve any of the means-ends tasks 9–12. Four of the children in our study did not solve object-permanence tasks 13–15 or means-ends tasks 9–12. We assumed that these children were in "stage 5" of their development, given their ages, though it is possible that they had not even reached this stage. In any case, the important point is that these children did not show any signs of possessing typical "stage 6" object-permanence or means-ends abilities. We analyzed the results of this study to test the claim that formal aspects of language are related to the development of "stage 6," and particularly that "stage 6" cognitive abilities are a prerequisite for language development.

Previous studies have found that children use words before they solve "stage 6" problems. However, the nature of these very early words was unclear. It is possible that these words are not produced spontaneously and productively, as later words are. For example, these words might simply be imitations of adult speech. Alternatively, a number of authors (Barrett, 1985; Bates et al., 1979; Greenfield & Smith, 1976) have suggested that very early words might be produced as part of limited specific routines. Barrett has described such uses most extensively and has described early words as being produced in particular "scripts." For example, a child might use "down" only at the end of a round of ring-a-rosy, or use "duck" only in the context of a particular walk to the lake, at a particular time, to view a particular duck. While these utterances are English words and are not simply imitations, they do not have the decontextualized, symbolic character we might expect from the first words on Piaget's account. If only these scripted words or imitated words occurred before "stage 6," Piaget's thesis might be salvaged.

More significantly, it would be interesting in general, independently of Piaget, to see if there are differences in the types of words children produce before and after they solve "stage 6" problems. We have suggested previously (Gopnik & Meltzoff, 1985a, 1985b) that children might use words productively in social contexts before they use them in more cognitive contexts. For example, children seem to consistently use words like "no" to encode a social concept, the concept of refusing another person's suggestion, before they use "no" to encode nonsocial concepts, such as the failure of a plan. Notice that these social uses of words are productive and arbitrary and are generalized across a wide variety of contexts. They are not limited to a single context. From a formal point of view these words are as symbolic as other words. But the things they sym- bolize are social relationships rather than physical ones. We might think of these words as analogous to adult constructions like "I promise" or "wife," which

TABLE 9.2
Four Children's Word Uses Before Stage 6

		Type of Use			
Subject	Sess. No.	Script[a]	Social[b]	Locative[c]	Name[d]
Peter	1				bus
Amy	1		mama		daddy
			up		ball
					bird
					dog
Patrick	1		hi		
			bye		
	2				
	3	egg	mama		daddy
					ball
					trees
	4		more		bottle
			that		cheese
					juice
					Cheerios
					Jess
					Craig
Adrian	1	up	mama	up(self)	daddy
		tick tick			car
	2	cock cock		down(self)	bottle
	3	cuckoo		up(object)	cookie

[a]Script uses occurred in one routinized context.
[b]Social uses occurred productively in a variety of contexts, to serve a particular social function.
[c]Locative uses occurred when the child moved himself or an object.
[d]Name uses occurred when the child referred to an object or class of objects.

encode fundamentally social concepts, but are fully productive linguistic forms. Similarly, Tomasello and Farrar (1984) have suggested that children might use words for visible movements before ''stage 6'' but only use words for invisible movements after they have passed ''stage 6'' object-permanence tasks.

We analyzed all the recorded language of the children in our study who did not solve object-permanence task 13 or means-ends task 9 at the first session, and were therefore classified as being in ''stage 5.'' The results suggest that children use words spontaneously and productively well before they show signs of ''stage 6'' abilities in other domains, but that there are changes in the content of children's language after they develop ''stage 6'' skills.

All four of the children in our study used at least some words before they solved the ''stage 6'' tasks. Table 9.2 lists all the recorded words. These words fell into several categories. Some words were only used in particular limited contexts or ''scripts.'' For example, Patrick only used ''egg'' in the particular context of eating his egg at breakfast, and Adrian only used ''up'' flicking up a particular switch. These early word uses do not necessarily challenge the Piagetian thesis. However, other words were used more productively, in a wide range of contexts, but were used in ways that served a particular social function. Thus, several children used "mama" when they wanted help of any kind, or used "hi" as a general greeting. We have classified these as "social" uses. It is important to note that these social uses of language are highly symbolic and arbitrary and according to Piaget's own work should count as language (Piaget, 1962). Similar words appear in Piaget's description of the first verbal schemas contemporaneous with "stage 6" (Piaget, 1962, p. 216).

Moreover, children used other words that were not limited to particular contexts or to particular social functions (see Table 9.2) but were used productively to refer to many types of objects or events. For example, "up" was used in a variety of circumstances in which the child tried to move up and one child used "down" when he moved objects down. This is consistent with Tomasello and Farrar's sugestions that visible movements might be encoded before stage 6.

But perhaps the clearest examples of productive word use in this period were the early names. Peter's "bus" and Adrian's "car" were used to refer to all moving vehicles, while Patrick's "ball" referred to all round objects, and his "tree" was used to refer to trees and hedges. These early names were applied to many different contexts, and did not seem to be limited to a single pragmatic function. From a formal point of view it is difficult to see how they are different from any other words in the one-word stage. Indeed, such overextended names have long been considered to be the paradigmatic "first words."

These early words could occur well before the advent of "stage 6" in our study. One child began to use words productively 3 months before the first signs of "stage 6" cognitive abilities. The evidence of this study, as well as the generally low correlation between formal linguistic measures and cognitive measures in previous studies, strongly suggests that "stage 6" cognitive abilities are not a prerequisite for language use. Nor was there any strong evidence for the "homologies" position. In this study, at least, children did not develop "stage 6" abilities and use their first words at the same time. Instead, the first words, including productive and decontextualized words consistently appeared before "stage 6."

However, we found that children began to use words to encode new types of meanings after they began to solve "stage 6" tasks. Several types of words did not appear until after the children solved object-permanence task 13 or means-ends task 9, the "stage 6" tasks according to Piaget (1952, 1954). These included words that encoded the success and failure of plans and the disappearance of objects. As we see below such words consistently appeared in conjunction with the solution of more difficult object-permanence and means-ends tasks—tasks that have traditionally been taken to signal the completion of "stage 6." Other types of words encoding other types of meanings also did not occur until after the children entered "stage 6." Before this time children did not use words like "more" to encode recurrence or use locative words like "up" and "down" to indicate movements that were not immediately caused by the child. All these uses of words did occur before the children completed the study, that is, before these children were 21-months-old. Moreover, while individual names were used in this very early period, the naming explosion did not occur until after the children entered stage 6.

THE SPECIFICITY HYPOTHESIS

The results of our analysis of language before "stage 6" suggest that there are no general relationships between productive language use and "stage 6" abilities. Instead, there seem to be relationships between specific semantic developments, including the development of "disappearance" and "success/failure" words, and "stage 6" cognitive developments.

So far we have followed the literature in talking about a general cognitive development, the development of "stage 6," which is reflected in both object-permanence development and means-ends development. But we have conducted other studies which suggest that when we study relationships between linguistic and cognitive development we should isolate specific cognitive developments as well specific semantic developments. In a previous study, for example, disappearance words were only closely related to object-permanence abilities, while success/failure words were more closely related to means-ends abilities (Gopnik & Meltzoff, 1984). We analyzed the results of the study just described, as well as past studies in our lab, to further investigate the sequencing and the specificity of these relationships between cognitive and linguistic developments (see also Gopnik & Meltzoff, 1986).

Looking first at the sequencing of the developments, we asked whether the cognitive developments preceded the linguistic ones or if the two types of developments could occur in reverse. We also examined the actual temporal gap between the linguistic and cognitive developments. How many days after one development did the other development take place? Finally, we looked at the correlations between the ages at which the linguistic and cognitive developments occurred. Were children who acquired a disappearance word early, also likely to solve the object permanence problems early?

These last two measures also gave us a way of operationalizing and testing the specificity hypothesis. If the hypothesis was correct, there should be short gaps between the development of object permanence skills and disappearance words, and between means-ends skills and success/failure words, but longer gaps between the development of object permanence skills and success/failure words and between the means-ends skills and disappearance words. Similarly, there should be high correlations between the related cognitive and semantic developments, and these correlations should remain high when the unrelated cognitive developments were partialed out. Moreover, the correlations between the related developments should be higher than those between the unrelated developments.

The testing procedures we used were essentially the same as those described earlier in the chapter. The subjects were 19 children ranging from 13–19 months-old at the time they were first observed. Three of these children were exposed to Finnish, Polish and Hebrew as well as English. Five of the subjects were tested approximately once a month, six were tested approximately once every 2 weeks, and eight were tested approximately once every 3 weeks. Testing continued for approximately 6 months. During the testing sessions children received the tasks described in Table 9.1. The scoring procedures for these tasks were the same as those described earlier.

The infants' mothers were asked to keep a record of their acquisition of disappearance and success/failure words, as well as some other words. In addition, any words they used during the testing session were recorded. Children were counted as having acquired a word if three spontaneous, appropriate uses of the word were recorded on the questionnaire or if they used the word spontaneously in one of the recording sessions.

Seventeen of the 19 children used a word to encode disappearance by the end of the study. Children used the English forms "gone" and "allgone" to encode disappearance. In addition, the two children in the study who were learning Finnish and Polish, used the Finnish "hukku" and the Polish "nema" to encode this concept.

All 19 children used some success/failure word by the end of the study. Children were counted as having acquired a success/failure word if they used a word in contexts involving success, or used a word in contexts involving failure. There was some variation in the actual words that were used. The English-speaking children used "uh-oh" and "no" to encode failure, while they used "there" and "good girl" to encode success. The Finnish-speaking child used "ae" for failure while the Hebrew-speaking child used "oy."

Sequencing of Cognitive and Linguistic Achievements

Previous studies (Gopnik & Meltzoff, 1984; Uzgiris & Hunt, 1975) suggest that there are at least two substages within the general development of "stage 6" object permanence—solving object-permanence task 13 (the simple invisible displacement task) and solving object-permanence task 14 (the serial invisible displacement task). Similarly, there are two levels of means-ends ability—solving means-ends task 9 (the string task) and solving tasks 10–12. From a Piagetian perspective, we can see the first substage in each domain as entering "stage 6" and the second as completing "stage 6." In this study each of these levels of cognitive development seemed to be related to linguistic development in a rather different way. Children seem to consistently reach the earlier level of development before they acquire the related words, but reach the higher level of development at about the same time that they acquire the related words.

Only two of the 19 children acquired a disappearance word before they solved

TABLE 9.3
Age in Days at Which Subjects First Solved Object-Concept and Means-Ends Tasks and
First Used Disappearance and Success/Failure Words

Subject No.	Object Concept Task 13	Object Concept Task 14	Means-Ends Task 9	Means-Ends Task 10-11	Dis-appearance Word	Success/ Failure Words
1	492	492	520	520	492	520
2	511	555	483	483	555	483
3	464	464	464	593	464	558
4	557	557	518	518	557	518
5	626	665	500	626	665	626
6	636	608	590	727	608	698
7	572	585	543	585	599	599
8	535	570	555	588	588	555
9	575	612	535	535	612	535
10	475	514	475	580	*	580
11	551	565	551	677	565	661
12	541	541	502	541	583	562
13	498	498	519	564	519	564
14	594	*	531	594	594	594
15	574	574	422	506	555	555
16	446	478	536	536	502	536
17	484	544	544	523	*	484
18	525	525	417	463	572	463
19	432	448	432	539	448	518

*These three subjects withdrew from the study before they solved Task 14 or used
a disappearance word.

the simpler object permanence problem (task 13) (see Table 9.3). In fact, many
of the children solved the task well before they used a disappearance word. On
average the gap between these two developments was 42.95 days. (The *gap* is
the absolute value of the temporal distance between two acquisitions.) Similarly,
none of the children used a success/failure word before they solved the simpler
means-ends task, means-ends task 9. The mean gap between these two developments was 57.47 days. These findings support the suggestion of other authors,
notably Tomasello and Farrar (1984), that children solve simple invisible displacement tasks before they use disappearance words. Moreover, they show that
children also solve means-ends task 9 before they acquire success/failure words.
Thus, in both domains the first cognitive substage is passed before the relevant
words are acquired.

  There was, however, a rather different relationship between these words and
the more difficult "stage 6" tasks—object-permanence task 14 and means-ends
tasks 10–12. These linguistic and cognitive developments could occur in either
order and often occurred contemporaneously. Eight children solved object permanence task 14 before they used a disappearance word, two children reversed
this order, and nine children acquired the word and solved the task in the same
session. Similarly, three children solved means-ends tasks 10–12 before they
used a success/failure word, six children reversed this order, and ten children
acquired the word and solved the task in the same session. Moreover, the mean

TABLE 9.4
Mean Gap in Days Between the First Solution of Object-Permanence
Task 14 and Means-Ends Task 10-12 and the First Use of
Disappearance and Success/Failure Words

Cognitive Achievements	Mean Gap in Days[a]
Object-permanence Task 14 and Disappearance Words	27.95
Object-permanence Task 14 and Success/Failure Words	55.68
Means-Ends Task 10-12 and Disappearance Words	64.63
Means-Ends Task 10-12 and Success/Failure Words	13.53
Object-permanence Task 14 and Means-Ends Task 10-12	59.84
Disappearance Words and Success/Failure Words	58.68

[a]The gap is the absolute value of the interval between one achievement and the other.

gaps between the related semantic developments and cognitive developments were very small. On average the gap between the solution of object-permanence task 14 and the acquisition of a disappearance word was only 27.95 days. Similarly, the average gap between the solution of means-ends tasks 10–12 and the acquisition of a success/failure word was only 13.53 days. These results suggest that these later cognitive developments occur concurrently with the related semantic developments (see Tables 9.3 and 9.4).

Testing the Specificity Hypothesis: Gap Scores

Not only were the temporal gaps between the related semantic and cognitive developments small, they were significantly smaller than the gaps between the unrelated cognitive and linguistic developments. The average temporal gap between the solution of object-permanence task 14 and the acquisition of success–failure words (mean = 55.68 days) is significantly longer than the average gap between the solution of this task and the acquisition of disappearance words, 27.95 days ($p < .05$). Similarly, the gap between the solution of the means-ends tasks 10–12 and the acquisition of a disappearance word (mean = 64.63 days) is significantly longer than the gap between the solution of this task and the acquisition of success/failure words, 13.57 days ($p < .01$). These findings suggest that these relationships are not only close, they are also highly specific. Rather than dealing with a general relationship between semantic and conceptual development we are dealing with two separate, dissociable and very specific relationships.

All four of these cognitive and linguistic achievements occur on average at about 18 months (the mean ages in months of these achievements are as follows: object-permanence task 14 = 17.90, means-ends tasks 10–12 = 18.52, disappearance words = 18.34, success/failure words = 18.37). However, there is a fair amount of individual variability. An individual child may solve one type of cognitive task several months before they solve the other task, or use one type of word several months before they use the other type. But, in spite of the fact that children acquire the cognitive abilities at different times, and acquire the semantic categories at different times, children do tend to acquire a disappearance word at about the same time that they solve the object-permanence problem, and similarly acquire a success/failure word at about the same time that they solve the means-ends problem.

Testing the Specificity Hypothesis: Correlations

Another way of testing the specificity hypothesis is to look at the correlations between the age of acquisition of linguistic and cognitive skills. This provides us with another measure of the relationship between the semantic and cognitive developments, and we can use partial correlations to test the specificity hypothesis more precisely. There are strong correlations between the age at which the children acquire disappearance words and the age at which they solve object-permanence task 14 ($r = .70$). Similarly, there are strong correlations between the age at which children acquire success/failure words and the age at which they solve means-ends tasks 10–12 ($r = .95$). There are much weaker correlations between the age of acquisition of disappearance words and means-ends tasks 10–12 and success/failure words and object-permanence task 14 ($r = .23$ and $r = .46$ respectively) (see Table 9.5).

It is also possible to partial out the effects of means-ends performance from the disappearance words/object permanence correlation. Similarly, we can partial out object permanence performance from the success/failure words/means-ends correlation. Partialling out the effects of the unrelated cognitive achievement has virtually no effect on the correlations which remain at $r = .68$ and $r = .94$ respectively.

These correlational results, then, also support the specificity hypothesis. They suggest that there are strong but very specific relationships between particular cognitive and linguistic developments. A child who solves object-permanence task 13 earlier is also likely to use a disappearance word earlier. A child who

TABLE 9.5
Pearson Correlation Coefficients Between the Age in Days of Solution of Object-Permanence Tasks 14 and Means-Ends Task 10-12 and the Acquisition of Disappearance and Success/Failure Words

	Disappearance Words	Means-Ends Task 10-12	Success/Failure Words
Object-permanence Task 14	.70[b]	.37	.46[a]
Disappearance Words		.23	.26
Means-Ends Task 10-12			.95[b]

[a] $p < .05$
[b] $p < .001$

solves means-ends tasks 10–12 earlier is likely to use a success/failure word earlier. The cross-correlations do not hold.

THE NAMING EXPLOSION AND CATEGORIZATION ABILITIES

So far we have shown that there is little evidence that formal properties of language are linked to general "stage 6" cognitive developments. However, there are at least two specific relationships between the content of early language and specific "stage 6" developments. We might predict that there would be other relationships between specific semantic and cognitive developments in this period. In particular, we have suggested that there might be a connection between the naming explosion and the development of new categorization skills during the transition from infancy to early childhood (Gopnik & Meltzoff, 1985b, 1986).

At around 18 months there are significant changes in the child's spontaneous classification behavior (Nelson, 1973; Ricciuti, 1965; Starkey, 1982; Sugarman, 1983). Before this point children who are given a set of objects belonging in two categories may spontaneously pick out one group of objects. For example, a 15-month-old who is given a group of dolls and cars may spontaneously pick out only the dolls. This behavior seems to indicate that the child recognizes that these different objects have some feature in common, a feature that is not shared by the other objects in the set. Similarly, there is some evidence from habituation studies that young infants can recognize rather abstract similarities between objects and respond differently to objects that belong in different categories (Cohen & Strauss, 1979). Both these findings suggest that infants can recognize that a particular object is more similar to some objects than to others and hence have some ability to recognize categories.

However, after around 18 months children will spontaneously sort all the objects in an array into two categories. For example, they will put all the dolls in one pile and put all the cars in another. This behavior suggests that, rather than simply recognizing the similarities between objects, they are actively trying to categorize the objects. They actively transform the objects so that their spatial arrangement reflects their division into categories. Moreover, children who behave in this way seem to be motivated to sort all the objects in the array into categories, rather than picking out just one category of objects. This active and spontaneous attempt to sort all the available objects into categories seems rather different from the infants' more passive recognition that an object shares features with other objects.

At around the same time that children start to sort all the objects in a group into categories, they also start to name all objects. Before around 18 months, children may use a few names for objects that are particularly important, desirable or interesting. As we have seen these names may occur before any signs of "stage 6" abilities and may be overextended. They are genuine names. However, at around 18 months children will often suddenly start to use many new names, a phenomenon that has been called "the naming explosion." During the naming explosion the child seems to discover that every object has a name. In fact, children rather compulsively ask for the names of objects in this period. The insight that every object has a name would seem *prima facie* to be related to the insight that all objects belong in categories. We designed a study to test whether there is an empirical relationship between these two areas of development.

Eight of the children described in the previous two studies also received a categorization task similar to the tasks used by Riccutti (1965) and Starkey (1981). The children were presented with three sets of eight objects. Each set could be sorted into two groups. There was a set of four toy clowns and four yellow rectangles, a set of four clear pillboxes and four caly balls, and a set of four dolls and four cars. The 8 objects in each set were presented to the child in a predetermined random arrangement on a table. The child was allowed to play with them for 3 minutes, and then they were removed. Each child received all three sets of objects interspersed among the cognitive tasks listed in Table 9.1. The three sets were presented in a randomly determined order. All test sessions were videotaped.

We followed the procedures of Ricciuti and Starkey for coding the children's behavior. We were particularly interested in seeing when the child would sort all 8 objects in a set into two groups, the highest level categorization behavior on the Ricciuti and Starkey scales. None of the children produced such behaviors at the start of the study, when they were 13–14 months old, but all the children produced such behaviors before they were 21-months-old. Most commonly, the children would place all the objects of one kind in one pile on the table and place all the objects of the other kind in another pile. As in the other cognitive tasks the decision about whether or not the children had classified the objects was made by a cognitive scorer who did not know the children's linguistic level. This scorer classified the children as having solved the task if they sorted all the objects in any one set into two groups.

Mothers were asked to record all the names their child used on the language questionnaire. The language scorer, who was not involved in the cognitive testing and did not know the child's cognitive level, went over the questionnaire with the mother at the start of each session and recorded the new names. Thus, as in the previous study language and cognition were scored independently. The language scorer only counted words as names if they were clearly applied to objects and were used in more than one social context. For example, a use of "mama" simply to obtain help from other people, or a use of "duck" only in the context of a particular walk to see a particular duck would not be counted as uses of names. This category primarily included words that would be described as general nominals in the adult language, but a few proper names, such as

"Daddy" were also included, as were a few onomatopoeic nouns such as "choo-choo" (systematically applied to trains) or "moo" (applied to cows).

Many different criteria could be used to define the naming explosion. In this case we decided that a very simple criterion would be most appropriate so we defined the naming explosion as the session in which the greatest number of new names were recorded. This criteria has also been used by Corrigan (1978).

The results suggest that there is a specific relationship between the development of the highest level categorization skill, sorting all the objects into two groups, and the naming explosion. The average gap between these two developments was 40.37 days. This gap was shorter than either the average gap between the naming explosion and the solution of object-permanence task 14 (56.7 days) or the average gap between the naming explosion and the solution of means-ends tasks 10–12 (55.87 days). (Object-permanence task 13 and means-ends task 9 were consistently passed well before the naming explosion or the solution of the sorting task.)

The correlational analysis provided further support for a relationship between the categorization task and the naming explosion. There was a significant correlation between the age at which the children first sorted all the objects into two groups and the age at which the naming explosion was first recorded ($r = .83$). There was no correlation at all between the age of solution of means-ends tasks 10–12 and the naming explosion ($r = .04$), though there was a correlation between the age of solution of object-permanence task 14 and the naming explosion ($r = .70$). However, the categorization/naming correlation remained high ($r = .76$) even when the effects of the object permanence task were partialled out, while the object permanence/ naming correlation disappeared when the effects of the categorization task were partialled out ($r = .18$). These results strongly suggest that the relationship between categorization and the naming explosion is a specific one.

As far as we know, these are the first results indicating a relationship between the development of categorization skills and linguistic skills, particularly the onset of the naming explosion. We have recently replicated this study with a larger sample of children and obtained similar results (Gopnik & Meltzoff, in press). These findings certainly suggest that there is another specific relationship between categorization and naming, which paraallels the specific relationships between disappearance words and object permanence and between success/failure words and means-ends abilities we have already reported.

CONCLUSION

The findings we have discussed in this chapter, taken with other results in the literature, suggest that there *are* relationships between linguistic and cognitive development in the one-word stage, but they do not have the characteristics that Piaget and others have supposed. First, there seems to be little relationship between formal aspects of language in this period, particularly the ability to use words productively, and the emergence of "stage 6" cognitive abilities. Our results suggest, however, that there are relationships between the content of early language and "stage 6" skills.

Second, these relationships do not necessarily involve cognitive prerequisites for linguistic developments. Some cognitive developments do consistently precede these semantic developments, for example, children seem to solve object-permanence task 13 before they use a disappearance word. However, slightly later cognitive developments appear to take place at the same time as the semantic developments. These cognitive and semantic developments occur concurrently.

Third, rather than finding a general relationship between semantic developments and some general "stage 6" cognitive development, we have found several different specific relationships between particular semantic developments and particular cognitive developments. So far we have found relationships between disappearance words and object permanence, success/failure words and means-ends understanding, and the naming explosion and categorization.

It seems likely that there are other specific relationships between semantic and cognitive developments analogous to those we have described here. For example, the early development of locative words could plausibly be related to the development of spatial abilities. Similarly, the development of "more" might be related to the ability to understand the abstract general concept of recurrence. Moreover, later semantic and syntactic developments, such as the expression of relationships between actions and objects, might be related to later specific cognitive developments.

Implications for Existing Theories

These findings would not be predicted by any of the prevailing theories of the relationship of linguistic and cognitive development in the one-word stage. Clearly, they are not consistent with Piaget's account. First, children can use words productively and symbolically before they show signs of "stage 6" developments in other domains. Second, we found strong and interesting concurrent relationships between semantic and conceptual developments rather than finding that conceptual developments always precede linguistic ones. Third, these relationships involve specific links between particular cognitive and linguistic achievements, rather than involving a general relationship between the ability to use words and "stage 6." Finally, these relationships involve semantic developments rather than general formal developments.

This last feature of these relationships also make them rather different from the relationships predicted by Bates et al., or Fischer and Corrigan. Both these accounts predict that formal properties of language will be related to cognitive developments. Our findings suggest that semantic rather than formal aspects of language development are related to cognitive development and that these semantic developments are related to specific cognitive achievements.

Our findings also suggest that the absence of relationships between more general measures of language and cognition previously reported in the literature reflects a genuine dissociation between these two aspects of development rather than reflecting the inadequacies of cognitive tests. Children's performance on the Uzgiris and Hunt tasks *is* related to their semantic development. This suggests that these tasks do measure genuine cognitive developments. The cognitive tasks aren't the problem. It's just that there isn't much relationship between the cognitive developments these task measure, and general formal aspects of language development.

An Alternative Model: A Shift from Social to Cognitive Functions of Language

The relationships we have discovered are all very specific. However, they share some general features. In each case, children acquire a word that encodes a particular concept at about the same time that they solve problems involving this concept. And many such words seem to emerge in the 15- to 21-month-old period. In fact, we suspect that most of the typical "one-word stage" words, relational words such as "gone," "there," "no," "uh-oh," "down," and "more" as well as the names of the naming explosion, are related to specific cognitive developments that take place in this period.

This is in contrast to the words that are used earlier in language development, the "script" words, social words, and specific names of the period preceding stage 6, and it is also in contrast to prelinguistic gestures and vocalizations. These earlier words seem to be more closely related to the children's communicative desires than to their cognitive interests. A social interactionist account may indeed be the best explanation for the use of these words, and similar words such as "please" or "byebye" that persist during the one-word stage. Of course, prelinguistic gestures and social words may be related to cognitive development in some way (see, for example, Bates et al., 1979). It would be rather surprising if they were not. But they are not related to specific cognitive developments in the way that later words are.

This pattern suggests to us that there is some general change in the child's language at around 18 months that *underlies* all the specific relationships between semantic and cognitive developments. This change, however, does not appear to involve the development of general linguistic abilities as Piaget, Bates et al., and Fischer and Corrigan would suggest.

We suggest that at around 18 months a new function of language emerges. At this point in their development children begin to talk about the specific cognitive problems they are working on at the moment. For example, a child who is in the middle of trying to understand complex object permanence problems may be particularly motivated to acquire a word like "gone" that is relevant to those problems, whereas a child who is working on means-ends problems may be more motivated to acquire success/failure words, and a child who is preoccupied with categorization may be more interested in early names. While all these relationships between language and cognition are quite specific, they reflect a common functional tendency to use words to try to solve difficult cognitive problems.

This cognitive, intrapersonal use of language is rather different from the more social, interpersonal functions of other early words and of prelinguistic communication. We suggest that at around 18 months children stop using language exclusively to communicate with other people, and begin to use language as a way of sorting out their own cognitive problems.

This raises the intriguing possibility that using language may actually facilitate these specific "stage 6" cognitive developments. It seems possible that acquiring an explicit, general word for disappearance, like "gone," might actually help the child to develop the general concept of disappearance that is necessary to solve the most difficult object-permanence problems. Similarly, acquiring words about means-ends relationships, like success and failure words, might facilitate the development of means-ends abilities, and understanding that every object has a name might help the child to understand that every object belongs in some category. The fact that the cognitive developments take place at the same time as the semantic developments, rather than being prerequisites for those developments, also suggests that there may be an interaction between these two areas of development.

Clearly, children's cognitive concerns shape the semantic structure of their early language. Equally, however, their early language may be influencing their cognitive development. Semantic and cognitive development are closely intertwined from the time children begin to use their first words.

ACKNOWLEDGMENT

The reserach reported in this paper was supported by a Natural Sciences and Engineering Research Council of Canada grant to the first author and a MacArthur Foundation grant to the second author. We are grateful to Guy Ewing, George Theodoris, Craig Harris and the parents of all our subjects for the assistance.

REFERENCES

Barrett, M. (1985). Early semantic representation and early word usage. In S. Kuczaj & M. Barrett (Eds.), *The development of word meaning* (pp. 39–67). New York: Springer-Verlag.

Bates, E., Benigni, L., Bretherton, I., Camaioni, L., & Volterra, V. (1979). *The emergence of symbols: Cognition-communication in infancy.* New York: Academic Press.

Bloom, L. (1973). *One word at a time: The use of single word utterances before syntax.* The Hague: Mouton.

Bloom, L., Lifter, K., & Broughton, J. (1981). What children say and what they know. In R. E. Stark (Ed.), *Language behavior in infancy and early childhood* (pp. 301–326). Elsevier: North Holland.

Bloom, L., Lifter, K., & Broughton, J. (1985). The convergence of early cognition and language in the second year of life: Problems in conceptualization and measurement. In M. Barrett (Ed.), *Single-Word Speech* (pp. 149–180). New York: Wiley.

Bonvillian, J. D., Orlansky, M. D., & Novack, L. L. (1983). Development milestones—Sign language acquisition and motor development. *Child Development, 54,* 1435–1445.

Brown, R. (1973). *A first language: The early stages.* Cambridge MA: Harvard University Press.

Bruner, J. (1975). From communication to language—A psychological perspective. *Cognition, 3,* 255–287.

Bruner, J. (1983). *Child's talk.* New York: W. W. Norton.

Chomsky, N. (1968). *Language and mind.* New York: Harcourt, Brace, Jovanovich.

Chomsky, N. (1980). *Rules and representations.* New York: Columbia University Press.

Cohen, L. B., & Strauss, M. (1979). Concept acquisition in the human infant. *Child Development, 50,* 419–424.

Corrigan, R. (1978). Language development as related to stage 6 object permanence development. *Journal of Child Language, 5,* 173–189.

Corrigan, R. (1979). Cognitive correlates of language: Differential criteria yield differential results. *Child Development, 50,* 617–631.

Dihoff, A., & Chapman, R. (1977). First words: Their origins in action. *Papers and Reports on Child Language Development, 13,* 1–7.

Fischer, K. W., & Corrigan, R. (1981). A skill approach to language development. In R. E. Stark (Ed.), *Language behavior in infancy and early childhood* (pp. 245–273). Elsevier: North Holland.

Fodor, J. (1983). *The modularity of mind.* Cambridge, MA: Bradford Books.

Gopnik, A. (1981). Development of non-nominal expressions in 1- 2-year-olds. In P. Dale & D. Ingram (Eds.), *Child language, an international perspective* (pp. 93–104). Baltimore, MD: University Park Press.

Gopnik, A. (1982). Words and plans: Early language and the development of intelligent action. *Journal of Child Language, 9,* 303–318.

Gopnik, A. (1984a). Conceptual and semantic change in scientists and children: Why there are no semantic universals. *Linguistics, 20,* 163–179.

Gopnik, A. (1984b). The acquisition of ''gone'' and the development of the object concept. *Journal of Child Language, 11,* 273–292.

Gopnik, A., & Meltzoff, A. N. (1984). Semantic and cognitive development in 15 to 21-month-old children. *Journal of Child Language, 11,* 495–513.

Gopnik, A., & Meltzoff, A. N. (1985a). From people to plans to objects: Changes in the meaning of early words and their relation to cognitive development. *Journal of Pragmatics, 9,* 495–512.

Gopnik, A., & Meltzoff, A. N. (1985b). Words, plans, things, and locations: Interactions between semantic and cognitive development in the one-word stage. In S. Kuczaj & M. Barrett (Eds.), *The development of word meaning* (pp. 199–223). New York: Springer-Verlag.

Gopnik, A., & Meltzoff, A. N. (1986). Relations between semantic and cognitive development in the one-word stage: The specificity hypothesis. *Child Development, 57,* 1040–1053.

Gopnik, A., & Meltzoff, A. N. (in press). The development of categorization in the second year and its relation to other cognitive and linguistic developments. *Child Development, 58.*

Greenfield, P. M., & Smith, J. H. (1976). *The structure of communication in early language development.* New York: Academic Press.

Harris, P. L. (1982). Cognitive prerequisites to language? *British Journal of Psychology, 73,* 187–195.

Lock, A. (1980). *The guided reinvention of language.* London: Academic Press.

McCune-Nicolich, L. (1981). The cognitive bases of relational words in the single word period. *Journal of Child Language, 8,* 15–34.

Morehead, D., & Morehead, A. (1974). From signal to sign: A Piagetian view of thought and language during the first two years. In R. L. Scheifelbusch & L. L. Lloyd (Eds.), *Language perspectives: Acquisition, retardation and intervention* (pp. 153–191). Baltimore, MD: University Park Press.

Nelson, K. (1973). Some evidence for the cognitive primacy of categorization and its functional basis. *Merrill-Palmer Quarterly, 19,* 21–39.

Piaget, J. (1952). *The origins of intelligence in children.* New York: W. W. Norton.

Piaget, J. (1954). *The construction of reality in the child.* New York: Basic Books.

Piaget, J. (1962). *Play, dreams, and imitation in childhood.* New York: W. W. Norton.

Ricciutti, H. N. (1965). Object grouping and selective ordering behaviors in infants 12 to 24 months old. *Merrill-Palmer Quarterly, 11,* 129–148.

Sinclair, H. (1970). The transition from sensory-motor behaviour to symbolic activity. *Interchange, 1,* 119–126.

Smolak, L., & Levine, M. P. (1984). The effects of differential criteria on the assessment of cognitive-linguistic relationships. *Child Development, 55,* 973–980.

Snow, C. (1979). Social interaction and language acquisition. In P. Dale & D. Ingram (Eds.), *Child language: An international perspective* (pp. 195–215). Baltimore, University Park Press.

Starkey, D. (1981). The origins of concept formation: Object sorting and object preference in early infancy. *Child Development, 52,* 489–497.

Sugarman, S. (1983). *Children's early thought: Development in classification.* Cambridge, England: Cambridge University Press.

Tomasello, M., & Farrar, M. (1984). Cognitive bases of lexical development: Object permanence and relational words. *Journal of Child Language, 11,* 477–493.

Uzgiris, I., & Hunt, J. M. V. (1975). *Assessment in infancy: Ordinal scales of psychological development.* Urbana: University of Illinois Press.

Wexler, K., & Culicover, P. (1980). *Formal principles of language acquisition.* Cambridge, MA: MIT Press.

10 Comprehending Concrete Metaphors: Developing an Understanding of Topic-Vehicle Interaction

Cathy H. Dent
University of North Carolina, Chapel Hill

INTRODUCTION

Children as young as three use statements in natural conversation such as "Look! They're flowers" about fireworks on the Fourth of July. Are those statements metaphors? Do children mean and understand such utterances the way adults would, or do they make "mistakes" of categorization? These are the questions to be discussed in this paper by presenting a model of metaphor and the cognitive abilities used to comprehend and produce metaphors (see Gardner, Winner, Bechhofer, & Wolf, 1978; Ortony, Reynolds, & Arter, 1978, for previous literature reviews). In addition, an empirical study of children's metaphor comprehension is presented that focuses on developing a nonverbal measure of preschoolers' understanding of simple concrete metaphors. The results of the empirical study are then related to the model and further research is suggested.

Theoretical Model

Metaphor is generally defined as a figure of speech in which a word or phrase, the *vehicle*, is applied to an object or concept, the *topic*, that it does not literally denote, but that bears some similarity to the object denoted literally; thus there is a *ground* for the statement, and it does make sense. For example, "My lawnmower is a wild animal" is a sensible comment about a lawnmower, although the statement is not literally true. In figurative utterances, as in any utterance, the topic and comment have referents (including actions and abstract entities as referents), but certain characteristics of the vehicle (figurative) term distinguish figurative utterances from literal utterances. The vehicle term in most metaphors occurring in nonpoetic discourse refers to concrete, perceivable objects or actions and the vehicle always entails a double reference, that is, simultaneous reference to the literally denoted object or action and temporary (within-an-utterance) reference to the topic object or action, resulting in an utterance that requires that knowledge of one domain be used to understand a different kind of domain (cf. Black, 1977).

The fact that vehicle terms in many metaphors and similes refer to common perceivable objects and events means that this type of language is particularly amenable to a realist theoretical explanation of the relationship between language and what it is used to communicate about. The realist approach to language (cf. Dent, 1986, 1987; Millikan, 1984; Rader & Dent, 1979; Schmidt & Dent, 1985; Verbrugge, 1985) proposes that language can be used to communicate about the physical world, as well as about physical and emotional internal states, because (1) what is to be described or talked about by a speaker is perceived by that speaker, and (2) the relationship between language and its referents is real, that is, has been perceived and experienced by both speaker and listener in the course of their previous experience with language in specific situations. It follows from these assumptions that the relationship between words and what they refer to is not arbitrary *in any one individual's experience,* that the meaning of much of language is the object or event being referred to, and that mental representation need not be invoked as a mediator between language and what it is used to describe or talk about. With regard to figurative language in particular, the realist approach specifies that what is crucial to using and understanding figurative language is detecting resemblances and perceiving the topic in light of the vehicle. This theoretical approach leads one to study the physical resemblances about which figurative language is used and to attend to the nonverbal aspects of metaphors. Thus, attention is directed to two areas of study in figurative language that have received minimal study, namely figurative language production (and the effects of physical context) and nonverbal components of meaning.

In addition to directing attention to new aspects of metaphor abilities, the realist approach has several theoretical advantages over an indirect or mentalist approach to meaning in language. First, the realist approach is parsimonious. If animals, including humans, directly perceive real objects, events, surfaces, and layouts in their environments (cf. Gibson, 1979), then they can also perceive the event of words and gestures being used about those objects and events. This idea is consistent with MacNamara's claim (1972) that children first learn the meaning of what is said and then learn the language. If people can perceive over time the permanent and changing aspects of the environment that are referred to with language, then feature lists or other types of mental representations which cannot be directly observed or manipulated are not necessary in a theoretical account of verbal meaning. The burden of proof for when and if mental mediation is required is on the theorist who claims the more complicated and unobservable explanation.

A second advantage of the realist approach to language pertains specifically to metaphor. When real resemblances are taken as the basis of metaphor then this type of language can be related systematically to the real world leading to a theory of how it is that a type of language which on the surface is "untrue" actually does reveal "how things are" (Black, 1977). This view of metaphor is particularly useful in developmental work because it focuses on nonverbal experience and abilities that even very young children have, thus guiding our efforts to detail the emergence of metaphor abilities.

While the idea that the ground or similarity between the topic and vehicle objects in many metaphors is real and is experienced (Dent, 1984; Verbrugge, 1980) has begun to be elucidated, it has not previously been noted that what characterizes metaphor is that the topic and vehicle refer to things that are different in kind. Although it has been established that for adults metaphors are about domains of objects, not individual objects, that is, both topic and vehicle reference groups or categories of objects or events (except those about individual people) (Kelly & Keil, 1987; Tourangeau & Sternberg, 1981; Verbrugge & MacCarrell, 1977), the idea of domains requires further specification.

The idea of natural kinds (Mill, 1884) is useful in determining principles for distinguishing literal from figurative similarity. A natural kind is a class of existing objects that have the same nature or character, although we cannot exhaustively enumerate the properties the objects have in common. Inasmuch as vehicles reference real objects and not a particular object they reference naturally occurring kinds. Furthermore, the topic must be a different kind of object than the vehicle. Metaphors are difficult to make about objects that are literally alike, that is, of the same kind, or about objects that are different in kind but share only a similarity that does not include the properties that make it a member of its kind. To quote Mill (1884):

> By a kind . . . , we mean those classes which are distinguished from all others not by one or a few definite properties, but by an unknown multitude of them: the combination of properties on which the class is grounded being a mere index to an indefinite number of distinctive attributes. The class horse is a kind, because the things which agree in possessing the characters by which we recognize a horse, agree in a great number of properties, as we know, and, it cannot be doubted, in many more we don't know. . . . But a combination of properties which does not give evidence of the existence of any other independent peculiarities does not constitute a kind. White horse, therefore, is not a kind, because horses which agree in whiteness do not agree in anything else, except the qualities common to all horses, and what even may be the causes of, or effects of that particular colour. (p. 460)

Therefore, it is difficult to construct a metaphor about a black shoe and a black horse, because even though shoes and horses are different in kind, black shoe and black horse are not kinds. Thus, the concept of naturally occurring kinds points out one direction for a theoretical specification of the difference between metaphoric and literal similarity and between metaphoric and literal language while capturing the fact that metaphors typically function by referencing real-world objects and events in order to communicate.

In comprehension of metaphor (Black, 1977), the hypothesized interaction of meaning between terms (possibly through some process of mental condensation or fusion) can take place precisely because the terms reference different kinds, thus allowing for each meaning to change the other; "fireworks are flowers" changes our understanding of both kinds, whereas "fireworks are explosions" changes only the meaning of fireworks. The idea that topic and vehicle domains interact so that when a metaphor has been comprehended both topic and vehicle meanings have been affected has been useful in psycholinguistic work with adults (e.g., Kelly & Keil, 1987; Verbrugge & MacCarrell, 1977). The present model, by focusing on the fact that topic and vehicle must be different in kind, leads to specifying how it is possible for topic and vehicle meanings to interact and affect each other. The developmental question is, do young children understand "A is B" concrete metaphors through an interaction of topic and vehicle as has been hypothesized and demonstrated for adults?

Empirical Research

In addition to the theoretical points raised above, the present study rests on previous empirical findings. First, nonverbal measures of metaphor comprehension, such as pointing to analogous parts of different things (Gentner, 1977) or enacting the action stated in a metaphor (Vosniadou & Ortony, 1986) have been shown to be effective measures of metaphor comprehension in preschool children. In general, nonverbal measures have indicated understanding of analogies, metaphors, and similes at younger ages than verbal measures such as paraphrase or explication. We are just beginning to understand children's metaphor abilities and one central issue is the actual inception or emergence of these abilities. For this reason studying young children's abilities is important. Also, we know very little about the relationship of nonverbal and verbal means of demonstrating comprehension of verbal material. Is nonverbal demonstration of comprehension a precursor to later abilities to verbally show comprehension? Although the present study does not directly investigate this latter question, both paraphrase and nonverbal measures are used in order to contrast within one age these different responses to metaphors. Related to issues of measuring comprehension is the question of the importance of context to a listener's comprehension of metaphor (cf. Dent, 1987; Verbrugge, 1979, 1986; Vosniadou & Ortony, 1987). Several studies have found that both verbal (Pearson, Raphael, TePaske, & Hyser, 1979; Windmueller, Massey, Blank, Gardner, & Winner, 1987) and nonverbal context (Gentner, 1977; Honeck, Voegtle, & Sowry, 1978) enhance figurative language comprehension. It has been shown that perceptual experience with metaphorically similar objects and events facilitates later comprehension of verbal metaphors about those objects presented in stories (Dent & Ledbetter, 1986) in children as young as five. Also, it has been shown that extensive verbal context aids children in understanding metaphors in stories even using only verbal measures of comprehension (Waggoner, Messe, & Palermo, 1985) at least as young as age seven. Thus, in order to study the emergence of metaphor abilities the present study employed both verbal and nonverbal context for the metaphors to be comprehended and verbal and nonverbal measures of comprehension.

A second category of empirical findings form part of the rationale for this study, specifically for the actual nonverbal measure of comprehension to be used. First, the instruction to think at the same time about two metaphorically similar objects or events was more effective in eliciting metaphors than instructions to compare the two (Dent, 1981, 1984). Also, adults sometimes report mental images of two metaphorically similar objects being fused or condensed into a single imaginal object as part of the comprehension of verbal metaphors (Evans, 1984; Verbrugge, 1977). These two findings are consistent with findings from studies in which visual information for fused objects was presented and metaphors were elicited as descriptions (Dent & Rosenberg, 1986; Rothenberg & Sobel, 1980). Specifically, concrete instances of fused objects, that is, miniature objects constructed to be fusions of two different-kind objects such as a wrinkled apple with a face, have been shown to be effective in eliciting metaphors from children as young as five (Dent & Rosenberg, 1986). In addition, superimposed slides of natural objects were superior to juxtaposed slides in eliciting high-quality metaphors from adults (Rothenberg & Sobel, 1980). Given the theoretical importance of topic-vehicle interaction (cf. Black, 1977; Kelly & Keil, 1987) and the empirical findings that depicted condensations were likely to elicit metaphors, the present study was designed to allow 4-year-old children to combine parts of depicted topic and vehicle objects in order to show nonverbally something of the meaning of simple concrete metaphors.

It was expected that children would show sensible depictions of topic-vehicle interaction even though they probably would not be able to paraphrase or explicate the metaphors. It was expected, also, that young children would sensibly condense objects in response to metaphors, but not to the highest degree, inasmuch as previous research has shown an increase in the degree of reported mental condensation with age when children 5 to 10 were asked to "think about two things (different in kind) at the same time" (Dent, 1984). Lastly, literal sentences should not elicit condensed pictures even when instructions paralleled those used for metaphoric sentences inasmuch as condensation of different-kind objects is a process that is, theoretically, unique to figurative language. This latter manipulation again was aimed at differentiating literal from metaphoric meaning and should thereby contribute to clearer definitions of both types of language.

METHOD

Subjects.   Twenty-eight 4-year-olds of middle class background participated; all were attending preschools and were native speakers of English. The
children were chosen randomly from those whose parents consented to the study;
one child refused to participate.

Materials.   The materials were photographs of realistic miniature objects
presented in pairs that could be talked about metaphorically, for example, a deer
leaping and a dancer leaping for ''the deer is a dancer.'' These pairs of objects
have been effective in eliciting metaphors from children as young as five (Dent.
1984; Dent & Rosenberg, 1986) so they were chosen as likely to be comprehensible to preschool children. Photographs of two pairs of stationary objects, a
wrinkled face and a wrinkled apple; a tall giraffe and a tall building (skyscraper)
and of two pairs of objects in movement, a dancer leaping and a deer leaping; a
ballerina spinning and a top spinning were used. All the photographs were
enlarged to 8″ by 10″ and the objects cut out. Then each object, approximately 4″
in height, was cut into four sections roughly corresponding to head, torso, upper
legs, and lower legs of the human figure. Children as young as two are able
analogously to map the human body onto inanimate objects (Gentner, 1977) so
that cutting the pictures into these parts should be understandable to preschoolers. The cutting lines were straight so that any two pieces could be easily
aligned. A practice pair, constructed as described above, was a lion and king.
For each pair of objects, a one-paragraph story was constructed that ended with a
metaphor about the two objects, and for each pair of objects there were two
stories, one wherein an object was the topic and the other object the vehicle and
another, wherein the order was reversed. Each story contained eight propositions; sample stories follow.

a. Johnny lived on a farm in the coun-   giraffe and skyscraper
try. One day his mother took him
to the city. They went to the zoo
and he saw giraffes with their long
necks. They went downtown and
he saw a tall, tall building. So
Johnny laughed and said, ''Look,
the building is a giraffe.''

b. Johnny lives on a farm in the coun-   giraffe and skyscraper
try. One day his mother took him
to the city. They went downtown
and he saw a tall, tall building.
Then they went to the zoo and saw
giraffes with their long necks. So
Johnny laughed and said, ''Look,
the giraffe is a building.''

In addition, stories ending in literal category statements were constructed about three literal pairings of these objects, that is, the deer and giraffe, king and face, dancer and ballerina. Each story contained five propositions. A sample story follows.

One day Johnny's mother took him to the zoo. He saw a giraffe and then in the next yard he saw a deer. He said, "The giraffe and the deer are both animals."

Procedure.   Half of the participants were read stories in which one simple object was the topic and the other the vehicle; the other half heard stories wherein the objects were reversed as topic and vehicle. Lion and king pictures were used for a practice trial with all the participants, which consisted of assembling each picture, side by side, on a felt board (left-right position counterbalanced) and asking the child to name each object and say how they are the same. Whatever similarity the participant provided, the experimenter agreed and then added that the lion and king were also both strong. Then the experimenter gave instructions to listen carefully to the story and try to understand it. After reading the story, the last line, the metaphor ("the king is a lion"), was repeated and the child was told to "use these two pictures (pointing to the object pictures) to show what that means" and the metaphor was repeated. In the practice trial after the child made a construction the adult modeled a construction wherein the lion's head was on the king's body (a condensed construction of the highest amount; see following section on Scoring). The same procedure, without any modeling of constructions, was used for the following four test trials. The experimenter was encouraging and supportive of whatever the child did and repeated the metaphor during the time that the child was constructing a new picture. For the test items, the grounds given by experimenter were leaping (with hand gesture) for dancer and deer, spinning (with hand gesture) for ballerina and top, wrinkled for face and apple, and tall for giraffe and skyscraper. Then, when the child had finished constructing, the experimenter asked "What does that mean (*metaphor*)" and "Why did X say that (*metaphor*)?" to check on their ability to paraphrase the metaphor. The finished pictorial constructions were photographed for later scoring.

As a control for possible demand characteristics of the task and to contrast literal and metaphoric language on this nonverbal comprehension measure, a literal sentence comprehension task that paralleled the metaphor comprehension task in all ways except that the sentence to be comprehended was a literal class membership sentence was conducted with 8 other children. A story was read and the child asked to make a picture to show what the last line meant. However, the two objects were of the same or similar kinds (chosen from the full set of objects described above), that is, deer and giraffe (both animals), king and face (both people), ballerina and dancer (both people and dancers). Five-year-olds often put these objects together in pilot tests in which they were asked to group together the things that were "the same kind" (cf. Dent, 1987) and the sentence to be comprehended was a literal class membership statement, for example, "the deer and giraffe are both animals." In order that the effects of modeling be constant across literal and metaphor conditions, the experimenter modeled a fused picture in the literal stories, too. For the literal stories the model corresponded to the sentence "the top is in the building" and consisted of overlaying the building on part of the top and leaving the rest of the top visible between the top and bottom part of the building (a condensed construction with the highest score, see Scoring below). The modeled literal sentence was not a class membership statement because the top and building as instances of artifacts would likely not be understood by 4-year-olds.

Scoring. Each photograph of the children's constructions was scored first for whether the object was condensed using the following rules. An object was not condensed if only one object was used in the construction, if two objects were used but not combined into one (e.g., two objects reconstructed side by side, or one constructed whole and the other parts around it), or if pieces from both objects were used but in an unsystematic way (e.g., a vertical sequence giraffe legs, top of building, giraffe head). Objects that combined pieces of the two original objects and those that were one object superimposed over another were scored as condensed. These photographs were then scored for amount of

TABLE 10.1
Condensation Scoring System

Scoring Category	Example Construction
Uncondensed:	
1. nonsensical arrangement of pieces	deer head deer legs dancer head deer body dancer torso deer legs dancer legs
2. reassembles objects, one or both, or one is whole with pieces of the other around it	eyes nose apple chin
Condensed:	
3. intermixes pieces in a sensible column	top of apple nose apple chin
4. one picture, whole or part, on top of the other, or analogous part replacement	dancer head deer body
5. top part of one object and bottom part of the other, or body of one with top and bottom of other above and below the body	ballerina head & arms body of top ballerina legs

condensation (cf. Dent, 1984). Specifically, responses scored as uncondensed were those in which pieces of different objects were not combined, or if combined, the combination was nonsensical (a score of 1) or one object was constructed whole and pieces of the other were arranged around it (score of 2). Condensed responses consisted of intermixing pieces in a sensible column or constructing one object over the other (score 3), analogous parts exchanged (score 4) or top part of one object was combined with bottom part of the other, or the top and bottom of one object was combined with the middle of the other object (score 5). Examples are given in Table 10.1. All the data were scored independently by two judges; agreement was 82% and disagreements were resolved by discussion.

RESULTS

Children readily used the pictures in response to the metaphors, but they almost never answered the question of why the speaker said the metaphor or what the metaphor meant with paraphrases of the metaphors. Only one response constituted a true paraphrase. One child when asked why the speaker in the story said "The deer is a dancer" replied "It went to ballet dance, it was dancing. It does a different dance." The adult said "What kind of dance does it do?" And the child said, "It jumps in the air like that" (making a leaping motion with her hands). The children provided a wide range of responses to the paraphrase questions including nonsense, no response, saying "I don't know," repeating the metaphor, saying that the two things were alike, saying how the two things were different, and repeating something from the story. Some children said the speaker did not know what the topic object was or that the topic object could not be the vehicle object. There were three types of response that were more relevant: stating the ground, for example, "they both spin," providing reasonable information as in "cause it (the top) looks like a ballerina," and the one paraphrase given above. A discussion of the relationship of answers to the paraphrase questions and type of pictorial construction follows.

The primary results concern the types of pictures the children constructed to show what the metaphors meant. One child did not produce any condensed pictures. Only 6 of the 80 picture constructions (7%) were scored nonsensical. For each story ending in a metaphor more children made condensed pictures than uncondensed and low-condensed responses (scores 3 and 4) were more frequent than high-condensed responses (score 5). The chi-square values for these differences are given in Table 10.2. Seventeen of the 19 children who produced condensed pictures received the same level of condensation score for at least 75% of their pictures.

The mean condensation scores of the picture constructions where the child provided the ground when asked why the speaker said the metaphor was 3.5 (1

TABLE 10.2
Frequencies of Different Types of Responses to Metaphors

Story	Uncondensed (Category 2)	Condensed (Categories 3,4,5)		
1	2	15	$x_2^2 = 9.94$	$p < .01$
2	4	16	$x_2^2 = 7.2$	$p < .01$
3	2	17	$x_2^2 = 11.8$	$p < .01$
4	1	17	$x^2 = 14.2$	$p < .01$

Story	Low Condensed (Categories 3,4)	High Condensed (Category 5)		
1	13	2	$x_2^2 = 8.06$	$p < .01$
2	15	1	$x_2^2 = 12.2$	$p < .01$
3	15	2	$x_2^2 = 9.94$	$p < .01$
4	13	4	$x^2 = 4.76$	$p < .05$

out of 12 was uncondensed) and the mean for when the ground was given in response to "what does (metaphor) mean?" was 3.7 (2 out of 18 were uncondensed).

The same average degree of condensation was found with either object taken as topic in the metaphor. "The deer is a dancer" and "The dancer is a deer." illustrate the contrasting orders. The degree of condensation was, on the average, 9.7 and 9.3 for different orders.

Also, the vehicle was predominant, in condensed responses, as often as the topic for all stories. For one order of objects the mean number of pieces used from the topic was 2.3 and from the vehicle 2.6; for the other order the corresponding means were 3.1 and 2.9. Overall, the number of cases where more pieces were used from the topic than vehicle object was 18 (2.3% of the total responses), in contrast the reverse dominance was shown in 24 instances (3% of the total responses). Those responses scored as most condensed had the same mean number of pieces from the topic as the vehicle object, that is, 2.2. Responses were equally likely to include the "head" piece from the topic as vehicle (15 and 20), the "feet" piece (17 and 11) and both the "head" and "feet" (32 and 35). One set of metaphors (one order) resulted in 18 constructions with more pieces of the vehicle than the topic, the other order resulted in only 6 such constructions. The metaphors that elicited more constructions where the vehicle was predominant were: the deer is a dancer, the apple is a face, the giraffe is a building, and the top is a ballerina. A t-test of difference between means for the number of constructions in which the vehicle object predominanted was significant; $t_{(18)} = 3.97$, $p < .002$, 2-tailed. The number of constructions in which more pieces of the topic than the vehicle were included was equivalent for the two orders, i.e., 10 and 8.

The metaphors based on motion similarity (ballerina and top and dancer and deer) elicited condensed constructions equally as often as stationary objects; 32 for motion (i.e., event) similarity and 33 for stationary objects with respective condensation means of 4.0 and 3.8.

TABLE 10.3
Frequencies of Different Types of Responses to Literal Statements

Story	Mean Score	Uncondensed	Condensed	(No High Scores)
1	2.4	6	2	$x^2 = 2.0$ ns
2	2.0	8	0	
3	2.1	7	1	$x^2 = 4.5$, $p < .05$

In contrast to the metaphors, literal sentences very rarely resulted in condensed constructions, whereas uncondensed constructions were frequent; 3 responses were condensed and 21 were uncondensed. The mean condensation overall was 2.2 on the above scale (see also Table 10.3). The predominant response to the literal sentences, such as "the deer and giraffe are both animals," was to take each picture apart and reassemble them side by side at a position below where the experimenter had placed them on the board.

DISCUSSION

The results show that young preschool children responded by sensibly combining depicted objects to show the meaning of a metaphor about those objects, although the amount of condensation was relatively low. The combined or condensed pictures that children produced might be an indication of the mental process of understanding a concrete "A is B" metaphor by seeing one object domain in terms of its similarities to a different-kind object domain, for example, seeing the "dancerness" of a leaping deer. Although the number of constructions in which either topic or vehicle object predominated was low, there was a preponderance of constructions in which the vehicle predominated for the set of metaphors wherein three of the four had human vehicles and nonhuman topics. Young children are more familiar with and, therefore, know people better than animals so it may have been easier for them to use parts of the human figure in constructing a depiction than parts of animals. These results bring up the interesting possibility that the interaction between topic and vehicle in metaphor comprehension is not a uniform process across all listeners and metaphors even within the subset of metaphors in which both topic and vehicle refer to concrete objects or actions. Perhaps the interaction process is different when the vehicle is more familiar than the topic than vice versa. We need much more data on metaphors young children actually produce and on what they know about the objects and actions they use in metaphors, in concert with further research on comprehension, to determine whether interaction between topic and vehicle occurs in different ways.

The children did not combine objects when asked to use the pictures to show the meaning of literal sentences. This is evidence that metaphors are not just ornamental or stylistic variations of literal comparison statements, that is, that metaphors have the same meaning as equivalent comparison statements that are literal (see Black, 1977; Verbrugge, 1979, for reviews of the different theories of metaphor). Specifically, although an "A is B" concrete metaphor has the same surface form as a class membership statement it is not such a statement. A metaphor leads to a new understanding of the topic, by drawing attention to resemblances not by saying what class the topic is a member of. The stories ending in metaphors did contain more propositions than those ending in literal statements, but both types of sentences were preceded by a coherent story context that included settings, protagonists and actions leading up to the descriptive statement (either literal or metaphoric) by the protagonist. It is doubtful that slightly more verbal context would lead to such different picture constructions when children were asked to show what a descriptive statement meant. Instead, the difference in constructions corresponds to the difference in meaning of the metaphors and literal statements.

The findings of the present study are relevant to general issues current in research on children's metaphor comprehension. First of all, the children did provide sensible pictorial responses to metaphors even though they could not paraphrase nor explicate the metaphors. They did show verbal evidence of understanding the ground or topic-vehicle similarity by stating the ground when asked or in response to the metalinguistic questions about the metaphors, so lack of understanding of the similarity on which the metaphors were based is not the reason for inability verbally to paraphrase. Although the stories were not as long as those used in some previous research (Waggoner, Messe, & Palermo, 1985) nonverbal context in the form of pictures was also present so the amount of context is probably not the critical factor either. Paraphrasing is a fundamentally different type of activity than either acting or contingently speaking in response to an utterance. While acting or replying in response to a speaker's utterance shows comprehension when appropriate, paraphrasing shows comprehension by translating one set of words into another set with a similar meaning. Many people, even adults, can use words appropriately without being able to provide another set of words that define a word's meaning and so it is not surprising that children have difficulty paraphrasing sentences, especially as those sentences in the typical study originate from adults and not from the children themselves or even from age peers. In any case, the present results are consistent with the ideas that verbal measures underestimate children's metaphor competence. In addition, the present measure has the advantage over enacting measures (cf. Vosniadou & Ortony, 1986) of potentially revealing more about the process of comprehension, that is, whether interaction of topic and vehicle is involved, and, therefore, of differentiating figurative and literal language if such interaction is characteristic of figurative language. Perhaps condensed pictures would facilitate young children's metaphor comprehension. If so we would have converging and validating evidence that the picture construction measure taps important metaphor abilities.

A second issue is that of whether topic and vehicle are equally affected in meaning by being used in a metaphor. Black (1977) describes the vehicle as a "filter" through which the topic is seen implying that a listener's understanding of the topic would be changed more than of the vehicle. Ortony (1979) in a related vein proposes that certain already salient aspects of the vehicle are applied to less salient aspects of the topic, again implying that the topic meaning would be changed more. The nonverbal measure of picture construction showed very little asymmetry in use of topic and vehicle object parts except that one set of metaphors was more likely than the counterpart set (in which topic and vehicle objects were reversed) to result in pictures where more parts of the vehicle were used than parts of the topic. This is only suggestive evidence at this point of any topic-vehicle asymmetry and we require much more data in order to know whether this measure is sensitive to such asymmetry and whether it exists in young children's metaphor comprehension. One possibility would be to use metaphors produced by same age children along with photographs that are divided into more pieces, and collect data on the actual process of the picture construction not just the end result to investigate whether either topic or vehicle object is used more, or kept more whole.

One final point is that there was no difference in amount of condensation to metaphors based on motion similarity, although motion information has previously proved an important variable in young children's metaphor production (Dent, 1984). It has been shown that motion information is more likely to be detected between objects different in kind by young children, but in the present case the similarity was made clear and provided before verbal metaphors based on the similarity. In this case, motion grounds did not affect children's metaphor comprehension. If actual motion had been present, there may have been an effect, and that question requires further empirical study.

In order to explore further the possibility that children do understand metaphors through the interaction of topic and vehicle domains further research should be done using the nonverbal measure of comprehension but with the addition of measures that are more process-oriented. For example, the process of making the condensed picture, not just the end point, might give us clues as to how children understand metaphors. Videotaping their actions as they produce the condensed pictures would provide the requisite data. In addition, changes with age in the process of object condensation should be charted, i.e., does degree of condensation increase with age? Is there a linear change with age?

To broaden the usefulness of this nonverbal measure, metaphors with varying types of grounds should be studied developmentally. For example, a 10-year-old child produced this metaphor, "the tree is the monarch of the field." This metaphor is based on a rather complex set of social relations, rather than on purely physical resemblance, and such relations as well as emotions can be depicted. However, the components of metaphor described in the model above are all present, including the possibility of topic-vehicle interaction. Perhaps the tree is seen to have king-like qualities, or be in relation to the shrubs around it as a king is to his subjects. Young children, who have limited experience with certain social relationships might not understand this metaphor, and, therefore might not sensibly condense pictures in response to it, while older children might produce a condensation that captured the meaning of the metaphor.

One final line of research would be useful, and that is to further validate the nonverbal measure developed herein by using the condensed pictures to elicit metaphors to see whether they represent the meaning of a metaphor well enough to lead to metaphors as descriptions. If this were the case, especially in children the same age as those who produced the picture, then picture condensation would be useful for elucidating not just comprehension but production of metaphor. Perhaps research on such seemingly commonplace events as young children's using and understanding metaphors will begin to provide some insight into the conundrum of what constitutes metaphoric meaning.

The orientation to metaphor outlined in the introduction has the advantage of detailing the relationship of the nonverbal and verbal aspects of metaphor and providing a focus for experimental studies of metaphor by directing attention to the perceptual information on which metaphors are based, and which children come to detect. The theoretical implications of the orientation outlined above are twofold. First, metaphoric similarity is defined as real, whether it is solely a physical resemblance or also includes social relationship and emotional response components. Second, metaphoric resemblance is differentiated from literal resemblance, then, not in being less real, but as existing between objects different in kind. Thus, the model relates one of the most fundamental aspects of perceiving and knowing, i.e., noting resemblance, to certain types of linguistic expression, and leads to empirical demonstrations that metaphoric resemblance is not an artifact of language but is actual, perceptible, and independent of linguistic expression. Linguistic expression, on the other hand, is intimately dependent on real-world resemblance. Specifically, it is difficult to use figurative language to talk about same-kind objects, and when metaphoric resemblance is talked about figuratively, the actual form of the utterance is affected by physical qualities of the resemblance (Dent, 1981). In the case of metaphor comprehension the model leads to a study of both verbal and nonverbal aspects of comprehension as in the present study where both types of measures were used. Thus, an important implication of the model is that all metaphor use includes necessary nonverbal components which can be demonstrated in comprehension as well as production.

ACKNOWLEDGMENTS

I thank Ellen Peisner for help in collecting data and the directors and children of Yates Baptist, Carrboro Methodist, and St. Marks preschools who generously cooperated. The work was supported by a Howells Memorial Fellowship from the University of Arkansas, Little Rock and a University Research Council Grant from the University of North Carolina, Chapel Hill. The author's current address is: Psychology Department, Miami University, Oxford, OH 45056.

REFERENCES

Black, M. (1977). More about metaphors. *Dialectica, 31,* 431–457.

Dent, C. H. (1981). Metaphors as descriptions of natural objects and events. *Parasession on Language and Behavior.* Chicago: Chicago Linguistic Society.

Dent, C. H. (1984). The developmental importance of motion information in perceiving and describing metaphoric similarity. *Child Development, 55,* 1607–1613.

Dent, C. H. (1986). The development of metaphoric competence. *Human Development, 29,* 223–226.

Dent, C. H. (1987, January). Developmental studies of perception and language: The twain shall meet. *Journal of Metaphor and Symbolic Activity, 2*(1).

Dent, C. H., & Ledbetter, P. (1986). Facilitating children's recall of figurative language in text using films of natural objects and events. *Human Development, 29,* 231–235.

Dent, C. H., & Rosenberg, L. (1985). *Metaphoric similarity, fused objects, and the development of figurative language.* (submitted)

Evans, M. (1984). *Metaphor and personality.* Unpublished doctoral dissertation. University of North Carolina, Chapel Hill.

Gardner, H., Winner, E., Bechhofer, R., & Wolf, D. (1978). The development of figurative language. In K. E. Nelson (Ed.), *Children's language Vol. 1* (pp. 1–38). New York: Gardner Press.

Gentner, D. (1977). Children's performance on a spatial analogies task. *Child Development, 48,* 1034–1039.

Gibson, J. J. (1979). *The ecological approach to visual perception.* Boston: Houghton-Mifflin.

Honeck, R., Voegtle, K., & Sowry, B. (1978). Figurative understanding of pictures and sentences. *Child Development 49,* 327–332.

Kelly, M., & Keil, F. (1987, January). Metaphor comprehension and knowledge of semantic domains. *Journal of Metaphor and Symbolic Activity, 2*(1).

MacNamara, J. (1972). Cognitive basis of language learning in infants. *Psychological Review, 79,* 1–13.

Mill, J. S. (1884). *A system of logic.* London: Longmans, Green.

Millikan, R. (1984). *Language thought and other biological categories.* Cambridge, MA: The MIT Press.

Ortony, A. (1979). Beyond literal similarity. *Psychological Review, 86,* 161–181.

Ortony, A., Reynolds, R. E., & Arter, J. A. (1978). Metaphor: Theoretical and empirical research. *Psychological Bulletin, 85,* 919–943

Pearson, P. D., Raphael, T., TePaske, N., & Hyser, C. (1979). The function of metaphor in children's recall of expository passages (*Technical Report, 131*). Center for the Study of Reading, University of Illinois, Champaign.

Rader, N., & Dent, C. H. (1979). A theoretical approach to meaning based on a theory of direct perception. In P. French (Ed.), *The development of meaning* (pp. 146–177). Hiroshima: Bunka Hyoron Publishing Co.

Rothenberg, A., & Sobel, R. (1980). Creation of literary metaphors as stimulated by superimposed vs. separated visual images. *Journal of Mental Imagery, 4,* 77–91.

Schmidt, L., & Dent, C. H. (1985). *The nature of lexical representation in natural language.* Paper presented at the International Linguistics Association, New York.

Tourangeau, R., & Sternberg, R. (1981). Aptness in metaphor. *Cognitive Psychology, 13,* 27–55.

Verbrugge, R. (1977). Resemblances in language and perception. In R. Shaw & J. Bransford (Eds.), *Perceiving, acting and knowing* (pp. 365–392). Hillsdale, NJ: Lawrence Erlbaum Associates.

Verbrugge, R. (1979). The primacy of metaphor in development. In E. Winner & H. Gardner, *Fact fiction and fantasy in childhood.* San Francisco: Jossey-Bass.

Verbrugge, R. (1980). Transformations in knowing: A realist view of metaphor. In R. Honeck & R. Hoffman (Eds.), *Cognition and figurative language* (pp. 87–125). Hillsdale, NJ: Lawrence Erlbaum Associates.

Verbrugge, R. (1985). Language and event perception: Steps toward a synthesis. In W. H. Warren & R. E. Shaw (Eds.), *Persistence and change: Proceedings of the First International Conference on Event Perception.* Hillsdale, NJ: Lawrence Erlbaum Associates.

Verbrugge, R. (1986). Research on metaphoric development: Themes and variations. *Human Development, 29,* 241–243.

Verbrugge, R., & McCarrell, N. (1977). Metaphoric comprehension: Studies in reminding and resembling. *Cognitive Psychology, 9,* 494–533.

Vosniadou, S., & Ortony, A. (1986). Testing the metaphoric competence of the young child: Paraphrase vs. enactment. *Human Development, 29,* 226–230.

Windmueller, G., Massey, C., Blank, P., Gardner, G., & Winner, E. (1986). Unpacking metaphors and allegories. *Human Development, 29,* 236–240.

Waggoner, J., Messe, M., & Palermo, D. (1985). Grasping the meaning of metaphor: Story recall and comprehension. *Child Development, 56,* 1156–1166.

11 Order of Acquisition in the Lexicon: Implications from Japanese Numeral Classifiers

Yo Matsumoto
Stanford University

INTRODUCTION

In this paper I discuss the following problems in the acquisition order of lexical items on the basis of my research on the child's acquisition of Japanese numeral classifiers: (1) What determine(s) the order of acquisition in the lexicon?, and (2) What kinds of relationship are there between types of acquisition order and types of lexical domains?

The numeral classifiers, which I examine here, are a set of morphemes that occur in a position adjacent to numerals, and whose choice depends on the nature of the entities whose number is being referred to (see Adams & Conklin, 1973; Allan, 1977; Denny, 1979; Dixon, 1982). Similar expressions in English include *sheet* in the phrase *two sheets of paper*. In many Asian, Micronesian, and other languages morphemes like this are required in talking about the number of (almost) every kind of countable entity. In Japanese, for example, speakers employ the classifier *-hiki* in talking about animals as in *ni-hiki-no saru* (two-CLASSIFIER-GENITIVE monkey) "two monkeys" and *-hon* in talking about long thin objects as in *ni-hon-no enpitsu* (two-CLASSIFIER-GENITIVE pencil) "two pencils." The acquisition of those items has been studied by Muraishi (1967), Sanches (1978), Kokuritsu Kokugo Kenkyusho (1983), and Matsumoto (1985b) in Japanese, Erbaugh (1985) in Mandarin, and Gandour et al. (1984) in Thai, but has not been discussed in relation to the theoretical questions of acquisition order.

First I review different theoretical hypotheses to see what predictions different views of the order of acquisition make in the acquisition of Japanese classifiers.

In later sections my research on the children's use of classifiers is reported, and some implications are discussed.

ORDER OF ACQUISITION IN THE LEXICON: A REVIEW

Determinant(s) of Acquisition Order

Theories of lexical acquisition must address the determinants of acquisition order. The hypothesis that caused much interest in this question was Eve Clark's Semantic Feature Hypothesis. By the order of acquisition in the lexicon she means the order in which adult meanings of lexical items are acquired,[1] and I use the term in this sense here. This order is different from what I would like to call the order of emergence, or the order in which lexical items enter children's vocabulary. Although some researchers have failed to discriminate between the two, this is an important distinction to maintain. Some different factors have been identified as determinants of acquisition order. Some of them are reviewed here.[2]

Semantic Complexity.   The most influential theory of acquisition order in the lexicon has been Clark's (1972, 1973) Semantic Complexity Hypothesis, which is a part of the general Semantic Feature Hypothesis. The hypothesis stated that children acquire semantically simpler terms first and then proceed to more complex ones, and that this relative complexity of meanings can be defined in terms of the number of semantic features that presumably comprise the meanings of the terms. That is, terms with fewer conditions placed on their use should be acquired prior to terms with additional conditions.

Clark and others have tested this hypothesis in several semantic domains. With respect to dimensional adjectives, for example, the semantic complexity view of acquisition order predicts that *big-small,* which can be used for talking about size in general, should be acquired prior to terms like *long-short* and *tall-short,* which refer to one-dimensional extensions of objects, which in turn should be acquired prior to terms like *wide-narrow, thick-thin,* and *deep-shallow,* which are applied to secondary one-dimensional extension (Clark, 1972). In this lexical

---

[1]It is actually very difficult to decide when an adult meaning of a lexical item is acquired, especially when we consider the argument of Bowerman (1985), who has claimed that the process of lexical acquisition is more dynamic and subtler than formerly believed. See Matsumoto (1985b) for a closer examination of how the adult meaning of the classifier -*hon* is acquired.

[2]Another possible determinant of acquisition order discussed in the literature is the role of nonlinguistic strategies (Clark, 1973b, Wilcox & Palermo 1974/75, Schwam, 1982). I did not take up this factor because it is now thought that nonlinguistic strategies do not actually determine the order of acquisition (Clark, 1983), and their role seems to be restricted to certain lexical items (e.g., spatial expressions), rather than to the lexicon as a whole.

domain researchers have found the following stable acquisition order, which Clark claims to match the prediction quite closely:[3] *big-small* → *long-short, tall-short,* → *high-low* → *thick-thin* → *wide-narrow, deep-shallow* (Bartlett, 1974, Brewer & Stone, 1975; Clark, 1972; Lindholm, 1982).

Other lexical domains where semantic complexity has been claimed to play an important role are verbs of possession: *have* → *give, take* → *trade, pay* → *buy, sell* (Gentner, 1975); spatial prepositions: *in, on, under* → *over, above, beside* → *in front of, between* (Clark, 1972; Johnston & Slobin, 1979); kinship terms: *father, mother* → *grandmother, grandfather* → *uncle, aunt* (Haviland & Clark, 1974); deictic terms: *I/you* → *here/there* → *this/that* → *come/go* → *bring/take* (Clark, 1978a).

While this view has been an influential one, there are a few problems with this view. First, the lexical domains to which this view can make predictions is limited. This view of acquisition order rests crucially on the notion of semantic features. Therefore, it provides no way to predict acquisition order in the lexical domains whose members cannot be described in terms of semantic features (e.g., color terms). In addition, recent studies of prototype semantics (e.g., Fillmore 1975, 1982, 1983; Lakoff, 1983; Rosch, Mervis, Gray, Johnson & Boyes-Braem, 1976) suggest that the words that can be analyzed within the framework of traditional semantic features are quite limited. Second, the attempt to define semantic complexity in terms of the number of features embodies a potential theoretical problem. Fillmore (1978), for example, warns that "such notions as the relative complexity of related vocabulary items can be given different appearances depending on the choice of primitives" (see also Kuczaj, 1981). Third, there are some empirical problems. For example, according to Carey (1982), the unmarked sense of *tall* as in "How tall is he?" should be acquired prior to the marked sense of *tall* as in "He is tall," since the former lacks the semantic feature of polarity (i.e., the former sense of *tall* is neutral as to whether the person referred to is actually tall or not.). However, Carey points out that children seem to acquire the marked sense of *tall* before the unmarked sense of the term. The semantic complexity view also makes an incorrect prediction about the order of acquisition of taxonomical terms (see below).

Frequency of Occurrence in the Input. Frequency of occurrence in the input has often been discussed as a determinant of acquisition order. The importance of this factor is emphasized by Carey (1982). On the basis of her discussion of dimensional adjectives, she claims that "order of acquisition is better predicted by frequency of usage than by semantic complexity, although it is roughly in accord with relative complexity" (p. 365).

The importance of frequency of occurrence should not, however, be over-

---

[3]The findings of Maratos (1973) and Ravn and Gelman (1984) suggest, however, a closer examination is needed.

emphasized for several reasons. First, it is doubtful that order of acquisition is solely determined by nonsemantic factors such as frequency. Frequency of occurrence itself cannot be related to the actual meanings that children give to lexical items, when order of acquisition has been discussed as the order in which adult meanings of lexical items are acquired (Clark, 1972). Frequency of occurrence may be more related to the order of emergence (Anglin, 1977). Second, some researchers suggest that frequency is not the only input factor that is important in semantic acquisition. Schwartz and Terrel (1983), for example, claim that the distribution of the occurrence of lexical items in the input is related to the speed of acquisition. Furthermore, Mervis and Pani (1980) show that children acquire a meaning faster when they are exposed to typical members of the semantic category than to atypical members of the category. This finding suggests that the pattern of use in the input is also an important aspect of the input in determining the order of acquisition. (See Baker & Nelson, 1984, and Nelson, Bonvillian, Denninger, Kaplan, & Baker, 1984, for a related discussion of the acquisition of syntax.)

Cognitive Complexity.   It has often been claimed that some lexical items are acquired before others because the semantic categories of the items are conceptually more basic or salient than others, and are therefore easier to map onto appropriate categories. I call this view the cognitive complexity view of acquisition order. Such a view is adopted by Johnston and Slobin (1979) in their cross-linguistic study of locative terms. They suggest that acquisition order of terms expressing seven basic locative relations, IN, ON, UNDER, BESIDE, BE-TWEEN, BACK, and FRONT, can be predicted by two kinds of factors. They are (1) cognitive complexity, which predicts, for example, the early acquisition of IN, ON, and UNDER on the basis of the basic primitive notion of containment, support and occlusion, and (2) salience of particular notions, which predicts, for example, relatively earlier acquisition of BACK in comparison to FRONT on account of the child's focus on disappearing or inaccessible objects, together with the improbability of asking about the location of a visible object. They also give some linguistic (formal) factors that might affect actual order of acquisition.

It should be noted that Clark's (1972) notion of semantic complexity may actually be one way to define cognitive complexity, which can be inferred from the following remark: "There is good reason to think that some situations are cognitively more complex than others, and it is this cognitive complexity that is reflected in the semantic structure of language. Therefore, examination of the relative semantic complexity of different words can provide a basis for making predictions about the order of acquisition" (p. 751). (See also Clark, 1983.)

This kind of complexity is also used as an explanation of the relatively early acquisition of basic level terms in comparison with superordinate terms (Rosch, Mervis, Gray, Johnson, & Boyes-Braem, 1976), and early acquisition of nouns in comparison with verbs (Gentner, 1982).

One problem of this view is that it is not always possible to find good objective conceptual grounds on which to make predictions. See Kameyama (1983) for a good example of the difficulty one might have in computing the relative cognitive complexity of meanings in the domain of Japanese clothing verbs.

Multiple-factor View. Actually, the researchers discussed above generally do not say that order of acquisition is determined solely by any one of the three factors; some,however, are especially explicit in claiming that order of acquisition is determined by various factors. Such is the recent position taken by Clark (1983), who claims that "patterns of use in the input, experience with the objects or situations being denoted and compatibility with a priori organizational principles, to name a few, may also contribute to the order of acquisition." Furthermore, Johnston and Slobin (1979) claim that in the acquisition of lexical terms like spatial prepositions, order of acquisition is determined by linguistic (or formal) factors such as placement of adposition and lexical diversity in addition to cognitive (or semantic) factors. This multiple-factor view seems to be a plausible one, given the limitation of any of the single factors discussed above. However, it is necessary to examine which factors actually contribute in what way to the acquisition order of lexical items.

Types of Acquisition Order and Types of Lexical Domains

Another problem is the relationship between types of acquisition order and types of lexical domains. This problem was first brought to attention by Clark (1978b, 1979), who discussed why the semantic complexity view cannot successfully predict the order of acquisition in animal and other taxonomical terms. Taxonomical terms are hierarchically organized. According to Berlin's study (Berlin, Breedlove, & Raven, 1973), for example, there are at most five different levels in biotaxonomical terms of the world: unique beginner (e.g., *animal, plant*), life forms (e.g., *tree, fish*), generic (e.g., *pine, dog*), specific (e.g., *lima bean*), and varietal (e.g., *baby lima bean*). Berlin's generic level corresponds to what Rosch and her colleagues call the basic level, which they also employ for terms in nonbiotaxonomies. In such a domain the semantic complexity view would predict that superordinate terms like *animal* should be acquired before basic-level terms like *dog*. However, children typically acquire (some) basic level terms prior to their superordinate ones (Rosch et al., 1976; Anglin, 1977), thus contradicting the semantic complexity view. This early acquisition of basic level terms has been attributed to factors like parental selection of terms of this level for children (Brown, 1958; Anglin, 1977) and/or the highest degree of differentiation of categories at this level (Rosch et al., 1976; Mervis & Crisafi, 1982). (The basic level terms are most differentiated because of a relatively high degree of both within-category similarity and between-category difference: Superordinate terms have too much variability within a category, and subordinate terms have too much similarity between neighboring categories.) This means that there are at least two patterns in the acquisition order. The first type is exemplified by the domain of dimensional adjectives, in which children's acquisition begins with the most general terms and more restricted terms are acquired later. The other is exemplified by the domain of animal terms, in which the acquisition begins at an intermediate level that usually matches the basic level. The first pattern is a *top-down acquisition order,* and the second, a *middle-first acquisition order.* Now the question that should be addressed is in which domains a top-down as opposed to a middle-first acquisition order typically occurs, or what is (or are) the characterizing feature(s) of the lexical domains where the former rather than the latter is observed.

On this problem Clark has suggested two possible factors. The first one is the distinction between the domains consisting of relational terms (terms that express relational information) and domains consisting of nonrelational terms (terms that do not express relational information) (Clark, 1979). Dimensional adjectives express relative extent or lack of extent by reference to a certain norm of the extension; verbs of possession express possessive relations; spatial prepositions express spatial relations, etc. Taxonomies are, on the other hand, made up of category terms, and are not relational in nature. I call this distinction the relational term view.

Clark's second suggestion is the distinction between *horizontal domains* and *vertical domains* (Clark, 1978b). Animal terms, she says, form a typical horizontal domain. In this domain the majority of terms contrast clearly at the same level called the basic level, and the number of levels from the highest superordinate to the lowest subordinate is quite restricted (see Berlin et al., 1973). She calls such domains horizontal domains because they are characterized by the predominance of horizontal contrasts (contrasts on the same level). In lexical domains like dimensional adjectives, on the other hand, there is no level comparable to the basic level on which the majority of terms contrast clearly, and the organization of the domains is characterized by a dominance of vertical contrasts (e.g., contrasts between *big-small* and *long-short,* between *long-short* and *wide-narrow*). Clark suggests that the predominance of vertical contrast or the lack of a basic level might be a crucial feature of the domains in which a top-down order of acquisition occurs. I call this the domain organization view.

It has been difficult, however, to choose between the two hypotheses since the major domains in which a top-down order has been observed are predominantly vertical domains that consist of relational terms.

PREDICTIONS FOR JAPANESE CLASSIFIERS

What predictions do the different views about the two problems discussed above make about the child's acquisition of Japanese numeral classifiers? In order to answer this question, one must look closely at the semantic system of Japanese classifiers.

In Japanese, numeral classifiers are realized as bound morphemes which occur in the position following numerals. The number of classifiers actually used by speakers varies from speaker to speaker and from register to register. Downing's questionnaire (Downing, 1984) given to 15 native speakers revealed that 120 items were claimed to be used by at least one speaker and 27 items were claimed to be used by all the speakers. Sanches (1978) estimated that the number of those classifiers that were actually used was around 30. Some of them are native morphemes while others are Sino-Japanese ones. There are two series of numerals: the native series and the Sino-Japanese series. There are cooccurrence restrictions between numeral series and classifiers. Generally speaking, the Sino-Japanese series tend to cooccur with Sino-Japanese classifiers, while the native series tend to cooccur with native classifiers. The semantic structure of these classifiers have been studied in recent papers (Denny, 1979; Downing, 1984; Matsumoto, 1985a, 1986, in press; Sanches, 1978). The full description of Japanese classifiers is beyond the scope of the present paper. A simplified description of main classifiers is given in Table 11.1, which is sufficient for the present purpose. It shows the meanings and some examples of their referents, as well as the numeral series with which they occur.

The basic semantic distinction made in the classifier system is that of animacy. Japanese adopts a three-way contrast: (1) human, (2) nonhuman animate, and (3) inanimate. The classifier -ri/-nin is used generally for human beings. Among the classifiers for nonhuman animate beings, -wa and -too are restricted in terms of shape (saliency of wings) and size (size larger than average human beings), respectively. The general classifier for nonhuman animate beings, -hiki, is not only used for those animate beings not referred to with -wa or -too, but also in cases where one refers to various animals together. There are many classifiers used for inanimate objects. The general classifier -tsu can be used for almost all kinds of inanimate entities, both concrete and abstract, although other specific classifiers tend to be preferred in actual use when the entity being referred to satisfies the conditions of those specific classifiers. There are four main classifiers that are conditioned solely by configurational properties of objects (configurational classifiers). They are -ko, a classifier for objects with no relatively salient extension along a specific dimension (Denny's [1979] "saliently three-dimensional objects"),[4] -mai, a classifier for saliently two dimensional or flat objects, -hon, a classifier for saliently one dimensional or long objects, and

---

[4]The classifier -ko is often said to have a restriction of size (smallness) on the grounds that it is not used for certain large objects like mountains. However, a closer examination of this classifier suggests that the relevant factor is not size but "spatial separatedness" (Matsumoto, 1985a). Evidence for this analysis includes the judgment that the classifier is not used for small spatially unseparated objects like noses and eyes, while it is used for large spatially separated objects like sattelites and advertisement balloons.

TABLE 11.1

Main Japanese Classifiers, The Numeral Series They Co-Occur With (S: Sino-Japanese Series; N: Native Series) Their Meanings, and Some Examples of Their Referents

Classifier	Numeral Series	Meaning	Example of Referents
-ri/	N (below 2)/	human beings	any human being
-nin	S (above 3)		
-hiki	S	animals in general	dog, squirrel, mouse, insect, fish, reptile
-wa	S	saliently winged animals	pigeon, sparrow, crow, chicken
-too	S	animals larger than average human beings	cow, horse, elephant, tiger
-tsu	N	inanimate entities in general	almost any inanimate entity
-ko	S	inanimate objects without a relatively salient dimension	apple, ball, stone, eraser, box, ring
-mai	S	saliently two-dimensional objects	paper, leaf, board, card, record
-hon	S	saliently one-dimensional objects	pencil, stick, string, tree, line
-tsubu	N	saliently zero-dimensional objects (tiny objects without a relatively salient dimension)	bead, grain of rice, sand
-dai	S	large mechanical objects	car, truck, TV set, refrigerator
-ki	S	airplane-like objects	jetliner, bomber, helicopter
-soo	S	boats	fishing boat, rowboat, canoe
-seki	S	ships	warship, tanker
-satsu	S	bound objects	book, notebook
-ken	S	houses	house, shop
-tsuu	S	letters	written postcard, enveloped letter
-chaku	S	outer garments	jacket, suit, coat, dress
-teki	S	drops of liquid	drop of water, oil, tears
-hai	S	fluid entity in open containers	bowlful of rice, glassful of water

236

-tsubu, a classifier for saliently zero dimensional (i.e., having little extension along any dimension) or very small objects with no relatively salient extension along any dimension.[5] There are many classifiers which are not solely characterized by configurational properties of objects (non-configurational classifiers). They include *-dai,* a classifier for large mechanical objects, *-ki,* a classifier for airplane-like objects, *-soo* and *-seki,* classifiers for boats and ships, respectively, *-satsu,* a classifier for bound objects, *-ken,* a classifier for houses, etc. For airplanes, the use of *-ki* is preferred over the use of *-dai,* although the use of *dai* is judged to be potentially correct by some native speakers.

Both Downing (1984) and Matsumoto (1985a) claim that we can recognize cases of vertical or superordinate-subordinate relationships between certain classifiers. Such a relationship can be found between *-tsu* and all the other classifiers for inanimate entities, between *-hiki* and the other two classifiers for animate beings, between *-dai* and *-ki,* and so on. At the same time, they claim, the system as a whole does not form a neatly organized taxonomical structure (see also Berlin, 1967 for a similar conclusion in Tzeltal classifiers). The relationship between configurational classifiers and nonconfigurational classifiers, for example, cannot be described in a taxonomy-like structure (see also Matsumoto (in press) for a discussion of this issue).

Now, what predictions can be made about the order of acquisition in the Japanese classifiers? The difference in the relative semantic complexity of classifiers would predict that classifiers with a relatively general application should be acquired prior to classifiers with additional restrictions on their application. For example, *-tsu* should be acquired prior to all the other classifiers for inanimate entities; *-hiki* should also be acquired prior to *-wa* and *-too;* *-dai* should be acquired prior to *-ki.* Among the configurational classifiers, it might be predicted that *-ko,* a classifier for objects of the most unmarked shape, should be acquired prior to *-hon* and *-mai,* classifiers for objects of specific shape, which in turn should be acquired prior to *-tsubu,* which can be regarded as having a restriction of size as well as shape, although these possible differences in the semantic complexity are not expressed in the analysis given above. (In fact, if one adopts the condition SALIENTLY ZERO-DIMENSIONAL rather than the conditions SMALL and NO RELATIVELY SALIENT EXTENSION ALONG ANY SPECIFIC DIMENSION for the meaning of *-tsubu,* there is no way to predict the order between *-hon* and *-mai* on the one hand and *-tsubu* on the other. This testifies to the flaw in the semantic complexity view that Fillmore and others point out: semantic complexity might differ according to different analyses.) No predictions can be made about the order of other pairs of classifiers.

How about the frequency of occurrence in the input? So far, there is no

---

[5]This restriction of shape is required because *-tsubu* cannot be used for very small saliently one-dimensional objects like staples and skin hairs.

TABLE 11.2
Relative Frequencies of Japanese Classifiers

| Caretaker | | Noncaretaker | |
1a. 2;0-2;5	1b. 3;6-3;11	2. Miyaji (1966)	3. Downing (1984)
1. *-tsu* 81%	1. *-tsu* 42%	1. *-tsu* 50%	1. *-nin* 40%
2. *-nin* 7%	2. *-nin* 36%	2. *-nin* 26%	2. *-tsu* 24%
3. *-mai* 6%	3. *-hai* 9%	3. *-mai* 5%	3. *-hiki* 6%
4. *-hon* 3%	4. *-dai* 7%	4. *-hon* 3%	4. *-hon* 6%
5. *-dai* 3%	5. *-hon* 2%	5. *-ko* 3%	4. *-mai* 6%
	5. *-mai* 2%	6. *-ken* 3%	6. *-ko* 2%
	7. *-ko* 1%	7. *-hai* 2%	6. *-ken* 2%
	7. *-satsu* 1%	8. *-hiki* 1%	8. *-mei* 1%
		8. *-mei* 1%	8. *-teki* 1%
		10. *-wa* 1%	10. *-tsuu* 1%
		10. *-dai* 1%	11. *-dai* 1%
		10. *-seki* 1%	11. *-seki* 1%
		10. *-ki* 1%	11. *-satsu* 1%
		10. *-teki* 1%	11. *-mej* 1%
			11. *-wa* 1%

1a) based on Koruritsu Kokugo Kenkyuusho (1982) (116 instances observed during the period when her child was 2;0 to 2;5)
1b) based on Kokuritsu Kokugo Kenkyuusho (1982) (72 instances observed during the period when her child was 3;6 to 3;11)
2) based on Miyaji (1966) (520 instances)
3) Downing (1984) 500 instances)

published data on frequency of use of classifiers in caretakers' speech to children. My own examination of a mother's speech in the corpus compiled by The National Language Research Institute (Kokuritsu Kokugo Kenkyuusho, 1982) revealed the relative frequencies shown in the first two columns of Table 11.2. The part of the corpus I examined was about 24 hours long, recorded during the periods her child was 2;0 to 2;5 (Data 1-a) and 3;6 to 3;11 (Data 1-b). The results indicate that *-tsu* is the most frequent classifier, and that other relatively frequent classifiers include *-ri/-nin, -hon, -mai,* and *-dai.* The frequency view of acquisition order predicts the acquisition of these classifiers before others, provided that the frequencies represented by the present data generally apply to other caretakers. There are two sources of data for frequency of use of classifiers in noncaretaker adult speech: Miyaji's (1970) *Frequency Dictionary of Japanese Words* (Data 2) and Downing's (1984) data (Data 3). The data are shown in the last two columns of Table 11.2. The differences in the data from these three sources indicate textual variation of the relative frequency of classifiers. It is natural that the frequency of classifiers, especially nonconfigurational ones, changes from text to text in accordance with the topic of the texts. For example, a relatively low frequency of *-dai* in the noncaretakers' speech contrasts with its high frequency in the mother's speech, in which there are frequent references to vehicles and toy vehicles, which are important referents of *-dai.*[6] This indicates

---

[6]Another reason for the relatively low frequency of *-dai* in the Data 2 in Table 11.2 is that this data is based on written materials published during the Taisho Era (1912–1926), when the reference to mechanical objects is undoubtedly fewer than in the present technologically developed age.

the limitation of the noncaretaker data as the data of the classifier frequencies to which children are exposed. At the same time, the following observations hold across the three sets of data:

1. *tsu* and *-ri/-nin* are the two most frequent classifiers and *-tsu* is more frequent than all the other classifiers for inanimate entities;

2. two configurational classifiers *-hon* and *-mai* stably retain higher ranks, and are more frequent than *-tsubu;*

3. *-hiki* is more frequent than *-wa* and *-too* (There is no occurrence of classifiers for animate beings in the caretaker's speech. This is because there was no occasion to talk about the number of animals in the conversation in that data.);

4. *-dai* is at least as frequent as *-ki.*

These observations suggest that classifiers with fewer restrictions placed on their use are used more frequently than classifiers with additional restrictions. In the Japanese classifier system, then, there tend to be a general correlation between frequency and semantic complexity in spite of the textual variation resulting from differences in topic. In fact, it is highly likely that the former is derived in part from the latter.

It should be noted that these three sets of data reveal relatively few uses of *-ko,* although there must have been many occasions in which this classifier was acceptable. This fact should be carefully evaluated, since an increasing use of *-ko* is a well-noted change in the Japanese numeral classifiers in recent years (Kenbo, 1976; Matsumoto, 1985a). Today many young speakers appear to prefer *-ko* over *-tsu* when both forms are acceptable, and the referential domain of *-ko* is widening to include the area where once *-tsu* alone was accepted (Matsumoto, 1985a). It is probably the case that *-ko* is now one of the most frequent classifiers at least in the speech of younger speakers, and the frequency of *-tsu* is correspondingly low. This should be kept in mind.

What predictions can be made in terms of cognitive complexity? Interestingly, some Japanese classifiers encode cognitively salient features of objects in their meanings: animacy and shape (cf. Clark 1977). It can be predicted, then, that those classifiers that are solely defined by those properties are acquired before the others. Thus, this sort of complexity makes more or less the same predictions as the two factors above.

Next, what contribution can the study of Japanese classifiers make to the problem of the relationship between types of acquisition order and types of lexical domains? Earlier, we saw two different views on the critical factor that distinguishes the domains where the top-down order of acquisition occurs from the domains where the middle-first order occurs. These two views make different predictions for Japanese classifiers. First, the relational term view predicts the nonoccurrence of a top-down order in the classifier system, since classifier meanings cannot be described relationally in Clark's sense.

How about the domain organization view? The system of Japanese classifiers cannot be charact ized as a predominantly horizontal domain, since it lacks a level comparable to the basic level in which the majority of terms contrast clearly. In fact, the system as a whole cannot be described as a neat multileveled taxonomical structure (Downing, 1984; Matsumoto, 1985a, in press). Do Japanese classifiers, then, form a predominantly vertical domain? The system of configurational classifiers might be similar to the vertical ⸺ganization of dimensional adjectives, since the classifiers are characterized by the presence or absence of the conditions of specific shape and size. However, the nonconfigurational classifiers cannot be regarded as forming a predominantly vertical domain, since there are no vertical contrasts among those items except for the contrast between -dai and ki. What is clear is that the classifier system differs from horizontal domains in the sense that there is no basic level. In this sense the Japanese classifier system can be characterized as a *nonhorizontal domain*. If Clark's domain organization view is slightly modified so that the crucial point is the lack of the basic level and not the dominance of vertical contrast, the revised view predicts that Japanese classifiers should exhibit a top-down order of acquisition.

These predictions are discussed below.

THE EXPERIMENTS

The acquisition of numeral expressions begins around the age of 1½ (Okubo, 1967; Iwabuchi & Maraishi, 1976). The first task that children cope with is the establishment of a numeral series. Until the age of 4 the use of classifiers is mainly limited to -tsu and/or -ko and -ri/-nin. My examination of a child's use of classifiers in the corpus from the National Language Research Institute (Kokuritsu Kokugo Kenkyuusho, 1982) during the periods between 2;0 and 2;5 and 3;5 and 3;11 revealed that -tsu was used 82% and 64% of the time respectively during each of the two periods, and -ri/-nin was used 13% and 23%. The use of other classifiers accounts for 5% and 13% of classifier use and almost all of them are restricted to contexts where the child's mother used the classifier in the preceding turn. No use of -ko was observed in the child studied. This result shows that those classifiers used frequently in a caretaker's speech are also used frequently by her child. However, this does not mean that such classifiers are used correctly. In fact, the child studied used -tsu instead of the correct classifier -ri/-nin for babies, suggesting that the contrast of -tsu and -ri/-nin had not yet been acquired.

The use of -tsu and -ko deserves further mention. It is generally the case that in the studies conducted before 1970 -tsu was the first and the most frequent classifier used by children (Iwabuchi & Muraishi. 1976; Okubo, 1967; Sanches, 1978). However, a study I conducted in 1983 shows that most of the 5-year-olds studied prefer to use -ko far more than -tsu as a general classifier for inanimate entities (Matsumoto, 1984b). The change seems to reflect the increasing use of -ko, and more generally, the increasing use of Sino-Japanese numeral expressions in adult speech. Furthermore, my production experiment with children of ages 3;8 to 5;3 conducted in 1984 (Matsumoto, 1985a), revealed that there were individual preferences in the choice of the two classifiers. Some children consistently used -tsu, and others -ko, for all the inanimate entities (and often animate beings as well), and still others tended to use either one depending upon the number of objects being referred to. As for other classifiers the experiment showed that there was an increasing use of -ri/-nin, and less frequently, -hiki, during the period observed.

Now I look more closely at a later development. Reported here are four cross-sectional production experiments conducted during 1983 and 1984. A noticeable point in these experiments was the inclusion of unfamiliar objects as well as familiar ones in the test materials. This was motivated by my view that a true adult-like semantic knowledge of a lexical item can be attributed to a child only when he or she correctly applies it to relevant novel objects.

CLASSIFIERS FOR NONHUMAN ANIMATE BEINGS: EXPERIMENT A

Japanese has three classifiers for nonhuman animate beings: -hiki, -wa, and -too. Experiment A was designed to explore children's acquisition of these three classifiers.

Method

Subjects.   Subjects were 38 preschool children, living in Tokyo. They ranged from 5;1 to 6;11 in age. They were divided into two age groups: nineteen 5-year-olds ($\bar{X}$ = 5;6) and nineteen 6-year-olds ($\bar{X}$ = 6;5).

Materials.   Materials were photographs or very detailed pictures of the following animals: (1) giraffes, elephants, *babary sheep, and *bison for -too; (2) crows, chickens, *Mandarin ducks, and *wagtails for -wa; and (3) dogs, monkeys, snakes, grasshoppers, *Japanese sables, and *marmots for -hiki. Asterisked animals were intended to be unfamiliar ones. Three pictures of each animal were prepared, each of which had 2, 3, or 4 instances of the animal. One of them was selected randomly for each subject. More than 6 pictures of inanimate objects were mixed in the test materials.

Procedure.   The experiment was carried out in a small room in a kindergarten. An experimenter interviewed subjects individually. First he instructed the child to describe the picture he was going to show them. Then he presented a picture in which there were a few instances of one of the animals listed above. While the child was looking at the picture, the experimenter helped him or her by asking a few questions. The questions included a request for the name and the number of instances of the animal in the picture. The latter question was *Do-redake iru?* "How many are there?" This is the vaguest or most general way of asking number or amount in Japanese and so offers no clue to an appropriate numeral expression. I employed this indirect way of questioning so that the children might not become too conscious about being tested on numeral expressions. The usual responses of children consisted of numerals and classifiers, of which only classifiers are relevant for the present discussion. If the subject did not identify the animal being presented or gave a wrong or inappropriate name (which was mostly the case with unfamiliar animals), the experimenter gave a correct name. Only one trial was conducted for each animal. Presentation order was randomized. The session began after one practice trial.

As control subjects, ten adult speakers were tested. When they were tested for production, using the procedure described above, all the pictured referents of *-hiki* drew responses with the expected classifier on 100% of the relevant occasions, those of *-wa* on more than 80%, and those of *-too* on more than 70%. All the responses other than the expected ones were with uses of *-hiki*. When these adults were tested for acceptability judgments, all of them acknowledged the acceptability of expected classifiers for all materials.

Results and Discussion

The results are presented in Table 11.3. It shows the percentage of responses with correct adult classifiers and those with other classifiers substituted for the correct ones for the referents of each classifier in each of the two age groups. The

TABLE 11.3
Results of Experiment A
Percentage Scores of Responses for the Referents of Each Animate Classifier

Responses		correct		Substitutions							
				-hiki		*-tsu/-ko*		*-ri/-nin*		others	
Correct Classifier	age	5	6	5	6	5	6	5	6	5	6
		%	%	%	%	%	%	%	%	%	%
-hiki (general)		74	89			14	3	5	0	7	8
-wa (winged)		17	34	61	62	12	0	5	3	5	1
-too (larger)		9	12	67	80	9	0	7	3	7	5

TABLE 11.4
Individual Response Patterns in Experiment A
("1" Represents "Acquired" and "0" Represents "Not Acquired")

Response Pattern	Response			Number of Subjects	Average Age
	-hiki	-wa	-too		
A	0[a]	0[b]	0[c]	6	5;7
B	1	0[d]	0[e]	21	6;0
C	1	1	0[f]	6	6;2
D	1	0[g]	1	2	6;0
E	1	1	1[h]	2	6;4
F	0	1	0[h]	1	(5;11)

Note. Consistent use of substitutions (the number of subjects who used a given classifier is shown)

[a] -tsu/-ko: 2
[b] -tsu/-ko: 2, -hiki: 2, -ri/-nin: 1
[c] -tsu/-ko: 1, -hiki: 1, -ri/-nin: 1
[d] -hiki 19
[e] -hiki 19
[f] -hiki 2
[g] -hiki 6
[h] -hiki 1

table shows that the use of -hiki was established in most 5-year-old children, and that there were relatively few (though increasing) responses with -wa and -too. There were many substitutions of -hiki for -wa and -too, which are not completely unacceptable for adults in their informal speech, and which some adult control subjects also employed. As to the familiarity factor, unfamiliar animate beings generally drew roughly as many correct responses as familiar ones, which shows that children who used correct classifiers generally had an abstract knowledge about the application of those items. (The differences in the correct responses to the familiar and unfamiliar referents of each classifier were: $\chi^2 = 0.25$, d. f. = 5, n. s. for -hiki, $\chi^2 = 3.97$, d. f. = 3, n. s. for wa,[7] and $\chi^2 = 1.00$, d. f. = 3, n. s. for -too, pooling all the subjects.)

The individual patterns of responses are described in Table 11.4. The patterns were analyzed in the following way. Children received a "1" for a classifier if they employed the classifier in at least 75% of the relevant trials (i.e., the classifier has been acquired), and an "0" if they did not achieve this level (i.e., the classifier has not been acquired). The scores for the three classifiers in each

---

[7]The bird which drew the most correct responses was the wagtail, an unfamiliar but prototypical referent of -wa. This suggests that the prototypicality of category members has more to do with the differences in the percentage of correct responses than with familiarity. The difference between correct responses to cars and tanks in Experiment D can also be explained in similar terms.

In their paper on Thai classifiers, Gandour et al. (1984) found that among the referents of a classifier, the house elicited more correct classifier use than a pavilion or a mosquito net (which is hung down from a ceiling and looks like a house). This phenomenon may also be explained in terms of the prototypicality of category members, although they explain it in terms of the difference in the frequency of the nouns that denote the three objects.

subject were examined, and 6 different patterns of responses were recognized, which presumably represent stages that children undergo during the course of acquiring these classifiers. The number and the average age of the subjects who responded with each pattern is given in the right-hand column of Table 11.4. Notes attached to the table show consistent uses of substitutions. They indicate the number of subjects who consistently (in at least 75% of the relevant trials) gave a nonadult-correct response in place of the correct one within each response pattern group. They show, for example, many cases of the consistent use of -*hiki* in place of -*wa* or -*too* in children who used only -*hiki* correctly (Pattern B).

The results show that there were significantly more cases of the consistent use of -*hiki* than that of -*wa* ($p < .001$ by the Sign Test) or -*too* ($p < .0001$). In fact, the consistent use of -*wa* or -*too* was observed almost always in cases where -*hiki* was used consistently (Patterns C, D, and E). The difference in the consistent use of -*wa* and -*too* did not reach the significant level of $p < .05$. These observations, as well as the average age of the subjects in each pattern, suggest the acquisition of these classifiers follows the order of stages represented by Patterns A → B → C or D → E, although there is one response pattern (Pattern F) that does not fit into this presumed order.

These findings suggest that at the age of 5, the unmarked classifier for nonhuman animate beings, -*hiki,* has been acquired by most children, and is used as a classifier for nonhuman animate beings in general unless the animate beings can be referred to with other already acquired classifier(s). This is exactly the way this classifier is used by adults. The other classifiers in question, -*wa* and -*too,* are acquired later. This observed order is consistent with the prediction based on the relative semantic complexity of these classifiers, as well as with the prediction based on frequency of use.

CONFIGURATIONAL CLASSIFIERS: EXPERIMENTS B AND C

As noted above, Japanese has several configurational classifiers. They include -*ko, -hon, -mai* and -*tsubu.* Experiment B was designed to examine order of acquisition of these classifiers.

EXPERIMENT B

Method

Subjects.   Subjects were 44 preschool children living in Tokyo. They ranged from 5;0 to 6;11 in age. They were divided into two age groups: 22 5-year-olds ($\bar{X} = 5;7$) and 22 6-year-olds ($\bar{X} = 6;6$).

Materials. Two kinds of real objects which satisfied the conditions of *-ko, -hon, -mai* and *-tsubu* were prepared. One of them was an object familiar to the children and the other was not familiar, and asterisked as before. The actual objects used were: apples and *paper clips for *-ko;* sheets of colored paper (origami) and *credit cards for *-mai;* pencils and *rasps for *-hon;* and grains of rice and *medical tablets called "jintan" for *-tsubu.*

Procedure. The procedure for this experiment was the same as in Experiment A except for the following points. This time an experimenter displayed various real objects before a subject, and told the subject to describe what was in front of him or her. He pointed to a few instances of one of the objects and asked the subject what they were and how many there were. The latter question was *Doredake aru* "How many are there?", this time with the use of *aru*, an existential verb for inanimate entities rather than *iru*, for animate beings. Two trials were given for each kind of object, each time with the different number of instances (3, 4, or 5) randomly determined for a subject. Therefore each subject was given 4 trials for the referents of each classifier.

All ten adult subjects acknowledged the acceptability of the expected classifier use for all our materials. When tested using the procedure described above for production, the subjects responded to the referents of *-ko* with the use of *-tsu* and *-ko* on 60% and 40% of the relevant occasions, respectively. All the referents of *-mai, -hon,* and *-tsubu* drew the expected responses on 100%, 100%, and more than 80% of the relevant occasions, respectively.

Results and Discussion

Results are shown in Table 11.5. It can be read in the same way as Table 11.3 . *-Tsu* and *-ko* have been treated together because both were actually used for the materials prepared for *-ko* by adult subjects. The problem of *-tsu* and *-ko* is discussed later.

Table 11.5 shows that *-tsu* and/or *-ko* were already used correctly for relevant objects by 5-year-olds, that the uses of *-mai* and *-hon* increased with age, and that *-tsubu* was used by relatively few children in the sample. The most frequent substitutions for *-mai, -hon,* and *-tsubu* were *-tsu* and/or *-ko.* As in Experiment A, the differences between correct responses to familiar and unfamiliar objects were slight ($\chi^2 = 0$, d. f. = 1, n. s. for *-tsu/ -ko*, $\chi^2 = 0.17$, d. f. = 1, n. s. for *-mai*, $\chi^2 = 0.31$, d. f. = 1, n. s. for *-hon*, and $\chi^2 = 1.38$, d. f. = 1, n. s. for *-tsubu*, pooling all the subjects), suggesting that those children who used these classifiers generally had an abstract knowledge of these meanings.

Table 11.6 presents the individual response patterns, analyzed in the same way as in Table 11.4. The Guttman Scaling analysis of the implicational order of the establishment of these classifiers showed the following coefficience of scalability: .90 for the order *-tsu/ -ko → -hon → -tsubu;* and .97 for the order *-tsu/ -ko*

TABLE 11.5
Results of Experiment B
Percentage Scores of Responses for
Referents of Each Configurational Classifier

Correct Classifier	Age	Responses Correct Classifier		Substitutions -tsu/-ko		Others	
		5	6	5	6	5	6
-tsu/-ko (general)		99%	98%			1%	2%
-mai (2-D)		48	60	49%	37%	3	2
-hon (1-D)		41	51	58	48	1	1
-tsubu (0-D)		7	14	84	84	9	2

→ -mai → -tsubu. No significant order could be established between -hon and -mai. These observations as well as the average age of each response pattern group suggest that the acquisition of these classifiers follows the stages represented by Patterns A → B or C → D → E, although there are two patterns that do not fit this order. The observed acquisition order of these classifiers appears to fit well with the prediction based on relative semantic complexity, as well as with the prediction based on frequency of occurrence in the input.

A problem remains, however, as to the semantic distinction between -tsu and -ko. The present experiment does not tell anything about this and it is therefore still unclear at what point children acquire the full adult meaning of -ko. The two

TABLE 11.6
Individual Response Patterns in Experiment B
("|" Represents "Acquired" and "0" Represents "Not Acquired")

Response Pattern	-tsu/-ko	Response -mai	-hon	-tsubu	Number of Subjects	Average Age
A	1	0 [a]	0 [b]	0 [c]	20	5;10
B	1	1	0 [d]	0 [e]	4	5;9
C	1	0	1	0 [f]	1	(6;10)
D	1	1	1	0 [g]	14	6;2
E	1	1	1	1	3	6;4
F	0	1	0	0 [h]	1	(6;3)
G	1	1	0	1	1	(6;11)

Notes. Consistent use of substitutions (the number of subjects who used a given classifier is shown)

[a] -tsu/-ko: 16
[b] -tsu/-ko: 17
[c] -tsu/-ko: 18
[d] -tsu/-ko: 2
[e] -tsu/-ko: 3
[f] -tsu/-ko: 1
[g] -tsu/-ko: 9
[h] -tsu/-ko: 1

classifiers share a large referential domain. All the referents of -ko can be referred to with -tsu. -Tsu can be used, however, for such nonreferents of -ko as abstract entities, spatially unseparated objects (e.g., mountains and noses) and intangible objects (e.g., clouds and fire). On this problem the result of Experiment C provides an indication of when these two classifiers begin to be used contrastively.

EXPERIMENT C

Method

Subjects. Subjects were 70 children, divided into 45 children between the ages of 5;0 and 6;3 (Group I; $\bar{X}$ = 5;8) and 25 children between the ages of 6;4 and 7;11 (Group II; $\bar{X}$ = 7;2).

Materials and Procedure. Subjects were tested, using the same procedure as in Experiment A, on classifier use for cups and erasers (referents of -ko) and mountains and clouds (nonreferents of -ko). Five trials, each with varying instances of objects from 1 to 5, were made for each of the two kinds of objects.

Results and Discussion

The results are shown in Table 11.7. In Group I there was no significant difference in their responses for the two kinds of entities (χ^2 = 1.30, d. f. = 2, n. s.). In most cases -ko was used for its referents (cups and earsers) as well as for its nonreferents (mountains and clouds). In Group II a significant difference was observed in the responses for the two kinds of entities (χ^2 = 15.25, d. f. = 2, $p < .001$). More responses of -ko were observed for its referents than for its nonreferents, and fewer responses of -tsu were observed for the referents of -ko than for the nonreferents of -ko. However, the use of -ko for its nonreferents was still as common as the use of -tsu. Table 11.8 presents the results of individual

TABLE 11.7
Results of Experiment c
Percentage Scores of Responses for
Referents of -ko and Nonreferents of -ko

Objects \ Response Group	-ko GI	-ko GII	-tsu GI	-tsu GII	Others GI	Others GII
	%	%	%	%	%	%
referents of -ko	70	68	18	26	12	6
nonreferents of -ko	66	44	19	41	16	15

TABLE 11.8
Individual Response Patterns in Experiment C

Response Pattern	Response		Number of Subjects	Average Age
	Referents of -ko	Nonreferents of -ko		
A	-ko	-ko	33	5;11
B	-tsu	-tsu	8	6;9
C	-ko	-tsu	3	7;5
D	-ko	inconsistent	9	6;1
Others	---	---	17	5;10

analysis. It shows that the dominant pattern was the use of -ko for both kinds of objects (Pattern A). There were some cases of a consistent use of -tsu for both kinds of objects (Pattern B), which provides no information about the meaning of -ko in those children. The consistent use of -ko for its referents and -tsu for the nonreferents of -ko (Pattern C), which evidences the knowledge of the distinction between the two classifiers, was observed only in three children, all of whom were over the age of 7. These findings suggest that most of the younger children studied do not possess the truly adult-like semantic knowledge of -ko. They seem to use it as a general classifier for inanimate entities, overextending it to cover the domain exclusively covered by -tsu for adults. The clear manifestation of the correct knowledge of -ko is observed only after the age of 7. This means that the full conditions of -ko may well be acquired even later than the acquisition of -mai and -hon.

Why is the full acquisition of -ko so late? This question can be rephrased as "Why don't young children use the two classifiers -tsu and -ko contrastively?" A few factors seem to be at work in the lack of a distinction in the early period. The first is the semantic similarity of the two classifiers: the two classifiers have a large referential domain in common. The overlap of the referential domains of the two classifiers would be more striking for children than adults might think, for children are not likely to receive sufficient exposure to the counting of abstract entities, for which only -tsu is acceptable. This means that if a child has either of the two classifiers he can do without the other in most cases. Another factor is a formal (morphological) difference between the two classifiers: they occur with different series of numerals. In this connection, Matsumoto (1984b) has found that individual children show a preference for using either the native or Sino-Japanese series, but not both. Because children correctly use -ko with the Sino-Japanese series, and -tsu, with the native series in most cases, this preference makes children favor one or the other of the two classifiers (see Clancy, 1985 for a further discussion of this problem). These two factors collectively influence children such that they adopt either one of the two classifiers as a general classifier for inanimate entities. In the case of the present subjects many of them chose -ko over -tsu probably because of the higher frequency of -ko over -tsu in the input for them, and this lead to the lack of the contrastive use of -ko and -tsu in early period. Thus, the present discussion suggests that the presence of a semantically similar item and the acquisition or use of formally related items, in conjunction with an effect of frequency, can also contribute to the order of acquisition.

This view is consistent with Slobin's view that acquisition order is determined by linguistic (formal) factors as well as cognitive (semantic) factors (Johnston & Slobin, 1979; Slobin, 1973). The present finding is also consistent with Johnston and Slobin's view that lexical diversity (the availability of more than one lexical item to pick up (almost) the same notion) delays the acquisition of those lexical items.

NONCONFIGURATIONAL CLASSIFIERS: EXPERIMENT D

In this section I examine the acquisition of five nonconfigurational classifiers: -dai, -soo, -ki, -satsu, and -ken.

Method

Subjects. The subjects were 36 children, living in Tokyo. They ranged from 5;1 to 7;11. They were divided into three age groups: 12 5-year-olds ($\bar{X} = 5;5$), 12 6-year-olds ($X = 6;5$), and 12 7-year-olds ($\bar{X} = 7;5$). Ten adult speakers were also tested as control subjects.

Materials. The materials used in this experiment were pictures of the following referents of the five classifiers. For -dai pictures of two vehicles were prepared: automobiles and *fantasy tanks (*jetto mogura*) or drill cars, and two nonvehicular machines: TV sets and *electric typewriters. The other pictured objects were fishing boats and *canoes for -soo; jet liners and *gliders for -ki; ordinary books and *atlases for -satsu; and ordinary houses and *thatched roofed houses for -ken. Asterisked objects were again intended for unfamiliar objects. Three pictures were prepared for each object, each of which has 2, 3, or 4 instances of one of the objects listed above. Two of them were selected randomly for each subject.

Procedure. The procedure was the same as in Experiment A, except that the relevant question was *Doredake aru?,* with the use of *aru.* Ten adult speakers were tested through the same method and it was found that all the objects drew expected classifiers on more than 85% of the relevant occasions. All the speakers accepted the use of expected classifiers for all the objects.

TABLE 11.9
Results of Experiment D
Percentage Scores of Responses for
Referents of Each Nonconfigurational Classifier

| Response | Substitutions | | | | | | | | | | | |
| | Correct | | | -tsu/-ko | | | -dai | | | Others | | |
Correct Classifier · Age	5	6	7	5	6	7	5	6	7	5	6	7
	%	%	%	%	%	%	%	%	%	%	%	%
-dai (vehicles)	27	56	67	71	44	31				2	0	2
-dai (nonvehicles)	0	10	17	98	88	73				2	2	10
-ki (planes)	0	6	0	70	42	40	23	48	56	6	4	4
-soo (boats)	0	13	2	69	58	40	29	25	42	2	4	17
-ken (houses)	0	27	31	92	71	50	6	0	13	2	2	6
-satsu (books)	19	42	50	75	55	33	0	0	0	6	4	17

The results in Table 11.9 show that the classifier -dai was used correctly for land vehicles early on, but was used for nonvehicular machines or appliances by few children, even among the 7-year-olds. -Soo and -ki were produced later than -dai. There were increasing uses of -satsu and -ken with age. The substitution columns show that the most frequent substitutions were the uses of -tsu and/or -ko. Many children used -dai for planes and boats in place of -ki and -soo. As for the familiarity condition, there were only negligible differences between correct

TABLE 11.10
Individual Response Patterns in Experiment D (on -dai, -ki and -soo)

	Response					
Response Pattern	dai for Nonvehicles	-dai for Land Vehicles	-ki	-soo	Number of Subjects	Average Age
A	0[a]	0[b]	0[c]	0[d]	18	6;3
B	0[e]	1	0[f]	0[g]	14	6;4
C	1	0	0[h]	0[i]	1	(7;5)
D	1[l]	1	0[j]	0	1	(7;5)
E	0[m]	1	1	0	1	(6;7)
F	0	1	0	1	1	(6;7)

[a] -tsu/-ko: 17
[b] -tsu/-ko: 14
[c] -tsu/-ko: 14, -dai: 1
[d] -tsu/-ko: 17, -dai: 1
[e] -tsu/-ko: 13
[f] -tsu/-ko: 5, -dai: 1
[g] -tsu/-ko: 1, -dai: 13

[h] -dai: 1
[i] -dai: 1
[j] -dai: 1
[k] -dai: 1
[l] -tsu/-ko: 1
[m] -tsu/-ko: 1

TABLE 11.11
Individual Response Patterns in Experiment D
(on -*satsu* and -*ken*)

Response Pattern	Response		the Number of Subjects	Average Age
	-*satsu*	-*ken*		
A	0[a]	0[b]	20	6;1
B	1	0[c]	9	6;8
C	0[d]	1	4	7;1
D	1	1	3	6;11

Note. Consistent use of substitutions

[a] -*tsu*/-*ko*: 17, -*mai*: 1
[b] -*tsu*/-*ko*: 19
[c] -*tsu*/-*ko*: 7, -*dai*: 1
[d] -*tsu*/-*ko*: 3, -*hon*: 1

responses to familiar and unfamiliar objects, except that there were more correct -*dai* responses to automobiles than to tanks ($\chi^2 = 3.12$, d. f. $= 1$, $p < .1$, pooling all the subjects).

The analysis of individual response patterns is shown in Tables 11.10 and 11.11. For the sake of simplicity the analysis is presented in two different tables. The two tables can be read in the same way as Table 11.4. Table 11.10 indicates the response patterns for the three kinds of vehicles (land-vehicles, i.e., automobiles and tanks; planes, i.e., jet liners and gliders; and boats, i.e., fishing boats and canoes) and for nonvehicular machines or appliances, i.e., TV sets and typewriters. What is interesting is that almost all the children who used -*dai* consistently for land vehicles (Patterns B, D, E, and F) also used it for planes, and most of them, for boats, in place of -*ki* and -*soo* respectively. Most children who did not use -*dai* for these objects (Pattern A) used -*tsu* and/or -*ko* consistently for them. A few cases of the consistent use of -*ki* and -*soo* is observed, in cases where -*dai* was established as a classifier for land vehicles (Patterns E and F). All this suggests that the earlier use of -*tsu* and/or -*ko* for vehicles is replaced by -*dai*, which is at first used as a classifier for vehicles in general and later replaced by -*soo* and -*ki* in the case of boats and planes, respectively. That is, acquisition proceeds from the stages represented by Patterns A → B → E or F. For lack of sufficient data no order among the stages C, D, E, and F can be determined. It should be noted, however, that the subject who consistently used -*soo* or -*ki* for their relevant objects (Pattern E or F) did not use -*dai* as adults do, for they failed to use it consistently for nonvehicular machines or appliances.

Table 11.11 presents the individual response patterns for books and houses. It suggests that after the period when referents of -*satsu* and -*ken* are covered by -*tsu* or *ko* (Pattern A), -*satsu* and -*ken* are acquired and used to refer to their relevant objects (Pattern B, C, and D). No order between -*satsu* and -*ken* could be established by the Sign Test.

The present experiment has revealed an interesting phenomenon about the children's use of -*dai*. The classifier emerged relatively early, and this seems to reflect a high frequency of the classifier in the input (see Data 1 in Table 11.2). In spite of its early emergence, however, the children's early meaning of the classifier was quite different from that of adults. Many children mapped this classifier onto the category "vehicle" rather than onto the adult's category of the classifier. The adult-like meaning of the classifier is attained quite late, and children often acquire -*ki* before they acquire the adult meaning of -*dai*. This observation is not consistent with the semantic complexity view of acquisition order, or with the frequency view of acquisition order, for these views predict that -*dai* should be acquired earlier than -*ki*. The order between -*tsu* and/or -*ko* and -*satsu* or -*ken* is consistent with either view.

What, then, are the factors that contribute to the observed order between -*dai* and -*ki?* The late acquisition of the full conditions of -*dai* is attributed to the early mismapping of the classifier onto the category "vehicle." This mismapping can be accounted for by two factors that presumably provide favorable conditions for the mismapping. The first one is the pattern of the use of this classifier in the input. This classifier is used far more frequently for vehicles (e.g., cars) than for nonvehicular machines (e.g., TV sets). (In the corpus of mother-child conversation examined above, for example, -*dai* occurs exclusively to refer to toy vehicles.) This factor may account for the children's failure to use the classifier for nonvehicular machines, but it alone does not explain the overextension of this classifier to planes and boats, for which adults would not usually use the classifier. Another factor that seems to be at work is the salience and the tightness of the category "vehicle." Vehicles form one of the categories about which children manifest considerable knowledge from an early age (Rescorla, 1981). In addition, the movement with which vehicles are associated appears to be a very salient feature for children (Clark, 1974). Such a category would be more likely to be selected as a category onto which to map a linguistic form than the cognitively less natural category of -*dai* in adults. Thus, it is likely that the availability of the salient category of "vehicles" and the frequent use of the classifier for certain kinds of vehicles made it easier to map -*dai* onto the category "vehicle" than onto the adult category of -*dai* (see Carey, 1982, for a similar account of the phenomenon reported in Kuczaj & Lederberg, 1977). The order of acquisition between -*dai* and -*ki* is, then, accounted for by what might be called mapping complexity, which is derived from an interaction of the two factors: the pattern of use in the input and the availability of salient conceptual categories.[8] The present experiment suggests that both these factors contribute to the order of acquisition.

---

[8]This notion of mapping complexity differs from the cognitive complexity above in that the former is determined by the interaction of the input data and conceptual categories in the child, while the latter does not seem to take the input data into account.

GENERAL DISCUSSION

The following overall picture of the acquisition of Japanese classifiers emerges from the experiments reported above. First, -*tsu* and/or -*ko* emerge as a general classifier before other classifiers begin to be used. Among the classifiers for nonhuman animate beings -*hiki* (a classifier for nonhuman animate beings in general) is acquired before the other classifiers. Among the configurational classifiers, the appearance of -*ko* is followed by the acquisition of -*mai* and -*hon* (classifiers restricted by shape), and -*tsubu* (a classifier restricted by size as well as shape) is acquired still later. Among the nonconfigurational classifiers, -*dai* emerges early as a general classifier for vehicles, and its overextended use for planes and boats is replaced by the more preferred use of -*ki* and -*soo* when these classifiers are acquired. -*Ken* and -*satsu* (classifiers for specific objects) are acquired relatively late to replace earlier use of -*tsu* and/or -*ko*.

These findings appear to be consistent in many cases with the predictions based on the semantic complexity view, as well as the frequency view of acquisition order discussed earlier. However, upon closer examination, the following phenomena reveal limitations of these two views: (1) the adult meaning of -*ko* is acquired very late, very probably later than the acquisition of -*hon* and -*mai;* (2) the full adult meaning of -*dai* is also acquired late, often later than that of -*ki.* These observations are contrary to the predictions seen earlier. They can be explained only by appealing to something other than semantic complexity and frequency of occurrence. Factors involved in the case of -*ko* are availability of semantically similar terms and the acquisition or use of formally related items. Factors involved in the case of -*dai* are the pattern of use for this classifier in the input, and the saliency of a related category. The present study suggests that these factors also contribute to the order of acquisition in lexical items, supporting the multiple factor view of acquisition order.

These various factors appear to play different roles in determining the order of acquisition of Japanese classifiers. Frequency probably plays a role in providing opportunities for a child to pay attention to a linguistic form and to work out the adult meaning of the item. Frequent use in the input, however, does not by itself lead to the early acquisition of the full adult meaning of the item; this can be seen in the late acquisition of a frequent classifier -*dai.* Semantic complexity seems to play two different roles. First, in some cases the complexity appears to determine the difficulty with which children discover adult meanings (cf. Clark, 1983). The relatively early acquisition of -*tsu* and -*hiki* most probably reflects the fact that children have fewer conditions to discover: All they have to find out are the conditions INANIMATE, or NONHUMAN and ANIMATE, respectively. (The saliency of the notion animacy may also be at work here.) Semantic complexity may also play a role in determining frequency of use and communicative usefulness, which will be discussed later. Other factors are relevant in the process of mapping classifiers onto the correct adult-like categories, as discussed in relation to -*ko* and -*dai*. These factors must be potentially at work in determining the order of acquisition in all lexical domains, although the importance of each factor in determining actual order may differ from one domain to another.[9]

The findings of this research have a further implication for the problem of the relationship between types of lexical domains and types of acquisition order. It was pointed out earlier that the order of acquisition in the Japanese classifier system, in which nonrelational terms form a nonhorizontal domain, might provide an answer to the problem of defining the lexical domains in which a top-down order of acquisition is observed. The present findings show that numeral classifiers to a large degree exhibit a top-down order of acquisition. This clearly indicates that the criterial feature is the organization pattern of lexical domains rather than the relational nature of lexical items that comprise those domains, thus supporting the domain organization view. That is, the top-down order occurs in the nonhorizontally organized domains or domains which lack the basic level of naming.[10]

Why, then, does acquisition begin with a different level in horizontal domains and nonhorizontal domains? The multiple-factor view provides an answer to this question. What is noteworthy in this connection is the similarity of the dimensional adjective and classifier systems, especially in the status of relatively general terms. General terms or less restricted terms in these nonhorizontal domains have a functional privilege. In dimensional adjectives the least restricted terms like *big-small* have a general purpose nature: they can be used successfully for a wide range of objects. In contrast, more restricted terms like *wide-narrow* are used in a restricted set of cases, and the use of such items leaves many other cases inexpressible. General terms are therefore a useful device for children, who have to utilize their limited vocabulary successfully to cover a large number of contexts. In addition, general terms occur very frequently in the input, and children are given ample opportunity to work out their meanings. A similar point

---

[9]A question may arise as to how many factors there are that are relevant to the order of acquisition. This issue is left open for future research. All that can be said at this point is that all aspects of input, children's conceptual structure, and adults' linguistic structure that are relevant to the child's discovery of adult meanings are possible factors that affect acquisition order.

[10]The view that the relational nature of meaning is irrelevant is also supported by a closer look at the acquisition of dimensional adjectives. The meanings of dimensional adjectives can be divided into two parts: dimensional features (e.g. [+vertical] for *tall* and *short*) which specify the dimension of extension to which these adjectives refer, and polarity features (e.g., [+polar] for *tall* and *long* which distinguish the two antonymous adjectives that are used for the same dimension of extension. It is the polarity features that make dimensional adjectives relational terms. However, Brewer & Stone (1975) found that children acquire polarity features before dimensional features. This means that what determines the order of acquisition in dimensional adjectives is not relational features of their meanings, but rather nonrelational features.

can be made about the system of action verbs, which lacks the basic level and which exhibits an order similar to a top-down order (Clark, 1978b).[11]

This is also the case with the classifier system in Japanese. In this domain relatively less restricted items (e.g., *-tsu, -ko,* and *-hiki*) have a general-purpose nature: they can be used for a large number of objects. On the other hand, the use of specific classifiers like *-satsu, -soo* and *-too* is limited to a small set of cases, and since they are not numerous enough, these classifiers as a whole cannot cover the whole referential domain of countable entities. General classifiers are therefore a useful device for children, just as general dimensional adjectives are. Moreover, general classifiers usually occur frequently in the input (although either of *-tsu* and *-ko* may be infrequent because of the competition between the two), so children receive ample opportunity to search for their adult meanings. Actually, specific classifiers might have an advantage for early acquisition. They are more similar to basic level terms in their internal structure, and therefore their categories must be more differentiated than less restricted ones. However, children seem to be unable to exploit this advantage because of the lack of functional privilege in these terms.

Terms in a taxonomy are quite different. The most superordinate terms in a taxonomy (e.g., *animal*) should be easy to acquire because of the small number of conditions to be discovered (cf. *-hiki*). However, these terms lack the functional privilege that characterizes general terms in dimensional adjectives and classifiers. They do not have a general-purpose nature. In fact, they are not specific enough to use in referring to their referents (animals in the case of *animal*) in most ordinary contexts. Nor are they highly frequent. On the other hand, basic level terms are the building blocks of the whole system. They pick up tight categories, and are most important in communication (Berlin et al., 1973; Rosch et al. 1976; see also Fillmore, 1983). In addition, basic level terms as a whole seem to cover nearly the whole referential domain of a taxonomy, which is not true of specific terms in the domains of dimensional adjectives or classifiers.

Thus, terms that are acquired first in the two kinds of domains are: (1) easier

---

[11]It is doubtful that action verbs have a neat vertically organized hierarchical structure (see Anglin 1985 for a related discussion). This also supports the present version of the domain organization view, which states that the critical point is the lack of the basic level rather than the dominance of vertical contrasts.

Interestingly, action verbs and classifiers exhibit a further similarity in the pattern of acquisition. Clark (1978b) observes that English-speaking children often use very specific denominal verbs (e.g., *button*) in addition to general-purpose verbs at an early stage of acquisition. Similarly, Gandour et al. (1984) observe that Thai-speaking children often employ very specific forms of classifiers called repeaters (Allan, 1977) in addition to the most general ones. These two phenomena are not observed in children learning Japanese, which has no repeaters or similar denominal verbs. Thus, in both domains children often use very specific options in addition to the most general ones provided that they are given models for these specific options by the input.

to map onto appropriate categories because of either the low semantic complexity or the high differentiation of the categories they pick up; and (2) functionally privileged (communicatively useful, frequently used). It is the combination of the effects of these two factors that presumably favors early acquisition of the least restricted terms in nonhorizontal domains, and the basic level terms in horizontal domains.[12] Thus, the different patterns of acquisition order are explained by the multiple-factor view, which states that an order of acquisition is determined by an interaction of different factors. Although this view must be examined further by considering other domains,[13] the present study suggests that this is a promising explanation of why different types of acquisition order occur in different types of lexical domains.

CONCLUSION

In this paper I have described the order of acquisition in Japanese classifiers and discussed the implications of my findings for the two problems of acquisition order in the lexicon. The findings suggest that order of acquisition is determined by the interaction of a variety of factors, some of which are interrelated. These include semantic complexity, the frequency and pattern of use in the input,

---

[12]In a paper on the acquisition of taxonomical categories at different levels, Mervis & Crisafi (1982) claim that a cognitive explanation (highest degree of differentiation at the basic level) provides a sufficient basis for the order of acquisition in taxonomical terms. However, the present findings provide a problem for this view. Very specific classifiers like -soo (for boats) and -ken (for houses) are more similar to basic level terms in terms of their internal structure (cf. Matsumoto, in press). Therefore, these classifiers represent more differentiated categories than general classifiers like -tsu and -hiki, which are similar to superordinate terms. However, as discussed above, relatively general classifiers are acquired before very specific ones. This shows that a cognitive factor is not enough to account for order of acquisition.

[13]It should be noted that not all the domains which have been claimed to exhibit a top-down order (semantic complexity predicts order of acquisition) can be characterized by the functional privilege (the general-purpose nature) of general terms. Take the system of deictic terms, for example. The most simple terms in this domain, I/you, cannot be characterized by the general-purpose nature: They cannot be used in place of other deictic terms like this/that without causing communicative difficulty. This phenomenon might seem to be inconsistent with the present view, which states that the functional privilege of general terms is a crucial feature of the domains in which a top-down order is observed. Does this view, then, lose force? Not necessarily, because deictic terms actually exhibit quite a different acquisition pattern from dimensional adjectives and classifiers, and therefore it would be a mistake to assume that the acquisition pattern of deictic terms is the same as those of classifiers and dimensional adjectives. The difference is that in classifiers and dimensional adjectives the use of a newly acquired term (e.g., thick) tends to replace the earlier use of already acquired terms (e.g, big). That is, new forms tend to express old functions formerly fulfilled by old forms in the same lexical domain. This is not the case with deictic terms. The use of demonstratives, for example, (which are acquired relatively late) does not replace the earlier use of personal pronouns. This observation strongly suggests the need of a finer typology of acquisition order than has been formerly found in the literature.

availability of related salient categories, the existence of semantically similar items, and acquisition and use of formally related items. I have also pointed out that a top-down order of acquisition like that of dimensional adjectives and classifiers typically occurs in lexical domains that lack a basic level of naming (nonhorizontal domains). Moreover, it is suggested that the occurrence of a top-down order in these domains is accounted for by the combination of the effects of low semantic complexity and functional privilege of general terms in these domains.

ACKNOWLEDGMENTS

This paper is based on my master's thesis that I presented to Sophia University, Tokyo (Matsumoto, 1985a). I would like to express my deep gratitude to the many teachers and friends who have helped me in my study. I am especially indebted to Eve Clark, Nancy Conklin, Peter Denny, Pamela Downing, Arnold Falvo, Yurika Hayakawa, Yoshihiko Ikegami, Takehiko Ito, John Nissel, Clifton Pye, Kozue Saito, and Kensaku Yoshida, who gave me invaluable help. Special thanks are due Cheryl Garcia, Keith Nelson and an anonymous reviewer of an earlier version of this paper for various suggestions toward improvement. Of course, they are not responsible for any remaining errors.

REFERENCES

Adams, K., & Conklin, N. (1973). Toward a theory of natural classification. In *Papers from the 9th Regional Meeting*, Chicago Linguistic Society.

Allan, K. (1977). Classifiers. *Language, 53*, 285–311.

Anglin, J. M. (1977). *Word, object, and conceptual development*. New York: Norton.

Anglin, J. M. (1985). The child's expressible knowledge of word concepts: what preschoolers can say about the meanings of some nouns and verbs. In K. Nelson (Ed.), *Children's language, Vol. 5* (pp. 77–128). Hillsdale, NJ: Lawrence Erlbaum Associates.

Baker, N. D., & Nelson, K. E. (1984). Recasting and related conversational techniques for triggering syntactic advances by young children. *First Language, 5*, 3–22.

Bartlett, E. J. (1976). Sizing things up. *Journal of Child Language. 3*, 205–219.

Berlin, B. (1967). *Tzeltal numeral classifiers*. The Hague: Mouton.

Berlin, B., Breedlove, D. E., & Raven, P. H. (1973). General principles of classification and nomenclature in folk biology. *American Anthropology, 75*, 214–242.

Bowerman, M. (1985). Beyond communicative adequacy: From piecemeal knowledge to an integrated system in the child's acquisition of language. In K. Nelson (Ed.), *Children's language, Vol. 5* (pp. 369–398). Hillsdale, NJ: Lawrence Erlbaum Associates.

Brewer, W. F., & Stone, J. B. (1975). Acquisition of spatial antonym pairs. *Journal of Experimental Child Psychology, 19*, 299–307.

Brown, R. (1958). How shall a thing be called? *Psychological Review, 65*, 14–21.

Carey, S. (1982). Semantic development. In E. Wanner & L. R. Gleitman (Eds.), *Language acquisition: The state of the art* (pp. 347–389). Cambridge, England: Cambridge University Press.

Clancy, P. (1985). The acquisition of Japanese. In D. I. Slobin (Ed.), *The crosslinguistic study of language acquisition* (pp. 373–524). Hillsdale, NJ: Lawrence Erlbaum Associates.

Clark, E. V. (1972). On the child's acquisition of antonyms in two semantic fields. *Journal of Verbal Learning and Verbal Behavior, 11*, 750–758.

Clark, E. V. (1973a). What's in a word? On the child's acquisition of semantics in his first language. In T. Moore (Ed.), *Cognitive development and the acquisition of language* (pp. 65–110). New York: Academic Press.

Clark, E. V. (1973b). Non-linguistic strategies and the acquisition of word meanings. *Cognition, 2*, 161–182.

Clark, E. V. (1974). Some aspects of the conceptual basis for first language acquisition. In R. L. Schiefelbusch & L. L. Lloyd (Eds.), *Language perspectives: acquisition, retardation and intervention* (pp. 105–128). Baltimore: University Park Press.

Clark, E. V. (1977). Universal categories: On the semantics of classifiers and children's early word meanings. In A. Juilland (Ed.), *Linguistic Studies offered to Joseph Greenberg: On the occasion of his sixtieth birthday* (pp. 449–462). Saratoga, CA: Anma Libri.

Clark, E. V. (1978a). From gesture to word: On the natural history of deixis in language acquisition. In J. Bruner & A. Garton (Eds.), *Human growth and development: Wolfson College lectures 1976* (pp. 85–120). Oxford: Oxford University Press.

Clark, E. V. (1978b). Discovering what words can do. In *Papers from the parasessions on the lexicon*. Chicago Linguistic Society.

Clark, E. V. (1979). Building a vocabulary: Words for objects, actions, and relations. In P. Fletcher & M. Garman (Eds.), *Language acquisition*. Cambridge, England: Cambridge University Press.

Clark, E. V. (1983). Meanings and concepts. In P. Mussen (Ed.), *Charmichael's manual of child psychology, Vol. 3, Cognition* (pp. 787–840). New York: Wiley.

Denny, P. (1979). Semantic analysis of selected Japanese numeral classifiers for units. *Linguistics, 17*, 317–335.

Dixon. R. M. W. (1982). Numeral classifiers and noun classes. In *Where have all the adjectives gone? and other essays in semantics and syntax*. Berlin, New York & Amsterdam: Mouton.

Downing, P. (1984). Japanese numeral classifiers: A semantic, syntactic, and functional profile. Unpublished doctoral dissertation, University of California, Berkeley.

Erbaugh, M. (1985). Taking stock: The development of Chinese noun classifiers historically and in young children. In C. Craig (Ed.), *Noun classification and categorization*. Amsterdam: Benjamins.

Fillmore, C. J. (1975). Alternatives to checklist theories of meaning. *Proceeding of the first annual meeting of Berkeley Linguistics Society*, 123–131.

Fillmore, C. (1978). On the organization of semantic information in the lexicon. In *Papers from the parasession on the lexicon* Chicago Linguistic Soceity.

Fillmore, C. J. (1982). Toward a descriptive framework for spatial deixis. In J. Jarvella & W. Klein (Eds.), *Speech, place and action* (pp. 31–59). New York: Wiley.

Fillmore, C. (1983). Frame semantics. In *Linguistics in the morning calm*. Seoul: The Linguistic Society of Korea.

Gandour, J., Petty, S., Dardranda, R., Dechongkit, S., & Mukegoen, S. (1984). The acquisition of numeral classifiers in Thai. *Linguistics, 22*, 455–479.

Gentner, D. (1975). Evidence for the psychological reality of semantic components: The verbs of possession. In D. Norman, D. Rumelhart, & the LNR Research Group, *Explorations in cognition*. San Francisco: Freeman.

Gentner, D. (1982). Why nouns are learned before verbs: Linguistic relativity vs. natural partitioning. In S. A. Kuczaj (Ed.), *Language development: Language, culture, and cognition*. (pp. 301–334). Hillsdale, NJ: Lawrence Erlbaum Associates.

Haviland, S. E., & Clark, E. V. (1974). This man's father is my father's son: A study on the acquisition of English kin terms. *Journal of Child Language, 1*, 23–47.

Iwabuchi, E. & Muraishi, S. (1976). *Yooji no yoogo* Tokyo: Nihon Hoosoo Shuppan.

Johnston, J. R., & Slobin, D. I. (1979). The development of locative expressions in English, Italian, Serbo-croation, and Turkish. *Journal of Child Language, 6,* 531–547.

Kameyama, M. (1983). Acquiring clothing verbs in Japanese. *Papers and Reports on Child Language Development, 22,* 66–73.

Kenbo, H. (1976). Gendai no josuushi. *Gengo Seikatsu, 66.*

Kokuritsu Kokugo Kenkyuusho. (1982). *Yooji no kotoba shiryoo* (Data on child language), vol. 4. *Nisaiji no kotoba no kiroku* (A record of a two-year old's speech.); vol. 6, *Sansaiji no kotoba no kiroku* (A record of a three-year old's speech). Tokyo: Shuueisha.

Kokuritsu Kokugo Kenkyuusho. (1983). *Yooji-jidoo no Gainenkeisei to Gengo.* Tokyo: Tokyo Shoseki.

Kuczaj, S. A. (1981). Review of *Ontogenesis of meaning* by E. Clark. *Journal of Child Language, 8,* 505–508.

Kuczaj, S. A., & Lederberg, A. (1977). Height, age, and function: Differing influence on children's comprehension of 'younger' and 'older'. *Journal of Child Language, 4,* 395–416.

Lakoff, G. (1983). Categories. In Linguistic Society of Korea (Ed.), *Linguistics in the morning calm.* Seoul: Hanshin Press.

Lindholm, K. (1982). Bilingual Children: Some interpretations of cognitive and linguistic development. In K. E. Nelson (Ed.), *Children's Language Vol. 2* (pp. 215–266). Hillsdale, NJ: Lawrence Erlbaum Associates.

Maratsos, M. P. (1973). Decrease in the understanding of the word 'big' in preschool children. *Child Development, 44,* 747–752.

Matsumoto, Y. (1984a). *Hito-, huta , mi-* vs *ichi, ni, san:* Kodomo no suushi-josuushi koozoo ni okeru soosa gensoku (The operating principles in children's numeral-classifier construction). In F. C. Peng, (Ed.), *Gengo no Dainamikkusu.* Hiroshima: Bunka Hyooron.

Matsumoto, Y. (1984b, March). *Gengoshuutoku ni okeru wa-kan suushikeiretsu.* [Native and Sino-Japanese numerals in language acquisition]. Paper presented at the 90th meeting of the society for the study of Japanese language.

Matsumoto, Y. (1985a). *Japanese numeral classifiers: Their structures and acquisition.* Unpublished master's thesis. Sophia University.

Matsumoto, Y. (1985b) Acquisition of some Japanese numeral classifiers: the search for convention. *PRCLD, 24.*

Matsumoto, Y. (1986). The Japanese classifier *-hon:* A prototype semantic analysis. *Sophia Linguistica, 20/21,* 73–81.

Matsumoto, Y. (in press). The Japanese classifiers *-ken* and *-mune:* prototype and background of existence. *Sophia Linguistica, 22/23.*

Mervis, C., & Crisafi, M. (1982). Order of acquisition of subordinate-, basic- and superordinate-level categories. *Child Development, 53,* 258–266.

Mervis, C., & Pani, J. (1980). Acquisition of object categories. *Cognitive Psychology, 12,* 496–522.

Miyaji, H. (1966). A frequency dictionary of Japanese Words. Unpublished doctoral dissertation, Stanford University.

Muraishi, S. (1967). Josuushi no choosa [A research on classifiers]. *Shotoo Kyooiku Shiryoo 214.*

Nelson, K., Bonvillian, J. D., Denninger, M. S., Kaplan, B. J., & Baker, N. D. (1984). Maternal input adjustments and non-adjustments as related to children's linguistic advances and to language acquisition theories. In A. Pellegrini & T. Yawkey (Eds.), *The development of oral and written language in social contexts* (pp. 31–56). Hillsdale, NJ: Lawrence Erlbaum Associates.

Okubo, A. (1967). *Yoojigengo no hattatsu.* [The development of child language]. Tokyo: Tookyoodoo.

Ravn, K. E., & Gelman, S. A. (1984). Rule usage in children's understanding of the word "big" in preschool children. *Child Development, 55,* 2141–2150.

Rescorla, L. (1981). Category development in early language. *Journal of Child Language, 8,* 321–335.

Rosch, E., Mervis, C., Gray, W., Johnson, D., & Boyes-Braem, P. (1976). Basic objects in natural categories. *Cognitive Psychology, 8*, 382–439.

Sanches, M. (1978). Language acquisition and language change: Japanese numeral classifiers. In M. Sanches & B. Blount (Eds.), *Socio-cultural dimensions of language change* (pp. 51–62). New York: Academic Press.

Schwam, E. (1982). Signs and strategies: The interactive processes of sign language learning. In K. E. Nelson (Ed.), *Children's language, Vol. 3* (pp. 392–436). Hillsdale, NJ: Lawrence Erlbaum Associates.

Schwartz, R. G., & Terrell, B. Y. (1983). The role of input frequency in lexical acquisition. *Journal of Child Language, 10*, 57–64.

Slobin, D. I. (1973). Cognitive prerequisites for the acquisition of grammar. In C. A. Ferguson & D. I. Slobin (Eds.), *Studies of child language development* (pp. 175–208). New York: Holt, Rinehart & Winston.

Wilcox, S., & Palermo, D. S. (1974/75). "In," "on," and "under" revisited. *Cognition, 3*, 245–254.

12 Children's Overgeneralizations of the English Dative Alternation

Lydia White
McGill University

1. INTRODUCTION

The English dative alternation has aroused much interest recently, both in theoretical linguistics and in language acquisition theory. In English there are many dative verbs which allow two possible complements of equivalent meaning; that is, they can be followed by [NP PP], as in (1a), or by [NP NP], as in (1b). Such verbs are known as alternating verbs, and the [NP NP] complement is often called the *double-object* construction.

1.a. John gave the book to Fred
   b. John gave Fred the book

In both cases, the noun phrase *the book* is the direct object, while *Fred* is the indirect object.

There are also verbs, in many cases identical in meaning, which do not allow the double object construction. That is, the [NP PP] complement is possible, as in (2a), whereas (2b) is ungrammatical:

2.a. John donated some money to the students
   b. *John donated the students some money

Baker (1979) discusses the learnability issue that these cases raise: if children acquire a transformational rule of dative-movement to derive (1b) from (1a), then they would also be expected to apply this rule generally to any dative verb, resulting in overgeneralizations like (2b). They would then be unable to *unlearn* the overgeneralization without negative evidence. In other words, they would have to be told explicitly that (2b) is ungrammatical, since there is nothing in the positive evidence to indicate that this is the case. Baker suggests that, instead of acquiring a movement rule, children subcategorize dative verbs conservatively, on the basis of positive evidence. On hearing sentences like (1a) and (1b), they will enter *give* in the lexicon as allowing both the [NP PP] and [NP NP] complements, whereas *donate* will be subcategorized for [NP PP], since only structures like (2a) will be exemplified in the input.

This analysis depends crucially on the assumption that forms like (2b) are nonoccurring in child language, since, if they do occur, the learnability issue is raised all over again, only this time for a lexical overgeneralization rather than a transformational one. In a recent paper, Mazurkewich and White (1984) present data showing precisely such overgeneralizations amongst older children and they suggest that failure to observe them up till now stems from the fact that verbs like *donate* are less likely to be understood and used by young children. David Ingram (personal communication) also has data from older children showing overgeneralizations like (2b). It seems that children are not as conservative in their approach to the acquisition of dative verbs as Baker's proposal suggests.

Mazurkewich and White propose a lexical analysis of the dative alternation, whereby the [NP PP] and [NP NP] forms are related by a lexical rule with two restrictions, one semantic and the other morphological. The morphological restriction dictates that alternating verbs must have native stems, rather than Latinate ones, accounting for the nonoccurrence of forms like (2b). They argue that this can be discovered by the child on the basis of positive evidence, leading to the loss of such overgeneralizations.

In addition to verbs like *give,* where the preposition in the [NP PP] complement is *to,* there are many verbs which alternate, where the indirect object occurs in a phrase introduced by the preposition *for,* as in (3):

3.a.   Mary bought a book for John
  b.   Mary bought John a book

There are also many verbs which can be followed by a prepositional phrase beginning with *for,* where the double object version is not possible, as in (4):

4.a.   John drove the car for Fred
  b.   *John drove Fred the car

Fischer (1971) suggests that the prepositional phrase in sentences like (4a) is not dative but, rather, benefactive; *Fred* is not a true indirect object. Sentences like (3a) are ambiguous between a dative and a benefactive reading. These benefactive *for*-phrases are not subcategorized by particular verbs. In other words, they are not arguments of verbs and they can occur in many different kinds of sentences. In addition, they can cooccur with true indirect objects, in both *to* and *for* datives, whether these are in the [NP PP] or [NP NP] form, as can be seen in (5):

5.a.   John brought a book to Mary for Fred
 b.   John brought Mary a book for Fred
 c.   John bought a book for Mary for Fred
 d.   John bought Mary a book for Fred

In all these sentences, *Mary* is the indirect object, the future recipient of the book, and *Fred* is the person on whose behalf John is performing the action. (We are not concerned here with the interpretation where [a book for Fred] is a complex NP.) Fischer suggests that these benefactive *for*-phrases hang from a higher level of structure than the indirect object *to*- and *for*-phrases, as shown in (6):

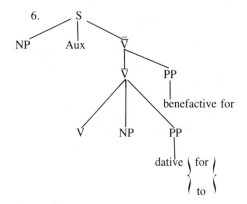

Many recent linguistic analyses have proposed that the distinction between alternating and nonalternating verbs is at least partly due to semantic factors, specifically that in the double-object construction, the indirect object must be the *prospective possessor* of the direct object (Fischer, 1971; Goldsmith, 1980; Mazurkewich & White, 1984; Oehrle, 1976; Stowell, 1981). This explains why forms like (4b) are impossible, since *Fred* is not the prospective possessor of *the car*. It also explains why (3b) can only have the dative interpretation, instead of being ambiguous like (3a). It appears, then, that true indirect objects must both be subcategorized by the verb, although their appearance is optional, and must carry a particular semantic role. Sentences containing *for*-phrases which do not meet these criteria do not have the alternate [NP NP] form.

The question arises as to whether children are aware of the syntactic and semantic differences between these two kinds of *for* phrases, and how they reach such awareness. Much of the crucial evidence which indicates that benefactives cannot occur in the double-object construction is negative evidence, for example, the fact that forms like (4b) are ungrammatical, the fact that (3b) does not have an ambiguous interpretation, the fact that in (5c) and (5d) the order must be dative before benefactive and not vice versa. Given the usual assumptions that negative data are not available to children or not used by them (Braine, 1971; Brown & Hanlon, 1970), the strongest hypothesis would be that children do not have to learn this difference at all, that the knowledge as to the possible syntactic behavior of certain semantic classes like benefactives is either given by Universal Grammar or is so transparent from the semantic roles involved as to be unproblematic. In either case, one would not expect errors like (4b) to occur in the course of acquisition.

Overgeneralizations like those in (7) have been observed by the author in the spontaneous speech of a number of children:

7.a. I'll brush him his hair (speaker aged 2;3)
  b. Pick me up all these things (speaker aged 5;2)
  c. Mummy, open Hadwen the door (speaker aged 6;0)

These sentences all share with (4b) the characteristic that the first NP after the verb is not the prospective possessor of the direct object and that it is not a true dative but a benefactive, and, hence, ineligible to occur in the [NP NP] construction.[1]

Anecdotal cases like (7) are comparatively rare in the literature. Bowerman (1983) reports some dative errors, including one involving a similar semantic overgeneralization, as in (8):

8. Button me the rest.

If such forms are more than passing performance errors, they are interesting precisely because they suggest *semantic* overgeneralization. They constitute cases similar to those discussed by Bowerman (1982, 1985), where the child makes overgeneralizations which suggest problems in working out the precise semantic class to which an already acquired syntactic or morphological rule applies. In other words, overgeneralizations like (7) and (8) suggest that the child has acquired the syntax of the double-object construction, but has not yet limited it to the class of true indirect objects, those NPs which will be the possessors of the direct object. As Bowerman (1982, 1985) points out, the existence of semantic overgeneralizations is problematic for accounts of syntax acquisition which assume that semantic roles are somehow transparent to children and that seman-

---

[1]Although in (7a) the indirect object does "possess" the direct object, this relationship existed prior to the action described by the verb. In the double-object construction in the adult grammar, the relationship of possession between the indirect and direct objects must be the result of the action of the verb.

tics serves as a necessary precursor to the acquisition of syntactic form. If anything, the acquisition of syntactic form in these cases seems to precede the acquisition of the precise semantic aspects of the structures in question.

In arguing against purely semantically based approaches to syntax acquisition, Maratsos (1979) and Maratsos and Chalkley (1980) also point out certain problems that arise for such accounts, particularly the fact that there is no one-to-one correspondence between semantic roles and structural positions, so that different semantic roles can be associated with the same structural position and phrase type. This is the case here; the *for*-phrases in the [NP PP] sentences are ambiguous between dative and benefactive readings, and the existence of overgeneralization of the benefactive role to the [NP NP] form suggests that children are unable to distinguish between the permitted syntactic positions for these two semantic roles.

In view of the paucity of data bearing on the issue of whether young children do or do not overgeneralize the semantic aspect of the dative alternation, an experiment was conducted to see whether forms such as those in (7) could be elicited.[2] I discuss the experiment and its results in Sections (2) and (3), and will then turn to the implications of the results in Section (4).

2. METHOD

2.i. Subjects. Twenty-two children, aged 3;8 to 5;8, attending McGill University Day Care Centre, were tested. Of these, twenty passed a pretest and continued to the main experiment. Thirteen of the children who passed the pretest were native speakers of English and the rest were fluently bilingual in English and some other language, in most cases French. Language background turned out to have no effect on the results. The average age of those taking part in the main experiment was 4;4.

2.ii. Tasks. The children were asked to perform two tasks, one an act-out task and the other an imitation task. In the act-out task, a number of toys were laid out in front of the child, and the experimenter read a sentence and asked the child to perform the action described in the sentence, using the relevant toys. For the imitation task, the child and the experimenter each held a puppet and the child was asked to make his or her puppet copy exactly what the experimenter's puppet said. Where a child failed to act out or to imitate a sentence, the sentence was repeated once more. The toys and the actions involved in the two tasks were the same. The order of presentation was randomized across subjects in both

---

[2]As far as I am aware, Fischer (1971) is the only person to include cases like (7) in her investigation of the acquisition of the dative alternation, although this is not the main focus of her study.

tasks. Some children performed the act-out task first, others the imitation task. There were 16 sentences in the act-out task and 18 in the imitation task. The test sentences are given in the Appendix.

Children varied enormously in the length of time they took to perform the tasks. Some children did one task immediately after the other, but those whose attention wandered during the first task did the second task on a consecutive day.

The children were all pretested for each task. They were pretested on all the vocabulary used in the test, and also on their ability to act out sentences and to imitate them. Since the issue to be investigated was the possible occurrence of overgeneralizations of double-object forms, it was important that the children should already have mastered that construction. Ten pretest sentences, involving *to*-dative verbs, were administered to establish that the children could act out and repeat both the [NP PP] and the [NP NP] complements. For example, children had to act out sentences like: *Give the book to the teddy, Show the monkey the ribbon,* and to repeat sentences like: *The doll is giving a book to the monkey, The monkey is bringing the doll a block.* Children making more than two mistakes on these sentences were eliminated from the testing. Fourteen of the children scored 100% on the pretests, five of them made one mistake, and one made two mistakes. In all cases, the mistakes involved the imitation part of the pretest, rather than the act out. Two children failed the pretest.

2.iii. Choice of Test Sentences.   The test sentences involved the following *for*-dative verbs which alternate in the adult grammar: *draw, get, build* and *find,* together with verbs which occur only with benefactive *for* phrases, and hence do not alternate for adults: *tie, open, wash* and *drive.* I shall refer to the latter as nonalternating verbs, even though they did "alternate" in the test, in that they were used with both complements. All verbs in the test were presented in both forms, so that the following range of sentence types occurred:

9.a.   The monkey is drawing a picture for the doll
  b.   The doll is drawing the teddy a picture
  c.   The teddy is opening the door for the monkey
  d.   The doll is opening the monkey the door

(9a) and (9b) represent the dative alternation with an alternating verb, whereas (9c) and (9d) represent the alternation with a verb that is, in fact, non-alternating, (9d) being ungrammatical. The monkey, doll and teddy were varied so that they all occurred at different times as subject and indirect object. In the imitation task, the verb was in the present progressive form; in the act-out task, the imperative was used, in order to reduce the number of NPs in the sentences and to concentrate on the direct and indirect objects.

In all sentences, full NPs were used rather than pronouns. A number of people find the ungrammatical double-object construction somewhat more acceptable in the case where the indirect object is a pronoun; that is, (7a), (7b) and (8) sound better than (7c) or (4b). Since it was the aim of this study to see whether children produce overgeneralizations that are unacceptable to adults, it was important to exclude the pronominal cases.[3]

In all the sentences, in both the [NP PP] and [NP NP] conditions, the indirect object was a toy animal or doll, i.e., it could be interpreted as being animate, whereas the direct object was inanimate, and the relationship between the direct and indirect object was always plausible. Problems with the [NP NP] construction are well known when both NPs are animate, as in (10a), or both inanimate, as in (10b), or when an animate object is given to an inanimate one, as in (10c) (Cook, 1976; Fischer, 1971; Roeper, Lapointe, Bing, & Tavakolian, 1981):

10.a.   John gave Mary Fred
   b.   John gave the cookie the stone
   c.   John gave the cookie the snake

Because the spontaneous overgeneralizations that have been observed were in normal situations, and because I did not want the children's acceptance or rejection of the [NP NP] construction to be confounded by difficulties in interpreting the rather peculiar sentences that result when animacy is controlled for, or when the relationship between the direct and indirect object is implausible, sentences like those in (10) were deliberately excluded. It is usually assumed that it is only by including such sentences that one can be sure that the syntax of the double-object construction has been mastered and that the child is not relying solely on semantic cues. For example, Roeper, Lapointe, Bing, and Tavakolian (1981) argue that *give* does not have an animacy requirement on the indirect object on the basis of sentences like:

11.   He gave the car a kick

However, such sentences are clearly idiomatic and different from other double-object sentences in that they can be paraphrased as:

12.   He kicked the car

This is not possible in the normal case. Sentences like (10b) and (10c) seem hard to interpret unless one imposes animate-like properties on the recipient, a point also noted by Fischer (1971). It would seem that the lexical entry for *give* and other dative verbs includes the information that the indirect object is animate and, hence, that factoring out animacy is not necessarily an appropriate way to test the child's command of the syntax of this construction.

---

[3]It is possible, in any case, that pronominal indirect objects are cliticized to the verb, so that they do not necessarily represent the same structure as the double-object construction with full NPs.

3. RESULTS

3.i. Results from the Act-out Task. In acting out the sentences, children either acted out the sentences fully, using the correct direct object and the correct indirect object,[4] or they acted them out by involving the direct object and ignoring the indirect object. For example, with sentences like (13a) and (13b), most children did involve the indirect object, in both the [NP PP] and the [NP NP] structure, that is, they would pick up the direct object and move it to the indirect object:

13.a.   Get the book for the doll
  b.   Get the monkey the car

On the other hand, with some verbs, most children did not involve the indirect object and again this was true of both complement types. Such was the case with the verb *draw,* for example. The same situation arose with the verbs that do not alternate in the adult grammar; for some of them, the indirect object was consistently acted out and for others not, regardless of the form of the complement. In other words, whether or not the indirect object was acted out *depended on the particular verb* (presumably the degree to which the indirect object seemed integral to the sentence meaning) and *was independent of either the complement type or the question of whether the verb alternates or not in the adult grammar.* These results are given in Table 12.1, where it can be seen that, although omission of the indirect object varies considerably from verb to verb, the children were very consistent in their treatment of each verb across the two complement types.

If the children were aware of a difference between true dative indirect objects and benefactives, one might expect them to be more inclined to omit the latter, particularly when a benefactive wrongly occurs in the [NP NP] structure. Whilst there is more omission of indirect objects with the nonalternating verbs than with the alternating ones, this difference is not significant. Furthermore, they were no more inclined to omit the benefactive from the [NP NP] forms of nonalternating verbs than from the [NP PP] versions of these verbs, suggesting that there is nothing special in their treatment of the sentences that are ungrammatical in the adult grammar.

The breakdown of these results by individual subjects is given in Table 12.2, which shows the number of totally correct act-out responses, i.e., those where the indirect object was included in the action. It can be seen that for most subjects whether a sentence is acted out correctly or not is *not* related either to the form of the complement ([NP PP] versus [NP NP]) or to the question of whether or not

---

[4]For convenience, I will refer to both dative and benefactive NPs as *indirect objects* when discussing these results.

TABLE 12.1
Results From the Act-Out Task (n = 20)

	NP PP			NP NP		
	Correct	I.O.Omitted	Other	Correct	I.O.Omitted	Other
Alternating Verbs						
draw	5	15	0	5	14	1
get	19	1	0	19	1	0
build	12	8	0	10	10	0
find	17	3	0	18	2	0
total	53	27	0	52	27	1
Nonalternating Verbs						
tie	13	6	1	13	6	1
open	14	6	0	10	8	2
wash	10	10	0	12	7	1
drive	7	13	0	7	12	1
total	44	36	1	42	33	4
Grand Total	96 (60%)	63 (39%)	1	94 (59%)	60 (37.5%)	6

Note. I.O. = indirect object

the verb alternates. Subjects 5 and 10 consistently fail to act out the indirect object for the nonalternating verbs in both the [NP PP] and [NP NP] conditions, suggesting that they treat benefactives differently from dative indirect objects. However, as Subject 10 also only fully acts out one alternating verb in the [NP NP] condition, this conclusion must be seen as tentative. Subjects 2 and 7 give

TABLE 12.2
Correct Act-Out Results, by Subject

		NP PP		NP NP	
Subject	Age	Alternating (n=4)	Nonalternating (n=4)	Alternating (n=4)	Nonalternating (n=4)
1.	3;8	3	1	2	1
2.	3;8	3	3	3	1
3.	3;11	3	2	3	3
4.	4;0	2	3	2	3
5.	4;0	3	0	2	0
6.	4;2	4	4	4	3
7.	4;3	3	2	3	1
8.	4;4	2	1	2	1
9.	4;5	3	3	3	3
10.	4;6	2	0	1	0
11.	4;8	2	2	1	2
12.	4;10	3	3	3	2
13.	4;10	1	2	2	2
14.	4;10	3	4	3	4
15.	5;4	1	4	4	3
16.	5;7	4	4	4	4
17.	5;7	4	2	2	4
18.	5;8	3	3	4	3
19.	3;9	2	1	2	1
20.	3;11	2	0	2	1

fewer correct act-out responses to the [NP NP] condition of the nonalternating verbs than to any of the other conditions, suggesting that they may be aware of the ungrammatical nature of these forms. Subjects 3,4,6,9,14,15,16,17, and 18 correctly act out three or four out of four nonalternating verbs in the [NP NP] version, suggesting overgeneralization of the double-object construction. For the remaining subjects, there does not seem to be a clear trend in either direction.

There were no truly incorrect responses. The 6 responses classified as *other* in Table 12.1 did not involve errors but irrelevant responses which suggested that the child's attention was wandering. No children took the first postverbal NP in the double-object construction to be the direct object. This would have been a perfectly plausible response in many cases, resulting in strings like "draw the doll," "get the monkey," "find the teddy," etc. The fact that the children never did this suggests that they never resorted to a linear strategy such as "first NP is the direct object," which has been proposed in the literature. On the contrary, they seemed quite clear as to which NP was the direct object in both the [NP PP] and the [NP NP] sentences, and if anything was omitted it was invariably the indirect object.

Failure to include the indirect object cannot be taken to indicate a lack of understanding of its role: because the true indirect object is always optional in *for*-datives, and benefactives are always optional as well, all the sentences make complete sense without acting out the indirect object.[5] It is noteworthy that one alternating verb, namely *draw,* and one nonalternating verb, namely *drive,* were particularly prone to having the indirect object omitted, again suggesting that this response is not based on the alternating status of the verb in the adult grammar.

On the basis of the act-out results, it appears that all the children can understand the dative alternation. The results involving correct acting out, that is including the direct and indirect objects in the action, indicate that many of the children can fully interpret sentences in which the [NP NP] complement is extended to a verb which does not alternate in the adult grammar, suggesting overgeneralization of this complement to verbs which do not, in fact, permit it.

3.ii. Results from the Imitation Task.   Of the twenty children who passed the pretest, one (Subject 19) refused to do the imitation task and another (Subject 20) did not understand that he was meant to copy the whole sentence and not just the puppet's last word. The results on the imitation task, therefore, are from eighteen of the children.

An imitation was counted as correct if it was totally correct or involved only minor lexical changes, such as *bear* for *teddy,* or *make* for *build.* An analysis of variance shows that there is a significant difference ($p < 0.01$) in the correct imitations of three conditions: children are most accurate on the [NP PP] sen-

---

[5]Fischer (1971) comments on the problems of devising *for*-dative sentences that can be fully acted out and this certainly seems to be a problem for some of the verbs tested here.

TABLE 12.3
Number of Correct Imitations (n = 18)

	NP PP	NP NP
Alternating Verbs		
draw	13	8
get	17	10
build	12	10
find	17	16
Totals	59 (82%)	44 (62.5%)
Nonalternating Verbs		
tie	16	5
open	18	11
wash	10	6
drive	16	10
Totals	60 (83%)	32 (44%)

tences (alternating and nonalternating verbs combined), next most accurate on the alternating [NP NP] verbs and least accurate on the nonalternating [NP NP] verbs. The overall results are given in Table 12.3.

These results suggest that the children as a group are aware of the ungrammaticality of the [NP NP] construction with only some of the nonalternating verbs. There are fewer correct imitations of the double-object construction with *tie* and *wash* than with *open* and *drive,* and the difference is significant, χ^2 (1, N = 72) = 6.80, $p < 0.01$. The number of correct imitations of the open/drive sentences in the [NP NP] form is not significantly different from the correct imitations of the [NP NP] construction with the alternating verbs.

The overall results are misleading in that they conceal the fact that individual children do imitate all the nonalternating [NP NP] forms as much as they imitate the alternating verbs in this condition. The imitation results from individual subjects are given in Table 12.4. It can be seen that six children (Subjects 1,8,13,15,17,18), ranging in age from the youngest to the oldest, correctly imitated three or four (out of four) nonalternating [NP NP] verbs. Only two children (Subjects 7 and 11) show imitation of multiple alternating [NP NP] forms and avoidance of nonalternating ones. Four subjects (3,4,6, and 14) correctly imitated only one [NP NP] form out of the total of eight, so that their avoidance of the double-object construction with nonalternating verbs cannot be taken as an indication that they are aware of a distinction between the two types of verbs. These four children showed the full range of error patterns discussed below, their predominant response for both the alternating and nonalternating [NP NP] forms being to convert them to [NP PP] ones. One child correctly imitated the [NP NP] version of a nonalternating verb and then commented that the sentence was "backwards," but there were otherwise few metalinguistic

TABLE 12.4
Correct Imitations, by Subject

Subject	Age	NP PP (n=8)	NP NP Alternating (n=4)	Nonalternating (n=4)
1.	3;8	7	4	4
2.	3;8	4	2	2
3.	3;11	8	1	0
4.	4;0	6	1	0
5.	4;0	6	3	2
6.	4;2	7	1	0
7.	4;3	6	3	0
8.	4;4	6	4	4
9.	4;5	7	2	2
10.	4;6	7	2	1
11.	4;8	6	2	0
12.	4;10	7	1	2
13.	4;10	8	3	3
14.	4;10	6	0	1
15.	5;4	6	4	3
16.	5;7	7	4	2
17.	5;7	7	3	3
18.	5;8	8	4	3

observations made by the children. I conclude from these results that *some of the children did overgeneralize the double-object construction and accept nonalternating verbs as alternating, though they did not necessarily accept all of them.*

The errors made by the children in their imitations are also of interest. In the case of sentences in the [NP PP] form, out of a total of 144 imitations, there were only 25 mistakes and 16 of these involved the child's repeating the structure correctly, but misnaming either the subject or the indirect object, usually resulting in the same NP being used for both. For example, in response to a sentence like (14a), some children repeated it as (14b) and others as (14c):

14.a.   The doll is washing the sweater for the teddy
　　b.   The teddy is washing the sweater for the teddy
　　c.   The doll is washing the sweater for the doll

There seemed to be no consistent pattern for individual children or across children; sometimes the NP they heard first would be used twice, at other times the NP they heard last. Occasionally, a toy not mentioned in the stimulus sentence would be named. Although classified as errors, such responses reveal that the child is aware of the structure of the stimulus sentences: in all these mistakes, the responses was still in the form of an [NP PP] complement.

For the [NP NP] sentences, there were 67 incorrect imitations, out of a total of 144. There were 4 main categories of error, of which one was the same as the error found for the [NP PP] sentences, that is, repeating the wrong toy as subject or as indirect object. Again, this error usually revealed an understanding of the form of the stimulus sentences, the response taking the form of an [NP NP] structure. However, in some cases, this error occurred in conjunction with another error, particularly the conversion error discussed below.

A second kind of error was for the [NP NP] structure to be converted to the [NP PP] form, as in (15b) for (15a):

15.a. The teddy is drawing the doll a house
   b. The teddy is drawing a house for the doll

Where such conversion errors occur for alternating verbs, this might be taken as an indication that the children who convert do not yet have command of the [NP NP] structure. However, in all the conversions that the children made, the roles of both the direct and indirect objects had been correctly understood in the [NP NP] form, but the alternate structure was used in the imitation, suggesting that they were perfectly well aware of the relationships involved in the [NP NP] complements. Such conversion errors are also reported by Fischer (1971). These conversions, where the direct and indirect objects had clearly been correctly indentified, contrast with conversion errors reported by Roeper et al. (1981), where children not only converted [NP NP] complements to [NP PP] ones but also reversed the direct and indirect objects, as in (16), where they repeated (16a) as (16b):

16.a. The cow gave the dog the pig
   b. The cow gave the dog to the pig

Such a response seems to reflect a genuine confusion about the double-object structure, a confusion which was absent in the subjects reported here, although this confusion may have been the result of their experimental task. (See Section 4.ii for further discussion). Other cases of systematic conversion of one syntactic structure to another in an imitation task are reported by Haber (1982), who found normal 4- and 5-year-olds would systematically alter passives that they could not repeat into actives. As she does not report on the exact nature of the conversion, it is not possible to tell whether these cases involved correct indentification of the semantic roles involved in the passives, parallel to the behavior of my subjects, or whether the conversion resulted in the reversal of the roles of the NPs, as is the case with the conversion reported by Roeper et al. Only the latter, I would suggest, can be taken to indicate that the children do not have command of the structures being tested.

Conversion of the stimulus sentences involving nonalternating verbs in the [NP NP] form could be argued to show that the children understand that [NP NP] complements are not, in fact, possible when a benefactive is involved. However, if that were so, one would expect a much higher proportion of conversions with nonalternating verbs than was actually found. Although there are more conversions for the nonalternating verbs, this can be attributed to the fact that one of the alternating verbs, namely *find*, received no conversions at all. The other alternating verbs received the same average number of conversions as the nonalternating verbs. Thus, it does not appear that conversion indicates any special sensitivity to the ungrammatical status of the double-object form with nonalternating verbs.

Another common error was for the indirect object to be omitted in the imitation task (as was also found in the act-out task), as in (17b) for (17a):

17.a.   The monkey is building the teddy a tower
   b.   The monkey is building a tower

There was only one case of an error involving the retention of the indirect object and omission of the direct object, again supporting the act-out data which show that these children never resort to a strategy of taking the first NP to be the direct object.

An interesting difference between the alternating and nonalternating verbs arises in the case of what might be termed *possessive* errors. That is, some children repeated a sentence like (18a) as (18b):

18.a.   The teddy is washing the monkey the pants
   b.   The teddy is washing the monkey's pants

This occurred 8 times for the nonalternating verbs but only once for the alternating ones.

The error totals for the imitations of [NP NP] sentences are given in Table 12.5. It can be seen that all the error patterns were found for both alternating and nonalternating verbs. Although most of the error totals were higher in the [NP NP] sentences with nonalternating verbs, the differences in the proportion of the various error types for the alternating versus the nonalternating verbs are not significant.

TABLE 12.5
Error Totals for Imitations of [NP NP] Sentences

Verbs	Wrong NPs	Omit I.O.	Possessives	Other	Conversions
Alternating					
draw	2	2	1	3	2
get	3	0	0	2	2
build	1	3	0	0	4
find	0	2	0	0	0
totals	6	7	1	5	8
Nonalternating					
tie	0	6	1	3	3
open	0	2	2	1	2
wash	2	1	3	3	3
drive	0	2	2	0	4
totals	2	11	8	7	12

Note. I.O. = indirect object.

The test included two additional sentences, not given in the tables of results above, where the double-object construction is obligatory, repeated here as (19) and (20):

19. The noise is giving the doll a headache
20. The car cost Daddy $5

These were included to test the proposal in Mazurkewich and White (1984) that the obligatory use of the [NP NP] form in such cases might force the relevance of the role of *possessor* to the child's attention and lead to a retreat from overgeneralization. Almost all the children found (19) very easy to imitate, with 15 out of 18 of them getting it right. On the other hand, many of them found (20) extremely difficult. Only half of the children got it right and many of these required the sentence to be repeated more than once, and their repetition was often slow and drawn out, in complete contrast to their other repetitions. However, the difficulties with (20) seemed to bear no relation to their performance on the other sentences; children who accepted nonalternating verbs in the [NP NP] form did not necessarily have problems with (20), whereas children who did not overgeneralize did have problems. Although it is clear that *cost* in this construction is difficult, it is not clear that this has any necessary connection with overgeneralization of the dative alternation, or retreat from it.

3.iii. Comparison of Results from the Two Tasks.   Eighteen of the subjects performed both of the tasks, and in both tasks the same verbs were employed. This makes it possible to compare the performance of individual children on the two tasks, as well as to see whether verbs are treated consistently across the tasks.

The results from individual subjects on the act-out task are given in Table 12.2, and their results on the imitation task are given in Table 12.4. As mentioned above, the results from Subjects 3,4,6,9,14,15,16,17, and 18 in the act-out task suggest that these children are overgeneralizing the double-object structure to nonalternating verbs. In the imitation task, the results from Subjects 1,8,13,15,17,18 suggest the same thing. Subjects 15,17, and 18, therefore, can be seen to overgeneralize across both the tasks. In addition, Subject 9, who overgeneralizes in the act-out task, has a response pattern in the imitation task which is consistent with overgeneralization, in that he correctly imitates an equal number of alternating and nonalternating [NP NP] forms. Subject 13, who overgeneralizes in the imitation task, has a response pattern in the act-out task which is consistent with overgeneralization, in that she acts out as many nonalternating as alternating [NP NP] forms. Thus, five of the subjects show responses to both tasks which suggest that they are overgeneralizers.

In the act out task, Subjects 2,5,7, and 10 showed behavior which suggested that they avoid overgeneralization of the [NP NP] structure to nonalternating verbs. Of these four subjects, only Subject 7 clearly shows the same avoidance in the imitation task.

There are two kinds of inconsistencies across the tasks. Some subjects perform much more accurately on all [NP NP] forms on the act-out task than on the imitation task; the subjects who avoided the double-object construction with both alternating and nonalternating verbs almost entirely in the imitation task (Subjects 3,4,6, and 14) nevertheless acted them out quite accurately. It is not clear whether these subjects have full command of the double-object structure at all. One might explain the discrepancy between the two tasks on the assumption that they adopt a comprehension strategy for the act-out task of treating the inanimate object as direct object and the animate object as indirect (see Section 4.ii for further discussion). On the other hand, Subjects 1,5, and 8 imitate more nonalternating [NP NP] forms than they act out. This might reflect the possibility that these children are particularly good imitators, so that their imitation ability overrides their awareness (revealed in the other task) that the [NP NP] form is odd with nonalternating verbs.

As far as the treatment of the various verbs across the two tasks is concerned, one can compare Table 12.1 and Table 12.3. Of the alternating verbs, accuracy on *find* is consistently high in both the tasks and in both the complement types. Responses to *get* are also very accurate for all but the imitations of the [NP NP] forms. *Build* is treated consistently, though not accurately, across the two tasks. In contrast to this, accuracy on *draw* is consistently low.

The response patterns for the nonalternating verbs are rather less consistent across the two tasks, except for *open* which was fairly consistently dealt with throughout. In the act-out task, *drive* was the verb which was least accurately acted out. However, this was true both with the [NP PP] and [NP NP] complements, suggesting that it is not the case that the children see this verb as problematic specifically in the [NP NP] version. With the verbs *tie* and *wash*, subjects were less accurate at imitating them in the [NP NP] version than in acting them out, and these verbs were less well imitated in the [NP NP] form than any other verbs in the test. Whilst the children's treatment of these verbs in the imitation task suggests that they may be aware of their nonalternating status, the act-out results do not suggest differential treatment of the double-object versions of these verbs.

4. DISCUSSION

4.i. The Existence of Overgeneralization.   The results from the two tasks suggest that overgeneralization of the double-object construction does occur and, hence, that the spontaneous overgeneralizations that have been noted in the literature cannot be dismissed as random performance errors. The comparison of individual performance across the two tasks shows that some of the children may reasonably be classified as overgeneralizers (Subjects 9,13,15,17,18). One child (Subject 7) can be classified as an avoider of overgeneralization; presumably this child has already worked out the semantic limitations on the dative alternation. The response patterns of some of the other subjects suggest overgeneralization on one of the two tasks whilst their behavior on the other is indeterminate; these children are potentially overgeneralizers as well. However, in spite of this evidence of overgeneralization amongst individuals, the response patterns to the various verbs show that some verbs are less likely to be overgeneralized than others, suggesting that this is not an across-the-board phenomenon but that it is lexically limited, a finding which is consistent with the view that the dative alternation is, in any case, a lexical phenomenon.

The age of the clear overgeneralizers is worthy of note: they range from 4;5 to 5;8, as compared with ages of 3;8 to 5;7 for nonovergeneralizers. In other words, this overgeneralization is not indicative of problems in the initial stages of acquisition. Rather, it constitutes another example of the kinds of overgeneralization discussed by Bowerman (1982, 1985), where older children fail to limit syntactic or morphological rules to the semantic class to which they apply in the adult grammar. I return to the implications of these late semantic overgeneralizations in Section 4.iii.

4.ii. Comparison with other Results.   In terms of the difference between [NP PP] and [NP NP] structures, these results, in their general trend, bear out other findings that the [NP PP] construction is preferred by children. However, this is only so for the imitation results. The act-out results show that both constructions were equally well acted out; although some verbs were less accurately acted out than others (compare *draw* with *get,* for example), this inaccuracy showed up in both the [NP NP] and [NP PP] complements. Furthermore, these subjects are generally better at the [NP NP] structure than others have found. Whilst this might simply reflect the fact that the subjects used in this experiment came from an academic community and were fairly advanced in their linguistic skills, there are other possible explanations for the differences.

Roeper et al. (1981) tested comprehension of the double-object construction (but not the [NP PP] complements) in children of various ages. Their youngest group was of kindergarten age, i.e., somewhat older than my subjects. As mentioned earlier, this group frequently responded by making a conversion error which involved taking the indirect object to be the direct object and vice versa, as in (16), repeated here as (21), so that (21a) was acted out as (21b):

21.a.   The cow gave the dog the pig
   b.   The cow gave the dog to the pig

This was true even in sentences where the indirect object was animate and the direct object inanimate. Out of 30 responses to an act-out task, only 10 were correct while 19 of them involved errors like (21b). I had no responses of this kind, either in the act-out or the imitation task.[6] I suggest that such a response is not necessarily indicative of the child's competence at all but rather reflects a strategy adopted to cope with certain kinds of experimental task. Since their test sentences included ones like those in (10), that is, sentences that are quite implausible in terms of the usual animacy requirements on the direct and indirect objects, it is quite possible that the children insert *to* into some of the sentences to render the meaning more plausible and then continue to do this throughout the task, even where it is inappropriate.

Cook (1976) also found in an act-out task that the youngest children he tested (5-year-olds) were only 31% correct on [NP NP] forms but 88% on [NP PP]. He reports them as doing better in [NP NP] structures where the indirect object was animate and the direct object inanimate but does not specify the proportion of correct responses in these cases. The kinds of errors made by his subjects are also not reported. As his sentences also varied animacy and plausibility, it is again possible that the children were confused by aspects of the task itself, so that their knowledge of the double-object construction is in fact being underestimated. However, as Cook notes, where the [NP PP] version of the sentence was implausible, the children had no problems of interpretation. They acted out forms like (22) correctly:

22.   Give the man to the car

It is arguable that the presence of the preposition in this case forces the implausible analysis, whereas if one hears (23), one's first assumption will be that one has misheard the sentence:

23.   Give the car the man

I suspect that adults would have as many problems as children with sentences like those in (10), (22) and (23); in other words they are a source of processing difficulty which is not indicative of lack of command of the [NP NP] complement.[7] However, in the experiments by Roeper et al. and by Cook, the alternation was tested exclusively with the verb *give*, which makes it impossible to make a direct comparison between their results and those reported here. It is conceivable that there might be something particularly problematic about the

---

[6]One child did make this error on one sentence in the pretest. He repeated (i) as (ii), and then commented ''that was a funny one'':

i.   Give the doll the brush
ii. Give the doll to the brush

[7]See Pinker (1984) for similar comments.

verb *give* which does not generalize to other dative verbs. This means that one should be wary of results obtained on the basis of one verb alone, especially if the alternation is lexical, as many people suggest.

In both my tasks, even where subjects made mistakes, these revealed that they had understood which NP was the direct object and which the indirect, except in the case of the *possessive* errors. As discussed in Section 3.ii, where the correct roles are maintained in converting on [NP NP] sentence to the [NP PP], this suggests understanding of the double-object construction, a point also noted by Fischer (1971).

It is, of course, possible that in order to interpret the sentences in the act-out task my subjects resorted to a purely semantic strategy based on animacy, that is that the indirect object is animate and the direct object inanimate. Roeper et al. propose such a strategy for their older subjects, but say that their youngest group did not make use of it. However, a strategy of this kind would seem only to make sense to explain successful acting out by children who do not actually produce [NP NP] forms. In other words, it would serve the child to interpret constructions which he does not yet fully control, so that it could be used to account for a discrepancy between comprehension and production. This strategy seems unnecessary in the case where children are in fact producing [NP NP] forms, as most of my subjects did. In other words, in the cases of Subjects 3,4,6, and 14, who acted out [NP NP] forms correctly but imitated only one out of eight, it might be that they were using an animacy strategy to interpret the act-out task sentences. However, it is implausible to explain the behavior of the rest of the subjects in this way. Comprehension strategies are irrelevant for production, so that children who can produce the [NP NP] complements as well as understand them must be assumed to have internalized the double-object construction, and hence not to need to resort to strategies to deal with it.

A strategy of this kind might also explain the successful acting out by my subjects of the nonalternating verbs in the [NP NP] form. That is, one could argue that these sentences are, in fact, interpretable by such a strategy and, therefore, that the act-out results do not indicate overgeneralization of the dative alternation at all. In that case one would expect a much higher proportion of conversion errors in the imitation task with the nonalternating verbs. The usual assumption behind imitation tasks is that children's imitations are revealing of their grammars and that children will be unable to repeat strings which are ungrammatical for them, or will modify them to make them fit the current grammar. If the act-out results were achieved by means of a semantic strategy which allowed the children to interpret structures which are not part of the grammar, then conversions would be expected on the imitation task which would indicate the children's awareness that benefactives can only occur in the [NP PP] form. As noted in the results, there is no significant difference in the proportion of conversion errors that occur with alternating and nonalternating verbs; conversions are found for all verbs except *find*, suggesting that the children do not treat the nonalternating [NP NP] forms differently from the alternating ones, and that the former are part of the grammar as well as the latter.

As far as I am aware, the only other study to consider whether children would accept or reject nonalternating verbs in the [NP NP] form is Fischer (1971), who found that children aged 3 to 4 show some awareness of the ungrammaticality of the alternation with certain verbs. She found that some verbs are more susceptible to overgeneralization than others, as is also indicated by my results.

4.iii. Semantics and Syntax Acquisition.   There have been a number of proposals in the acquisition literature that syntax acquisition is somehow assisted by semantics. These proposals range from the assumption that early grammars are semantically based rather than syntactic (Schlesinger, 1971), to claims that semantics may be used to *bootstrap* the child into syntax (Pinker, 1984, 1985), or the idea that prototypical meanings can somehow aid the acquisition of syntactic rules (de Villiers, 1980). Even those who argue against purely semantically based grammar acquisition (Maratsos, 1979; Maratsos & Chalkley, 1980) note that syntactic rules may nevertheless be limited to a semantic subclass in the child grammar, whilst they are not so limited in the adult grammar. For example, Maratsos, Fox, Becker, and Chalkley (1985) report a number of experiments in which children limit the passive to action verbs, suggesting undergeneralization, since passive is not semantically constrained in the adult grammar. The results reported here suggest the opposite of this. Rather than being limited to a semantic subclass, the children who overgeneralize the double-object construction are extending it beyond the class to which it applies in the adult grammar.

De Villiers (1980) suggests that syntax acquisition of certain constructions like the passive might proceed by the child's identifying *prototypical* verbs. She shows that children trained to form passives with prototypical action verbs will not extend the passive to nonprototypical verbs, but children trained on nonprototypical verbs will generalize the passive to prototypical verbs. This difference in the treatment of prototypical and nonprototypical verbs could explain the difference in my subjects' responses to some of the alternating verbs; for example, one might argue that their problems with *draw* in both tasks stem from the fact that *draw* is not a prototypical dative verb, and hence that they do not realize that this verb subcategorizes for an indirect object. Of course, this argument assumes that one can identify prototypes in the first place, which is itself open to question. (See Maratsos & Chalkley, 1980, for discussion). However, the prototype argument runs into difficulties with the nonalternating verbs. As Maratsos and Chalkley (1980) point out:

> When an item is considered to be a more peripheral or "worse" member of a category (in that it less accurately embodies the "essence" of the defining class characteristics), *it is also more restricted as to which class operations it can participate in.* Thus a "better" member of a prototypical class generally partici-

pates in all the operations that a peripheral member does, and more besides. (p. 177, italics added).

In other words, the prototype analysis predicts semantic undergeneralization, not overgeneralization. If we assume that the alternating verbs in my test are prototypical datives and the nonalternating ones are not, the children ought *not* to extend the double-object complement from the prototypical to the nonprototypical cases, contrary to the results reported here.

The finding of overgeneralization of the double-object construction is more consistent with the kinds of late overgeneralization discussed in Bowerman (1982, 1985), and raises the same kinds of issues. She reports on semantic overgeneralizations which occur after a period of correct usage. One case concerns the reversative *un-* morpheme, which occurs in verbs like *undo, unbuckle, uncover,* etc. Novel uses, such as *uncome, unshorten, unbend, unopen,* revealed that children understood the reversative meaning of the morpheme but had not limited it to the semantic class of verbs with "covering, enclosing, and surface-attaching meaning." Another case discussed by Bowerman is similar to the cases reported here, in that it also involves the question of the degree to which certain semantic roles fit certain syntactic patterns. These are sentences which involve verbs taking three noun arguments, where the subject has the semantic role of agent, and the two other arguments are theme and goal. Some verbs obligatorily express the theme as the direct object and the goal in a prepositional phrase, as in (24a), while others do the converse, as in (24b):

24.a. John spilled water (theme) onto the floor (goal)
   b. Bob covered the bed (goal) with a blanket (theme)

Bowerman reports frequent late errors that involve the child's treating verbs like *cover* in (24b), which obligatorily require the direct object to be the goal, as if they were like *spill* in (24a), where the direct object is the theme. Errors which involve making the goal the direct object for verbs which obligatorily require the theme in this position are also found, but are less frequent. Examples of these errors are given in (25):

25.a. Feel your hand (theme) to that (goal)
       (= Feel that with your hand)
   b. I spilled it (goal) of orange juice (theme)
       (= I spilled the orange juice on it)

In these cases, the children have correctly understood which semantic roles the verbs in question take, but have confused the syntactic forms (NP or PP) and grammatical relations (direct object or oblique object) by which these roles must be realized. Although the dative cases are not completely parallel, because benefactives are not subcategorized by verbs, the confusion nevertheless is a very similar one. Bowerman (1985) argues that errors of this type suggest that children have to *learn* the meaning structure of their language, and that theories of acquisition that assume that meaning is somehow transparent from non-linguistic cognitive development overlook this point. She suggests that "the child can . . . develop or notice meanings as a consequence of observing the way linguistic forms are used" (1985, p. 383), a point I return to in the next section.

4.iv. Learnability Implications.   The existence of such overgeneralizations raises the question of how children subsequently *unlearn* them. It has already been mentioned that negative evidence, in the form of correction, is not considered to be reliably available to children, nor used by them when it does occur. In a recent paper, Hirsh-Pasek, Treiman, and Schneiderman (1984) suggest that a form of negative evidence may be available in that mothers more often repeat, and in the process correct, ungrammatical utterances. However, they found this to be true only for errors made by 2-year-olds.

Since the overgeneralizations discussed here are produced by older children, this form of negative data would not appear to be available. Even if it were, it is not clear that it could work in cases like the dative alternation, where two forms are possible with many verbs. That is, if a child produced a sentence like (1b) and the mother repeated it as (1a), it would be misleading if the child interpreted this as a form of correction. It is not clear how the child is to know when a repetition which is somewhat altered by the parent is to count as a correction and when it is not. It seems, therefore, that retreat must be by means of additional information in the positive data.

Recall that there are two factors that disallow the double-object construction for adults in cases like (4b), repeated below as (26b):

26a.   John drove the car for Fred
  b.   *John drove Fred the car

One is the semantic condition which states that the indirect object must be the prospective possessor of the direct object, and the other is the fact that the *for* phrase in (26a) is not subcategorized by the verb because it is a benefactive, and hence it cannot enter into a lexical rule like the one that relates (3a) and (3b), repeated below as (27):

27.a.   Mary bought a book for John
   b.   Mary bought John a book

Recognition of either of these factors might provide a potential line of retreat from overgeneralization.

In Mazurkewich and White (1984), the semantic line of retreat is proposed for such cases. It is suggested that in cases involving inalienable or prior possession, the relevance of the possessor role might be forced to the child's attention, so that the child would then drop the [NP NP] complement in those cases where the first postverbal NP could not be construed as the possessor of the direct object. The results from the sentences involving inalienable or prior possession do not seem to bear out this hypothesis, although since only 2 sentences were used here, this should be further investigated with other sentences of this type.

Alternatively, the fact that benefactive *for* phrases are not subcategorized might provide a possible way out of overgeneralizations. Presumably, children who accept sentences like (26b) have also misanalyzed sentences like (26a) as having a subcategorized *for* phrase; that is, they assume that in the tree diagram it hangs off $\bar{v}$ instead of $\bar{\bar{v}}$ (see 6), page 263.[8] The potential diagnostic for whether a *for* phrase is or is not subcategorized, namely whether it does or does not occur in the double-object construction, can clearly not serve for these children, since this is precisely the observation that they have apparently failed to make. However, there are other sentences which might draw to the child's attention the fact that in certain circumstances *for* phrases cannot be subcategorized. For example, if the child hears a sentence with a nonsubcategorized constituent before the *for* phrase, this should indicate that the *for* phrase in question cannot be the indirect object. An example of such a sentence is given in (27):

27.   John washed the car in the driveway for Fred

Since *wash* does not subcategorize for a locative (a fact the child would presumably already know), the only possible relevant structure for this sentence would be one where $\bar{v}$ contains only the direct object NP, whilst $\bar{\bar{v}}$ contains both the PPs. (Again, we are not concerned with the interpretation where [a car in the driveway] can be a complex NP.) Sentences like this would force the child to amend the lexical entries of those verbs where a benefactive had mistakenly been assumed to be subcategorized, leading to a loss of overgeneralization. In other words, by observing the way the *for*-phrase is used in such sentences, children may obtain the kind of linguistic evidence which contributes to their eventual knowledge of the restrictions on the syntactic occurrences of benefactives. Thus, Bowerman's suggestion that the child will learn meaning as a consequence of observing the way linguistic forms are used provides a potential line of retreat from overgeneralization in this case. Presumably, some children will encounter the relevant evidence earlier than others, and they may encounter it for some verbs before others, accounting for the relative infrequency and inconsistency of dative overgeneralizations of this type. That is, the question of whether overgeneralization will occur is dependent on the child's prior linguistic experience.

---

[8]Other cases of children hanging constituents from the wrong level of structure are reported in Goodluck (1981) and Tavakolian (1981).

In conclusion, in the adult grammar, verbs like *open* subcategorize for a direct object noun phrase. They may also be followed by a benefactive *for*-phrase which is *not* a subcategorized dative indirect object. These verbs do not allow a double-object complement, since the [NP NP] form is only possible where the verb subcategorizes for a direct and indirect object, and where the latter is the prospective possessor of the former. The comprehension and production of forms like (28) by the children reported on here suggests that they overgeneralize the dative alternation and extend the double object complement to verbs which do not allow it:

28.   The monkey is opening the doll the box

The potential source of this overgeneralization is the fact the true indirect objects and benefactives both occur in prepositional phrases introduced by *for,* as in (29):

29.a.   John bought a book for Mary (dative indirect object)
  b.   John washed the car for Fred (benefactive)

Two different semantic roles, dative and benefactive, have the same syntactic realization, a PP, presumably leading the children to suppose that when they hear one of them, the dative, in a double-object complement like (30), this is also possible for the other, namely the benefactive:

30.   John bought Mary a book

The age of the clear overgeneralizers suggests that this is a late error, and the fact that spontaneous forms of this type are infrequent in the literature indicates that the overgeneralization is subject to individual variation, presumably due to the fact that there is a variety of linguistic evidence to indicate the nonsubcategorized status of benefactives, and different children may be exposed to this evidence, or notice its relevance, at different times. Occurrence of semantic overgeneralization of the dative alternation supports Bowerman's contention that syntactic restrictions on certain meanings have to be learned. The constraints on the occurrence of benefactive phrases do not appear to be obvious from the child's nonlinguistic knowledge of the world, nor do they seem to be directly given by Universal Grammar.

ACKNOWLEDGMENT

I am grateful to the McGill Family Community Centre for their cooperation in this testing.

APPENDIX TEST SENTENCES

Act-out Task

1. Draw a picture for the teddy
2. Draw the doll a house
3. Get the book for the doll
4. Get the monkey the car
5. Build a tower for the monkey
6. Build the teddy a tower
7. Find a ribbon for the doll
8. Find the teddy a block
9. Tie the ribbon for the doll
10. Tie the teddy the shoe lace
11. Open the box for the monkey
12. Open the doll the box
13. Wash the sweater for the teddy
14. Wash the monkey the pants
15. Drive the car for the monkey
16. Drive the teddy the car

Imitation Task

1. The noise is giving the doll a headache
2. The car cost Daddy $5
3. The monkey is drawing a picture for the teddy
4. The teddy is drawing the doll a house
5. The teddy is getting the book for the doll
6. The doll is getting the monkey the car
7. The teddy is building a tower for the monkey
8. The monkey is building the teddy a tower
9. The monkey is finding a ribbon for the doll
10. The monkey is finding the teddy a block
11. The teddy is tying the ribbon for the doll
12. The doll is tying the teddy the shoe lace
13. The doll is opening the box for the monkey
14. The monkey is opening the doll the box
15. The doll is washing the sweater for the teddy

16. The teddy is washing the monkey the pants
17. The teddy is driving the car for the monkey
18. The monkey is driving the teddy the car

REFERENCES

Baker, C. L. (1979). Syntactic theory and the projection problem. *Linguistic Inquiry, 10,* 533–581.

Bowerman, M. (1982). Reorganizational processes in lexical and syntactic development. In E. Wanner & L. Gleitman (Eds.), *Language acquisition: The state of the art* (pp. 319–346). Cambridge, England: Cambridge University Press.

Bowerman, M. (1983). How do children avoid constructing an overly general grammar in the absence of feedback about what is not a sentence? *Papers and Reports on Child Language Development.* Stanford University.

Bowerman, M. (1985). Beyond communicative adequacy: from piecemeal knowledge to an integrated system in the child's acquisition of language. In K. E. Nelson (Ed.), *Children's language, Vol. 5* (pp 369–398). Hillsdale, NJ: Lawrence Erlbaum Associates.

Brown, R., & Hanlon, C. (1970). Derivational complexity and order of acquisition in child speech. In J. R. Hayes (Ed.), *Cognition and the development of language* (pp. 11–53). New York: Wiley.

Braine, M. (1971). On two types of models of the internalization of grammars. In D. Slobin (ed.), *The ontogenesis of grammar* (pp. 153–186). Orlando, FL: Academic Press.

Cook, V. (1976). A note on indirect objects. *Journal of Child Language, 3,* 435–437.

de Villiers, J. (1980). The process of rule learning in child speech: A new look. In K. E. Nelson (Ed.), *Children language, Vol. 2* (pp. 1–44). New York: Gardner Press,

Fischer, S. (1971). *The acquisition of verb-particle and dative constructions.* Unpublished doctoral dissertation, MIT.

Goldsmith, J. (1980). Meaning and mechanism in grammar. In S. Kuno (Ed.), *Harvard Studies in Syntax and Semantics* III.

Goodluck, H. (1981). Children's grammar of complement subject interpretation. In S. Tavakolian (Ed.), *Language acquisition and linguistic theory* (pp.139–166). Cambridge, MA: MIT Press.

Haber, L. (1982). An analysis of linguistic deviance. In K. E. Nelson (Ed.), *Children's language, Vol. 3* (pp. 247–285). Hillsdale, NJ: Lawrence Erlbaum Associates.

Hirsh-Pasek, K., Treiman, R. & Schneiderman, M. (1984). Brown and Hanlon revisited: Mothers' sensitivity to ungrammatical forms. *Journal of Child Language, 11,* 81–88.

Maratsos, M. (1979). How to get from words to sentences. In D. Aaronson & R. Rieber (Eds.), *Psycholinguistic research: Implications and applications* (pp. 285–353). Hillsdale, NJ: Lawrence Erlbaum Associates.

Maratsos, M., & Chalkley, M. A. (1980). The internal language of children's syntax: the ontogenesis and representation of syntactic categories. In K. E. Nelson (Ed.), *Children's language, Vol. 2* (pp. 127–214). New York: Gardner Press.

Maratsos, M., Fox, D., Becker, J., & Chalkley, M. A. (1985). Semantic restrictions on children's passives. *Cognition, 19,* 167–191.

Mazurkewich, I., & White, L. (1984). The acquisition of the dative alternation: Unlearning overgeneralizations. *Cognition, 16,* 261–283.

Oehrle, R. (1976). *The grammatical status of the English dative alternation.* Unpublished doctoral dissertation, MIT.

Pinker, S. (1984). *Language learnability and language development.* Cambridge, MA: Harvard University Press.

Pinker, S. (1985). Language learnability and children's language: A multifaceted approach. In K. E. Nelson (Ed.), *Children's language, Vol. 5* (pp. 399–442). Hillsdale, NJ: Lawrence Erlbaum Associates.

Roeper, T., Lapointe, S., Bing, J., & Tavakolian, S. (1981). A lexical approach to language acquisition. In S. Tavakolian (Ed.), *Language acquisition and linguistic theory* (pp. 35–58). Cambridge, MA: MIT Press.

Schlesinger, I. (1971). Production of utterances and language acquisition. In D. Slobin (Ed.), *The ontogenesis of grammar*. Orlando, FL: Academic Press.

Stowell, T. (1981). *Origins of phrase-structure*. Unpublished doctoral dissertation. MIT.

Tavakolian, S. (1981). The conjoined-clause analysis of relative clauses. In S. Tavakolian (Ed.), *Language acquisition and linguistic theory* (pp. 167–187). Cambridge, MA: MIT Press.

13

Some Observations from the Perspective of the Rare Event Cognitive Comparison Theory of Language Acquisition

Keith E. Nelson
The Pennsylvania State University

This chapter is concerned with the *mechanisms* of the child that lead to progress in language acquisition and also with the *conditions* which contribute to the child making successive advances in language acquisition. In part, the discussion draws upon selected data and viewpoints presented in the preceding chapters of this Volume 6 of *Children's Language*. In addition, much other recent work including work of my own will appear with the comparisons and conclusions drawn. In line with "learnability" theorists, such as Wexler and Collicover (1980) and Pinker (1985), the argument will stress the necessity of attributing to the child only those mechanisms which are in line with what we know about children's cognitive and linguistic development and of assuming as input conditions only those conditions which actually occur. However, the evidence we cite requires a substantially different picture of both learning mechanisms and the conditions of learning than have been painted by learnability theorists to date.

The chapter begins with a consideration of the nature of the learning mechanism which children bring to the task of acquiring language, including the acquisition of syntax, semantics, phonology, and discourse structures and rules. Following this, we consider the kinds of methods and the kinds of findings and conclusions that have so far appeared concerning the interactional conditions which provide the substance and the context for the input the children use in abstracting and inducing new linguistic structures. In addition, we consider how the child uses the available learning mechanisms to very selectively attempt to store, retrieve, analyze, and extrapolate from particular patterns within the input at particular stages in language acquisition. A related issue is the consideration of how different children end up following different paths to many advances in language subsystems and to the language system overall at a mature level of mastery.

RARE EVENT COGNITIVE COMPARISONS

The mechanism the child brings to bear on language acquisition is powerful and it is selective. These adjectives are supported very strongly by the last 3 decades of research on infancy and early childhood. In the first 12- to 18-months the child brings to bear powerful analytic and memory skills for the acquisition of considerable phonology as well as the rudiments of early semantics and very early syntax. From 18 months on the system becomes very powerful indeed and continues to increase in power with the child's development generally through ages 3½- to 4-years-of-age. By these latter age periods a typical child will have in place a sufficiently powerful learning mechanism to deal with language structures of any known complexity when they are presented within appropriate discourse contexts. We first give an overall brief summary of the analytic mechanism, and then consider the many different components that are essential to the remarkable effectiveness of this mechanism in combination with typical input in the creation of extremely complex language systems in most children during the first 5 or 6 years of life.

An Overall Description

The analytic mechanism we characterize is, in general, pegged to children in stage 2 or stage 3 according to Brown's (1973) stages of development, with the assumption that the system has less power at earlier stages of development and, as noted earlier, increases in power as the child advances in cognitive and language stage and age generally up to about the age of 4. The system is extremely powerful in abstracting, storing, retrieving, and applying structural description for every part of the language system.

Rare Events and Cognitive Comparisons

The child's acquisition mechanism is termed a "rare event" mechanism because it is only rarely that the child successfully attends to new input and arrives at new structural descriptions that advance the language system and are used in processing further utterances from others and in producing new utterances by the child. In each of the subareas of phonology, semantics, syntax, and discourse (and in their interrelationships), the system is engaged very selectively so that analytic and long-term memory capacities are applied to particular new structural acquisitions at particular stages, rather than spread in scatter-shot fashion across a very wide range of structures at any particular point in acquisition. It must also be stressed that the system is extremely open—it is ready to analyze, store, and use any rich patterns of communication in any mode. But the input patterns must be presented in such a way that the child can observe the use of the communication system by truly expert users and can engage in a process of emotional and social and communicative exchange with such experts.

Cognitive comparisons between old structures and new structures are crucial within each domain. Here, for purposes of illustration we take syntactic structures as a case in point. When a cognitive comparison occurs between a new sentence structure, for example, "The alligators will swim," and a current sentence structure, for example, "The alligators swim," three outcomes are possible: (1) there is no discrepancy between the structures, and the child codes this as confirmation of the usefulness of the current structure, (2) a discrepancy exists, but the child cannot in any way encode the discrepancy, or (3) a codable or partially codable discrepancy is noted. Only in the third case does the child's skill domain gain information from explicit differences between current structures and structures in the input set. However, codable discrepancies are rarely noted by the child. This is true because there are limitations of memory, attention, and motivation, and because most of the highly specific kinds of new structures children require for comparison at each stage do not occur very frequently in input. A complete absence of such required forms for a period will lead to a plateau in acquisition; conversely, a relatively high incidence of such forms in easy-to-process contexts will tend to accelerate the child's progress. This latter assumption is directly tested in several of the studies presented below in domains as various as semantic skills, drawing skills, sign language syntactic skills, and spoken language syntactic skills.

Assigning Old Structural Descriptions to Match New Input Strings

This component really provides the background for new analysis. Of course, as long as the new input string can be successfully matched to an old structural description the child will simply interpret the new input according to the old rules and structures. This background of repeated assimilation of new input to old structures (cf. Langer, 1969; Piaget, 1954) is necessary to keep the child engaged in successful communication with other people on the basis of whatever system rules are already available. Furthermore, this background activity prepares the child for turning the power of the analytic system and its tremendous long-term storage system to dealing with certain kinds of input strings that cannot be assimilated using the old structural descriptions.

Tentatively Abstracting Foci (TAF)

A new focus or several new foci for intensive structural analyses can be established in a variety of ways. Sometimes these arise because new examples come along in input which in effect draw attention to themselves and which trigger off the establishment of new areas or foci for analysis. In other instances, what the child has already learned about language may effectively prepare the child to look for certain kinds of new information and new structures. These kinds of new foci would not have been looked for before many foundations, elements, and structures had been established. Regardless of how the areas for intensive structural analysis arise, these areas or foci become "hot spots" that receive priority for the allocation of attention, storage, retrieval, comparison, and hypothesis-monitoring. The child's learning system is extremely powerful but it is not powerful enough to analyze everything at once. Instead the system is highly selective and works intensively on selected structural description problems that arise at particular stages in development. This selective work involves simultaneous and coordinated efforts at improving production along with comprehension whenever possible. As the child moves on, these problems are solved for a particular stage and a new foundation becomes established for creating a new round of foci for intensive analyses, and so on, until basically the entire language system has been learned. For individuals who continue to look for new and flexible ways in which language can be used, as described under Nelson and Nelson's (1978) cognitive pendulum theory at a final, stage 5 level of development (cf. also Dreyfus & Dreyfus, 1986; Fischer & Papp, 1984; Sternberg, 1984), these cycles of new analysis with new centers or foci for analysis will continue to be created throughout the life span.

Within Tentatively Abstracted Foci, Finding Mismatches between New Input Strings and Old Structural Descriptions

If the child is going to work out new and more sophisticated structural descriptions than those already in the system, mismatches must be found between the current structural descriptions and new input strings. Most such potential mismatches will not be "attended to" or engaged by the child's system, will not be a hot spot for analysis, and so will not lead to new storage, comparison, and to new abstraction of structures. However, the particular mismatches which are within an intensive focus for attention and analysis lie at the heart of language learning. These selected mismatches together with their analyses by the child comprise the "rare events" that fuel language acquisition despite widely varying overall input to children.

In dealing with the kinds of mismatch noticing and analysis which are crucial to understanding language development, it is necessary to consider in successive sections the processes of attention, storage, retrieval, comparison, and hypothesis monitoring. For the moment it will serve to give an example or two that may illustrate how the child at a particular level of language mastery may begin to deal with new kinds of mismatches which were not the focus of analysis in learning at the preceding stages. So, imagine a child who in first learning language has learned to produce and understand sentences such as "The dog chases the pony." Underlying structural descriptions within the language system have been acquired that permit the child to precisely understand the structure syntactically and semantically of these kinds of simple, declarative, active sentences with noun phrases that are limited to one noun and one modifier at the maximum. I believe that the child at this level would often be ready to establish new hot spots of analyses which would concern some new structural details represented in such input strings as the following: (1) The pony is chased by the dog. (2) The pony is being chased by the dog. (3) The dog is chasing the pony, isn't he? (4) The big old white dog chases the shaggy brown pony. (5) The shaggy brown pony is being chased by the old white dog. (6) The dog will chase the pony.

By considering multiple examples like this, each of which might occur within the same kinds of conversational turns and might become involved in central foci of analyses, we immediately raise the question of which kinds of details might be processed by a particular child during a limited time, such as a few weeks or a few months. It is likely that different children might select somewhat different foci from the same available input. These selections would depend on the overall patterns in the input, which might influence the salience of certain kinds of structures, as well as on the patterns of structural description already established in the child's language system. From the internal system point of view, some children might be better prepared to analyze passive structures while other children might be more likely to first direct their attention and analyses to structures such as the tag question forms that example (3) represents. Still other children might be more likely to form foci of analyses that concern structure within noun phrases at a level of complexity beyond the current kinds of simple noun phrases as presumed at this developmental level.

In understanding how the child selectively assigns processing time to and works out the analysis of a new structural form it is important not to put the cart before the horse. That is, it is important not to do what Wexler and Collicover (1980) do, which is to provide the child as given and ready-made those structural descriptions (as foundations for learning) that in fact have to be constructed or abstracted by the child in the course of learning. Let us make reference to our prior examples above. If the child is acquiring tag question forms then we cannot assume that the reasons the child's system pays attention to examples in the input which take the form known to us as tag questions is that the child's system already has good structural descriptions for tag questions and is looking for them in the input.

Instead, what we assume is that there are several levels in the acquisition process which have to be carried through in sequence before a complete and consolidated analysis can be constructed by the child. The very first stage is one of selectively reattending to examples which do not match current structural descriptions and which are coded at first simply as mismatches or discrepancies from the current system. Thus a child may first form a hot spot for analysis in terms of auxiliary use in questions and may selectively attend to tags as interesting but initially uncodable input strings which are stored selectively in relation to current known descriptions (e.g., for auxiliaries). Once some further coding of the discrepancies occur, then selective attention can be refined and then refined again through many cycles until very particular details of input strings may be selectively attended to in relation to the structure of tag questions. So, at a late stage in the acquisition of tag sentence structures the child may be coding very precisely the occurrence of particular pronouns and particular auxiliaries which lie behind contrasts such as "Isn't he?" versus "Weren't they?". The selective attention of the child's system—often at the subconscious level—clearly works in coordination with the storage and retrieval and comparison processes but to some extent can be isolated.

Certainly it is fundamental to see that the effective deployment of attention, towards particular kinds of new structural descriptions and towards relevant input strings for these structural descriptions, is a necessary component of the learning mechanism which leads to rapid and effective language acquisition by most preschool children. As Kuczaj (1982) has noted, it is the "uptake" of input strings that contributes to learning rather than simply the occurrence of a structural string in the input. In discussing below issues raised by Mannle and Tomasello, by Roth, by Conti-Ramsden and Friel-Patti, by Snow, Perlmann, and Nathan, and by Speidel (all in this volume), I will argue that one of the very substantial contributions of styles of language use by parents and of the particular scripted or unscripted context variations that children encounter lies in the area of directing the learning mechanisms to attend to or engage certain kinds of information at the cost of certain other kinds of information.

Selective Storage

When the power of the comparison system is selectively focused on mismatches within particular foci of analysis, there are several levels of selective storage which take place for selected input strings. Discrepancy tagging is the first such level. When this process is applied, then the child's system has simply noticed that an input string such as a future-tense question is discrepant from any retrieved structural description, and the input string is tagged for storage in connection with the closest structural description which was successfully retrieved. So, for example, the child who can retrieve a structural description for "The dog chases the pony" may selectively tag as discrepant an input string consisting of "The dog will chase the pony, won't he?". The system at this point does not know how to describe the discrepancies between the input and the available structural description for a simple active sentence. However, by selectively storing in gestalt form all or most of the complete sentence from the input that does not match with available structural descriptions, along with coordinated storage of related sentences for which a full structural description is available, the child sets the stage for further rounds of selective attention and storage and analysis (cf. Peters, 1983; Shatz, this volume). Notice that here again the full power of the system is applied in a very selective sort of way. There is no claim that every input string that the child attends to is stored in a complete and unanalyzed form. Instead, the claim is a very limited one that within current central foci of analyses the child does have the inclination and the cognitive power to selectively store complete input strings that are not yet given a full structural description together with selectively retrieved prior input strings and input descriptions which are "similar"—in ways to be specified and clarified by further examples and analyses in the future. Those examples from long-term storage are then re-entered in long-term storage along with the new input strings and tags and codes for both new and old examples.

The further the child goes in working out new levels of structural descriptions for to-be-acquired forms,the more specific the child's selective tagging and storing will be. This means that as the child works out a tentative structural description for a tag question with one auxiliary and one pronoun as in "The dog is chasing the pony,isn't he," the more specific the memory tags and therefore the later retrieval will be. What the child is able to do even by 18 months or so is to set up files in long-term memory which can be addressable according to particular structural details of interest. This means that in the process of working out the final details of an analysis of tag questions, the child who encounters a new tag question in the input will be able to store the input string along with considerable precision in the structural description for that input string. The child also will locate and use the related tentative wholistically stored input strings from earlier rounds of analysis, as well as related structural descriptions concerning all the relevant details of auxiliary choice, positive negative valence, pronoun choice, and word order. Because the system can be so selective and efficient in storage, the child typically will be able to tolerate considerable scatter—across time and conversations—of the needed examples for working out a particular new structural description. Similarly, another child may draw together in storage and comparison widely scattered examples of future tense verbs, as in "The dog will chase the pony, won't he?" and in "The girl will climb the hill." To put it another way, the child is not dependent upon having the needed examples in input all closely-spaced and specifically called to the child's attention in order to acquire new semantic, syntactic, phonological, or discourse forms. Instead, again within the limits of particular stages and the limits of selective attention and analysis, the child will be able to carry in memory a large number of selectively tagged and stored examples and tentative structural descriptions which will then be used later as necessary to fuel further rounds of comparison, analysis and hypothesis testing.

Selective Retrieval

The counterpart to selective storage is selective retrieval. The child who selectively tags a new input string as an interesting mismatch with current structural descriptions will be able to selectively retrieve previously stored examples that are related to the same kind of mismatch and to the same kind of overall wholistically stored input string. This means that the child will be able to put together within a short-term processing space a whole series of related examples, and to conduct pattern analyses on the basis of the accumulated set of related examples including the most current example. Through parallel processing within the child's system complex searches, complex pattern analyses, and ongoing conversation can co-occur (cf. MacWhinney, 1986, 1977a, 1980; K. E. Nelson, 1986a, 1986b; McClelland & Rumelhart, 1986).

At some point the child will accumulate enough related examples for comparison and the successful abstraction of new structural descriptions will actually occur. These successful abstractions are the central "rare events" in language acquisition. They are the "cracking the code" events that rest upon the information provided in a series of input strings, but that go well beyond that information to construct new descriptions. In the absence of evidence to the contrary, it is safest to consider these powerful abstraction processes to be general cognitive abstraction processes which are richly fueled by the complexity of the language system and the dense overall input that most children receive. It is likely that most of these successful abstraction events do rest upon the very recent occurrence of some crucial input strings, as in the case of a newly abstracted structural description for passive sentences or for tag questions. For example, it is likely that passive structures are abstracted successfully after a history of selective attention, storage, and retrieval of a series of related examples and that the final step in the formation of a complete structural description (still to be further monitored and tested against input for a period) rests upon a passive which has just occurred in conversation. Similarly, crucial abstraction steps for tag questions are likely to be triggered by the occurrence of new tag questions which provide additional information to supplement that already available from the child's long-term storage system.

However, it cannot be overlooked that sometimes the child may in effect trigger her own new abstraction steps by searching through long-term storage in the absence of particular new triggering input examples. One way in which this may happen is that the child may be engaged in private play and thinking and in the course of this may retrieve certain kinds of language structures. In the course of using those language structures, the child may hit upon some connections within long-term storage between the examples that had not previously been selectively stored and related together. In that case, the child would put into comparison new sets of examples and structural descriptions that had not previously been placed within the same pattern of comparison and analysis. All the information was available in the child's long-term storage, but it had not been related in a particular pattern of comparison before. When this happens, exactly the same abstraction mechanisms that apply in the case of conversational triggering of successful new abstractions would still apply. But the information that enters the analysis process would be different than had previously occurred in the child's thinking or in the child's communication in conversational contexts. So, there is nothing inconsistent about allowing some crucial new steps of abstraction to occur within the context of conversation under the immediate triggering influence of highly relevant input strings that relate to hot spots of analysis, but also allowing that within hot spots of analysis the child even in private thinking may be led to notice some new connections between stored input strings and structural descriptions available within the language system. Thus, new abstraction steps can also occur during lulls in conversation and in the absence of new input strings for a period. Active retrieval and comparison processes along these latter lines are suggested by Bowerman (1985) in her discussions of relatively ''late'' acquisition reformulations and errors and by Shatz (this volume) in her discussions of some ''expansion operations.''

Selective Analysis

In analysis, patterns of input strings are placed together in working memory according to similarities in their currently available structural descriptions and similarities in the gaps or discrepancies in these available structural descriptions. What enters working memory depends both on recent input strings and on the selective retrieval of related information from long-term memory. Selectivity comes in at this point in several ways. First, processing time is limited so only a limited number of comparisons will be carried out on the assembled set of structural descriptions, wholistically stored input strings, and fragments of stored input strings. Second, within the limited number of comparisons possible the child will concentrate on the hot spots or ''tentatively abstracted foci'' of a particular developmental stage or substage. To be more concrete, a child might search through six or eight different examples of well described active sentences in present tense along with less fully described but semantically similar passive examples and ignore many details of the sentences that are not related to working out the by-clause and other details directly related to the active-passive distinction. At another point in time, using superficially somewhat similar sets of sentences for comparison, the child might organize in working memory a set of examples that are concerned with noun phrase structures. The child would then actively seek, within a preselected focus, comparisons that concern the way in which modifier types are combined to produce complex noun phrases such as, ''The shaggy brown pony.''

The consequences of an attempted analysis of new structural detail may be that nothing new is coded and the assembled examples are simply tagged again and long-term memory is ready for some future more successful analysis attempt. Another consequence of an attempted analysis of new patterns of language structure is that the child may not work out a new full structural description but may reorganize the examples within working memory so that particular kinds of similarities or discrepancies are tagged as particularly salient and deserving of intense analysis in future rounds of comparison. Selective attention, selective storage, and future selective analyses will then be influenced by the reorganization of the available information in long-term memory. Finally, in some instances the analysis may succeed in generating a new structural description which is complete enough to be ready for testing out. Below, we refer to a tentative new structural description as simply an hypothesis. These new hypotheses about language structures will then be monitored in both comprehension and production. Over a period of time successful hypotheses that lead to no discrepancies against input strings or very few discrepancies against input strings will be consolidated and removed from the hot spot category. In short, once analysis succeeds in abstracting reasonably successful new structural descriptions the processor will move on to other, new, tentatively abstracted foci which will receive the benefit of very powerful selection in the attentional, storage, retrieval, analyses and monitoring mechanisms. There is an obvious "progressive" nature in these cycles of abstraction and monitoring, but it should not be overstated. At certain points children strongly consolidate and treat as "successful" structural descriptions that are "regressions" or other "serious errors" from the viewpoint of an observer who maps the longitudinal language growth for a child. Often the child imposes a well established structural description from language or cognition on input strings that require considerably different descriptions. Witness the imposition of expected, probable-event interpretations and similar nonsyntactic strategies on sentences such as "The mommy was fed by the child." (Schwam, 1982; Strohner & Nelson, 1974). Such diversions from "steady progress" have been of great interest to successive generations of child language scholars. The point is not that a child's system always leads to the same predictable successive steps in acquisition, but rather that an open and powerful system works in similar qualitative fashion for each child, and through countless cycles of activity usually evaluates and replaces weaker tentative structural descriptions with better ones.

Selective Hypothesis Monitoring and Consolidation

Let us imagine that the child has worked out a tentative description structurally of how tag questions are formed, a structural description that includes the appropriate coordination of a positive main clause with a negative tag or vice versa, the coordination of pronoun use, and the coordination of the auxiliary in the tag with the verb chosen in the main clause. The child will actively monitor the success of the new structural description against selected new input strings. This means that in the period soon following the establishment of a new structural hypothesis the child will be very highly attentive to any input strings that appear to bear close relationship to the hypothesis about tag question structure. The comparisons that take place will be comparisons on match and mismatch. This is precisely what we have described above. When input strings perfectly match with the available structural description, then during this period of intensive monitoring special record keeping will occur in long-term memory that will establish how often the structural description is successful. In many cases this will result in wholistic storage of matching input strings. Naturally, any mismatches will be noted and will result in further rounds of attention, retrieval, storage, analysis, and monitoring. These rounds of discrepancy tagging, analysis, and monitoring will continue until a reasonable criterion of success is achieved for the latest structural hypothesis. Although authors such as Wexler and Collicover (1980) prefer to stress distinctions between grammaticality and ungrammaticality, it is more likely that the child's comparisons are based upon match-mismatch comparisons and that a very wide range of possible hypotheses can be entertained. Both for an individual child and across children it is likely that the same kinds of evidence may be used to generate quite different hypotheses. In line with the discussion above, the child's "attention" to multiple hypotheses and relevant input strings can proceed primarily at the subconscious or tacit level. The child's learning mechanism attends to extensive structural details that lie outside the child's immediate awareness.

These considerations lead to a recognition that style differences in attention, processing, the formation of hypotheses to be tested, and the monitoring of hypotheses may be very important. To the extent that this is true, a model of language acquisition actually becomes a series of related models with different children eventually achieving similar success by considerably different routes involving contrasts in analytic style and evidence use, productive style, comprehension style, and discourse style. Once again, it is important not to put the cart before the horse. If we provide powerful structural descriptions to the child that precede the child's abstraction of structural descriptions then we misrepresent the process of language acquisition and we underestimate the attentional, memory, analysis, and monitoring skills that even young preschool children bring to bear on language acquisition. These same skills can be applied to the acquisition of any other complex, rule-governed, emotionally ladened, communicative system. The hallmarks of first language acquisition processes are extremely powerful cognitive abilities that are at the same time extremely open and flexible; they are ready to process and make sense of any kind of rich exchange system that the child becomes familiar with. The powerful and selective analytic skills and hypothesis monitoring and consolidation skills that the young child employs can equally be used for the acquisition of story skills (Johnson, 1983), of written language (Söderbergh, 1977), of a single spoken first language (Brown, 1973), of several spoken first languages acquired simultaneously by bilingual and trilingual children, and for the acquisition of sign language alone or in combination with spoken and written languages (Bonvillian, Charrow, & Nelson, 1983; Bonvillian, Nelson, & Charrow; 1976; Maxwell, 1983; Nelson, 1977a, 1980, 1981, 1982, 1985a, 1986a, 1986b; Prinz & Prinz, 1981).

Given a heavy bias across every culture for exposing children primarily to a single spoken first language, then what we nearly always see is the acquisition of a rich first spoken language. But negative evidence and exceptions in the area of the science of developmental psychology, as in every other science, are often even more informative than the most typical kinds of examples. We shall argue below that most children receive an extremely rich input cushion for a first spoken language which obscures how very powerful the child's information processing capacities are. When the child is given relatively thin, but adequate, interaction experiences in a language system, then we can arrive at reasonable estimates of the limits of the child's attention, storage, retrieval, and analytic capacities. Similarly, when children acquire an atypical language such as a written language or sign language with the same ease that we usually see in the case of spoken first language acquisition—given only limited but fluent interactions with adults or older children who are indeed expert in using written language or in using sign language—then we see that the learning mechanism is indeed flexible and open and capable of remarkable feats of selective analysis, storage and retrieval, hypothesis formation or construction, and hypothesis monitoring and consolidation (Bissex, 1980; Maxwell, 1983; Söderbergh, 1977). In each case, whether atypical or typical, what we see is that the extremely powerful and selective processes necessary for learning are applied first to a few of the structural details of a communication exchange system, and then with those first details in place the child goes through round after round after round of actively seeking out new foci or hot spots for attention and analysis until essentially the complete system is worked out.

An illusion is created by the age of 5 or 6 that each person who has become reasonably fluent in using a spoken or written or sign language code is using exactly the same system. In fact, whenever we have been able to look closely at the individual details of acquisition processes we see some startling differences in the way in which children analyze, test out, and deploy their communication resources (Clark, 1982; Lieven, 1978; Nelson, 1981; Nelson & Bonvillian, 1978; Peters, 1983; van Kleeck & Street, 1982). Because the central activities of the learning mechanism are not usually under active conscious control or reflection, the child's extremely flexible and powerful learning mechanism results in different children establishing different centers of attention, different files or subnetworks of examples and structural descriptions which will be at the heart of working out new analyses and new hypotheses. Thus, in the end, we see a mature, well-established and efficient system which works for each child with high success but which rests upon some continued widespread differences between children in what information is activated in the course of producing and comprehending comparable sentences and comparable discourse sequences. Nevertheless, fluent users of a particular language in a particular mode have sufficiently similar structural descriptions and sufficiently similar ready access to stored input strings to limit miscommunication to a small zone under most social and physical conditions. Similarly, there is a sufficient degree of overlap in the available structural descriptions to yield highly similar patterns of grammaticality ratings when these are explicitly sought. Behind the scenes, so to speak, however, considerable individual differences in the information storage networks and the organization of the rich structural descriptions and in preferences or biases for readily using and comprehending certain language structures rather than certain other language structures continue to exist. And, as noted earlier, these differences at the level of mature or fluent language use rest upon individual roots to language mastery, which also show considerable differences between children. The combination of high power and high flexibility in the learning mechanism coupled with much more diversity in input than most models of language acquisition have recognized, lead to extensive differences in the accessibility and organization of particular discourse, semantic, and syntactic rules and the availability of particular input fragments and whole input strings. In consequence, the pattern of communication, thinking, feeling, and, indeed one's theory about the world and about the role of communication in the world, continue to reflect the vast differences in the details of the paths taken by different children to reasonable levels of language mastery (cf. Cook-Gumperz, 1985; Kearney, 1984; Schieffelin, 1979).

Finally, it is important to note here that at the level of monitoring and consolidation of hypotheses that far from everybody within a culture succeeds in a nearly perfect mastery of the language system. Linguistic and psychological studies have been heavily biased towards describing the most fluent and the most communicative members of society. Evidence is accumulating that a significant minority of 6- to 16-year-olds as well as many mature adults plateau at only a moderate degree of language mastery (e.g., Whyte, 1983). In such cases the usual contexts of language use do not challenge or test out the limitations on language mastery that have been achieved. Further, it is far from automatic that every member of a culture will receive all the input that is needed to work out full structural descriptions of a language system, or that given apparently adequate input that the learning mechanism will always succeed in seeking new rounds of selective attention, analysis, storage and retrieval, and hypothesis monitoring and consolidation until virtually all discrepancies or gaps between inputs and structural descriptions are resolved. As in any other problem-solving activity the task of continuing to generate new hypotheses and to test them effectively against available evidence is complex. For this complex activity, different language system outcomes arise because different individuals may have somewhat different levels of power or capacity in the learning mechanism and because the interactional evidence varies considerably for different individuals. In addition, the system itself learns as it goes along, so that learning to learn processes when they are proceeding well lead to ever increasing powers of hypothesis generation, selective retrieval and abstraction, and monitoring. When these processes are not going well the top limits on the learning mechanism itself may not be reached. Since motivational, social, and emotional processes are also fundamental to the engagement of the learning mechanism in the continued rounds of new analyses that are needed to fully work out a language system, it is not surprising that by rigorous standards of language mastery a substantial minority of individuals within every culture that has been studied end up consolidating their language systems at far from complete mastery.

VARIATIONS IN THE ACTIVE ENVIRONMENT OF INTERACTION

Here we concern ourselves with what most people in the literature have labeled input effects or context effects. We have chosen to emphasize an active interactional environment because the mere availability of input examples is much less important than the particular kind of availability that occurs within specific interactional sequences. Similarly, the labeling of context in terms of play context, or instructional context, or fantasy context, or whatever, provides less information than specific descriptions of the kinds of interactional sequences that are occurring within a particular setting at a particular time. In considering the ways in which environmental interactions vary, four different categories are presented below. The use of these categories will help to differentiate the varied ways in which *language learning* is affected by specific kinds of interactions and also the ways in which language use or *language deployment* are affected by variations in specific interactional details.

Effects of Input Variations on Deployment of Already Available Language Skills

Very often when studies purport to show that variations in input and interaction influence the child's acquisition of new language skills the designs are inadequate for testing such an hypothesis. Very often such studies fail to provide a clear baseline assessment which even approaches adequacy in terms of specifying which language skills the child has prior to the interactions which are the focus of study. Within such designs it is very probable that when children over the course of repeated interactions of a certain sort begin to display certain modeled and targeted language structures, the increased use of these structures are simply increases in the frequency of displaying structures already available at the onset of the study. Here we would like to stress that these deployment effects absolutely must be differentiated from genuine acquisition sequences in which we know the children lack certain language structures, experience certain kinds of interactional conditions, and then either acquire the targeted language structures or do not acquire the targeted language structures. These points apply equally to language therapy outcome studies and to theoretically oriented investigations.

In addition, it is important to recognize that increased deployment of available language structures is a phenomenon of interest in its own right. And as we argue below, in some cases there may be fairly complex and subtle ways in which increased deployment of some language structures may influence the probability that certain kinds of genuine new acquisitions will occur. In the present volume it is clear that several authors argue that varied deployment levels for children's language structures very often can be attributable to differences in the kinds of interactions that are encouraged by a mother across varying contexts and goals, and even by different mothers who are in the same setting and seemingly sharing similar goals. For example, when Roth argues that responses by the mother which occur within one second or less of the offset of a child's utterance will in turn markedly increase the probability that the child in the next turn of conversation will display language of any complexity, this fits within this category of "variation affecting language deployment." Also, the observations of Speidel on children in classroom situations and of Conti-Ramsden and Friel-Patti and of Snow et al. in varied preschool situations also bear on the ways in which language deployment can be affected by variations in who is talking with the child, with what purpose in mind, and with what stylistic variations. Part of the theorized effect of highly "scripted" interactions, such as certain book-reading routines and certain bathing routines, consists of an increased deployment by the child, in the direction of greater complexity, of language structures. High scriptedness perhaps will also lead to a greater overall rate of deployment of language structures. Portions of Shatz' discussion of bootstrapping operations in language acquisition periods bear on shifts in deployment of available language skills as much as on advances in the child's language structures.

It appears that varied interactional context and styles, with their accompanying specific interactional sequences and adult deployment of specific language structures of varying rate and complexity, indeed lead to variations by children in the levels of their language structures displayed. To the extent that this is true, there are strong implications for methods of assessing children's language levels. Clearly, if a child were observed under conditions which tend to optimize the child's display of available language complexity and another child were observed under less optimal conditions, then we would confound language level differences between children with differences between the observed conditions. This means that perhaps most researchers should take more care, even in apparently straightforward home taping of mother-child conversational samples, of equating the conditions of interaction. Naturally there are limits on how much equating in conditions can occur and in many instances a goal of the investigation will be to describe how different mothers and different situations contribute to children's language deployment and to children's language learning. However, even more than most of us have attempted to date, we should consider the possibility that observing children in some instances with adults other than their parents and with siblings or friends, in combination with observations of interaction with the mother or father, may tell us a great deal about language structures that we may miss by relying on the most often used methods of collecting data on children's language levels. Certainly the work by Manle and Tomasello (this volume) shows us that interactional sequences are often strikingly different when we move the child from the mother to the father to a sibling and compare the respective conversations. Work by Hall and Cole (1978) and by John Dore (1978) also demonstrate how strongly deployment of language structures can be influenced by who the child is talking to and whether the goal of the conversation from the adult point of view is to conduct an examination of what the child knows, to share information in a give and take fashion with the child, or to accomplish other purposes (cf. Wilcox & Webster, 1980).

Because we have stressed the relevance of a processing model for understanding children's language acquisition and how they make use of available information from conversational context, it is worth speculating on the ways in which deployment shifts might in complex ways affect the child's success in extracting needed information for language growth from certain kinds of interactional sequences. Recall that selective attention, selective comparison, and selective storage, retrieval, and hypothesis monitoring are all essential components of the learning mechanism that the child employs in working out new language structures. To learn something new in terms of language structure the child must not simply encounter a relevant new example of the structure in input but must actively attend to that challenging structure, compare it in selective ways with previously stored information, formulate tentative hypotheses, and then check and monitor these hypotheses against further carefully highlighted and selected input strings. If we get the child through particular styles of conversation in particular contexts to deploy their highest levels of language structure actively in conversation, then there may be powerful catalytic effects on learning about new structures. There may be very interesting combinations of certain positive effects on attention and analysis of "optimal" deployment paired with facilitation through interactional sequences which carry the challenging language structures that the child needs to attend to and analyze. Consider, for example, triggering kinds of interaction sequences incorporating "growth recasts" that not only pick up on the child's meaning but provide in a high-attention position the target structures the child may be about to acquire. The impact of such sequences may be further enhanced when the child is displaying the highest level of complexity in his initial utterances, which the adult then responds to through recasting and similar techniques.

Cross-Sectional Clues to Input Variation Effects on Language Advances

Most of the literature of a theoretical sort and most of the literature of an empirical sort which discusses input variation effects falls within this category, with clues drawn from cross-sectional observations of children at one time period only or of children at different time periods who are not linked in terms of measures of progress for the same children between time periods. In short, what most people observe and argue about, or speculate about theoretically, has been centered on the kinds of input that are observed which *might* have a potential for positively influencing the child's language growth. But language growth is not measured, so these correlational and often very abundant clues about possible effects of input variations need to be treated cautiously until other evidence begins to back them up. Nevertheless, it is essential to begin a search for the roles that input plays in observations of the kinds of interactional sequences that children actually encounter. In many respects what we know even at this level is still remarkably vague. The field remains young.

Mannle and Tomasello (this volume) illustrates some valuable and innovative work in specifying new kinds of conversations which have been neglected in prior research—namely, the kinds of conversations that children in the preschool period have with their siblings and with their fathers. Their conclusions are interesting because in some respects they show how very different inferences can be drawn about possible advantages and disadvantages of certain interactional characteristics depending upon the angle from which they are viewed. What they find is that fathers and siblings are both less "tuned in" to the young child's language levels and apparent intentions than are mothers. The data they present shows that relative to the mother of a language learning young child, a father or sibling engages in fewer and shorter episodes in which the child shares with a partner joint attention, that they more often give off-topic replies to the child's prior utterances, and that they are less likely to pick up on the joint attentional focus with a "follow in" kind of reference. But are these tendencies on the part of fathers and siblings disadvantages for the language learning child, or advantages, or a complex mixture of both? In most other writing on the kinds of adjustments or fine tuning that are made to a language learning child, the characteristics shown by fathers and siblings rather than by mothers in the Mannle and Tomasello work would be interpreted as detrimental to the child's opportunities for efficiently and rapidly learning new language structures. Mannle and Tomasello, however, emphasize that a child may learn some important things from siblings and fathers that are not learned from mothers (cf. Nelson, 1977a, 1980). In particular, their discussion centers on the possibility that by dealing with siblings the child may learn more about dealing with conversations with other children, and that by dealing with fathers—who typically are spending less time than mothers with children and are less familiar with the child's knowledge and skills than mothers—they may be learning to better "bridge" the gap to conversations with complete strangers who know nothing about the child's particular background and knowledge and style and skills and so will not be in a position to make any dramatic adjustments to the child on the basis of such special knowledge. Given that children learn to hold conversations with a wide variety of people within and outside their families, then the less finely tuned conversational strategies and styles of fathers and siblings may contribute in their own ways to the child learning certain kinds of new language skills. I would argue that particularly in the area of discourse rules and the development of alternative conversational plans for different conversational goals, for different conversational partners, and for different settings, the "bridging" hypotheses of Mannle and Tomasello are most likely to be verified by future follow-up work. An important portion of such work will need to rely on some of the remaining categories in this chapter, which try to determine whether clues from cross-sectional work hold up when additional methodological forays are undertaken.

Before leaving the Mannle and Tomasello work it is appropriate to also note that there is another kind of clue about language learning in some of their data. A subset of fathers, those tending to use relatively high levels of nonacknowledgments and minimal or off-topic replies, tended to have children whose style was relatively high in terms of percentage of general nominals. To put it another way, these children tended to show a referential rather than social-expressive kind of style. It would be very surprising if additional research does not show relationships between the kinds of styles that children develop and the patterns of conversations which they hold not only with their mothers but across all siblings, fathers, and others they converse with on any regular basis, even if a particular partner may talk with the child only 30 minutes or so per week. These kinds of hypothesized effects are fully in line with what I have termed the "rare event hypothesis" that quite a small amount of interaction can have very clear effects on children's language advances and on the style or bias or orientation that children show in their language (cf. Ahlgren, 1986; Cook-Gumperz, 1985). To extend this notion just a bit here, as long as certain kinds of interactional sequences have a clear and distinctive structure to them they may contribute to the child's learning of particular kinds of language structures and language strategies that may not be learned at all or may not be learned as easily in other particular kinds of interactional sequences. I believe that Mannle and Tomasello are distinctly on the right track in trying to consider the diverse ways in which children may draw upon conversational partners and sequences for establishing a variety of language skills and for learning their preferred styles of communicating. Along the way the children perhaps will also learn some alternate but less perferred ways of holding conversations with other people. Cook-Gumperz (1985) has similarly stressed that a lot of language learning does take place when children are talking together, both in fantasy oriented and more realistic conversations, and that through such child-to-child exchanges over a period of time children really make language their own and form their own distinctive orientations and styles for communication. Alhgren has observed an interesting and valuable variation on such child-child influences—when Swedish deaf children, with little communication and with no prior contact with deaf children (of deaf parents) who know considerable sign language, are given opportunities to converse occasionally with the latter young "experts" in sign, new communication styles as well as rapid mastery of sign language are stimulated. Thus, not just language skills but personality and culture to some extent are shaped in the same crucibles of conversation for child-child pairs and for children paired with varying adult partners (cf. Doi, 1985; Harre, 1983; Kearney, 1984; Sinha, 1980).

Analyses from the Mannle and Tomasello chapter were for 12- to 24-month-old children. Roth (chapter 6) looks at the very early side of this period, interactions between 12-month-old infants and their mothers. She also comes up with an innovative analysis of what takes place in infant-mother communicative interactions. A prime finding for Roth is that prompt responding by mothers to infant's vocalizations tend to be highly associated with the mother' use of semantic encoding responses, responses that pick up on the child's current focus of activity or attention. What is novel about this is that it suggests that mother's behaviors often come in packages and that many analyses which look one-by-one at separate indices of mother's verbal behavior could possibly miss important clues in patterns of maternal response. Roth clearly acknowledges that any facilitating effect on the child's language growth beyond 12 months is beyond her frame of analysis for this particular set of data. But she strongly argues that there are reasons to expect that the child will better be able to attend to and process replies by the mother which do follow the child's activity and attentional foci and which occur within less than 1 second of the offset of the child's own vocalizations.

Another set of clues about possibly facilitating aspects of conversation for children's language growth comes from the now controversial area of "scripts" and situational structure. It is not easy to give a definition of scripts that is iron clad or fully operational. However, most attempted definitions at least share a recognition that some event sequences are recurrent, become familiar, and have many sequentially well-structured properties that are similar across different instances of the event sequence. Thus, for many children "scriptedness" appears to be a reasonable label for recurrent book reading, bathing, mealtime sequences. Beyond this, the details of a script as they govern the conversational content and structure for the child and for the mother or other conversational partners become much less easy to agree on. Work by Snow and her colleagues (this volume; Snow & Goldfried, 1983), Nelson and her colleagues (in K. Nelson, 1986), and by Conti-Ramsden and Friel- Patti (this volume) have begun to provide some very interesting detail about the structure of mother-child exchange in situations which vary along scriptedness kinds of features. Snow et al. report two very interesting and related findings. One is that in such routine and familiar sequences as those occurring when the child and mother are reading books together, mother's speech shows higher semantic contingency than in less scripted and less routine situations. The second feature that ties in with this is that the mothers also show relatively *less* fine tuning of the structural level of their utterances to the structural levels of the the children's utterances in the "scripted" versus "unscripted" interactional episodes. In terms of the processing model discussed above, I would argue that the semantic contingency of the mothers may lead to relatively high attention by the children to the structural properties of the mothers' speech. In addition, the relatively low degree of structural match to the child's level may provide relatively high levels of new structural information that is more advanced than the child's current level, and so the child could analyze and learn from such structure. However, because relatively few examples of specific structures which are currently in the "hot spots" of attention and analysis will occur in any particular conversation, it would not be expected that the child's concurrent language use during a particular episode of reading books would show jumps forward in language complexity. Instead, the child within a particular episode can be expected to attend to and selectively store those examples that are well placed in the conversation in the sense of making it easy to see the meaning of the utterances and to begin to analyze their structure, in preparation for subsequent comparison with other related examples that will lead to the child's abstraction of new structural descriptions beyond their current language system.

It is clear that Snow et al. had many other interesting things to say about their data. But here again I would like to stress that there is certainly an interesting set of clues about the *possibly* facilitating aspects of *some* scripted kinds of interactions between children and adults. These clues are entirely consistent with other cross-sectional clues and with experimentally convergent data on the kinds of exchanges that directly trigger children's acquisitions of new language structures. As we see below, in some instances the convergent work directly deals with story reading kinds of routines (Baker et al., 1985; Pemberton & Watkins, 1987). Furthermore, work by Snow and Goldfried (1983) for the book-reading routine of a child and his mother are also consistent with a possible enhancement of certain aspects of processing within routine situations. In this instance, the focus should be on retrieval processes. The child observed in this case study appeared to be using utterances on new occasions of the book-reading routine that were directly traceable to things that the mother had said in previous episodes. In terms of the processing model, then, selective retrieval and analysis of certain contents and structures may be facilitated by the many familiar cues within a particular book to not only what the characters and the narrator may be "saying" (through the voices of the mother or child) but also to the spontaneous but predictable and recurrent kinds of comments and observations that the child and mother may generate each time the book is read. Finding related examples for comparison and analysis may become more probable when stored context cues are highly similar for the variations across readings of particular story components. With more children observed carefully over a longitudinal period, it certainly might be possible to demonstrate that children in such book-reading routines are able to draw upon storage and retrieval facilitation from the recurrent context. Moreover, this in turn could lead to facilitation of the pace at which the child could assemble together for analysis in working memory some closely related examples and could then abstract new structural descriptions. At this point in time many speculative and inferential steps have been necessarily included in this kind of argument. Nevertheless, it would appear that one aspect of scripted situations that deserves differentiated discussion is of possible ways in which attention and memory processes may be shifted by the structure of a script and by its recurrent nature, so that effects on acquisition of new language structures could in part be attributed to these shifts in attention and memory processes.

Results reported by Conti-Ramsden and Friel-Patti (this volume) are informative on dialogue aspects of mother-child conversation, particularly when different situations and tasks are examined. They argue that in a situation where a new toy is introduced for the child and mother to explore that a low level of "scriptedness" applies. Higher levels of scriptedness are argued to describe a waiting kind of situation (without toys) and a play situation with many familiar kinds of toys available. They find, as did Snow et al. (this volume), that semantic contingency is highest for the mother in the high-scripted situations. Additional information on the child's conversational behavior is particularly interesting. Here they find that in the two more scripted situations the children show more complex conversational structure in the sense of taking more turns that initiate conversations on a topic and that they also seize the floor for longer times and for longer sequences of utterances within a particular conversational turn. These kinds of results provide clues that the development of conversational complexity, in addition to any semantic or syntactic complexity advances, might possibly be facilitated by some aspects of highly familiar and structurally predictable scripted sorts of episodes. To the extent that this is true, it is important to consider, on the one hand, how the child may be exposed to particular conversational devices and sequences and replies that could provide the structures for analysis and entry into the child's own language system of more complex conversational devices. On the other hand, the support of attention and memory processes within a scripted kind of situation could strongly influence the child's utilization of available input even if the scripted situation did not provide higher or more appropriate levels of conversational structure than contrasting, less-scripted conversations. Conti-Ramsden and Friel-Patti directly argue that the contribution of memory "support" for learning new language structures could be a very important role that familiar, predictable, highly scripted kinds of interactions could provide (cf. K. Nelson, 1986). As in all phases of language learning, progress at both comprehension and production levels can be expected to profit when script facilitators or other facilitators have an impact.

Longitudinal Growth Clues to Input Variation Effects on Language Advances

One recent exemplar of work in this category is that of Speidel (this volume) on conversational exchanges in the classroom for Hawaiian children who are learning standard English dialect. Speidel argues that the same kinds of conversational replies to children that have been implicated in facilitating first language acquisition, such as recasts and elaborations of the child's previous utterance, can also be facilitating of advances in a new dialect. Cross-sectional clues that school children were receiving the possibly facilitating discourse structures were followed up with convergent longitudinal testing to determine if relative to a control group who did not receive planned conversational sessions, the conversational group did in fact make stronger gains in standard English dialect acquisition. Speidel concludes as follows ''The series of process analyses of how such learning can occur show remarkable similarity to how young children acquire their first language, namely through the analysis and use of responsive input in the form of repetitions, expansions, focus functions, recasts, and requests for clarifications . . . It should be emphasized once again, that the nature of the message oriented talk in the conversational approach is different from message oriented talk in classrooms in which the teacher talks at length at the children or asks rounds of questions to find out what the children have learned.'' (Speidel, this volume, p. 129).

In following up cross-sectional clues about which kinds of replies to children's utterances and which kinds of other elements in the conversation may be facilitative of children's language growth in particular areas of language at particular stages of growth, it is essential to avoid three very common design and analysis errors. These errors are:

1. Mixing together in a longitudinal follow-up children of widely differing ages and language ability, thereby obscuring the ways in which different forms of selective attention and analysis will operate on different input structures at different points in language development.

2. Emphasizing categories of maternal speech tabulated regardless of whether these utterances occur immediately following a child utterance of any kind (rather than following another maternal utterance) and regardless of the relationship between the structure of the child's utterance and the immediately following or closely following adult utterance.

3. Grouping together in analysis qualitatively different kinds of replies which have been shown in previous research to have very different kinds of probable effects on children's language growth. For example, grouped ''imitations by the mother'' of what the child said often include a mixture of exact repetitions (for which clues strongly point to a negative effect on the rate of children's language growth), expansions and recasts of children's utterances where the maternal expansions and recasts carry *new* structural information beyond the child's current level, (for which there are the strongest clues about facilitating impact on the child's language growth available in the literature), and recasts and expansions of the child's utterances that are presenting variations on what the child said but which in fact are not presenting any new structural information that the child is not already using in the system as evidenced by other utterances that the child produces (which logically cannot facilitate language advances).

In many instances studies have incorporated all three of these kinds of errors. In such cases the data can best be described as *mush* and no matter how thinly you slice mush and try to discuss it and interpret it and speculate from it, each new slice is still mush and such data is largely irrelevant to and inadequate for assessing whether and how different kinds of adult utterances and discourse strategies at different points in children's language development have positive or negative effects on language growth (in this regard examine Newport et al., 1977, and follow-up analyses on the same data set).

The need to analyze discourse *sequences* cannot be overemphasized. In conversation, children and their conversational partners are engaged in multiple tasks, with each influencing what the other may say and do next. Active processing by the child of new, challenging linguistic information (*challenging* relative to the child's current level) is likely to depend on *how* the information is placed in the recent flow of verbal and nonverbal events. Some potential challenges will be flooded or rushed away, while others will stand out for sustained attention. As Shatz (this volume) emphasizes, the child is not just an active processor but also is an active *elicitor* of communication from others. By gesture, by questions, by pauses, and by the forms of their utterances children in many instances appear to stimulate the production by others of challenging and informative new utterances (Bohannon & Marquis, 1977; Bohannon & Warren-Leubecker, 1985; Lewis & Rosenblum, 1974). In addition, if the child's eliciting operations are guided by hot spots under special scrutiny, then the child who has just posed an eliciting utterance of a particular form may be especially primed to process any relevant growth recasts or related replies. The frame of analysis the child sets up in working memory (cf. Baddeley, 1984; Hitch, 1984) can also incorporate immediately subsequent conversational turns in which the child or a partner provides variations, expansions, and reductions for further comparisons. On the child's part, Shatz refers to the latter as part of a set of "expansion operations." It is clear that Shatz and I both see the child as a limited capacity processor who is remarkably efficient at using such capacity for intensive activities relevant to current areas of growth. These selective activities include coordinated steps of elicitation, active variation on utterance form, attention and storage, retrieval and comparison, abstraction of hypotheses, and testing and monitoring and consolidation of hypotheses. It should be valuable to pursue convergent work that seeks to specify more precisely how the child's own eliciting and expansion operations contribute to language growth.

Convergent Clues to Input Variation Effects on Language Advances

When the available literature is put together with the rare-event processing model outlined earlier, then a fairly clear picture of highly facilitating kinds of discourse interactions for language advances can be constructed. In such interactions the child is engaged in emotionally ladened, meaningful, and interesting conversation with a fluent adult who is using over a series of many turns the kinds of initiations and replies that maintain the child's interest, that introduce into the conversation language forms that are more complex than the child's current forms, and which in a minority of cases specifically pair challenging language forms with contingent replies that pick up on the child's immediately preceding utterance. These latter replies are "growth recasts," which simultaneously present a challenging language form and present it embedded in discourse immediately after one of the child's own utterances that is related closely in meaning but which differs in form from the adult's reply. What we are emphasizing here are the probabilities that the child will attend to and process and selectively encode relevant new structural information and relevant new holistic input strings. These probabilities depend not just on the adult utterance in isolation and not just on a single instance of pairing an adult utterance with the previous reply, but also on the pattern of conversation over many turns. To the extent that this description is accurate, then it requires that we view with even more caution than the criticisms early in this paper suggest, any attempt to characterize input effects from analyses of transcripts in which adult utterance types are tallied in isolation from related pieces of discourse. For example, simply counting the number of auxiliary-fronted questions (Newport, Gleitman, & Gleitman, 1977) regardless of how these are embedded in discourse will provide very weak clues, indeed, about how and when a child at particular language levels might make use of and attend to those kinds of questions. Instead, there is another way of interpreting the clues from cross sectional and longitudinal naturalistic studies which is highly consistent with the processing account that considers patterns of language events over many turns in conversation. Namely, in work by Barnes, Gutfreund, Satterly and Wells (1983), by Cross (1977, 1978), by Furrow, Nelson, and Benedict (1979; see also Furrow & Nelson, 1986), by Libergott et al. (1984), and by Nelson et al. (1984), we see redundant clues that mothers who have children who are progressing relatively rapidly in language acquisition are using packages or patterns of discourse strategies over many turns. In such dyads the children receive relatively high frequencies of easy-to-process new challenging language structures, and also the pattern of discourse within which these occur also enhances the probability that the child will attend to and analyze those high-potential input challenges when they do occur. In particular, it is likely that there is a "synergistic" effect, to borrow a term from Cross, in which mothers who are likely to continue the child's topic even when not recasting also: (1) provide relatively high levels of growth recasts (though at any language age, seldom more than 5 to 10% of all opportunities for replying), and (2) provide elaborations and recasting of the mother's own utterances by the mother within the same turn, so that the child can attend to and compare relationships between utterance forms and meanings within a turn by the mother and not just within frames consisting of a child utterance—mother utterance pair.

In one piece of convergent work, Nelson et al. (1984) presented a pattern analysis which follows up on this kind of theoretical analysis. In a longitudinal design in which language growth between 22- and 27-months-of-age was examined, the results were clearcut. Children who were relatively high in the rate of language advance received substantially more of a particular discourse package—maternal use of topic continuations and recasts. Children high in syntactic growth received such a package on 57% of the possible occasions when their mothers replied to the children's utterances, as compared with only a 31% rate for children whose syntactic growth was low during this intermediate period of language growth between 22- and 27-months-of-age.

This same result also serves to illustrate a related point. The above result was based on topic continuations and recasts of a particular sort, those recasts which were simple in the sense of changing only one main part of the child's sentence. Meaning was maintained in such simple recasts, but relative to the child's preceding utterance the adult simple recast changed only the subject, only the verb, or only the object. Recall that the children in this study were at ages of 22- to 27-months. Our reasoning is that children are led to pay closer attention to adult utterances when their mothers are using many topic continuations and simple recasts, all of which pick up on what the child has just said. In addition, we expect that the child is at these ages better able to process and selectively encode relatively simple challenging structures which are beyond the child's current level. Thus, simple recasts, when they receive the benefit of the child's high attention, are most likely to pay off in the child's storing, comparing, and abstracting processes so that the child successfully abstracts new structural descriptions over time. But suppose we had, as some investigators have done, simply lumped together all kinds of contingent replies by the mother that picked up on the child's meaning regardless of whether these contingent replies were exact or partial imitations without any additions or changes by the mother—which we found to be negatively associated with the child's language growth, complicated recasts that changed two or more main elements of the child's utterance—which we also found to be negatively associated with language growth, as well as the simple recasts and topic continuations which we found were definitely and strongly associated with children's rapid advances in syntax. That kind of broad and gross analysis of whether contingent replies are associated with language advances in children would completely miss the action in terms of what parts of conversational sequences at particular stages in language growth have positive and negative influences on the child's success in working out new language structures. The child's system is a selective system. The child is only selectively working on the acquisition of a small to moderate number of hot spots or foci at any given time, and the child's selective attention, encoding, retrieval, and comparison will lead to a sensitivity to certain kinds of new input structures when they come along in certain discourse contexts. For the same reasons, there will be very low or total insensitivity to other input structures which at subsequent points in language development might in turn become the focus of strongly selective attention and analysis.

Similarly, it appears from convergent work in both naturalistic conversations and in specially tailored experimental conversations that the adult input which is likely to be selected and used in facilitating language process by the child occurs in very selective portions of what the adult says. Consider parents and experimenters and therapists who succeed in providing growth recasts that are above the child's current level, and that are embedded immediately following what children have said or that are embedded in a sequence of adult utterances in such a way that they draw attention to relationships among the adult utterances. All of the ways in which these adults succeed in providing useful and challenging comparison material for the child to attend to and analyze usually are carried by less than 10% of the adult replies to what children say and often by far less than this 10% level. From this minority, this small minority of *potentially* highly useful examples for analysis, the child almost certainly selects only a subset for actual strong attention and analyses. It is argued that *the crux of language growth lies in these rarely occurring instances in which potentially challenging and useful input strings are actually seized by the child's system and put into storage and into comparison with other previously stored and tagged exemplars of a similar sort.* Notice again, that the fundamental event that is called a "rare event" is not an input string considered in isolation, but rather the complex event consisting of the child's attending to, tagging and storing, retrieving and comparing, a small set of related exemplars so that the child goes on to successful abstraction of new structures and their subsequent monitoring and evaluation. To the extent that this process is occurring as we have inferred from clues from naturalistic investigations of a convergent sort, then experimental work of a convergent sort should be able to demonstrate that particular new language structures can in fact be readily triggered by experimentally tailored conversational sequences. Convergent interventions thus may fit with this analysis of the child's processing system and of the kinds of interactional sequences which a child will best be able to learn from. Here we will consider, in summary form, some of the kinds of experimental convergent evidence that bear upon these issues.

1. If the processing system is open, then growth recasts and related discourse events in sign language could be expected to have a facilitating effect on sign language growth just as the evidence suggests growth recasts in speech facilitate language growth in a spoken first language. Work by Prinz and Masin (1985) demonstrates precisely such an effect. Teachers and parents were trained to use recast replies that were growth recasts above the children's predominantly one-sign productive level of development. These intervention procedures proved sufficient to trigger the acquisition of new sign language structures.

2. Children who are delayed in language acquisition—if they receive conversational sequences that incorporate stage appropriate levels of growth recasts—

should also be expected to profit from the availability of conversational sequences with growth recasts as long as the children's processing systems are similar to those of normally progressing children. That is, if there are similar levels of development in terms of attention, storage, retrieval, comparison, abstraction, and monitoring processes. Sometimes differences or deficiencies in such processes of necessity must be studied together within a clinical setting along with the effects of intervention techniques. So the issues will always be a bit complicated when intervention for language delayed and language disordered children is considered. Nevertheless, there are encouraging examples of the successful use of growth recasting techniques to trigger new language structures and new language levels in language delayed children (Schwartz, 1986; Wilcox, 1984).

In a similar theoretical vein, Sigel & Saunders (1979) and Sigel & McGillicuddy-Delisi (1983) argue that language and cognitive growth can be stimulated in behind-norm as well as in at-norm children by conversational exchanges that provide challenge to and "distance" from the child's current representations of events.

3. If the child is particularly ready to pay attention to and to store, retrieve, and analyze input strings that occur in the form of growth recasts or similar attention-comparison-enhancing discourse sequences, then such growth recasts should have a positive effect in experimental studies for more than one or two kinds of language structures. Reasonably broad evidence that many different kinds of structures can be triggered for acquisition by the child should be expected. Nelson and his colleagues (Nelson, 1977b, 1980, 1981; Baker & Nelson, 1984; Baker, Pemberton, & Nelson, 1985; Nelson & Baker, 1986) present evidence for quite a range of syntactic structures that have been triggered by growth recasts within the range of 2- to 4-years for children acquiring English as a first language. For these triggered structures, growth recasting proved a sufficient trigger for acquisition within 5 to 6 hours of recasting at the most with less than 10% of those hours devoted to recasting of the target structures. The studied structures include the following: tag questions, passives, relative clauses, gerunds, reflexive pronouns, future tense and conditional verbs, auxiliaries, and complex noun phrases. In related intervention work Scherer and Olswang (1984) report acquisition of two-term semantic relations by 2-year-olds.

4. Limits on the kinds of structures that children at a particular language level might be able to selectively attend to, analyze, and incorporate into their language system often may be understood more precisely from experimental work combined with naturalistic work than from naturalistic work alone. Take the example of passive sentences. These have been acquired in a series of different growth recasting studies involving different children and different experimenters. Prior literature had suggested that it would be very unusual for children below 3½-years-of-age with MLU's of below 5 words to acquire passive structures. Instead, it was often observed that productive control of the passive was

not achieved until after 8- or 9- or even 10-years-of-age (e.g., Horgan, 1978; Sinclair-de-Zwart, 1969). Nevertheless, many children at the early language learning levels just mentioned did, in fact, acquire productive control of the passives including a wide range of verbs and including truncated and full passives with a good variation of animate and inanimate objects. This outcome reveals levels of power in the storage and analysis and monitoring capacities of these young children that are not so readily obvious from naturally obtained transcripts of what children say and what their conversational partners say to them.

Something approaching the limits of what children are able to do with their powerful processing mechanism may be seen only when the input is exceptional. In the case of growth recasts presenting relatively challenging structures like passives to these young children, we can see how much complexity the child is able to handle and how quickly children are able to work out new structures on the basis of relatively rare or infrequent input strings when these strings actually enter close analysis and tracking by the learning mechanism. The evidence suggests that the reason that most children have not worked out passive structures by age 3½ is that the occurrence in input in comparison-facilitating interactional frames that contain the passive is exceptionally low for most preschool children. Here again, we can see a new kind of convergence by looking at the naturally occurring input for the same children who received experimentally provided growth recasts and who succeeded in acquiring passive structures. Their conversations before intervention with their mothers typically showed either no maternal passive occurrences at all or just one passive occurrence in a single sample of conversation lasting from 40 to 60 minutes. Of even greater importance, the occurrence of growth recasts that specifically carry passive structures is virtually nil across all mothers sampled in these experimental studies. Thus, the evidence suggests that the child typically by 3- or 3½-years-of-age is not waiting for new advances in processing and thinking capacity before structures such as passives can be analyzed and incorporated into the child's language system, as in such proposals as that of Sinclair-deZwart (1969) that concrete operational thinking of the sort Piaget described is necessary for dealing with passive structures and their reversible character. Instead, the young child is waiting for selective engagement of the learning mechanism to turn round to the passive structure so that it becomes a hot spot for analysis and also for relatively easy-to-analyze occurrences of passives to come along in the input.

5. There is yet another kind of convergent evidence which has been very seldom seen in the literature but which would be extremely valuable whenever it can be obtained. What is needed is evidence concerning successful acquisition of new language structures by children under circumstances in which there are well-documented steps in the child's progress from lacking the structure, to initial hypotheses and exploration of the structure in production, to successful mastery and consolidation of the structure, along with clearly documented records of the input that the child is receiving from all sources. Under such carefully docu-

mented circumstances we may see that some children succeed in acquiring structures under input and interaction conditions which are surprising—just as the successful acquisition of passive structures by young children who are given growth recasts under experimental conditions has been a surprise in revealing how powerful the child's system really is at an early age. Similarly, we may be able to bracket the range of input conditions under which children can work out successful analyses of new language structures of a specified sort by carefully documenting how children under very different input conditions either succeed or do not succeed in acquiring new language structures. There is strong reason to believe that most children in Western cultures who have been in contact with university communities, and so have entered most of the language acquisition studies of the last 25 years, are exceptional in terms of having a relatively high "input cushion" consisting of a higher proportion of language facilitating kinds of discourse sequences. This speculation, though it is shared by many (e.g., Schieffelin, 1979; Shatz, this volume; Snow et al., this volume), needs to be more carefully documented in America, Australia, Germany, Italy, Sweden, England, and other Western cultures than has so far occurred. In apparently contrasting cultural conditions where less adult-child speech interactions occur (see, for example, Pye, 1986) or where different kinds of sequences are prevalent (e.g., Schieffelin, 1979; Slobin, 1985) the same kind of careful documentation of both language growth and of interactional sequences will also be necessary before the cross-sectional clues from these settings about the processes of language acquisition will carry very much weight.

6. Another area for further exploration concerns the way in which a common cognitive learning mechanism might prove to underlie a broad variety of acquisitions. Acquisition may occur whenever the interactional conditions expose the child to a full range of language structures within a context that is emotionally laden and involving, and that includes a reasonable frequency of some sorts of language-growth-facilitating sequences. Here again what can be learned from atypical children may be at least as rich as what we can learn from typical children. Children who acquire multiple spoken languages or who acquire sign language and speech in a bilingual fashion or who acquire reading and writing systems at an early age all are relevant to the kind of attention and storage and retrieval and analysis and monitoring mechanisms which children possess. Well-documented case studies will be useful in helping to differentiate which aspects of the child's system—if any—are specific to the analysis of a first spoken language, to a first sign language, and to subsystems such as syntax rules, semantic structures, or discourse rules (cf. Fodor, 1984).

Another Approach on Input: Assuming the Irrelevance of Input Variations for Language Advances

Some authors have assumed that input variations are essentially uninteresting and will tell us little about the learning system and how advances are made by the child in language. Certainly some of Chomsky's writings fall in this category (e.g., Chomsky, 1968). Here two particular lines of theoretical work are briefly discussed.

Bickerton (1984) has referred to a "language bio program hypothesis." He assumes that Hawaiian Creole has been derived from Hawaiian pidgin in a single generation. In attributing to the child a very strong, innately given, language-specific language acquisition mechanism, Bickerton takes some very questionable positions concerning what input is available—rather than observing and studying the evidence available in input—and the ways in which children might in successive rounds of analysis use the input in different and increasingly powerful ways. He assumes rather than documents that native language speakers of English and fluent or semifluent second language learners of English are *not* the main influence on the development of Creole. And he further assumes rather than documents that there is "not enough data" (p. 184) for the child to operate on in the "pidgin input." When he refers to some other discussions of the way in which children might work out complex language structures on the basis of some rarely occurring specific examples of input, as when Maratsos and Chalkley (1980) talk about complex pattern searching and inference mechanisms that children apply to evidence patterns, he says that the clues that the child might be using would have to be characterized as "extremely slight and elusive." Well, as Maratsos and Chalkley argue, and as I have argued here and in other contexts, many infrequent events can be utilized precisely because the child's cognitive mechanism when applied to the interactional data for language results in the abstraction gradually of very sophisticated language structures and simultaneously in the progressive development of the abstraction mechanisms themselves, so that there is a kind of learning how to learn effect with increasing efficiency in using data for new abstractions of structure. These effects are greatest when there have been many previous cycles of working out simpler levels of structure and when an extensive storage and retrieval system has also had opportunity to become more efficient with use (cf. also, MacWhinney, 1986, 1987). For the Creole learning situation that Bickerton describes, it is relevant to know that children at 2½ to 3½-years-of-age who would not ordinarily develop passive structures or relative clause structures or tag question structures in English at that age go ahead and acquire these structures when growth recasting kinds of opportunities are presented to the children in reasonably fluent and emotionally engaged conversational encounters (Baker & Nelson, 1984). Thus, in young learners of Creole we can infer that the mechanism is, indeed, ready to selectively attend to and analyze in a rapid manner some fairly infrequent and "slight" interactional sequences that bear upon structures currently in the focus of attention and analysis. As mentioned above, in understanding the learning mechanisms which are applied to language learning it will be revealing to have well-documented instances of unusual language acquisition under unusual interactional conditions. However, from Bickerton's writing it is impossible to determine either what the input has been for the acquisition of Creole or how a child who succeeded in acquiring Creole made use of the input that was available. In short, Bickerton has appropriately laid out the territory of Creole acquisition as an extremely interesting problem for anyone interested in language learning mechanisms and the role that input variation plays in the child's development of different language systems besides those in typical first language learning situations. Precise accounts of what happens in such territory await careful empirical research.

In a different way Wexler and Cullicover (1980) discuss some speculative mechanisms for advances in children's language systems. By giving a simulation mechanism only the "input" which they make up in a very convenient form, they completely ignore any actual input the children may be receiving. In their model the child is conveniently "presented" within their simulation with grammatical sentences and accompanying structural descriptions. The questions then concern how the child organizes and uses this information to work out new structural descriptions. All the examples the model presents itself are complete grammatical sentences, or, in Wexler and Cullicover's terms, "positive instances" of grammatical sentences. Through this procedure these authors place their entire theoretical concern on grammatical versus ungrammatical structures and in patterns among these. They ignore how the "preanalysis" is accomplished that could lead to a learning mechanism receiving these well-formed and only these well-formed grammatical sentences and accompanying structural descriptions. Despite many clues from the literature on interactional sequences with language-learning children, they assume that the child does not get evidence from discourse concerning which sentences may be poorly formed. Certainly children do not get evidence all of the time concerning this, and usually they do not get explicit labeling such as "this is a nongrammatical sentence" or "this is an error." But interactional clues in terms of noncomprehension, imitation, acknowledgment, topic continuation, recasting, and so on provide powerful and usable information for the child's learning mechanism about the well-formedness of many sentence examples (e.g., Bohannon & Warren-Leubecker, 1985; Ninio, 1986; Snow & Goldfried, 1983; Wilcox & Webster, 1980). Given the child's powerful learning system, it is safe to assume these clues can and are used in language acquisition. Wexler and Cullicover completely ignore such evidence except in a few inconsistent, contradictory footnotes.

All in all, Wexler and Cullicover choose to posit an extremely powerful language specific learning mechanism that does not need or use input in a powerful way to fuel abstractions of new structural descriptions, which then lead to new foci of attention and analysis and still newer structural descriptions, and so on in a continuing cycle. Wexler and Cullicover make unsupportable assumptions about the nature of the input available. They fail to see that, as Bruner, Roy, and Ratner (1982) and Shatz (this volume) would say, powerful "bootstrapping operations" are possible given the child's general learning mechanisms applied through repeated cycles to the kinds of input that are usually available in the form of interactional sequences for most preschool children. They choose an appropriate summary phrase—"the child is primarily responsible for language acquisition. . . ." (Wexler & Cullicover 1980, p. 75) but for the wrong reasons. It is the state of the child's current language system and the state of the current conversation and the state of the child's current attention which determines in large part which parts of an interactional sequence will be noticed by the learning mechanism, stored, and entered into important comparative analyses. And only if the child's learning mechanism is reasonably intact in terms of attention and memory and analysis processes will the child succeed in learning language under the actual input conditions that occur within known cultures. But not quite all children with such intact learning mechanisms do encounter favorable enough environments for learning language and not all children who do learn language successfully end up acquiring it at the same rate or to the same level of completion. Nor do they always acquire exactly the same grammatical system just because they are within the same culture. The child's learning mechanism may, indeed, steer the child down the road of communicative interaction, but the child's style of acquisition and rate of acquisition and eventual language system at mastery levels all will be greatly influenced by the particular interactional input sequences that occur along those communicative pathways. The child succeeds under most chosen pathways through the available input, not because the child is powerfully preset with language structures, but for precisely the opposite reason. The child is extremely open to learning from input that is encountered. And the cognitive system applied is one that is powerful and very flexible, so that children can proceed by different routes in working out from important variations in input conditions remarkably similar levels and details of language complexity within a language community. Studying how the child uses input at different points in language development, and how particular children successfully analyze input when their styles and processing biases vary, lies not at the periphery of understanding how language learning occurs but right at the heart.

How Current Language and Cognition Levels Both Facilitate and Limit What Will Be Learned Next

We have assumed that the child brings to a typically rich set of interactional sequences in language a highly selective and highly powerful learning mechanism. Briefly in the above discussion it has been emphasized that what the child will attend to and learn depends on the child's current level of development. Just because a child at 2½ to 3½ under appropriate interactional conditions may quite rapidly acquire surprisingly complex language structures, this does not mean that the child at that level or at an earlier level is prepared to analyze and structurally incorporate new concepts or new language rules regardless of differential complexity or regardless of how they might fit in or fail to fit in with already acquired language and cognitive structures. At this point it should be interesting to consider a few particular ways in which the studies and model presented above might bear on the interactions between the child's current language and conceptual system with new components of language and the conceptual system that may be about to be acquired.

Valuable discussions along these lines are provided by Gopnik and Meltzoff (this volume) concerning the ways in which new words and new sensorimotor achievements may be related. Recall that in earlier discussions above on the way in which interactional sequences might or might not influence syntactic advances, it was strongly stressed that very global analyses of input could easily "mush" together qualitatively different kinds of input in learning events. Under such circumstances investigators often have prematurely concluded that there are low levels of relation between mothers' language variations and their children's rates of acquisition of new language structures, rather than concluding that the measures used were too global and too insensitive and not sufficiently interactional in nature to reveal the ways in which children make differential use of different kinds of input sequences. Similarly, Gopnik and Meltzoff say that claims of low relationships between sensorimotor levels and language progress in terms of the acquisition of first words and first semantic relations reveal more about the measures used than about the ways in which language and cognition are related to each other. In their own studies Gopnik and Meltzoff find that words concerning disappearance, words like *gone,* appear in close conjunction with the acquisition of Stage 5 levels in object permanence. At these levels the child learns to predict the reappearance of hidden objects in certain ways and learns to uncover objects behind coverlets and otherwise rediscover through action that an object does, in fact, continue to exist and can be found quickly when hiding sequences are carefully observed. One acquisition may proceed or follow the other by a few weeks, with disappearance words occurring simultaneously with or shortly before or after the mastery of the Stage 5 object permanence tasks. In contrast, in another area of semantic content, words concerning failure (such as "uh oh") or success are not as closely timed to Stage 5 object permanence as they are to another sensorimotor achievement, the mastery of means-ends relationships. Both of these findings of parallels between specific content in the semantic system and achievement of particular kinds of sensory motor conceptual success fit very comfortably with the above model and discussions above concerning language growth in relation to available input. A child who has already acquired many concepts of a semantic nature (even though most of them are at the comprehension level) and some early sensorimotor foundations may form a focus or hot spot of analysis that is concerned with the disappearance of objects, their continued existence, and ways of referring to such event sequences (cf. Nelson, 1982, 1985b). Given that the child may form a hot spot of analysis and may then very selectively attend to, encode and tag, retrieve and analyze, and monitor what happens in this selective area, then it should be no surprise that the child may in a short period of time work out both new words and new problem-solving techniques in relation to this area of intense attention and analysis. Whether the child abstracts new language structures or abstracts new search and problem solving techniques first, may depend very much on accidents concerning which kinds of interactional sequences, including which kinds of labeling sequences by others, the child happens to encounter. Precisely because the system is highly open and flexible, a new focus of analysis for particular kinds of event sequences may be primed and ready to analyze relevant event sequences regardless of whether they are richer at the nonverbal level, richer at the verbal level, or rich at both levels within the same short period of time. As in the acquisition gradually of an impressive number of new syntactic structures within a few preschool years, in these first 18-months-of-life the child does not acquire everything at once. The establishment of one new focus of attention and analysis may lead to rapid acquisition in that area but may temporarily slow down or preclude certain other kinds of analyses occurring simultaneously. What Gopnik and Meltzoff have done is to present intriguing data within this age period that suggests a very powerful learning mechanism may be selectively turned on to certain contents in a semantic system and to certain sensorimotor problems at about the same time. Once again, though, it is essential to see that very general measures of the child's semantic system or the child's sensorimotor conceptual system might miss not only the relationships which Meltzoff and Gopnik observed but also might miss many other particular and interesting and short-lived relationships between language, cognition, and possible variations of input that may enter intense foci of analysis and mastery.

Another area in which these results concerning cognitive and language relationships converge is in the area of individual differences. It is surprising to learn when experimental studies are done in which input for the formation of new rules and new concepts is quite carefully controlled across different children that remarkably strong individual differences still emerge (Baker & Nelson, 1984; Cohen & Strauss, 1979; Nelson, 1982; Nelson & Bonvillian, 1978; Leonard & Schwartz, 1985; Younger, 1986). A reasonable inference is that when children's different tendencies to form particular foci and to form rules or hypotheses or categories of varying structure are interfaced with strong differences in the patterns of data available under normal everyday conditions for children, the observed levels of individual differences in the structure of language rules and the structure of concepts will be greatly magnified. In short, the research so far has only begun to scratch the surface of individual differences in forming individual new rules and concepts, in working out final systems which vary in all probability in structural detail, and in the many overall pathways to those final systems.

In contrasting ways, the chapters in this volume by Matsumoto, by White, and by Pye, Ingram, and List all touch on differential pathways. White finds that rules for the English dative are overgeneralized across contrasting verb forms by some preschool children but not by others. This outcome raises the essential question of the origins of individual differences in language rules during the rapid acquisition phases of the preschool period. Related work on verbs by deVilliers (1980) strongly indicates that differential evidence patterns children encounter could orient different children toward different rule patterns. Work by Nelson et al. (1985) suggests that further contributions to rule acquisition and rule deployment may be the child's early cognitive and emotional style along with the extent of opportunities for interacting with closely spaced siblings. The latter factor obviously ties in again with the view of Mannle and Tomasello (this volume) that siblings can play a special and important role in influencing younger children's language acquisition. In Matsumoto's work, children are observed cross-sectionally so here too there are wide open questions about the origins of observed individual differences. But what is beyond doubt is that in mapping Japanese classifiers to semantic concepts there are some strong and intriguing differences between children. Perhaps some of this variation for Matsumoto's semantic classes, such as land vehicles, could rest in children's relative degrees of interest in and thus contact patterns with exemplars for different semantic concepts. This would tie in with observations that some preschool children actively seek domain-specific evidence and become conceptually very sophisticated in the preschool years in dealing with selected concepts like dinosaurs (Carey, 1985; Chi & Koeske, 1983). Across languages the role of evidence patterns on acquisition can also be discerned. Pye et al. (this volume) argue convincingly that the children's phonological systems develop with so much sensitivity to the local input, Quiché or English, that acquisition theories require modification. At the semantic and syntactic levels Bowerman (1986) recently has made similar arguments. It would be surprising if theoretical accounts of language over the next decade do not build considerably on these kinds of foundations to provide much richer accounts of children's styles, evidence pattern variations, and the interactions of these two factors. As argued earlier in this chapter, rather than a single theory, what may be required are a *related set of theories* that account for the many different pathways by which individual learners of language reach mastery and a mature style or orientation in language deployment.

CONCLUDING COMMENTS

All evidence is not created equal. In this chapter we have sorted evidence on possible influences on children's language use and language advances into contrasting categories. Some evidence is too flawed to tell any clear story. Other evidence on close inspection concerns deployment of already available language skills but not introduction of new rules and new skills into the child's language system. This area of deployment deserves more direct investigation and discussion. If we take seriously the findings in this volume and other recent work, then there is a strong need to recognize how widely the child's use of language can fluctuate from partner to partner and situation to situation. Given that conclusion, it follows that assessment procedures should capture rather than ignore such fluctuations and should do so on both production and comprehension levels. A related conclusion is that "false positive" effects of language therapy could easily result from pretreatment assessments that measure low deployment and later assessments that measure higher deployment of an unchanged level of language mastery.

In the detection of how genuine advances in the child's language system and subsystems (phonology, semantics, syntax, discourse) occur, it is essential not only to see that many observations on children's language do not shed light on these questions but also to seek out convergent methods that together can provide powerful patterns of disconfirming or confirming data for theoretical hypotheses. We have argued here that naturalistic longitudinal group studies plus experimental intervention group studies should be coordinated with case studies of both sorts on typical as well as atypical children and typical and atypical language-learning circumstances. From the limited amount of such convergent evidence currently available, the argument is drawn that the central events in the child's language progress occur fairly rarely. These *rare events* consist of sequences in which the child happens to: (1) encounter a challenging, above-current-level language structure in input; (2) attends to this example and retrieves for comparison highly relevant and highly selected examples from short- and long-term memory; (3) abstracts and stores in long-term memory a new and more advanced structural description. Adults can help to provide favorable circumstances, but they cannot guarantee when a rare-event sequence will be carried through. Such rare-event sequences are triggered infrequently in most naturalistic contexts because the complexity level of the input and the quality of the child-partner discourse rarely support all three of the necessary steps in the sequence. But when conditions are right, the young child's cognitive system is prepared. The learning mechanism is both powerful and flexible. It incorporates strong pattern analyzing and abstracting capabilities. And it fuels new abstractions through highly selective storing-and-tagging and retrieval processes.

Arguments that the acquisition mechanism is primarily cognitive rather than specific to language learning have been expanded upon in other papers (Baker & Nelson, 1984; Bonvillian, Nelson, & Charrow, 1976; Nelson, 1977a, 1977b, 1980, 1981, 1982, 1983, 1986a, 1986b; Nelson & Nelson, 1978). It has been proposed that similar conversational procedures of giving "growth recasts" could stimulate rule advances regardless of whether such recasting occurs for moral reasoning rules (cf. Kohlberg, 1976), language rules, or rules in any socially shared and complex domain. Some recent work on how acquisition of new graphic skills can be triggered rapidly in preschool children when recasting and similar conditions supporting rare-event sequences are provided is certainly encouraging in this respect (Cox & Freeman, 1986; Nelson, Pemberton, & Rollenhagen, 1986; Nelson, Aronsson, & Flynn, 1986; Pemberton & Nelson, 1985; Phillips, Innal, & Landers, 1986; Pratt, 1984). In the graphic skill domain, even more so than in language acquisition, the usual conditions of child-expert partner interaction often leave the child on a plateau of development where for long periods no new challenges to the child's level of development occur in ways that promote successful attention and analysis. In short, for long periods no new rare-event sequences may occur even though the child is prepared to analyze new challenges. The good side of that coin is that when an expert (child or adult) in a domain can interact meaningfully and smoothly with a child learner and provide challenging growth recasts and similar responses, then the probabilities of rapid growth in the domain may be elevated quickly and substantially. In some instances, the kinds of highly scripted routines (e.g., reading in predictable ways) discussed in this volume will carry precisely the rich challenges that promote growth. Much work remains in specifying when such script effects can be expected. Nevertheless, child-expert patterns of discourse as related to syntactic growth, discourse as related to semantic growth, discourse as related to the phonological and conversational subsystems, and discourse as related to graphic and other nonlanguage domains are beginning to converge. In the latter categories, there is research by Prinz, Pemberton, and Nelson (1985) and Nelson, Dalke & Prinz (1987) indicating that recast-incorporating discourse for text and sign language can facilitate deaf children's text skill and sign skill acquisition, and that growth in both skill areas can be triggered by instructional-conversational sessions pairing the child with an interactive computer coordinated with a conversationally responsive adult. Similarly, when parents and teachers experimentally provide growth recasts to deaf children in sign, the children make sign language advances (Prinz & Masin, 1985).

Badly needed in future work is convergent work of yet another sort. This work would build on and test the replication of established studies that have helped to isolate and explain specific, well-documented acquisitions of new language rules by children. In addition, the new studies would use a variety of convergent methods to provide a much richer account of the attentional, tagging-and-sorting, retrieval, and monitoring components during the acquisition and consolidation of new rules. The work in this volume is heuristic in this regard, because it suggests that such convergent work might coordinate within research efforts methodologies that are sensitive to timing details (cf. Roth), joint attentional focus (this chapter; Speidel; Mannle & Tomasello), elicitation aspects of the child's behavior (Shatz; this chapter), abstraction and storage processes (Matsumoto; Shatz; Conti-Ramsden & Friel-Patti; Gopnik & Meltzoff; Dent; this chapter), generalization and monitoring processes (White; Shatz; this chapter), and culture and situation (Pye et al.; Snow et al.; this chapter), as well as the details of input elements within and across conversational turns (see especially,

Bernstein-Ratner; this chapter; Snow et al.). Richer work along these lines is needed in phonology, syntax, semantics, and discourse. In direct contrast to Fodor's (1984) theorizing on "modules" in language, the present empirical review and theoretical interpretation finds many more similarities than differences across the subdomains in terms of acquisition mechanisms. Work by Macken & Ferguson (1983), Fischer & Papp (1984), Karmiloff-Smith (1981), Nelson & Nelson, (1978), and Sternberg (1984) draws similar conclusions. One of the interesting commonalities across these diverse authors covering diverse subtopics in language and cognitive development is that at least three to four general stages are seen in each area of development, and another common emphasis in these views is that different areas can reach mastery in individual children at staggered times relative to other areas and to overall measures of cognitive development. Early stages allow for considerably broad rules and a lot of idiosyncracy between children in rule content. Extensive sets of rules are acquired, coordinated, and consolidated in middle stages. And in each domain of development the most advanced stages move beyond an already-efficient use of system rules to higher-level organizations and abstractions that allow both continued efficiency in typical situations and an enhanced ability to apply the system in new ways and in new situations.

ACKNOWLEDGMENTS

Preparation of this report and conduct of reviewed studies was supported in part by Grants G008302959 and G008430079 from the U.S. Department of Education, a grant from The Hasbro Children's Foundation, and National Science Foundation Grant BNS-8013767.

Many thanks to Joy Creeger for assistance on the manuscript and to Steven Camarata for stimulating discussions.

REFERENCES

Ahlgren, I. (1986, June). *Recent research on Swedish sign language.* Paper presented to the Center for the Study of Child and Adolescent Development, The Pennsylvania State University, University Park, PA.

Baddeley, A. (1984). Reading and working memory. In P. A. Kolers, M. E. Wrolstad, & H. Bouma (Ed.), *Proceedings of the Conference on Visible Language* (pp. 311–322). New York: Plenum.

Baker, N., & Nelson, K. E. (1984). Recasting and related conversational techniques for triggering syntactic advances by young children. *First Language, 5,* 3–22.

Baker, N. D., Pemberton, E. F., & Nelson, K. E. (1985, October). *Facilitating young children's language development through stories: Reading and Recasting.* Paper presented at the Boston University Conference on Language Development, Boston, MA.

Barnes, S., Gutfreund, M., Satterly, D., & Wells, G. (1983). Characteristics of adult speech which predict children's language development. *Journal of Child Language, 10,* 65–84.

Bickerton, D. (1984). The language biogram hypothesis. *The Behavioral and Brain Sciences, 7,* 173–221.

Bissex, G. L. (1980). *GNYS AT WRK: A child learns to read and write.* Cambridge, MA: Harvard University Press.

Bohannon, J., & Marquis, A. L. (1977). Children's control of adult speech. *Child Development, 48,* 1002–1008.

Bohannon, J., & Warren-Leubecker, A. (1985). Theoretical approaches to language acquisition. In J. B. Gleason (Ed.), *The development of language* (pp. 173–226). Toronto: Merrill.

Bonvillian, J. D., Charrow, V. R., & Nelson, K. E. (1973). Psycholinguistic and educational implications of deafness. *Human Development, 16,* 321–345.

Bonvillian, J. D., Nelson, K. E., & Charrow, V. R. (1976). Language and language-related skills in deaf and hearing children. *Sign Language Studies, 12,* 211–250.

Bowerman, M. (1985). Beyond communicative adequacy: From piecemeal knowledge to an integrated system in the child's acquisition of language. In K. E. Nelson (Ed.), *Children's language, Vol. 5* (pp. 369–398). Hillsdale, NJ: Lawrence Erlbaum Associates.

Bowerman, M. (1986). What shapes children's grammars? In D. I. Slobin (Ed.), *The cross-linguistic study of language acquisition* (Vol. 2, pp. 1257–1319). Hillsdale, NJ: Lawrence Erlbaum Associates.

Brown, R. (1973). *A first language.* Cambridge, MA: Harvard University Press.

Bruner, J., Roy, C., & Ratner, N. (1982). The beginning of request. In K. E. Nelson (Ed.), *Children's language, Vol. 3* (pp. 91–138). Hillsdale, NJ: Lawrence Erlbaum Associates.

Carey, S. (1985, November). *Children's conceptual development.* Paper presented to the Center for the Study of Child and Adolescent Development, The Pennsylvania State University, University Park, PA.

Chi, M. T. H., & Koeske, R. D. (1983). Network representation of a child's dinosaur knowledge. *Developmental Psychology, 19,* 29–39.

Chomsky, N. (1968). *Language and mind.* New York: Harcourt, Brace, Jovanovich.

Clark, R. (1982). Theory and method in child-language research: Are we assuming too much? In S. A. Kuczaj (Ed.), *Language development: Syntax and semantics* (pp. 1–36). Hillsdale, NJ: Lawrence Erlbaum Associates.

Cohen, L. B., & Strauss, M. S. (1979). Concept acquisition in the human infant. *Child Development, 50,* 419–424.

Cook-Gumperz, J. (1985, May). *The child's acquisition of languages and world views.* Paper presented at the Georgetown Roundtable on Linguistics, Georgetown University, Washington, DC.

Cox, M. V., & Freeman, N. H. (Eds.). (1986). *The creation of visual order.* Cambridge, England: Cambridge University Press.

Cross, T. G. (1977). Mother's speech adjustments: The contribution of selected child listener variables. In C. E. Snow & C. A. Ferguson (Eds.), *Talking to children.* Cambridge, England: Cambridge University Press.

Cross, T. G. (1978). Mothers' speech and its association with rate of linguistic development in young children. In N. Waterson & C. Snow (Eds.), *The development of communication.* New York: Wiley.

deVilliers, J. (1980). The process of rule learning in child speech: A new look. In K. E. Nelson (Ed.), *Children's language, Vol. 2.* (pp. 1–44). Hillsdale, NJ: Lawrence Erlbaum Associates.

Doi, T. (1985). *The anatomy of self.* New York: Kodansha International Ltd.

Dore, J. (1978). Variation in preschool children's conversational performance. In K. E. Nelson (Ed.), *Children's language, Vol. 1* (pp. 397–444). New York: Gardner Press.

Dreyfus, H. L., & Dreyfus, S. F. (1986). *Mind over machine: The power of human intuition and expertise in the era of the computer.* New York: Macmillan.

Fischer, K. W., & Papp, S. L. (1984). Processes of cognitive development: Optimal level and skill acquisition. In R. J. Sternberg (Ed.), *Mechanisms of cognitive development* (pp. 45–80). New York: Freeman.

Fodor, J. A. (1984). *The modularity of mind.* Cambridge, MA: The MIT Press.

Furrow, D., & Nelson, K. (1986). A further look at the motherese hypothesis: A reply to Gleitman, Newport, & Gleitman. *Journal of Child Language, 13,* 163–176.

Furrow, D., Nelson, K., & Benedict, H. (1979). Mothers' speech to children and syntactic development: Some simple relationships. *Journal of Child Language, 6,* 423–442.

Hall, W. S., & Cole, M. (1978). On participants' shaping of discourse through their understanding of the task. In K. E. Nelson (Ed.), *Children language, Vol. 1.* (pp. 445–465). New York: Gardner Press.

Harre, R. (1983). *Personal being: A theory for individual psychology.* Cambridge, MA: Harvard University Press.

Hitch, G. J. (1984). Developing the concept of working memory. In G. Claxton (Ed.), *Cognitive psychology, new directions* (pp. 154–196). London: Routledge & Kegan Paul.

Horgan, D. (1978). The development of the full passive. *Journal of Child Language, 5,* 65–80.

Johnson, N. S. (1983). What do you do if you can't tell the whole story? The development of summarization skills. In K. E. Nelson (Ed.), *Children's language, Volume 4* (pp. 315–384). Hillsdale, NJ: Lawrence Erlbaum Associates.

Karmiloff-Smith, A. (1981). The grammatical marking of thematic structure in the development of language production. In W. Deutsch (Ed.), *The child's construction of language* (pp. 121–147). Orlando, FL: Academic Press.

Kearney, M. (1984). *World view.* Nevato, CA: Chandler and Sharp.

Kohlberg, L. (1976). Moral stages and moralization: The cognitive-developmental approach. In T. Lickona (Ed.), *Moral development and moral behavior* (pp. 31–53). New York: Holt.

Kuczaj, S. A. (1982). On the nature of syntactic development. In S. A. Kuczaj (Ed.), *Language development: Syntax and semantics* (pp. 37–72). Hillsdale, NJ: Lawrence Erlbaum Associates.

Langer, J. (1969). Disequilibrium as a source of development. In P. Mussen, J. Langer, & M. Covington (Eds.), *Trends and Issues in Developmental Psychology,* (pp. 68–91). New York: Holt.

Leonard, L. B., & Schwartz, R. G. (1985). Early linguistic development of children with specific language impairment. In K. E. Nelson (Ed.), *Children's language, volume 5* (pp. 291–318). Hillsdale, NJ: Lawrence Erlbaum Associates.

Lewis, M., & Rosenblum, L. A. (Eds.). (1974). *The effect on the infant of its caregiver.* New York: Wiley.

Liebergott, J., Menyuk, P., Schultz, M., Chesnick, M., & Thomas, S. (1984, April). *Individual variation and the mechanisms of interaction.* Paper presented to the Southeastern Conference on Human Development, Athens, GA.

Lieven, E. V. M. (1978). Conversations between mothers and young children: Individual differences and their possible implications for the study of language learning. In N. Waterson & C. Snow (Eds.), *The development of communication* (pp. 173–187). New York: Wiley.

Macken, M. A., & Ferguson, C. A. (1983). Cognitive aspects of phonological development: Model, evidence, and issues. In K. E. Nelson (Ed.), *Children's language, Vol. 4* (pp. 256–282). Hillsdale, NJ: Lawrence Erlbaum Associates.

MacWhinney, B. (1987). Competition, variation, and language learning. In B. MacWhinney (Ed.), *Mechanisms of language acquisition.* Hillsdale, NJ: Lawrence Erlbaum Associates.

MacWhinney, B. (1986). Hungarian language acquisition as an exemplification of a general model of grammatical development. In D. I. Slobin (Ed.), *The crosslinguistic study of language acquisition* (Vol. 2, pp. 1069–1156). Hillsdale, NJ: Lawrence Erlbaum Associates.

McClelland, J. L. & Rumelhart, D. (1986). *Parallel distributed processing, vol. 2.* Cambridge, MA: The MIT Press.

Maratsos, M., & Chalkley, M. (1980). The internal language of children's syntax: The ontogenesis and representation of syntactic categories. In K. E. Nelson (Ed.), *Children's Language, Vol. 2* (pp. 127–214). Hillsdale, NJ: Lawrence Erlbaum Associates.

Maxwell, M. (1983). Language acquisition in a deaf child of deaf parents: Speech, sign variations and print variations. In K. E. Nelson (Ed.), *Children's language, Vol. 4* (pp. 283–314). Hillsdale, NJ: Lawrence Erlbaum Associates.

Nelson, K. E. (1977a). Aspects of language acquisition and use from age two to age twenty. *Journal of the American Academy of Child Psychiatry, 16,* 584–607. Also reprinted in S. Chess & A. Thomas (Eds.), *Annual progress in child psychiatry and child development,* Vol. 11. New York: Bruner/Mazel.

Nelson, K. E. (1977b). Facilitating children's syntax acquisition. *Developmental Psychology, 13,* 101–107.

Nelson, K. E. (1980). Theories of the child's acquisition of syntax: A look at rare events and at necessary, catalytic, and irrelevant components of mother-child conversation. *Annals of the New York Academy of Sciences, 345,* 45–67.

Nelson, K. E. (1981). Toward a rare-event cognitive comparison theory of syntax acquisition. In P. S. Dale & D. Ingram (Eds.), *Child language: An international perspective* (pp. 229–240). Baltimore, MD: University Park Press.

Nelson, K. E. (1982). Experimental gambits in the service of language acquisition theory: From the Fiffin Project to operation input swap. In S. A. Kuczaj (Ed.), *Language development: Syntax and semantics* (pp. 159–199). Hillsdale, NJ: Lawrence Erlbaum Associates.

Nelson, K. E. (1983). Abstract of Keynote Address to the 1982 Child Language Seminar. *First language, 4,* 51–62.

Nelson, K. E. (1985a, January). *Rare events and other common processes in children's acquisition across many domains.* Paper presented to the Max-Planck Institute for Psycholinguistics, Nijmegen, Holland.

Nelson, K. E. (1985b, July). Categories and category formation in children from 10 to 54 months. In B. Benelli & G. Pieraut-Le Bonniec (Chairs). *Conceptual development in children.* Symposium conducted at the meeting of the International Society for the Study of Behavioral Development, Tours, France.

Nelson, K. E. (1986a, April). Discussion. In J. N. Bohannon (Chair), *New approaches to language acquisition: Learnability theory, processing constraints, and the negative evidence issue.* Symposium conducted at the Conference on Human Development, Nashville.

Nelson, K. E. (1986b, October). Strategies for first language teaching. Invited paper and chapter in R. L. Schiefulbusch & M. Rice (Eds.), *Teachability of language.* (Conference sponsored by the University of Kansas.)

Nelson, K. E., Aronsson, K., & Flynn, M. A. (1987). *Process, culture and style in children's art.* in preparation.

Nelson, K. E., & Bonvillian, J. D. (1978). Early semantic development: conceptual growth and related processes between 2 and 4½ years of age. *In* K. E. Nelson (Ed.), *Children's Language, Vol. 1* (pp. 467–556). New York: Gardner Press.

Nelson, K. E., & Baker, N. D. (1986, October). *Theoretical and applied implications of experimentally-induced advances in children's language.* Paper presented at the Boston University Conference on Language Development, Boston.

Nelson, K. E., Baker, N. D., Denninger, M., Bonvillian, J. D., & Kaplan, B. J. (1985). *Cookie* versus *do-it-again:* Imitative-referential and personal-social-syntactic-initiating language styles in young children. *Linguistics, 23,* 433–454.

Nelson, K. E., Dalke, D., & Prinz, P. M. (1987, April) *Refinement and replication of communicative gains through interactive microcomputer instruction for communicatively handicapped children.* Paper presented to the Society for Research in Child Development. Baltimore, MD.

Nelson, K. E., Denninger, M. M., Bonvillian, J. D., Kaplan, B. J., & Baker, N. D. (1984). Maternal input adjustments and non-adjustments as related to children's linguistic advances and to language acquisition theories. In A. D. Pellegrini & T. D. Yawkey (Eds.), *The development of oral and written languages: Readings in developmental and applied linguistics.* Norwood, NJ: Ablex.

Nelson, K. E., & Nelson, K. (1978). Cognitive pendulums and their linguistic realization. In K. E. Nelson (Ed.), *Children's language, Vol. 1* (pp. 223–286). Hillsdale, NJ: Lawrence Erlbaum Associates.

Nelson, K. E., Pemberton, E. F., & Rollenhagen, C. F. (1986). *Cross-cultural replication of graphic recasting effects.* Unpublished manuscript, The Pennsylvania State University, University Park, PA.

Nelson, K. (1981). Individual differences in language development. *Developmental Psychology, 17,* 170–187.

Nelson, K. (1986). *Event knowledge: Structure and function in development.* Hillsdale, NJ: Lawrence Erlbaum Associates.

Newport, E. L., Gleitman, H., & Gleitman, L. R. (1977). Mother, I'd rather do it myself: Some effects and non-effects of maternal speech style. In C. E. Snow & C. A. Ferguson (Eds.), *Talking to children.* New York: Cambridge University Press.

Ninio, A. (1986, April) Clarification demands by mothers in three age groups. In J. N. Bohannon (Chair), *New approaches to language acquisition: Learnability theory, processing constraints, and the negative evidence issue.* Symposium conducted at the Conference on Human Development, Nashville.

Pemberton, E. F., & Nelson, K. E. (1985). *Using graphic recasting and modelling to foster young children's drawing ability.* Unpublished manuscript, The Pennsylvania State University, University Park, PA.

Pemberton, E. F., & Watkins, R. V. (1987). Language facilitation through stories: Recasting and modeling. *First language, 7,*(1), 1–15.

Peters, A. (1983). *The units of language acquisition.* Cambridge, England: Cambridge University Press.

Phillips, W. A., Innal, M., & Lander, E. (1986). On the discovery and storage of graphic schema. In M. V. Cox & N. H. Freeman (Eds.), *The creation of visual order.* Cambridge, England: Cambridge University Press.

Piaget, J. (1954). *The construction of reality in the child.* New York: Basic Books.

Pinker, S. (1985). Language learnability and children's language: A multifacted approach. In K. E. Nelson (Ed.), *Children's language, volume 5* (pp. 399–442). Hillsdale, NJ: Lawrence Erlbaum Associates.

Pratt, F. A. (1984). A theoretical framework for thinking about depiction. In W. R. Crozier & A. J. Chapman (Eds.), *Cognitive processes in the perception of art.* Amsterdam: North-Holland.

Prinz, P. M., & Masin, L. (1985). Lending a helping hand: Linguistic input and sign language acquisition in deaf children. *Applied Psycholinguistics, 6,* 357–370.

Prinz, P. M., Pemberton, E., & Nelson, K. E. (1985). ALPHA interactive microcomputer system for teaching reading, writing, and communication skills to hearing-impaired children. *American Annals of the Deaf, 130,* 444–461.

Prinz, P. M., & Prinz, E. A. (1981). The acquisition of American Sign Language and spoken English in a hearing child of a deaf mother and hearing father: Phase II—initial combinatorial patterns of communication. *Sign Language Studies, 30,* 78–88.

Pye, C. (1986). Quiche Mayan speech to children. *Journal of Child Language, 13*(1), 85–100.

Scherer, N. J. & Olswang, L. B. (1984). Role of mothers' expansions in stimulating children's language production. *Journal of Speech and Hearing Research, 27,* 387–396.

Schwartz, R. (1986, November). *Personal communication.* American Speech and Hearing Association annual meeting, Detroit.

Schieffelin, B. B. (1979). Getting it together: An ethnographic approach to the study of the development of communicative competence. In E. Ochs & B. Schieffelin (Eds.), *Developmental pragmatics.* New York: Academic Press.

Schwam, F. (1982). Signs and strategies: The interactive processes of sign language learning. In K. E. Nelson (Ed.), *Children's language, Vol. 3* (pp. 392–430). Hillsdale, NJ: Lawrence Erlbaum Associates.

Sinclair-de-Zwart, H. (1969). Developmental psycholinguistics. In D. Elkind & J. H. Flavell (Eds.), *Studies in cognitive development: Essays in honor of Jean Piaget,* New York: Oxford University Press.

Sigel, I. E., & McGillicuddy-Delisi, A. V. (1984). Parents as teachers of their children: A distancing model. In A. D. Pellegrini & T. D. Yawkey (Eds.), *The development of oral and written language in social contexts* (pp. 71–92). Norwood, NJ: Ablex.

Sigel, I. E., & Saunders, R. (1979). An inquiry into inquiry: Question asking as a instructional model. In L. Katz (Eds.), *Current topics in early childhood education, Vol. II.* (pp. 169–193). Norwood, NJ: Ablex.

Sinha, C. (1980). Representational development and the structure of action. In G. Butterworth & P. Light (eds.), *Social cognition: Studies of the development of understanding.* London: The Harvester Press.

Slobin, D. (Ed.). (1985). *The cross-linguistic study of language acquisition, volumes 1 and 2.* Hillsdale, NJ: Lawrence Erlbaum Associates.

Snow, C. A., & Goldfried, B. A. (1983). Turn the page please: Situation-specific language learning. *Journal of Child Language, 10,* 551–570.

Söderbergh, R. (1977). *Reading in early childhood: A linguistic study of a preschool child's gradual acquisition of reading ability.* Washington, DC: Georgetown University Press.

Sternberg, R. J. (1984). Mechanisms of cognitive development: A componential approach. In R. J. Sternberg (Ed.), *Mechanisms of cognitive development.* New York: Freeman.

Strohner, H., & Nelson, K. E. (1974). The young child's development of sentence comprehension: Influence of event probability, nonverbal context, syntactic form, and strategies. *Child Development, 45,* 567–576.

Tager-Flusberg, H. (Chair). (1986, October). *Theoretical issues in the acquisition of grammar.* Symposium with papers by U. Bellugi, R. Cromer, and E. Bates, presented to the Boston University Conference on Language Development, Boston.

van Kleeck, A., & Street, R. (1982). Does reticence mean just talking less? Qualitative differences in the language of talkative and reticent preschoolers. *Journal of Psycholinguistic Research, 11,* 609–630.

Wexler, K., & Cullicover, P. W. (1980). *Formal principles of language acquisition.* Cambridge, MA: The MIT Press.

Whyte, J. (1983). Metaphor interpretation and reading ability in adults. *Journal of Psycholinguistic Research, 12,* 457–466.

Wilcox, M. J. (1984). Developmental language disorders: Preschoolers. In A. Holland (Ed.), *Language disorders in children.* San Diego, CA: College-Hill Press.

Wilcox, M. J., & Webster, E. (1980). Early discourse behavior: An analysis of children's responses to listener feedback. *Child Development, 51,* 1120–1125.

Younger, B. (1986, April). *Development of feature abstraction capabilities in infants.* Paper presented to the Conference on Human Development, Nashville.

Author Index

Subject Index